BARRON'S

GRE®

VERBAL WORKBOOK

2ND EDITION

Philip Geer, Ed.M.

BARRON'S

Dedication

Dedicated to my English teacher colleagues in Singapore, America, Britain, Hong Kong, and Australia, especially Dr. Peter Saunders and Dr. Robert Wilks, with whom I enjoyed many interesting discussions about the English language and other subjects over the years. And especially, and as always, to B.B.

I would like to thank Wayne Barr at Barron's for bringing me on board. Thanks also to my conscientious editor, Pat Hunter.

About the Author

Philip Geer has taught English language and literature for many years in the United States and abroad. He is the author of several textbooks and test preparation books, including *Essential Words for the GRE* and *Wordfest!* both published by Barron's, and is the academic director of Mentaurs Educational Consultants. You can contact Philip Geer at director@mentaurs.com for guidance in your GRE Verbal Reasoning and Analytical Writing preparation.

© Copyright 2014, 2011 by Barron's Educational Series, Inc.

All inquiries should be addressed to:
Barron's Educational Series, Inc.
250 Wireless Boulevard
Hauppauge, New York 11788
www.barronseduc.com

ISBN: 978-1-4380-0379-5
ISSN 2160-1585

PRINTED IN THE UNITED STATES OF AMERICA
9 8 7 6 5 4 3 2 1

CONTENTS

Preface

Serious students preparing for the Verbal Reasoning section of the GRE know that the best way to prepare is to do exercises similar to those that appear on the actual test, and they are always looking for high-quality practice exercises. However, there is a shortage of such material. Therefore, I have written Barron's *Verbal Workbook for the GRE*. This workbook offers three complete verbal reasoning tests and extensive practice on each type of question that appears on the test, so that students will have the skills to do well. Each answer is clearly explained, ensuring that students will easily understand why it is correct.

The revised GRE requires a greater number of high-order reasoning skills than the past test, so I have included quite demanding reading passages on a wide variety of topics with correspondingly more difficult questions on them. Thus, after completing the book students will not only have improved their comprehension and other verbal skills, but they will also have become comfortable with a range of topics in the arts and sciences. This is important because the test-makers say that "reading passages are drawn from many different disciplines and sources." In addition, I have written the sentence equivalence and text completion exercises so that they develop high-order thinking skills as they provide useful information about a range of topics.

A feature of this book is the GRE Dictionary, which gives definitions of words likely to appear on the test, as well as a brief sentence illustrating how each word is used. Difficult words used in this book are defined, so students can efficiently expand their vocabulary as they work through the exercises.

Of course, students should not rely on only one book in their preparation for the test. They should also read widely in a variety of areas. One of the best ways to become familiar with different areas of thought is through reading high-quality periodicals, such as *The New York Times*, *The Atlantic*, *The Economist*, and *Scientific American*. This has the additional benefit of further developing vocabulary. Students who lack a solid vocabulary foundation should consider embarking on a systematic vocabulary building program, such as *Wordfest!* and *Essential Words for the GRE*, both published by Barron's.

The New GRE

The Educational Testing Service (ETS) revised the Graduate Record Exam (GRE) General Test in August 2011. There are two ways of taking the test:

1. The **computer-based test**, which lasts about 3 hours and 45 minutes, is made up of the following:

   - Analytical Writing: one section with two distinct tasks separately timed; 30 minutes per task
   - Verbal Reasoning: two sections; 20 questions per section; 30 minutes per section
   - Quantitative Reasoning: two sections; 20 questions per section; 35 minutes per section

   Also, there may be one section after the analytical writing section that will either be identified or unidentified but that will not count toward your score.

   Most students take this version of the test. New features allow test-takers to mark questions and return to them, move around to different questions within sections, and change and edit answers within a section.

2. The **paper-based test** is offered in areas where the computer-based test is not available. This version of the revised GRE General Test consists of the following:

   - Analytical Writing: one section with two distinct tasks separately timed; 30 minutes per task
   - Verbal Reasoning: two sections; 25 questions per section; 35 minutes per section
   - Quantitative Reasoning: two sections; 25 questions per section; 40 minutes per section

Other than the few relatively minor differences in duration and number of questions, the material and question types on the computer-based GRE and the paper-based GRE section are the same.

This workbook is designed to help students prepare for both versions of the GRE Verbal Reasoning section. Since most students take the computer-based test, the number of questions per section and the time allowed per section in the diagnostic and practice tests in this book follow the computer-based version. Students preparing for the paper-based version of the test should remember that the time allowed for each section and the number of questions on each section will be somewhat different, as outlined above.

The New Verbal Reasoning Section

![chevron pattern bar]

ETS gives a clear statement of what is assessed in the revised GRE Verbal Reasoning section:

"The Verbal Reasoning measure assesses your ability to analyze and evaluate written material and synthesize information obtained from it, analyze relationships among component parts of sentences and recognize relationships among words and concepts." According to ETS, the revised Verbal Reasoning section of the GRE has a greater number of advanced reading passages, with more demanding questions, than the earlier verbal section of the test. Also, it has longer, more complex sentence completion type questions. Another important difference is that it no longer contains either antonym questions or analogy questions. In addition, two new types of reading comprehension questions and two new types of sentence completion questions have been introduced on the revised test. These are discussed in detail below.

The scoring system for the Verbal Reasoning section has been changed. Formerly, scores were reported on a scale of 200 to 800 with score increments of 10 points. The revised scoring system places scores on a scale of 130 to 170, with score increments of one point.

ETS says that the new Verbal Reasoning section has "greater emphasis on higher cognitive skills and less dependence on vocabulary knowledge alone." This means, as mentioned above, that reading passages and questions on them are more difficult, requiring a greater number of abstract and inferential thinking skills. It also means that text completion questions are more complex, requiring the ability to follow a complicated line of reasoning and to understand the meaning of words in context. Therefore, it is vital to make sure you have the appropriate skills to perform well.

Before taking the Diagnostic Test in this book, which will give you a good idea of how good your skills are, let's look at the skills you need for the Verbal Reasoning section. After that, we will examine some sample questions.

SENTENCE EQUIVALENCE SKILLS

The Sentence Equivalence question is the first kind of sentence completion type question on the new GRE. A single sentence with one blank and six answer choices will appear. You must select two correct answer choices that fit the overall meaning of the sentence and produce completed sentences that are basically equivalent in meaning. *Answers that are not fully correct do not receive any credit.*

To answer this type of question correctly, you must have the ability to make a correct judgment about what constitutes a complete and meaningful sentence. You must also have a good vocabulary, because quite a few of the words in the answer choices, and in some cases in the question sentence as well, will be quite advanced words. In nearly all cases the two correct answer words will be very close in meaning, and in many cases the two answer words will be synonymous. However, be careful in choosing two words simply because they are synonymous because very often there will be two pairs of synonyms among the six answer choice words.

Evaluate each sentence, paying attention to its structure and general sense. Note words and phrases that give clues about the structure of the sentence, such as *however, on the other hand, although, moreover, if,* and *unless.* Often such words will help you to determine how the parts of the sentence are related to one another. If, after analyzing the sentence, you don't have any idea what the correct answers are based on the structure of the sentence but you have identified two synonyms, go ahead and choose them. The odds will be on your side because there are only rarely more than two pairs of synonyms.

TEXT COMPLETION SKILLS

The skills needed for text completion questions are similar to those needed for the Sentence Equivalence questions. You must be able to understand the overall sense of the sentence (or sentences), understand relationships among different parts of the sentence (or sentences), and analyze how changes in one part of the sentence (or sentences) affect the meaning of other parts of the sentence (or sentences). Also, advanced words frequently appear in both the sentence (or sentences) and in the answer choices.

In this workbook, text completion questions requiring one blank to be filled in are referred to as *Text Completion Questions: Single Blank.* This type of question consists of one sentence with five answer choices for the blank. Text completion questions requiring two blanks to be filled in are referred to in this book as *Text Completion Questions: Double Blank.* This type of question consists of one to five sentences with three answer choices for each blank. Text completion questions requiring three blanks to be filled in are referred to in this workbook as *Text Completion Questions: Triple Blank.* This type of question consists of one to five sentences with three answer choices for each blank.

Text Completion Question: Single Blank questions are often the easiest of these questions because there is no need to consider how an answer choice for the blank affects answer choices for other blanks.

Text Completion Question: Double Blank questions are considerably more complex, but they usually do not consist of more than two sentences, so it is usually not difficult to follow the reasoning. Frequently, in fact, there is only one sentence in this type of question, so it is only necessary to understand the meaning and structure of this sentence to determine the best answer choices.

Text Completion Question: Triple Blank questions are by far the most complex because they require you to follow an extended line of reasoning and to determine how different answer choices affect the overall meaning. They can be regarded as a type of short reading comprehension question because you need to be able to comprehend an entire passage rather than only one or two sentences. If you find you are having difficulty determining the correct answer choices on a Text Completion: Triple Blank question, you might consider going on to other questions and returning to it later if you have sufficient time left. No more credit is given for answering a difficult text completion question correctly than answering an easy one correctly, so it makes sense to not use too much time on questions you find very difficult if this means you have insufficient time for other questions.

It is important to remember that, as with the Sentence Equivalence question, no credit is given for partially correct answers. This means, for example, that even if you select two out of three correct answer choices in a Text Completion: Triple Blank question, you will receive no credit.

You should first read each Text Completion question to get a sense of its meaning and structure. Note key words and phrases that help to organize the sentence. After selecting your answer for each blank, read the passage again to make sure it is logically coherent.

READING COMPREHENSION SKILLS

Because ETS says that the GRE tests more advanced skills than it previously did, there will almost certainly be more questions requiring you to not only understand the meaning of a text but to evaluate it critically, make inferences, and reach conclusions based on information in it. ETS provides a list of skills required for the Reading Comprehension questions, which is summarized below. Note that the skills become increasingly more advanced. You must be able to:

1. **Understand the meaning of individual words and sentences.**
   This skill is fundamental. You can't develop higher-level reading skills unless you are able to comprehend the literal meaning of words and sentences. Thus, as mentioned before, knowledge of advanced vocabulary is necessary to do well, as is the ability to follow the logic of sentences. ETS stresses that there will be an increased variety of types of texts tested, which means you will encounter quite a few different types and styles of writing.

2. **Understand the meaning of paragraphs and larger bodies of text.**
   You have to synthesize the meaning of words and sentences to arrive at a more general meaning. To do this, you must be able to understand the function of sentences. Does a sentence elaborate on an idea? Question an idea? Provide a link to another idea? You must also be able to see how sentences combine to form larger units.

3. **Distinguish between major and minor points.**
   You need to be able to evaluate the main argument and determine how important various points are in that argument. For example, the author might raise additional points that are related to the main topic but that are not central to the main topic under discussion.

4. **Summarize a passage.**
   Quite often a question will require you to determine the main idea or ideas presented in a passage. This involves some of the skills in objective 3 above, as well as being able to see how the major ideas form one unified concept.

5. **Draw conclusions from information provided.**
   Another term for a conclusion reached from information provided is "inference." This is one of the most important skills for the GRE, and it will be tested often. Reasonable people can infer different things from the same information, so students often have trouble understanding why one answer is considered better than another

answer on this type of question. The best advice is that the test-makers expect you to base your answer closely on the information provided in the passage. An inference may be reasonable but not follow logically from what is stated in the passage.

6. **Reason from incomplete data to infer missing information.**

Questions requiring this skill are not as common as ones requiring you to draw conclusions from information, described in objective 5 above. These types of questions are typically less difficult because generally it is easier to see what information is needed than it is to reach a conclusion. This type of question might, for example, ask you to say what scientific evidence not mentioned in the passage would best support a particular scientific theory. Again, the best advice is to be logical and to stick to the information given in the passage.

7. **Understand the structure of a text in terms of how the parts relate to one another.**

Questions requiring an understanding of the structure of the text are fairly common. By "structure" the test-makers are referring mainly to the *argument* presented and the means used to advance that argument. This is because most texts on the GRE present an argument in some form. It is important to be able to follow the main lines of an argument not only to answer this type of question but to answer most of the other types of questions as well. Once you have figured out the logical structure of the passage, you will be able to answer questions about how a particular part of the text fits into the argument and relates to the other parts of the text. Texts can be organized in many different ways, so don't assume, for example, that there will be first an introduction, next a major proposition advanced, then support given for the proposition, followed by a qualification of the proposition, and finally a conclusion reached. Also, keep in mind that all sentences, paragraphs, and passages are structured in a particular way, and that you may be asked questions on any of these and on the logical relationships between them or parts of them.

8. **Identify the author's assumptions and perspectives.**

As mentioned in objective 7 above, understanding the argument of a passage not only enables you to answer questions about the structure of a text but about other types of questions as well. Every writer makes certain assumptions about the topic under discussion, but normally these are not discussed explicitly in the relatively short passages such as the ones on the GRE. Therefore, you need to consider the argument and determine what assumptions are implicitly made. For an example, an author may cite insights from psychoanalytic theory without discussing the validity of that area of thought. An implicit assumption would be that psychoanalytic theory has some validity.

"Perspective" is a more general term than "assumption" and refers to the author's overall outlook and the attitude he or she takes to the topic, as well as all of the assumptions he or she makes about the subject.

9. **Analyze a text and read conclusions about it.**

Once again, if you are able to identify the main argument presented in the text, you should be able to arrive at reasonable conclusions about it. This type of question is similar to many of the other types of questions, particularly 5, 7, and 8 discussed above and 10 and 11 discussed below. Many sorts of questions will be asked requiring you to analyze a text and reach conclusions about it, but some of the common sorts of questions ask you to consider the central proposition advanced, its premises, the logic and persuasiveness of the argument, as well as the sufficiency of the evidence offered for the proposition. ETS says that "Reading and understanding a piece of text . . . requires active engagement with the text, asking questions, formulating and evaluating hypotheses and reflecting on the relationship of the particular text to other texts and information." Think actively and critically as you read, posing questions about the assertions made. However, be as objective as you can be. You may, for example, disagree with something the author says, but ask yourself whether your objection is truly a valid one. Remember, the test is about your understanding of the ideas of others, not about your ideas.

10. **Identify strengths and weaknesses of a position.**

As mentioned above, questions that test this skill require a good understanding of the argument of a text. Nearly every argument will be stronger in some areas than others. Also, limited space may not allow a particular aspect of an argument to be fully developed, thus making it weak. As with objective 9 discussed above, this type of question will most frequently be about the premises on which an argument is based, the logic and persuasiveness of the argument, and the sufficiency of the evidence offered. You may also be asked to consider the unstated implications of the assertions made. Remember that you may not be asked about the primary argument made in the text, but rather about a secondary, perhaps supporting, argument.

11. **Develop and consider alternative explanations.**

This type of question appears the least frequently on the GRE. Once again, however, a sound understanding of the argument, especially its assumptions, logic, persuasiveness, and evidence will help you to answer questions that test this skill. If you read actively, "formulating and evaluating hypotheses" as ETS suggests, alternative explanations will occur to you.

After working through the Reading Comprehension exercises in this workbook, you will have acquired the skills discussed above. Also, you will have become familiar with a wide variety of topics and writing of the type that will appear on the test. This is important because the test-makers say that the passages are selected from "the physical sciences, biological sciences, social sciences, arts, and humanities."

The length of passages on the test will vary from one to several paragraphs. There will be from 12 to 15 passages and from one to about six questions on each passage. There will be three types of Reading Comprehension questions:

1. **The five-choice multiple-choice question** in which you need to choose the *one* answer you think is correct.

2. **The three-choice multiple-choice question** in which you need to choose *one, two,* or *three* answers you think are correct.

3. **The select-in-passage question** in which you need to select the sentence in the passage that best meets the description given in the question. Note that on the computer-based test you will be asked to highlight the correct sentence on the screen. Because most students take the computer-based version of the test, a similar format is used in this book in which you are asked to write the first three words and the last three words of the sentence you choose as the answer. Students taking the

paper-based test will be given a multiple-choice question with five sentences from the passage as answer choices.

Answering Reading Comprehension Questions

Read the passage carefully, following the main argument. In many cases there will be two or more interrelated arguments, which may or may not reflect the author's viewpoint. If you find a passage difficult, it may be necessary to quickly look back at the important parts of the passage you aren't clear about.

After you have a reasonable understanding of the passage, read each question on it, making sure that you understand what the question is asking. Often there will be a key word in the question that will help you to identify what is being asked and the associated skill you need to answer it. Some of the most important of these words are *proposition, assumption, premise, argument, attitude, evidence, implication, connotation, ambiguous, implicit, conclusion, inference, perspective, generalization, qualification, fallacy, perspective, paradox,* and *tone.* Make sure you know the meanings of these words.

Remember to use only information in the passage to answer questions. Frequently, you will be required to make inferences. Your inferences should be reasonable and limited to the scope of what is discussed in the passage.

Read all the answer choices before selecting your answer, remembering that some answers might be reasonable but not answer the question as precisely as the correct answer. For the question type that requires you to select one, two, or three answers, keep in mind that there is no credit given for partially correct answers. For example, if the correct answers are A and C and you select C, you will receive no credit.

Examining the Questions

THE SENTENCE EQUIVALENCE QUESTION

The Sentence Equivalence question requires you to select *two* correct answer choices that fit the overall meaning of the sentence and produce completed sentences that are basically equivalent in meaning. Answers that are not fully correct do not receive any credit.

EXAMPLE 1

In the view of some people, a problem the field of political science faces is that the _____ of its practitioners are predominantly liberal, whereas those of the subjects of their inquiry are often conservative.

(A) habits
(B) inclinations
(C) politics
(D) proclivities
(E) protégés
(F) students

Answers: **B** and **D**

It makes sense that a problem is created in the field of political science because some people believe that political scientists are predominantly liberal, whereas many of the people they study have conservative political views. (B) *inclinations* and (D) *proclivities* both mean *tendencies*, which refers to the tendencies of political scientists and the subjects of their inquiry. (C) *Politics* is a good choice but there is no synonym for it. (A) *habits*, (E) *protégés*, and (F) *students* all make some sense but are not synonyms and don't make as much sense as (B) *inclinations* and (D) *proclivities*.

On this type of question, some choices will often make sense but will not be synonymous with any of the other choices. Also, a pair of synonyms other than the correct pair will sometimes appear.

EXAMPLE 2

Luddites were English workers who, in the early nineteenth century, rioted in protest against laborsaving machinery in the textile industry in the belief that such machinery would lead to _____ in employment for workers.

(A) an increase
(B) a dichotomy
(C) a diminution
(D) an expansion
(E) a regression
(F) a reduction

Answers: **C** and **F**

(C) *a diminution* and (F) *a reduction* are synonyms. The Luddites rioted to protest laborsaving machinery, so it makes sense that they thought such machinery would lead to *a reduction* or *a diminution* in employment for workers. In this example, none of the other choices fits the overall meaning of the sentence.

THE TEXT COMPLETION QUESTION

Let's first examine the first type of Text Completion question, the single blank sentence with five answer choices.

EXAMPLE 1

One of the criteria for determining whether a government is a dictatorship or not is whether there is _____ use of power against citizens or other countries.

| metaphorical |
| preordained |
| pragmatic |
| disinterested |
| arbitrary |

Answer: **arbitrary**

Arbitrary has several meanings, all of which make sense in this context. One meaning of *arbitrary* is "determined by whim," a meaning that can be applied to a dictatorship. *Arbitrary* also means "not limited by law," which also makes sense because a characteristic of a dictatorship is to exceed the limits of the law. None of the other choices makes sense.

EXAMPLE 2

Gradually, engineers have made the internal operation of personal computers "invisible," so that to people uninitiated into the _____ world of computer hardware, computers are simply black boxes that allow software to run.

nascent
syncretistic
ephemeral
arcane
ersatz

Answer: **arcane**

The sentence contrasts the limited familiarity with the operation of computer hardware of the "uninitiated" with the expertise of engineers. It makes sense that to the uninitiated the world of computer hardware is *arcane* (understood by only a few; obscure). None of the other choices makes good sense.

Next we turn to the Text Completion Question: Double Blank with three answer choices per blank. *Answers that are not fully correct do not receive any credit.*

EXAMPLE 3

It has been argued that belief in ethical relativism became pervasive as the social sciences (i) _____ the idea that values can only be judged on the basis of their usefulness in a particular society. According to ethical relativists, what is considered (ii) _____ in one society might rightly be considered perfectly normal and moral in another.

(i)	(ii)
disseminated	analogous
lambasted	reprehensible
explicated	passé

Answers: **disseminated** and **reprehensible**

The sentence says that it has been argued that many people came to believe in ethical relativism as the social science *disseminated* (spread) the idea that values are not absolute and can only be judged on how well they work in particular societies. Ethical relativists believe that what is "moral" in one society might be considered *reprehensible* (blameworthy) in another society.

The following are some of the technological developments that have proven to be "breakthrough technologies," creating (i) _____ new ways of doing things and having far-reaching (ii) _____ for human culture and thought: paper, books, movable type, sail, steam engine, mass production, digital computer, transistor, radio and television, internal combustion engine, and electric light, generator, and motor.

(i)	(ii)
desultory	implications
myriad	allegories
a paucity of	inferences

Answers: **myriad** and **implications**

It makes sense that "breakthrough technologies" would create *myriad* (a large number of) new ways of doing things and have far-reaching *implications* (implicit significance) for human culture.

Finally, let's examine the Text Completion Question: Triple Blank, which also offers three answer choices per blank. Once again, answers that are not fully correct do not receive any credit.

Modern science generally takes a (i) _____ view of reality, believing that the most plausible and (ii) _____ is that all events (including ideas) can be explained in terms of physical phenomena. According to this view, other types of substances, such as soul, are (iii) _____ .

(i)	(ii)	(iii)
tendentious	original hypothesis	immutable
solipsistic	heuristic device	illusory
materialistic	utilitarian theory	enigmatic

Answers: **materialistic** and **utilitarian theory** and **illusory**

Materialistic (relating to materialism, the philosophy that physical matter is the only reality) is the best choice for column (i) because the sentence says that everything can be explained in terms of "physical phenomena." For column (ii), all of the choices make some sense. However, *utilitarian theory* is the best choice because it is reasonable that science would place a high value on a theory that has practical value. For column (iii), the best choice is *illusory* (based on illusion) because the phrase "other types of substances" contrasts with "physical phenomena."

EXAMPLE 6

Cyril Burt, a British psychologist, defined intelligence as "innate general
(i) _____ capacity." The last two words of this definition would meet
with broad agreement; that is, intelligence refers to the ability of an organism to
think, understand, and know. However, the extent to which this ability is genetically
transmitted and how far it may be (ii) _____ experience of the environment
is arguable, and it may also be argued whether or not intelligence is a "general"
ability or the combination of certain specific abilities. It has been felt, for example,
that since certain people seem to possess a greater ability to, say, understand
mathematical problems than to express themselves in language ((iii) _____),
these abilities may be independent of each other.

(i)	(ii)	(iii)
affective	enhanced	(albeit not perfectly)
psychological	limited by	(or vice versa)
cognitive	affected by	(and so on, ad infinitum)

Answers: **cognitive** and **affected by** and **or vice versa**

In column (i), *cognitive* (related to thinking and knowledge) is the best choice because the paragraph says "intelligence refers to the ability of an organism to think, understand, and know." In column (ii), the best choice is *affected by* because there is a contrast between the genetic transmission of intelligence and intelligence determined by experience. In column (iii), the best choice is *or vice versa* because the sentence is giving examples that could just as reasonably be reversed.

THE READING COMPREHENSION QUESTION

You will be presented with a prose excerpt, followed by questions to test your understanding. There are three types of reading comprehension questions:

1. **the five-choice multiple-choice question** in which you need to choose *the one* answer you think is correct.
2. **the three-choice multiple-choice question** in which you need to choose *one, two, or three* answers you think are correct. To get credit, all must be correct.
3. **the select-in-passage question** in which you need to select the sentence in the passage that best meets the description given in the question.

Examples of each type of reading question are given after the passage below. Read the passage, and then answer the questions on it.

Since human beings make noises, use gestures, employ combinations of objects or actions in order to convey meaning, there is a place for a discipline which would analyze this kind of activity and make explicit the systems of convention on which it rests.

Line

(5)   Semiotics is based on the assumption that insofar as human actions or productions convey meaning, insofar as they function as signs, there must be an underlying system of conventions and distinctions which makes this meaning possible. Where there are signs there is system. This is what various signifying activities have in common, and if one is to determine their essential nature one must treat them not in

(10) isolation but as examples of semiotic systems.

   Various typologies of signs have been proposed, but three fundamental classes of signs seem to stand out as requiring different approaches: the icon, the index, and the sign proper (sometimes misleadingly called "symbol"). All signs consist of a signifier and a signified, a form and an associated meaning or meanings; but the

(15) relations between signifier and signified are different for each of these three types of sign. An *icon* involves actual resemblance between signifier and signified: a portrait signifies the person of whom it is a portrait less by an arbitrary convention than by resemblance. In an *index* the relation between signifier and signified is causal: smoke means fire because fire is generally the cause of smoke; clouds mean rain if they are

(20) the sort of clouds which produce rain; tracks are signs of the type of animal likely to have produced them. In the *sign* proper, however, the relation between signifier and signified is arbitrary and conventional: shaking hands conventionally signifies greeting; cheese is by convention an appropriate food with which to end a meal.

The Five-Choice Multiple-Choice Question with Only One Correct Answer

EXAMPLE 1

Select the best answer choice for the following question.

Which of the following statements would the author of the passage be least likely to agree with?

(A) Nearly any human activity might convey meaning.

(B) An advertising firm might make more effective advertisements if they made use of the insights of semiotics.

(C) Semiotic systems only function when everyone involved understands explicitly the system of conventions on which they are based.

(D) Semiotics is a legitimate academic discipline.

(E) Signs must be examined not individually but rather in relationship to other signs.

Answer: **C**

(A) A wide range of activities are mentioned—"noises . . . gestures . . . combinations of objects or actions" to "convey meaning," so the author would probably agree with this statement.

(B) The author describes the new field of semiotics, saying there is a place for "a discipline that would analyze this kind of activity and make explicit the systems of convention on which it rests." We can infer that the author would probably agree that an advertising firm might make more effective advertisements if it had a good understanding of semiotics because advertising often makes use of various signs.

(C) As mentioned above, the author says "there is room for a discipline which would make explicit the systems of convention on which it rests." We can infer that since these systems are not explicit now most people do not understand them explicitly. Thus, the author would almost certainly not agree that the functioning of semiotic systems depends on their being known explicitly by everyone involved.

(D) The author would agree with this because he says "there is place" for such a discipline.

(E) The author would agree with this because he says "if one is to determine [signifying activities'] essential nature one must treat them not in isolation but as examples of semiotic systems."

The Three-Choice Multiple-Choice Question with One, Two, or Three Correct Answers

---

EXAMPLE 2A

Consider each of the three choices separately and select all that apply.

Based on the author's description of the three fundamental classes of signs, which of the following would be considered a sign proper?

(A) The use of a white flag by an army to signal a desire to surrender to an enemy
(B) A fossil of an organism that died 100 million years ago
(C) A bell in a school sounding at the end of class

Answers: **A** and **C**

In a sign proper, according to the author, "the relation between signifier and signified is arbitrary and conventional." Thus,

(A) the use of a white flag by an army to signal a desire to surrender to an enemy would be considered a sign proper because the use of a white flag is arbitrary; for example, the flag could be another color in a different system of conventions

(B) a 100-million-year-old fossil would convey information and could be an index, but it would not be a sign proper because there is no arbitrary, conventional relation between signifier and signified

(C) a bell in a school indicating the end of class would be a sign proper because the use of a bell is arbitrary; for example, a buzzer could be used

Consider each of the three choices separately and select all that apply.

If a sign proper is not understood within the context of a particular semiotic system, which of the following is also true?

(A) It cannot convey meaning to others.
(B) It is necessarily based on a causal relationship between signifier and signified.
(C) The sign proper will almost certainly acquire a universally understood meaning.

Answer: **A**

The author says that the meaning conveyed by signs depends on "an underlying system of conventions." A sign proper especially depends on a system of conventions because the relation between signifier and signified is entirely arbitrary and conventional. Thus,

(A) a sign proper cannot convey meaning to others unless it is understood in the context of the semiotic system of which it is a part

(B) there is nothing said to suggest that the meaning of a sign proper not understood within the context of a particular semiotic system would depend on a causal relationship between signifier and signified

(C) there is nothing in the passage that suggests that a sign proper that is not understood with the context of a particular semiotic system would be likely to acquire a universally understood meaning. It is possible that such a sign proper would acquire other meanings, but it is very unlikely that such meanings would be universally understood because there are many semiotic systems

The Select-in-Passage Question with a Sentence Choice That Best Meets the Description Given in the Question

Students taking the paper-based test will be given a multiple-choice question with five sentences from the passage as answer choices. Because most students take the computer-based version of the test, which requires you to identify one sentence by highlighting it on the screen, a similar format is used in this book. In this book this question requires you to write the first three words and the last three words of the sentence you choose as the answer.

EXAMPLE 3

Select the sentence that states what approach must be taken to finding the truth about signs. Write the first three words and the last three words of the sentence on the lines below.

_____

_____

Answer: **"This is what . . . of semiotic systems."**

To determine the "essential nature" of signifying activities, their relationship to semiotic systems must be studied.

Diagnostic Test

ANSWER SHEET
Diagnostic Test

SECTION 1

1. Ⓐ Ⓑ Ⓒ Ⓓ Ⓔ Ⓕ
2. Ⓐ Ⓑ Ⓒ Ⓓ Ⓔ Ⓕ
3. Ⓐ Ⓑ Ⓒ Ⓓ Ⓔ Ⓕ
4. Ⓐ Ⓑ Ⓒ Ⓓ Ⓔ Ⓕ
5. Ⓐ Ⓑ Ⓒ Ⓓ Ⓔ Ⓕ
6. _____
7. _____
8. _____
9. (i) _____
   (ii) _____

10. (i) _____
    (ii) _____
11. (i) _____
    (ii) _____
    (iii) _____
12. (i) _____
    (ii) _____
    (iii) _____

13. Ⓐ Ⓑ Ⓒ Ⓓ Ⓔ
14. Ⓐ Ⓑ Ⓒ
15. Ⓐ Ⓑ Ⓒ
16. _____
    _____
17. Ⓐ Ⓑ Ⓒ Ⓓ Ⓔ
18. Ⓐ Ⓑ Ⓒ Ⓓ Ⓔ
19. Ⓐ Ⓑ Ⓒ
20. _____
    _____

SECTION 2

1. Ⓐ Ⓑ Ⓒ Ⓓ Ⓔ Ⓕ
2. Ⓐ Ⓑ Ⓒ Ⓓ Ⓔ Ⓕ
3. Ⓐ Ⓑ Ⓒ Ⓓ Ⓔ Ⓕ
4. Ⓐ Ⓑ Ⓒ Ⓓ Ⓔ Ⓕ
5. Ⓐ Ⓑ Ⓒ Ⓓ Ⓔ Ⓕ
6. _____
7. _____
8. (i) _____
   (ii) _____
9. (i) _____
   (ii) _____

10. (i) _____
    (ii) _____
    (iii) _____
11. (i) _____
    (ii) _____
    (iii) _____
12. (i) _____
    (ii) _____
    (iii) _____

13. Ⓐ Ⓑ Ⓒ Ⓓ Ⓔ
14. Ⓐ Ⓑ Ⓒ
15. Ⓐ Ⓑ Ⓒ
16. Ⓐ Ⓑ Ⓒ
17. Ⓐ Ⓑ Ⓒ Ⓓ Ⓔ
18. Ⓐ Ⓑ Ⓒ Ⓓ Ⓔ
19. Ⓐ Ⓑ Ⓒ
20. _____
    _____

SECTION 1

Time: 30 minutes

20 questions

> Choose the best answer to each of the following questions in this section.

> Fill in the blank in each sentence by selecting two answer choices that fit the overall meaning of the sentence and produce completed sentences that are equivalent in meaning.

1. The difficulty in using an example as evidence to prove a thesis is that an opponent can contend that the example is unique, and therefore not _____.
   - (A) sophistical
   - (B) satirical
   - (C) apropos
   - (D) credible
   - (E) lucid
   - (F) germane

2. Some observers see multinational companies as the means by which an elite class that will exploit the labor of the rest of the world is emerging, while those with a more _____ view see them as precursors to a world government that will bring harmony to a strife-torn world.
   - (A) prescient
   - (B) sanguine
   - (C) gloomy
   - (D) refined
   - (E) optimistic
   - (F) melancholy

3. Due process of law prevents government from making _____ charges against citizens, and helps to ensure that they receive a fair and expeditious trial.
   - (A) deleterious
   - (B) false
   - (C) explicit
   - (D) sophistical
   - (E) spurious
   - (F) criminal

4. In the American federal system of government, the will of the legislature can be
_____ by that of the executive or the judiciary, whereas in the parliamentary
system virtually all power is vested in the parliament.
(A) queried
(B) tempered
(C) reinforced
(D) stymied
(E) stanched
(F) thwarted

5. Judaism, Christianity, and Islam are described by many theologians as essentially
dualistic, in that they believe in two _____ principles of good and evil.
(A) inexorable
(B) opposite
(C) analogous
(D) antithetical
(E) amorphous
(F) unyielding

> **Fill in all of the blanks in the sentences by selecting one entry from the correspond-
> ing column of choices in the way that best completes the text.**

6. The literary critic Susan Sontag uttered a famous aesthetic _____ :
"Taste has no system and no proofs"—by which she meant that artistic taste
is subjective, since there are no unbiased criteria for assessing art.

cognomen
diatribe
apologia
injunction
dictum

7. In nineteenth-century Britain the writings of Thomas Malthus engendered a mass
movement to control population in order to _____ mass starvation due to
population growth outrunning growth in food supply.

husband
romanticize
lampoon
proscribe
forestall

8. The difficulty of finding synonyms for words can be illustrated by comparing the word *belief* and the word *dogma*: *belief* is neutral, with no _____ or favorable connotations; *dogma*, however, can connote a rigid, inflexible belief.

facetious
pejorative
periphrastic ·
tangential
rhetorical

9. (i) _____ of a single world government are sometimes described as (ii) _____ because such a government is seen as unrealistically based on the power of existing governments being severely curtailed.

(i)	(ii)
Advocates	putting the cart before the horse
Critics	building castles in the air
Opponents	justifying the means by the ends achieved

10. Much of Western history can be viewed as a (i) _____ the ideals of (ii)_____ civilization, with its emphasis on the heroic, noble, tragic, and generally human, and the Hebraic, with its emphasis on God and His relationship to humanity in history.

(i)	(ii)
dialectic between	Semitic
dichotomy between	contemporary
qualification of	Hellenic

11. Under Chief Justice Earl Warren, the U.S. Supreme Court rewrote much of the corpus of constitutional law. During Warren's tenure, the Supreme Court ruled that the "one person, one vote" principle must be the basis of all legislative apportionment; (i) _____, there has been electoral reform, shifting voting power from rural districts to urban and suburban areas. Critics of the "one person, one vote" principle argue that the framers of the Constitution were aware that representation would not be equal, and that if they had wanted a "one person, one vote" system, they would have specified it in the Constitution; (ii) _____, they believe that the Warren Court exceeded its constitutional prerogatives and (iii) _____ power to itself that properly belongs to Congress.

(i)	(ii)	(iii)
unexpectedly, therefore	based on this reasoning	ascribed
as a result	on the other hand	attributed
unfortunately, however	nevertheless	arrogated

12. A common objection to utilitarianism is that goodness cannot be fairly or reliably (i) _____ . An example is a situation in which ninety percent of society is made extremely happy by making ten percent of it extremely unhappy, resulting in an increase of total happiness but leaving the minority more unhappy. The increased unhappiness of the minority might (ii) _____ the increased happiness of the majority, thus (iii) _____ .

(i)	(ii)	(iii)
assessed	still outweigh	illustrating the subjectivity of human beings
quantified	necessitate	rendering the action wrong
explained	hardly prove	obfuscating the situation

> **Read the passages below, and then answer the questions that follow them based on the information in the passages themselves and in any introductory material or notes. The correct answer may be stated or merely suggested in the passages.**

Questions 13–16 are based on the following passage.

We must first give ourselves the semantic reminder that there is no such *thing* as Art. Art is not an entity, any more than life is an entity. It is a word, a general term conveniently but often loosely used to cover a certain rather wide-ranging type of human
Line activity and its products. It is impossible to delimit either the type or its range with
(5) precision. Here I shall use the word "art" to cover the effective organization of experience into integrated forms which are emotionally significant and aesthetically satisfying. This includes some of the practice and some of the products of activities like painting and sculpture, literature and drama, dance and ritual celebration, music and architecture. But, of course, in the spectrum of all of these activities art slips
(10) over into non-art, for example literature grades into straightforward information and into propaganda. The essential distinctness of art, I would say, is that it provides a qualitative enrichment of life, by creating a diversity of new experience. For one thing, art can tap emotional resources of human personality which might otherwise remain unutilized, either individually or socially. It is a process of extending
(15) ourselves, through our sensibilities and our imagination, to something we have not reached before. It is a process of discovery about ourselves and about life. Art helps us to assimilate the experience provided by our senses and our emotions.

But although art is in general a process of differentiation and proliferates variety, it is in particular a process of integration and synthesis. Any work of art, however
(20) humble, brings together a number of separate (and sometimes apparently disparate) elements and moulds them into an organic unity.

Art can exert the most profound effects on the minds of men. To many people poetry or painting or music have conveyed an overwhelming sense of revelation. At the play, we can be "purged by pity and fear" or gripped by powerful and liberating

(25) collective emotion, and many people have found their first visit to the theatre was also their induction into a new and compelling mode of experience. We are not quite the same after we have read Tolstoy's *War and Peace*. And Beethoven's posthumous quartets can transport us to another world, make us free of another realm of being.

That is the point. Art opens the doors of that other world in which matter and

(30) quantity are transformed by mind and quality. Art is sometimes contemptuously dismissed as escapism. But we all need escape. Apart from our modern need to escape from the dullness of routine and from the overmechanized life of cities, there is the universal and permanent need to escape from the practical and actual present in which we have of necessity to spend so much of our lives, and above all from the

(35) prison of our single and limited selves.

The artist can utilize intellectual ideas and moral concepts among the raw materials which he organizes, thus transmuting reason and morality into art and giving a further dimension to his work. In painting, we need only think of the concepts of maternity and divinity in pictures of the Madonna and Child. Inferior artists will be

(40) incapable of organizing these non-aesthetic elements into an aesthetic unity, and their work will not rise above the didactic or the propagandist, the moralistic or the merely representational. But the good artist can fuse them into a richer whole in the creative crucible of his imagination.

Select one answer choice for the following question.

13. In the last paragraph the author probably chose to use the word "transmuting" rather than "transforming" in order to
(A) emphasize that in the artistic process the materials of art must undergo a change akin to an alchemical one
(B) make clear that reason and morality must be separated from pure art in the crucible of the artistic imagination
(C) remind the reader that art always involves an element of the sleight-of-hand that distances it from conventional moral norms
(D) make the point that art is superior to reason and morality
(E) help defend art from the charge of being merely escapist

14. Which of the following points make up part of the author's defense of art against the criticism that it is escapist?
    (A) Art helps fulfill a necessary need to escape from the concerns of everyday life.
    (B) Art provides an important way for us to escape from our limited selves.
    (C) Art deals with important moral issues, making them relevant to our everyday lives.

15. Which of the following statements would the author be likely to agree with?
    (A) All ritual is art.
    (B) The greatest art is fundamentally realistic.
    (C) A work of literature is not art to the degree that its purpose is to convince people of the truth of a particular idea.

Select the sentence that contrasts two opposing tendencies in art.

16. _____

Questions 17–20 are based on the following passage.

If you look at the sky from a dark site, far from city lights, you can see the Milky Way arching over you, its diffuse stream of light interrupted by dark patches. These are interstellar clouds. The dust particles in them block starlight and make them opaque
Line to visible light. Consequently, those of us who seek to observe star formation face a
(5) fundamental problem: stars cloak their own birth. The material that goes into creating a star is thick and dark; it needs to become dense enough to initiate nuclear fusion but has not done so yet. Astronomers can see how this process begins and how it ends, but what comes in the middle is inherently hard to observe, because much of the radiation comes out at far-infrared and submillimeter wavelengths
(10) where the astronomer's toolbox is relatively primitive compared with other parts of the spectrum.

Astronomers think that stars' natal clouds arise as a part of the grand cycle of the interstellar medium, in which gas and dust circulate from clouds to stars and back again. The medium consists primarily of hydrogen; helium makes up about one
(15) quarter by mass, and all the other elements amount to a few percent. Some of this material is primordial matter barely disturbed since the first three minutes of the big bang: some is cast off by stars during their lifetimes; and some is the debris of exploded stars. Stellar radiation breaks any molecules of hydrogen into their constituent atoms.

(20)   Initially the gas is diffuse, with about one hydrogen atom per cubic centimeter, but as it cools it coagulates into discrete clouds, much as water vapor condenses into clouds in Earth's atmosphere. The gas cools by radiating heat, but the process is not straightforward, because there are only a limited number of ways for the heat to escape. The most efficient turns out to be far-infrared emission from certain

(25) chemical elements, such as the radiation emitted by ionized carbon at a wavelength of 158 microns. Earth's lower atmosphere is opaque at these wavelengths, so they must be observed using space–based observatories such as Herschel Space Observatory, launched last year by the European Space Agency, or telescopes mounted in airplanes, such as the Stratospheric Observatory for Infrared Astronomy (SOFIA).

(30)   As the clouds cool, they become denser. When they reach about 1,000 atoms per cubic centimeter, they are thick enough to block ultraviolet radiation from the surrounding galaxy. Hydrogen atoms can then combine into molecules through a complicated process involving dust grains. Radio observations have shown that molecular clouds contain compounds ranging from hydrogen up to complex organ-

(35) ics, which may have provided the wherewithal for life on Earth. Beyond this stage, however, the trail goes cold. Infrared observations have revealed nascent stars deeply embedded in dust but have trouble seeing the earliest steps leading from molecular cloud to these protostars.

        The situation for the very earliest stages of star formation began to change in the

(40) mid-1990s, when the Midcourse Space Experiment and the Infrared Space Observatory discovered clouds so dense (more than 10,000 atoms per cubic centimeter) that they are opaque even to the thermal infrared wavelengths that usually penetrate dusty regions. These so-called infrared dark clouds are much more massive (100 to 100,000 times the mass of the sun) than clouds that had been previously discovered

(45) at optical wavelengths. Over the past several years two teams have used the Spitzer Space Telescope to make a comprehensive survey of them: the Galactic Legacy Infrared Midplane Survey Extraordinaire (GLIMPSE) led by Edward B. Churchwell of the University of Wisconsin—Madison and the MIPSGAL survey led by Sean Carey of the Spitzer Science Center. These clouds appear to be the missing link between

(50) molecular clouds and protostars.

        In fact, dark clouds and dense cores could represent the crucial formative stage of stars when their masses are determined. The clouds come in a range of masses; small ones are more common than large ones. This distribution of masses closely mimics that of stars—except that the clouds are systematically three times more

(55) massive than stars, suggesting that only one third of the mass of a cloud ends up in the newborn star. The rest is somehow lost to space.

        Whether this similarity in distributions is causal or just coincidental remains to be proved. Whatever sets the mass of a star determines its entire life history: whether it is a massive star that dies young and explodes catastrophically or a more modest star

(60) that lives longer and goes more gently into that good night.

17. Which sequence best describes the current thinking about star formation discussed in this passage?
    (A) Extremely dense, massive, infrared dark clouds form; natal clouds form as interstellar medium cools and becomes denser; protostars form; stars form.
    (B) Molecular clouds form as interstellar medium cools and becomes denser; protostars form; extremely dense, massive, infrared dark clouds form; stars form.
    (C) Material from exploded stars coagulates to form molecular clouds; extremely dense, massive infrared dark clouds form; nuclear fusion is initiated; protostars form; stars form.
    (D) Natal clouds form as interstellar medium cools and becomes denser; extremely dense, massive infrared dark clouds form; protostars form; stars form.
    (E) Molecular clouds form out of cooling interstellar medium; massive infrared dark clouds form; nuclear fusion is initiated; protostars form; stars form.

18. Present knowledge of the relationship between infrared dark clouds and stars
    (A) shows conclusively that a star's mass is determined primarily by the mass of the cloud in which it is found
    (B) strongly suggests that a star's mass will always be approximately one-third that of the cloud in which it is formed
    (C) shows clearly that there is no causal relation between the mass of a cloud and the mass of a star
    (D) suggests that a star's mass may be determined by the mass of the cloud in which it was found
    (E) suggests that there is little relation between a star's mass at birth and its life expectancy

19. Which of the following are true?
    (A) New stars are made up partially of material from exploded stars.
    (B) Organic compounds have been observed in molecular clouds.
    (C) A star's mass at birth has little relation to how long it will live.

Select the sentence that draws an analogy between two processes.

20. _____

SECTION 2

Time: 30 minutes
20 questions

> Choose the best answer to each of the following questions in this section.

> Fill in the blank in each sentence by selecting two answer choices that fit the overall meaning of the sentence and produce completed sentences that are equivalent in meaning.

1. Hindus believe that God incarnates in different epochs in various guises, taking _____ form such as Krishna, Buddha, and Jesus.
   (A) an ethereal
   (B) a protean
   (C) a seraphic
   (D) a bodily
   (E) an intangible
   (F) a corporeal

2. Lord Byron, a handsome and dashing figure, was something of _____, his many love affairs with high-born women making him notorious.
   (A) a raconteur
   (B) a Casanova
   (C) a dilettante
   (D) a Lothario
   (E) a hedonist
   (F) an epicurean

3. A difficulty faced by researchers in parapsychology is that many psychologists regard such studies as a waste of resources on a search for _____ phenomena.
   (A) occult
   (B) practical
   (C) chimerical
   (D) pragmatic
   (E) mystical
   (F) fanciful

4. The X-ray machine is _____ example of pure scientific research leading, on a completely unforeseen path, to the development of a revolutionary diagnostic tool; it gave doctors a totally new way to diagnose injuries and diseases.

(A) a putative
(B) a conspicuous
(C) a salient
(D) an ephemeral
(E) a singular
(F) a unique

5. Anarchists believe that since people are autonomous agents, they should not allow themselves to be _____ by the restrictions of the state.

(A) emancipated
(B) liberated
(C) bemused
(D) constrained
(E) circumscribed
(F) perturbed

> **Fill in all of the blanks in the sentences by selecting one entry from the corresponding column of choices in the way that best completes the text.**

6. Laymen sometimes _____ the use of jargon by doctors and lawyers, but they should realize that the need for precise meaning makes the use of some technical terms inevitable.

| obfuscate |
| approve of |
| elicit |
| belie |
| decry |

7. In 1787, when the U.S. Constitution was written, it was proposed that it abolish slavery immediately, but opponents of the measure forced a compromise whereby slavery would not be _____ until early in the next century.

| impugned |
| interpolated |
| proscribed |
| fomented |
| arbitrated |

8. In biological (i) _____ , the relationship between the lord of the manor and the vassal was (ii) _____ , in that in Europe in the middle ages there were many belligerent forces abroad, and thus the lord needed the vassal as a soldier and the vassal needed the security provided by being part of a large institution.

(i)	(ii)
nomenclature	pathological
research	symbiotic
hierarchies	decorous

9. Some contemporary thinkers believe that the theory of evolution solves the philosophical problem of (i) _____—the fact that nature seems to possess (ii) _____ goals toward which life moves—by establishing that there are no such goals, rather merely continuous adaptation by organisms to their habitat.

(i)	(ii)
etiology	inherent
teleology	ancillary
epistemology	concomitant

10. Although the double-edged sword is (i) _____ image, it sometimes loses its effectiveness and becomes (ii) _____ , since there are (iii) _____—from guns to the Internet—that can be aptly described as double-edged swords.

(i)	(ii)	(iii)
a discordant	a solecism	myriad things
an enigmatic	a cliché	few entities
an evocative	a malapropism	a modicum of things

11. One of the reasons attempts to (i) _____ the study of politics have met with some success is the development of public opinion polls, which have become so (ii)_____ that some political scientists fear the advent of governments that do not lead the people, but rather (iii) _____ public opinion.

(i)	(ii)	(iii)
systematize	unreliable	ignore the complexities of
extend	ubiquitous	follow the vagaries of
quantify	subjective	allow for differences in

12. Formal education systems have been criticized on a number of grounds, the most radical criticisms advocating that schools be (i) _____. For example, Ivan Illych, the author of a book entitled *Deschooling Society*, argues that schooling is wasteful in terms of the money and time spent on it, and that it encourages people to regard knowledge and skills acquisitively, and (ii) _____ with material acquisition. He also makes a distinction between organizations which are imposed on people by force like schools and prisons, and those which people participate in by choice, declaring himself in favor of the latter. This last criticism follows from certain assumptions with regard to (iii) _____. Illych's proposals are individual-centered rather than society-centered, which is to say that according to him the individual rather that the society has the right to decide what, how, with whom, and where he or she learns.

(i)	(ii)	(iii)
abolished	equate its acquisition	metaphysics
better funded	juxtapose it	what is socially desirable
countenanced	confound it	factors beyond our control

> Read the passages below, and then answer the questions that follow them based on the information in the passages themselves and in any introductory material or notes. The correct answer may be stated or merely suggested in the passages.

Questions 13–16 are based on the following passage.

Sunlight is not the only forceful breeze that emanates from the Sun. There is another, known as the solar wind. The solar wind is a flood of plasma, protons and electrons, that streams out constantly from the Sun in all directions at a velocity
Line of about 500 hm/s. We never encounter it here on Earth, because we are protected
(5) from it by the Earth's magnetosphere.

If the Earth's magnetosphere blocks the solar wind, it must be creating drag, and therefore feel a force as a result. Why not create an artificial magnetosphere on a spacecraft and use the same effect for propulsion? This was an idea that Boeing engineer Dana Andrews and I hit on in 1988. The idea was timely. In 1987,
(10) high-temperature superconductors had been discovered. These are essential to making a magnetic propulsion device practical, as low-temperature superconductors require too much heavy cooling equipment and ordinary conductors require too much power. The amount of force per square kilometer of solar wind is much less even than that created by sunlight, but the area blocked off by a magnetic
(15) field could be made much larger than any practical solid solar sail. Working in collaboration, Dana and I derived equations and ran computer simulations of the solar wind impacting a spacecraft generating a large magnetic field. Our results: If practical high-temperature superconducting cable can be made that can conduct

(20) electrical current with the same density as the state-of-the-art low-temperature superconductors such as niobium titanium (NbTi)—about 1 million amps per square centimeter—then *magnetic sails* or "magsails" can be made that will have thrust-to-weight ratios *a hundred times* better than that of a 10-micron-thick solar sail. Furthermore, unlike an ultra-thin solar sail, the magsail would not be difficult

(25) to deploy. Instead of being made of thin plastic film, it would be made of rugged cable, which due to magnetic forces would automatically "inflate" itself into a stiff hoop shape as soon as electrical current was put in it. It would take power to get current flowing through the cable, but because superconducting wire has no electrical resistance, once the current was in the cable, no further power would be

(30) needed to keep it going. In addition, the magsail would shield the ship completely against solar flares.

A magsail can exert enough force in the direction away from the Sun to completely negate the gravitational attraction, or it can have its current turned down so as to negate whatever portion of the Sun's gravity is desired. Without going into

(35) details here, this capability would allow a ship co-orbiting the Sun with the Earth to shift itself into orbits that take it to any planet in the solar system, just by turning the magsail power up and down. And it all can be done without an ounce of propellant.

Select one answer choice for the following question.

13. Which of the following would increase the power of a magnetic sail?
   (A) An increase in the velocity of the solar wind
   (B) An increase in the strength of the Earth's magnetosphere
   (C) An increase in the electric current supply to the magsail
   (D) A decrease in the strength of the magnetic field generated by a spacecraft using a magnetic sail
   (E) A decrease in both the frequency and duration of solar flares

---

Consider each of the three choices separately and select all that apply.

14. Which of the following are true?
   (A) The solar wind creates far less force by square kilometer than does sunlight.
   (B) A magnetic sail propulsion system would leave occupants of the spacecraft more vulnerable to solar flares than would a solar sail.
   (C) The development of useful magnetic sails is dependent on further advances in superconductivity technology.

15. Which of the following are advantages of using a magnetic sail as opposed to a solar sail to propel a spacecraft?
    (A) The solar wind is a steadier, more reliable source of energy than sunlight.
    (B) A magnetic sail would be easier to deploy than a solar sail.
    (C) Once the magnetic sail is running, it would require no further electrical power.

16. Which of the following are true?
    (A) A magnetic sail would not be dependent on the Earth's magnetosphere blocking the solar wind.
    (B) The solar wind is concentrated tightly in a direction determined by the Sun's magnetosphere.
    (C) A spacecraft traveling in the solar system propelled by a magnetic sail would not require a propellant.

Questions 17–20 are based on the following passage.

SHIVA-NATARAJA, the Lord of the Dance, is a metaphysic in stone—or bronze or copper or whatever material it happens to be made from, the material being immaterial to its meaning. For me, it is the greatest sculpture there is. But I'm obviously
Line speaking out of my own cultural preferences. For someone else, the four arms, the
(5) ring of fire, the dwarf underfoot, might seem unnatural, even revolting. But for an Indian, each of those features would have a symbolic significance, and the whole would resonate in his mind as powerfully, say, as the Sistine Chapel might in a Christian's, or images of the Buddha might in a Buddhist's.

But what do those symbols mean? How do they fit together? Many Hindus would
(10) have a representation of Nataraja in their homes but many would also have forgotten what it means. That is perhaps the fate of traditional art today. How many Christians now would recall that the Cross was not just two pieces of wood that Christ was crucified on, but was understood, in traditional Christian iconography, as the axis mundi, the temporal order (the horizontal) turning upon the eternal (the vertical)?
(15) To understand that—to understand any traditional art—one must know how to read the symbols. Traditional art, as art scholar Ananda Coomaraswamy explains, is not an expression of mood or feeling. Its effect does not depend on affect, but on understanding a symbolic order of meaning: "The object itself is a point of departure and a signpost . . . we are to see, not the likeness made by hands but its archetype. Sym-
(20) bols cannot be understood "apart from the references which they symbolize." What follows is derived from Coomaraswamy's well-known exegesis in *The Dance of Shiva*.

Shiva is bejeweled, and his locks whirl in the dance. He wears a man's earring in his right ear, and a woman's in his left. He is dancing, of course, and the dance represents his five aspects: creation, preservation, destruction or evolution, embodi-
(25) ment or illusion, release or grace. His upper right hand holds the drum, summoning creation into existence; his upper left hand fire, from which destruction and evolution issue. The lower right hand is uplifted, signifying "Do not fear." And the lower left points downwards, at both the right foot squashing the demon Muyalaka, who symbolizes ignorance, as well as at the raised left foot, which symbolizes release or
(30) grace. The whole stands on a lotus pedestal, from which issues an arch of fire, symbolizing the material universe.

The significance of Shiva's dance is threefold: Firstly, the dance is the source of all movement within the cosmos, as represented by that arch. Secondly, the purpose of the dance is to release souls from illusion. And thirdly, the place of the dance is (35) within each human heart.

Aldous Huxley, in his novel *Island*, has a lovely poetic description of Nataraja, drawing on this skeletal framework: Shiva dances "in all the worlds at once," he says, beginning with "the world of matter."

"Look at the great round halo," Huxley continues, "fringed with fire, within which (40) the god is dancing. It stands for Nature, for the world of mass and energy . . . Nataraja at play among the stars and in the atoms. But also, at play within every living thing . . . Rub-a-dub-dub, the creation tattoo, the cosmic reveille, sounded by the drum . . . But now look at the uppermost of Shiva's left hands. It brandishes the fire by which all that has been created is forthwith destroyed. He dances this way—what (45) happiness! Dances that way—and oh, the pain, the hideous fear, the desolation! For Nataraja it's all play, and the play is an end in itself. He dances because he dances, and the dancing is his maha-sukha, his infinite and eternal bliss. 'Eternal bliss'? For us there's no bliss, only the oscillation between happiness and terror and a sense of outrage at the thought that our pains are as integral a part of Nataraja's dance as our (50) pleasures, our dying as our living.

"Now look at Shiva's other pair of hands. The lower right hand is raised and the palm is turned outwards. That gesture signifies 'Don't be afraid; it's All Right'. But how can anyone in his senses fail to be afraid? How can anyone pretend that evil and suffering are all right? Nataraja has the answer. Look now at his lower left hand. (55) He's using it to point down at his feet. Look closely and you'll see that the right foot is planted squarely on a horrible little subhuman creature . . . the embodiment of ignorance, the manifestation of greedy, possessive selfhood. Stamp on him, break his back! And that's precisely what Nataraja is doing . . . But notice that it isn't at this trampling right foot that he points his finger; it's at the left foot, the foot that, as (60) he dances, he's in the act of raising from the ground. That lifted foot, that dancing defiance of the force of gravity, it's the symbol of release, of moksha, of liberation.

"Nataraja dances in all the worlds at once—in the world of physics and of chemistry, in the world of ordinary, all-too-human experience, in the world finally of Suchness, of Mind, of the Clear Light."

(65) The extraordinary power of traditional art, of various cultures and religions, is its ability to define a totality, in an instant, a gestalt. That explains its enduring power, as well as our difficulty, accustomed as we are to the fractured and fleeting image, in understanding it.

Select one answer choice for the following questions.

17. "A metaphysic in stone" most nearly means
    (A) the use of physics to express and interpret the underlying laws of the universe
    (B) the greatest stone sculpture ever created by human hands
    (C) a sculpture made of stone that expresses a fundamental philosophical principle
    (D) a metaphor for the physical universe
    (E) a piece of sculpture that exists on a metaphysical plane beyond this universe

18. Which of the following statements would the author of this passage be most likely to agree with?
    (A) What makes Siva-Nataraja such a great work of art is that it shows the mood of the artist in a way that is easy for people to relate to.
    (B) Art is a universal language that transcends the limitations of culture.
    (C) It would be impossible for a Christian to have any real understanding of Hindu art due to the different theological presuppositions of Christianity and Hinduism.
    (D) The ultimate aim of any art form is to take us away from our ordinary way of experiencing the world and really make us *feel*.
    (E) Traditional art sometimes seeks to portray underlying reality through the use of symbols.

Consider each of the three choices separately and select all that apply.

19. Which of the following statements would the author of this passage be most likely to agree with?
    (A) Art has progressed greatly since the days when the traditional art that survives today was produced.
    (B) Most people today have difficulty understanding and appreciating traditional art.
    (C) The great popularity of film and television has hindered the ability of many people to appreciate traditional art.

Identify the sentence by writing its first three words and last three words on the line below.

Select the sentence that uses a word that refers to a set of traditional symbolic forms associated with the theme of a work of art.

20. _____

ANSWER KEY
Diagnostic Test

Section 1

1. C, F
2. B, E
3. B, E
4. D, F
5. B, D
6. dictum
7. forestall
8. pejorative
9. Advocates/quixotic
10. dialectic between/Hellenic
11. as a result/based on this reasoning/arrogated
12. quantified/still outweigh/rendering the action wrong
13. A
14. A, B
15. C
16. "But although art...integration and synthesis."
17. D
18. D
19. A, B
20. "Initially the gas . . . in Earth's atmosphere."

Section 2

1. D, F
2. B, D
3. C, F
4. B, C
5. D, E
6. decry
7. proscribed
8. nomenclature/symbiotic
9. teleology/inherent
10. an evocative/a cliché/myriad things
11. quantify/ubiquitous/follow the vagaries of
12. abolished/equate its acquisition/what is socially desirable
13. A
14. A, C
15. B, C
16. A, C
17. C
18. E
19. B, C
20. "How many Christians . . . eternal (the vertical)?"

CORRECT ANSWERS	SCORE
1–6	VERY POOR
7–12	POOR
13–18	BELOW AVERAGE
19–24	AVERAGE
25–30	GOOD
31–36	VERY GOOD
37–40	EXCELLENT

ANSWER EXPLANATIONS

Section 1

1. **(C), (F)** *Sui generis* and *unique* both mean *one of a kind*. If the example is one of a kind it might not be relevant.

2. **(B), (E)** *Sanguine* and *optimistic* both mean *expecting a favorable outcome*. "While" in the sentence signals a contrast of this outlook with the pessimistic outlook described in the first part of the sentence.

3. **(B), (E)** *False* and *spurious* both mean *contrary to the truth*. Due process prevents government from making such charges.

4. **(D), (F)** *Stymied* and *thwarted* both mean *defeat the plans of*. The executive and judiciary branches of government can both defeat plans made by the executive branch.

5. **(B), (D)** "Dualistic" in the sentence means that these religions believe that there are two fundamental principles. *Opposite* and *antithetical* are synonymous. Good and evil are opposite principles.

6. **dictum** *Dictum* (authoritative statement) is the best choice because the statement "Taste has no systems and no proofs" is a definite statement of a principle. The statement is famous, so it can be called authoritative.

7. **forestall** Malthus's writings made many people want to control population in order to *forestall* (*prevent or delay*) mass starvation.

8. **pejorative** *Pejorative* means *having bad connotations*. The word "belief" has no unfavorable or favorable connotations.

9. **Advocates/quixotic** *Advocates* (people who support a cause) of a single world government are often described as *quixotic* (impractical) because the plan for such a government is unrealistically *based on curtailing* (limiting) the power of existing governments.

10. **dialectic between/Hellenic** A *dialectic* is a process of arriving at the truth through a process of debate. *Hellenic* refers to Greek civilization, whose ideals have conducted what can be described as a debate with the ideals of Hebraic civilization.

11. **as a result/based on this reasoning/arrogated** The Supreme Court ruling on apportionment required that members of legislatures be distributed so that every person's vote has equal weight. This has resulted in (*as a result*) electoral reforms. Critics of the Supreme Court ruling reason that there is no evidence that the writers of the Constitution intended such a system. *Based on this reasoning*, these critics believe that the Supreme Court seized power for itself (*arrogated* power to itself) that actually belongs to Congress.

12. **quantified/still outweigh/rendering the action wrong** *Quantified* (expressed as an amount) is the best choice because the sentence is about attempts to measure amounts of happiness. *Still outweigh* is the best choice because the increased unhappiness of the minority would nevertheless be a greater consideration in determining total happiness than some quantified sum of everyone's happiness. Because the increased unhappiness of the minority would be more significant than the increased happiness of the majority, the action would be wrong (*rendering the action wrong*).

13. **A** *Transmuting* and *transforming* have a similar meaning, which is *change*. However, *transmuting* has a stronger suggestion of a fundamental change in the inner nature of a substance. The author is emphasizing that reason and art undergo a change that produces art similar to the process in which alchemists tried to transmute lead into gold.

14. **(A), (B)** The author says, "Apart from our modern need to escape from the dullness of routine and from the overmechanized life of cities, there is the universal and permanent need to escape from... the prison of our single and limited selves."

15. **(C)** The author says, "But, of course, in the *spectrum* of all of these activities art slips over into non-art, for example literature grades into straightforward information and into *propaganda*."

16. **"But although art is in general a process of differentiation and proliferates variety, it is in particular a process of integration and synthesis."** This sentence says that the process of art creates, on the one hand, variety, while, on the other hand, it creates synthesis.

17. **(D)** The passage is mainly about attempts to find out what happens *after* natal clouds form as the interstellar medium becomes denser and *before* protostars form: "Infrared observations have revealed nascent stars deeply embedded in dust but have trouble seeing the earliest steps from molecular cloud to these protostars." The discovery of infrared dark clouds provides what the author calls "the missing link between molecular clouds and protostars."

18. **(D)** The author says, "In fact, dark clouds and dense cores could represent the crucial formative stage of stars when their masses are determined. . . This [the clouds'] distribution of masses closely mimics that of stars . . . Whether this similarity in distributions is caused or just coincidental remains to be proved."

19. **(A), (B)**   (A) The interstellar medium consists partially of "the debris of exploded stars." Since stars form eventually out of the interstellar medium new stars are made up partially of exploded stars. (B) "Radio observations have shown that molecular clouds contain compounds ranging from hydrogen up to complex organics."

20. **"Initially the gas is diffuse, with about one hydrogen atom per cubic centimeter, but as it cools it coagulates into discrete clouds, much as water vapor condenses into clouds in Earth's atmosphere."** This sentence draws an analogy between the process in which the gas that makes up the interstellar medium coagulates to form individual clouds and the process in which water vapor in the Earth's atmosphere condenses to form clouds.

Section 2

1. **(D), (F)**   "Incarnate" means to take *corporeal/bodily* form.

2. **(B), (D)**   Byron's many love affairs made him notorious (brought him disrepute). *Casanova* and *Lothario* have a similar meaning, although *Lothario* has a stronger negative connotation.

3. **(C), (F)**   Many psychologists regard parapsychology research to be a waste of resources because it is a search for non-existent phenomena. Such phenomena are *fanciful/chimerical*.

4. **(B), (C)**   The X-ray machine was a revolutionary new device, so it is a *conspicuous/ salient* example of pure research leading to an extremely useful practical application.

5. **(D), (E)**   Anarchists believe that government is bad and that people should not allow themselves to be restricted (*constrained/circumscribed*) by it.

6. **decry**   Doctors and lawyers sometimes need to use jargon when they need to be precise, so laymen should not *decry* (condemn) this.

7. **proscribed**   A compromise was reached on the issue of slavery that outlawed (*proscribed*) it at a set time in the future rather than immediately.

8. **nomenclature/symbiotic**   *Nomenclature* (terms used in a particular field of knowledge) refers to the use of the word *symbiotic* (mutually helpful) to describe the relationship between lord and vassal.

9. **teleology/inherent**   *Teleology* is belief in a purposeful development toward an end. Nature appears to have such goals toward which it moves. It is reasonable that these goals would be *inherent* (existing as an essential part) goals in nature.

10. **an evocative/a cliché/myriad things**   *Evocative* (tending to call to mind) is a good choice because it contrasts with the negative "it sometimes loses its effectiveness." *Cliché* (overused expression) is appropriate because "double-edged sword" . . . "sometimes loses its effectiveness" and because many things can accurately be termed double-edged swords.

11. **quantify/ubiquitous/follow the vagaries of**   Public opinion polls measure opinion, so *quantify* (express the amount) the study of politics makes good sense. Some political scientists fear that governments might follow public opinion rather than provide

leadership because opinion polls have become so *ubiquitous* (widespread). They fear that governments will *follow the vagaries* (erratic behavior) of public opinion.

12. **abolished/equate its acquisition/what is socially desirable** *Abolished* is the best choice because it describes "the most radical criticisms." *Equate its acquisition* makes sense because "acquisitively" means "demonstrating a strong desire to gain and possess." *What is socially desirable* is a good choice because the sentence following describes what Illych regards as socially desirable.

13. **(A)** Since a magnetic sail depends on the drag produced by blocking the solar wind, we can infer that an increase in the velocity of the solar wind would increase the power of a magnetic sail.

14. **(A), (C)** (A) "The amount of force per square kilometer of solar wind is much less even than that created by sunlight." (C) "If practical high-temperature superconducting cable can be made that can conduct electrical current with the same density as the state-of-the-art low-temperature superconductors such as niobium titanium (NbTi) . . . then *magnetic sails* or 'magsails' can be made that will have thrust-to-weight ratios *a hundred times* better than that of a 10-micron-thick solar sail."

15. **(B), (C)** (B) "Furthermore, unlike an ultra-thin solar sail, the magsail would not be difficult to deploy." (C) "It would take power to get current flowing through the cable, but because superconducting wire has no electrical resistance, once the current was in the cable, no further power would be needed to keep it going."

16. **(A), (C)** (A) The principle of the Earth's magnetosphere blocking the solar wind and the artificial magnetosphere of a spacecraft is the same, but they function independently of each other. (C) Because the ship is propelled by the drag created by blocking the solar wind, no propellant is required. ("And it all can be done without an ounce of propellant.")

17. **(C)** A *metaphysic* is an underlying philosophical principle. Shiva-Nataraja is a sculpture that is sometimes made of stone that expresses such a fundamental principle.

18. **(E)** According to the author, traditional art such as Shiva-Nataraja seeks to express a deep philosophical truth about the world through the use of symbols. In the case of Shiva-Nataraja this truth is about the nature of creation and the part played by human beings in it. He says "to understand any traditional art . . . one must know how to read the symbols" and "Traditional art . . . does not depend on affect, but on understanding a symbolic order of meaning."

19. **(B), (C)** (B) The author says that many Hindus and Christians have forgotten the symbolism underlying the art of their religion. Without "understanding [this] symbolic order of meaning" it is not possible to understand and appreciate traditional art. He says "This is the fate of traditional art today." (C) The author says "That [the ability of art to define a totality] explains its [traditional art's] enduring power, as well as our difficulty, accustomed as we are to the fractured and fleeting image, in understanding it." It can be inferred that the author would agree that film and television have played a part in making us accustomed to the fractured and fleeting image and thus hindered our ability to appreciate traditional art.

20. **"How many Christians now would recall that the Cross was not just two pieces of wood that Christ was crucified on, but was understood, in traditional Christian iconography, as the axis mundi, the temporal order (the horizontal) turning upon the eternal (the vertical)?"** "Christian *iconography*" refers to the traditional symbolic forms associated with the themes of Christian art.

Sentence Equivalence Questions

Fill in the blank in each sentence by selecting <u>two</u> answer choices that fit the overall meaning of the sentence and produce completed sentences that are equivalent in meaning. Answers that are not fully correct will receive no credit.

1. _____ of vegetarianism have anticipated objections that universal vegetarianism would cause unemployment in the meat industry by pointing out that vegetarianism could be introduced gradually, and that jobs could be found for these people in farming.
   (A) Proponents
   (B) Opponents
   (C) Exemplars
   (D) Critics
   (E) Dilettantes
   (F) Advocates

2. As the fields within classical physics (such as electricity and magnetism, mechanics, and optics) came to have utilitarian value, it became _____ for universities to set up separate engineering departments specializing in the application of these fields to real-life problems.
   (A) praiseworthy
   (B) apocryphal
   (C) difficult
   (D) laudable
   (E) expedient
   (F) appropriate

3. A sizable diminution in levels of ozone in the atmosphere was detected over Antarctica in 1985, _____ scientists who had issued warnings in the early 1970s that chlorofluorocarbons and other types of industrial chemicals might cause a reaction that would deplete ozone in the upper atmosphere.

(A) demeaning

(B) critiquing

(C) vindicating

(D) undermining

(E) justifying

(F) humiliating

4. Contraception as a government policy has been the subject of often _____ debate, but leaders of countries with very large populations such as China believe that they have no realistic alternative to taking steps to limit population growth.

(A) vociferous

(B) acrimonious

(C) tendentious

(D) bitter

(E) endless

(F) exemplary

5. Many of the laws of nature formulated by modern physics challenge conventional thinking and are so _____ that they cannot be understood by lay people; however, most people accept them on the authority of reputable scientists.

(A) recondite

(B) tenuous

(C) esoteric

(D) singular

(E) cogent

(F) logical

6. A criticism of democracy as it has existed in practice is that the power to vote for leaders is of _____ importance in societies in which there are powerful vested interests that control the economy, the media, and other powerful areas.

(A) tremendous

(B) peripheral

(C) vestigial

(D) paramount

(E) secondary

(F) primary

7. Sociologists are investigating why people of certain societies have a greater _____ for violence than those of other societies.
   (A) liking
   (B) nomenclature
   (C) proclivity
   (D) ability
   (E) predilection
   (F) capacity

8. Most extrapolations as to what human society will be like in the far future are little more than _____ .
   (A) archetypes
   (B) excuses
   (C) rationalizations
   (D) rhetoric
   (E) speculation
   (F) conjecture

9. Oceans play a major role in climate, often serving to _____ extremes of hot or cold.
   (A) exacerbate
   (B) moderate
   (C) obscure
   (D) conceal
   (E) augment
   (F) temper

10. A number of scientific studies have provided evidence _____ the hypothesis that the Earth is undergoing global warming caused by humanity's activity, creating a "greenhouse effect."
    (A) supporting
    (B) misconstruing
    (C) questioning
    (D) obfuscating
    (E) corroborating
    (F) undermining

11. Plate tectonics explains the _____ of the Himalayan mountain range as the result of a collision between the Eurasian plate and the smaller Indian plate, each carrying a continent.
    (A) height
    (B) genesis
    (C) morphology
    (D) size
    (E) homogeneity
    (F) origin

12. Bill Gates, a canny entrepreneur, foresaw a market for software that would make using computers less threatening to the _____.
    (A) elderly
    (B) neophyte
    (C) unscrupulous
    (D) technocrats
    (E) tyro
    (F) status quo

13. The discovery of the New World made it _____ that more accurate maps be devised in order to allow reliable navigation.
    (A) moot
    (B) imperative
    (C) essential
    (D) incontrovertible
    (E) academic
    (F) debatable

14. The quest for absolute zero, the lowest temperature theoretically possible, has become, for some scientists, _____ to the search for the Holy Grail.
    (A) subordinate
    (B) comparable
    (C) impervious
    (D) ancillary
    (E) analogous
    (F) cognate

15. People who believe that technology is largely _____ to both human beings and nature are sometimes referred to as "neo-luddites."
    (A) deleterious
    (B) opaque
    (C) inimical
    (D) anthropogenic
    (E) obscure
    (F) amoral

16. The framers of America's Constitution initially were _____ to include provisions explicitly defining civil liberties because they wanted to minimize the role of government, even in defending precious individual liberties; however, several years after the Constitution was ratified, the Bill of Rights was added as the first ten amendments to the Constitution, guaranteeing, among other things, freedom of speech, religion, press, and assembly.

    (A) keen
    (B) encouraged
    (C) loath
    (D) reluctant
    (E) enabled
    (F) eager

17. These famous words of the American Declaration of Independence _____ state the doctrine of natural law as applied to relations between government and the governed: "We hold these truths to be self-evident, that all men are created equal, that they are endowed by their Creator with certain unalienable Rights, that among these are Life, Liberty and the pursuit of Happiness—That to secure these rights, Governments are instituted among Men, deriving their just powers from the consent of the governed."

    (A) succinctly
    (B) cogently
    (C) jocularly
    (D) definitively
    (E) jocosely
    (F) concisely

18. Although it is true that some jargon is unnecessary, much of it is used legitimately by experts, especially in _____ fields.

    (A) holistic
    (B) diverse
    (C) varied
    (D) recondite
    (E) abstruse
    (F) technical

19. Countries like Singapore, whose economies depend greatly on trade, tend to _____ the advantages of free trade.

    (A) laud
    (B) belittle
    (C) disparage
    (D) exaggerate
    (E) lament
    (F) praise

20. To the physicist, the nucleus of an atom is a combination of myriad forces that to the lay person are _____ .
    (A) a presupposition
    (B) an enigma
    (C) a mélange
    (D) a shibboleth
    (E) a misnomer
    (F) a mystery

21. Conservatism has its roots in the upheavals of the French Revolution, which resulted in the _____ of the influence of the Church, the monarch, and the landed aristocracy in Europe.
    (A) consummation
    (B) waning
    (C) juxtaposition
    (D) burgeoning
    (E) dissolution
    (F) decline

22. Arguably, the Internet exacerbates the _____ between rich and poor countries because the economies of countries with access to it become more competitive, whereas those without access to it lag behind.
    (A) inequality
    (B) histrionics
    (C) tension
    (D) enmity
    (E) disparity
    (F) dispute

23. The hypothesis that life is _____ throughout the universe is plausible, but on the available evidence it can not be proved or disproved.
    (A) sentient
    (B) prevalent
    (C) innocuous
    (D) very common
    (E) extremely rare
    (F) fecund

24. Some economists believe that the free enterprise system should be the _____for all societies, regardless of the nature of their cultures.
    (A) paradigm
    (B) ethos
    (C) best motif
    (D) icon
    (E) economic engine
    (F) model

25. A number of historians have claimed to have discovered _____ laws governing the unfolding of events, but the consensus of contemporary historians is that they do not meet the criteria for scientific laws because there are numerous reasonable objections that can be raised against them.
    (A) immutable
    (B) antiquated
    (C) pernicious
    (D) scientific
    (E) unchangeable
    (F) empirical

26. In a manner similar to the automobile, which freed people from the necessity of living near their work places, the Internet allows people to live in _____ areas and "telecommute"—that is, do their work and interact with colleagues through a computer link.
    (A) isolated
    (B) remote
    (C) proximate
    (D) urban
    (E) pastoral
    (F) nearby

27. There exists a tradition that literature should, _____ , strive to teach worthwhile moral lessons.
    (A) fortuitously
    (B) inexplicably
    (C) inconspicuously
    (D) cryptically
    (E) unobtrusively
    (F) rhetorically

28. In order to properly diagnose disease, doctors normally try to be _____ in their examination of the patient.
    (A) puerile
    (B) dispassionate
    (C) accurate
    (D) impartial
    (E) fatuous
    (F) empathetic

29. _____ people are often caught in a vicious circle: because they are poor they cannot afford a good education and so can't find a good job, which means they can't make much money and so remain poor.

(A) Affluent

(B) Indigent

(C) Indolent

(D) Autonomous

(E) Rich

(F) Impoverished

30. A Marxist theory that has had continuing influence in the social sciences is economic determinism—the idea that social and political institutions are decided not by _____ but by the material conditions in which people live.

(A) ideology

(B) pragmatism

(C) consensus

(D) political machinations

(E) political beliefs

(F) fiat

31. In a debate one might be tempted to use techniques such as exaggeration and appeals to emotion, but generally these ultimately _____ one's argument.

(A) undermine

(B) disprove

(C) weaken

(D) support

(E) embellish

(F) buttress

32. Orthodox Judaism, Christianity, and Islam tend to see mysticism as _____ to their teachings and to their followers, whereas Hinduism and Buddhism tend to encourage their adherents to pursue mystical experience.

(A) harmful

(B) vital

(C) tangential

(D) inimical

(E) central

(F) irrelevant

33. The newspaper editorial suggests that a plan to _____ poverty through a network of concerned people that would redirect twenty percent of the resources of the developed world to poor countries is just pure fantasy.
    (A) eliminate
    (B) perpetuate
    (C) eradicate
    (D) reduce
    (E) continue
    (F) ameliorate

34. Political debate in democratic countries is very much concerned with finding a middle ground between groups with opposing views so that _____ can be reached.
    (A) a dilemma
    (B) a consensus
    (C) a solution
    (D) an agreement
    (E) an impasse
    (F) autonomy

35. Although the amount of energy in an isolated system cannot change, energy in one form can be _____ into another form.
    (A) diffused
    (B) transmuted
    (C) incarnated
    (D) inculcated
    (E) mutated
    (F) changed

36. During the Crusades, leaders of the Catholic Church urged the faithful to war, and Moslems defended their lands with equal _____ .
    (A) enthusiastic devotion to a cause
    (B) disregard for human life
    (C) ambivalence
    (D) aplomb
    (E) zeal
    (F) dispassion

37. Several popular historians have created fictional scenarios in order to _____ what history would have been if earlier events had been different.
    (A) delineate
    (B) pontificate about
    (C) speculate about
    (D) obviate
    (E) rhapsodize about
    (F) conjecture about

38. The trend toward what some historians have called the "imperial Presidency" started early in the twentieth century with the activist presidency of Theodore Roosevelt, and reached its _____ under President Franklin D. Roosevelt, who planned and implemented his New Deal policies despite considerable opposition from Congress and the Supreme Court.

(A) zenith

(B) low point

(C) epitome

(D) conclusion

(E) nadir

(F) acme

39. _____ hypothesis is that human behavior is too complex to be meaningfully described or predicted by scientific laws, especially at the social level.

(A) A dubious

(B) An inductive

(C) A conclusive

(D) A meretricious

(E) A credible

(F) A plausible

40. Cultural imperialism occurs when one country imposes its values, views, or _____ on the people of another country.

(A) mores

(B) ideology

(C) religion

(D) constitution

(E) jurisprudence

(F) customs

41. It seems likely that herd mentality plays a part in depressions; as an economy slumps, some people panic, others _____ this panic, and something akin to mass hysteria ensues.

(A) revel in

(B) belittle

(C) imitate

(D) disparage

(E) emulate

(F) escape

42. Fundamental to democracy is the idea of natural rights—the belief that certain rights are inherent in human beings, and that no agency can _____ these rights.
   (A) interpolate
   (B) guarantee
   (C) invalidate
   (D) nullify
   (E) query
   (F) ascertain

43. Physicists have compiled _____ evidence that the total energy of an isolated system remains constant over time.
   (A) empirical
   (B) quantitative
   (C) incontrovertible
   (D) putative
   (E) convincing
   (F) indisputable

44. Since humankind depends on topsoil for food, it seems _____ to ensure that it is not eroded by irresponsible land development and strip mining.
   (A) myopic
   (B) ineffectual
   (C) short-sighted
   (D) prudent
   (E) skeptical
   (F) wise

45. Some observers see the rapid growth of big business as _____ of a new world political system in which the dominant political entities are not nation states, but multinational companies.
   (A) the epitome
   (B) the harbinger
   (C) the archetype
   (D) the dream
   (E) the forerunner
   (F) a perversion

46. One of the most _____ uses to which humanity has put electro-magnetic radiation is radio broadcasting, which allows information to be sent in the form of electrical waves.
   (A) theoretical
   (B) anachronistic
   (C) efficacious
   (D) divergent
   (E) abstract
   (F) effective

47. Estuaries are particularly at risk because in addition to being affected by off-shore drilling, they often also receive industrial and other effluents that can _____ many of the species in their ecosystem.
    (A) devastate
    (B) deplete
    (C) decimate
    (D) identify
    (E) protect
    (F) safeguard

48. Climatologists are trying to unravel the _____ trends in the temperature of the Earth's climate, but are often stymied by their incredible complexity.
    (A) complicated
    (B) clear cut
    (C) ephemeral
    (D) convoluted
    (E) straightforward
    (F) salient

49. It is often argued that tyrannical governments cannot be _____ for long by a policy of appeasement on the part of other countries.
    (A) placated
    (B) castigated
    (C) mollified
    (D) buttressed
    (E) chastised
    (F) controlled

50. A juror can be dismissed if it is shown that he or she has _____ against the defendant for reasons of race or religion.
    (A) a bias
    (B) a predisposition
    (C) litigation
    (D) a grudge
    (E) a stricture
    (F) animosity

ANSWER KEY
Sentence Equivalence Questions

1. A, F		**26.** A, B	
2. E, F		**27.** C, E	
3. C, E		**28.** B, D	
4. B, D		**29.** B, F	
5. A, C		**30.** A, E	
6. B, E		**31.** A, C	
7. C, E		**32.** A, D	
8. E, F		**33.** A, C	
9. B, F		**34.** B, D	
10. A, E		**35.** B, F	
11. B, F		**36.** A, E	
12. B, E		**37.** C, F	
13. B, C		**38.** A, F	
14. B, E		**39.** E, F	
15. A, C		**40.** A, F	
16. C, D		**41.** C, E	
17. A, F		**42.** C, D	
18 D, E		**43.** C, F	
19. A, F		**44.** D, F	
20. B, F		**45.** B, E	
21. B, F		**46.** C, F	
22. A, E		**47.** A, C	
23. B, D		**48.** A, D	
24. A, F		**49.** A, C	
25. A, E		**50.** A, B	

ANSWER EXPLANATIONS

1. **(A), (F)** *Proponents* and *advocates* are people who speak in favor of something. They "have anticipated objections," so they are supporters of vegetarianism.

2. **(E), (F)** "Utilitarian value" suggests that practical applications were feasible, so setting up engineering departments was *expedient/appropriate*.

3. **(C), (E)** "A sizeable diminution" shows that scientists who issued warnings were correct, thus *vindicating/justifying* them.

4. **(B), (D)** All the choices are possible. However, *acrimonious* and *bitter* are the only synonyms and make good sense.

5. **(A), (C)** "Cannot be understood by lay people" suggests that the laws are difficult to understand (*recondite/esoteric*).

6. **(B), (E)** "A criticism of democracy" suggests that the power to vote for leaders is of *secondary/peripheral* importance. Also, it is stated that there are "powerful vested interests that control the economy, the media, and other areas."

7. **(C), (E)** (A) *liking* and (F) *capacity* make sense. (B) *Nomenclature* makes some sense but is odd usage. (D) *Ability* also makes some sense. However, *proclivity/predilections* make the best sense and are synonyms meaning "tendency."

8. **(E), (F)** "Extrapolations" are estimates made by projecting known information. "What human society will look like in the far future" suggests extrapolations. It makes sense that extrapolations about the far future would be little more than *speculation/conjecture* (conclusions based on insufficient evidence).

9. **(B), (F)** "Extremes of hot and cold" are *moderated/tempered* by the ocean.

10. **(A), (E)** All the choices make sense. However, the only synonyms are *supporting/corroborating*, which make good sense.

11. **(B), (F)** All the choices are reasonable. However, the only synonyms are *genesis/origin*, which make sense because the collision of two plates could create a mountain range.

12. **(B), (E)** A market for software that would make using computers less threatening" suggests that there are people who are not experienced in using computers (*neophyte/tyro*).

13. **(B), (C)** "To allow reliable navigation" after "the discovery of the New World" it was very important (*imperative/essential*) to have more accurate maps.

14. **(B), (E)** The search for the Holy Grail (a cup believed to have been used by Jesus Christ at the Last Supper) is *comparable/analogous* to the quest for absolute zero because both are extremely difficult.

15. **(A), (C)** The only two synonyms are *deleterious/inimical*, and they make good sense in the sentence. It is reasonable that some people think that technology is *harmful* to both human beings and nature. Luddites were early nineteenth-century British workers who destroyed laborsaving machinery they thought would cause unemployment.

16. **(C), (D)** The framers of the Constitution were *loath/reluctant* to include provisions of any kind that would increase the role of government.

17. **(A), (F)** Choices A, B, D, and F all make some sense. However, *succinctly* and *concisely* are synonyms and make good sense.

18. **(D), (E)** "Used legitimately by experts" means that jargon is used properly by specialists in various fields. It makes sense that experts would especially use jargon in fields that are difficult to comprehend (*recondite/abstruse*).

19. **(A), (F)** It makes sense that countries whose economies depend greatly on trade would *laud/praise* the advantages of free trade.

20. **(B), (F)** Physicists understand the forces of the nucleus, whereas to lay people they are *a mystery/an enigma*.

21. **(B), (F)** It is reasonable that "the upheavals of the French Revolution" weakened existing powerful institutions, leading to the *waning/decline* of their influence.

22. **(A), (E)** Countries with access to the Internet (rich countries) "become more competitive" whereas those without access to the Internet (poor countries) "lag behind." This exacerbates (worsens) the *inequality/disparity* between rich countries and poor countries.

23. **(B), (D)** All the choices make some sense. However, *prevalent* and *very common* have the same meaning and make good sense.

24. **(A), (F)** *Paradigm* and *model* have the same meaning. There are no other synonyms and they make good sense because it is reasonable that many economists believe strongly in the value of the free market system.

25. **(A), (E)** *Immutable* and *unchangeable* have the same meaning and make good sense. (B) "antiquated" and (C) "pernicious" make little sense. (D) "scientific" and (F) "empirical" make some sense but are not synonyms.

26. **(A), (B)** The Internet allows people to "do their work and interact with colleagues through a computer link," so it makes sense that it allows people to live in *isolated/remote* areas.

27. **(C), (E)** *Inconspicuously* and *unobtrusively* have the same meaning and make good sense because people tend not to like moral lessons in literature to be conspicuous.

28. **(B), (D)** *Dispassionate* and *impartial* have the same meaning. It makes sense that doctors try to be impartial in diagnosing disease.

29. **(B), (F)** The sentence describes a vicious circle involving the poor. *Indigent* and *impoverished* are synonyms meaning very poor.

30. **(A), (E)** The sentence contrasts "the material conditions in which people live" with something very different. *Ideology* and *political beliefs* have the same meaning and contrast logically with material conditions.

31. **(A), (C)** One might be tempted to use exaggeration or other such techniques in a debate. However, "ultimately" (in the end) they *undermine/weaken* one's argument.

32. **(A), (D)** Hinduism and Buddhism encourage their followers to seek mystical experience, so it is reasonable to infer that they regard such experience as harmless and even beneficial. In contrast, Orthodox Judaism, Christianity, and Islam see mysticism as *harmful/inimical* to their followers.

33. **(A), (C)** The newspaper editorial suggests that the plan is "just building castles in the air," so it makes sense that it is an unrealistic plan to *eliminate/eradicate* poverty. Ameliorate means "improve," so it is not as close in meaning as are *eliminate* and *eradicate*.

34. **(B), (D)** Finding a middle ground between groups with opposing views will result in *a consensus/an agreement*.

35. **(B), (F)** It makes sense that although the amount of energy cannot change energy can be *transmuted/changed* from one form to another.

36. **(A), (E)** Leaders of the Catholic Church "urged the faithful to war," so it makes sense they were full of *zeal/enthusiastic devotion to a cause*. Muslims are described as having equal *zeal/enthusiastic devotion to a cause*.

37. **(C), (F)** Fictional scenarios allow historians to *speculate about/conjecture about* how history would have been different assuming certain changes in earlier events.

38. **(A), (F)** The sentence describes a trend toward an "imperial presidency" that reached its high point (*zenith/acme*) under President Franklin D. Roosevelt.

39. **(E), (F)** *Credible* and *plausible* are the only two words with the same meaning (believable) and make good sense.

40. **(A), (F)** All the choices make some sense. However, only (A) *mores* and (F) *customs* are synonyms, and they make good sense.

41. **(C), (E)** A herd mentality can produce something like mass hysteria in which people *imitate/emulate* the panic of others.

42. **(C), (D)** If certain rights are "inherent" in human beings, no agency [can] *invalidate/nullify* these rights.

43. **(C), (F)** All the choices make sense, but the only two words with the same meaning are *incontrovertible* and *indisputable*, which make good sense.

44. **(D), (F)** Since humankind depends on topsoil for food it is *prudent/wise* to prevent its erosion.

45. **(B), (E)** If big business continues its rapid growth, it is possible that multinational companies will be the dominant political entities. Thus, it is possible to see the rapid growth of big business as the *harbinger/forerunner* of a new world political system.

46. **(C), (F)** Radio broadcasting allows information to be sent in the form of electrical waves, so it makes sense to describe this use of electromagnetic radiation as *efficacious/effective*.

47. **(A), (C)** Estuaries are described as being "particularly at risk," so it's reasonable that industrial and other effluents can *devastate/decimate* many of the species in their ecosystem.

48. **(A), (D)**   Climatologists are "often stymied by" the "incredible complexity" of trends in the temperature of the Earth's climate, so it makes sense that these trends are *complicated/convoluted*.

49. **(A), (C)**   A policy of appeasement by definition seeks to appease an aggressive country. It is reasonable to argue that tyrannical governments cannot be *placated/mollified* for long because they are committed to their aggression.

50. **(A), (B)**   Since it is the duty of the court to ensure that jurors are fair in the judgment of a case, it makes sense that a juror can be dismissed if it is shown that he or she has a *bias/predisposition* against the defendant.

Text Completion Questions: Single Blank

> Fill in the blank in each sentence below by selecting one entry from the corresponding column of choices in the way that best completes the text.

1. By coincidence, the image of the sun as viewed from Earth is nearly _____ that of the moon as viewed from the Earth.

concomitant with
homogeneous with
congruent with
tantamount to
consonant with

2. In the 1960s the U.S. Supreme Court assumed the role of social activist because a majority of justices believed that some of the states were _____ in implementing federal laws due to factors such as racial prejudice, which made authorities reluctant to act lest they lose the support of their constituents.

dispassionate
robust
phlegmatic
saturnine
dilatory

3. The Greeks believed that three judges decide the fate of souls, heroes going to the Elysian Fields and _____ going to Tartarus.

reformers
refugees
malefactors
bohemians
paragons

4. The nineteenth-century British satirist Thomas Love Peacock _____ the metaphysical speculation of thinkers like Samuel Taylor Coleridge as pretentious and nonsensical.

| documented |
| palliated |
| interpolated |
| lampooned |
| husbanded |

5. One of the interesting things about maps is that to make a map certain decisions must be made about what to include in it and how to represent this information; from such decisions _____ can be made about the outlook of the mapmakers.

| prognostications |
| stories |
| inferences |
| suggestions |
| premises |

6. _____ technologies created the factory system of mass production and specialization that allowed the industrial revolution.

| Innovative |
| Frenetic |
| Nominal |
| Meretricious |
| Terrestrial |

7. The Austrian _____ Konrad Lorenz was a pioneer in the study of animal behavior under natural conditions, untainted by human interaction with the subjects.

| entomologist |
| ethologist |
| ethnologist |
| ecologist |
| etymologist |

8. Nineteenth-century _____ for capitalism provided a rationalization for the exploitation of the poor by the rich by drawing an analogy between the free market of capitalism and the struggle for existence described by Darwin, in which the fit survive.

| pedants |
| polyglots |
| demagogues |
| apologists |
| satirists |

9. Like abstract art, expressionist art seeks to portray subjective reality by distorting external reality; however, unlike abstract art, which emphasizes the cognitive, expressionist art is largely concerned with _____ states of mind.

| aberrant |
| subjective |
| normative |
| affective |
| subliminal |

10. A sizable diminution in levels of ozone in the atmosphere was detected over Antarctica in 1985, _____ scientists who had issued warnings in the early 1970s that chlorofluorocarbons and other types of industrial chemicals might cause a reaction which would deplete ozone in the upper atmosphere.

| undermining |
| admonishing |
| vindicating |
| surprising |
| critiquing |

11. Because of its political problems and _____ inflation for long periods after World War II, some economists have cited Argentina as a country that nearly fell from the ranks of developed countries to become an underdeveloped country.

| falling |
| salutary |
| intractable |
| scant |
| commensurate |

12. One of the great triumphs of modern medicine has been the prevention, largely through inoculation, of many cases of diseases such as typhoid, poliomyelitis, and diphtheria that previously were among humanity's greatest _____ .

attributes
paroxysms
scourges
pathogens
specters

13. An ethical _____ sometimes faced by drug companies is whether they should sell drugs more cheaply in poor countries than in affluent countries, thus foregoing profits that would recompense them for the high cost of the research required to develop new drugs, or sell them at the market price and thus have sufficient funds to continue the development of new drugs.

vicissitude
dilemma
peccadillo
paradigm
pretext

14. One of Sigmund Freud's famous _____ remarks about the field of psychoanalysis was, "Sometimes a cigar is just a cigar," implying that he felt that the mind does not always attach a symbolic meaning to objects.

misanthropic
gnomic
semiotic
jocular
psychic

15. The Roman goddess Venus has had many _____ in the Mediterranean world, but today she is most commonly known throughout the region as the goddess of love and beauty.

friezes
admirers
scruples
incarnations
proclivities

16. Primary malnutrition is a deficiency in the consumption of food, whereas secondary malnutrition is due to the inability of the body to properly utilize ingested food or excessive excretion; in secondary malnutrition, a disease is usually _____ as the cause.

| insinuated |
| implicated |
| obliterated |
| impugned |
| obviated |

17. Laypeople regard antimatter, which is material made up of antiparticles, as _____ and improbable substance, but physicists assure us that it exists because it has been observed.

| an immaterial |
| an inanimate |
| an exotic |
| an incipient |
| an ostentatious |

18. Modern communications has increasingly made use of the very high-frequency segment of the radio spectrum, partly because of the _____ of communications satellites that allow line-of-sight transmission, which is well suited for such very high frequencies.

| parity |
| expense |
| manifestation |
| advent |
| inducement |

19. As conductors approach absolute zero, they achieve _____ called "super-conductivity," allowing them to transmit electrical current with great efficiency.

| an attribute |
| a hegemony |
| a malady |
| a prowess |
| a validity |

20. Thomas Love Peacock, the classically oriented contemporary of the English romantic poets, believed that they had strayed too far from reality and were creating a _____ universe of their own in which they wallowed complacently.

subliminal
solipsistic
maudlin
corporeal
pantheistic

21. Because electromagnetic waves travel at the speed of light, radio communication between astronauts on the moon and the Earth would be _____ by delays of only several seconds, whereas astronauts voyaging to the planets would face communications delays of minutes or even hours.

bolstered
hampered
enervated
facilitated
ravaged

22. Albert Einstein stated that he would not have lent his _____ to the cause of the proponents of building the atomic bomb if he had known in advance that the Germans would not develop one.

empathy
notoriety
credibility
prescience
accolades

23. The concept of the biosphere has helped to _____ the idea of life on Earth as a fragile and interdependent system that humanity disrupts at its peril.

obfuscate
parody
refute
disseminate
transcend

24. _____ is intrinsic to language, but writers should nevertheless strive to be as precise as possible.

| Equivocation |
| Malapropism |
| Ambiguity |
| Grandiloquence |
| Innuendo |

25. One indicator of a warming trend in the Earth's climate is that glaciers are melting more rapidly than previously; a glacier near Chile, for example, is _____ losing seven meters of its surface per year.

| inviolably |
| ironically |
| inexorably |
| inexplicably |
| subjectively |

26. It is now clear that ice ages, far from being _____ , occur regularly.

| glacial |
| pervasive |
| prodigious |
| aberrant |
| sublime |

27. Although antimatter has _____ existence in our locality of the universe since it is very quickly destroyed by ordinary matter, scientists believe that it exists more abundantly elsewhere.

| a synergetic |
| a platonic |
| a viable |
| an ephemeral |
| a precipitous |

28. Not only has organic chemistry provided invaluable insight into the nature of life, it has also proven to be of great _____ value, allowing chemists to create the organic compounds used in thousands of petrochemical, pharmaceutical, and other products.

experimental
scientific
utilitarian
heuristic
theoretical

29. Chemists _____ many organic compounds from petroleum, which is composed of the remains of microscopic marine organisms.

misconstrue
squander
sequester
synthesize
quantify

30. Photosynthesis is one part of the carbon cycle, allowing molecules of carbon dioxide to be incorporated into plants, which are then eaten by animals and made _____ part of their tissue.

a nascent
a fecund
a sovereign
an alchemical
an intrinsic

31. Like most movements in art, surrealism became _____ fairly quickly, but its influence is still pervasive.

bourgeois
extant
enervated
germane
inviolable

32. Words acquire connotations as they are used in various contexts; thus, a word may have a straightforward _____ but its connotations may be quite complex.

| delineation |
| denotation |
| archetype |
| etymology |
| neologism |

33. A recurrent issue in literary criticism is whether a work of literature should be _____—that is, whether it should merely entertain or whether it should teach moral values.

| culpable |
| viable |
| ephemeral |
| didactic |
| prurient |

34. A tradition of great poets (Chaucer, Shakespeare, Donne, Pope, Eliot, and Yeats, for example) is held by some critics to exist in a line of succession, each adding his contribution to the line, thereby creating _____ of work, which, although diverse, is unified by being part of this tradition.

| a pastiche |
| an oeuvre |
| a parody |
| a gamut |
| a corpus |

35. The fact that irony is _____ means that the listener (or reader) who "gets it" is able to feel superior to those who do not understand it.

| subtle |
| humorous |
| situational |
| generic |
| gratuitous |

36. Knowledge of the _____ of similar words allows a writer to choose the most appropriate word for each situation.

argot
juxtaposition
nuances
ambiguities
cognates

37. To establish the validity of the _____ that cigarette smoking causes lung cancer, epidemiologists had to establish that the higher rate of lung cancer in smokers is caused solely by smoking and not by other factors.

caveat
misapprehension
leitmotif
ontology
induction

38. Part of the genius of the English poetic tradition is the way it can accommodate _____ challenges to it, such as the revolutionary work of the romantic poets of the nineteenth century.

radical
occasional
multifarious
obscure
innocuous

39. Some science fiction writers believe that one of the responsibilities of the genre is to analyze present trends in science and society and _____ them into the future so that their possible impact can be assessed.

promulgate
sustain
scrutinize
extrapolate
protract

40. Champions of the command economy contend that, unlike the free market, which responds mostly to short-term fluctuations in the market, the command economy has the advantage of being able to effectively incorporate long-term strategies, such as resource _____ and management of the impact of economic activity on the environment.

honing
husbanding
paring
juxtapositioning
utilization

41. Some critics argue that everything a writer "says" in a work of fiction should be interpreted in the context of the author's life; however, others contend that a text is more fruitfully regarded as _____ , existing independently of its creator, similar to a creation of God or nature.

impromptu
autonomous
inviolable
salient
sacrosanct

42. According to political scientist Stephen F. Knott, the United States has engaged in _____ operations—ranging from kidnapping to covert efforts to overthrow foreign governments—regularly since its founding.

superfluous
sententious
clandestine
putative
inviolable

43. Pragmatism is similar to Utilitarianism in its belief that human _____ is primarily an instrument to help human beings to live good lives.

dudgeon
lassitude
approbation
ratiocination
catharsis

44. A catch-22 facing modern composers—and one that nearly _____ their compositions from being heard publicly—is that only music that is familiar to audiences is likely to be played in concert halls, but that for music to become popular it must be played in concert halls.

precludes
discourages
deters
obviates
induces

45. In a sense, everyone is a prisoner of his or her preconceptions and _____ experience, which inevitably give rise to prejudices.

cosmopolitan
convoluted
quintessential
meretricious
circumscribed

46. Countries such as Sweden and Denmark are sometimes criticized for providing so many benefits for their citizens that they lose their incentive to work, but it is _____ fact that the Scandinavian "welfare states" have some of the most dynamic, innovative, and productive economies in the world.

an academic
a serendipitous
an incontrovertible
a melancholy
an apocryphal

47. Some observers see multinational companies as the tools by which an elite class that will exploit the labor of the rest of the world is emerging, while those with a more _____ view see them as precursors to a world government that will bring harmony to a strife-torn world.

unpalatable
collateral
prescient
sagacious
sanguine

48. It is important for writers to make their frame of reference clear so that readers will have some idea of the _____ from which they are starting.

| premises |
| implications |
| tropes |
| platitudes |
| precursors |

49. Historians generally agree that Prohibition significantly reduced the amount of alcohol consumed in the United States, but that the cost to society due to the rise of gangsterism, as well as the _____ of respect for law that came with widespread breaking of the prohibition laws, made its repeal sensible.

| articulating |
| sanctioning |
| undermining |
| implementing |
| attenuating |

50. An important element in the modern _____ is an almost unquestioning belief in science and ratiocination.

| karma |
| pantheon |
| proletariat |
| juggernaut |
| zeitgeist |

ANSWER KEY
Text Completion Questions: Single Blank

1. congruent with
2. dilatory
3. malefactors
4. lampooned
5. inferences
6. Innovative
7. ethologist
8. apologists
9. affective
10. vindicating
11. intractable
12. scourges
13. dilemma
14. jocular
15. incarnations
16. implicated
17. an exotic
18 advent
19. an attribute
20. solipsistic
21. hampered
22. credibility
23. disseminate
24. Ambiguity
25. inexorably
26. aberrant
27. an ephemeral
28. utilitarian
29. synthesize
30. an intrinsic
31. enervated
32. denotation
33. didactic
34. a corpus
35. subtle
36. nuances
37. induction
38. radical
39. extrapolate
40. husbanding
41. autonomous
42. clandestine
43. ratiocination
44. precludes
45. circumscribed
46. an incontrovertible
47. sanguine
48. premises
49. undermining
50. zeitgeist

ANSWER EXPLANATIONS

1. **congruent with** The image of the sun as viewed from Earth nearly coincides with or is *congruent with* that of the moon when it is superimposed on the image of the moon. *Consonant with* means "consistent with" or "in agreement with," so this is not as good a choice.

2. **dilatory** "Authorities [were] reluctant to act" signals that states were *dilatory* (slow; tending to delay) in implementing federal laws.

3. **malefactors** *Malefactors* (doers of evil) is the best choice because it contrasts with "heroes."

4. **lampooned** Thomas Love Peacock considered the metaphysical speculation of thinkers like Coleridge "pretentious and nonsensical," so it makes sense that he *lampooned* (attacked with satire) it.

5. **inferences** *Inferences* (conclusions) can be made about the outlook of the mapmakers "from such decisions" they made creating their maps.

6. **Innovative** *Innovative* (original) technologies created the factory system of mass production and specialization that led to the industrial revolution.

7. **ethologist** An *ethologist* is a scientist who studies animal behavior. Konrad Lorenz was "a pioneer in the study of animal behavior under natural conditions."

8. **apologists** *Apologists* (persons who defend or justify a cause) "provided a rationalization for the exploitation of the poor by the rich."

9. **affective** *Affective* (relating to the emotions) is the best answer because expression-ist art is contrasted with abstract art, which stresses the cognitive (relating to mental processes by which knowledge is acquired).

10. **vindicating** Scientists issued warnings in the early 1970s of a reaction "which would deplete ozone in the upper atmosphere." These scientists were *vindicated* (had their claim supported) when a sizable diminution in levels of ozone in the atmosphere was detected in 1985.

11. **intractable** Argentina's "political problems and *intractable* (not easily managed) inflation" led some economists to consider labeling Argentina an underdeveloped country.

12. **scourges** Typhoid, poliomyelitis, and diphtheria previously were among humanity's greatest *scourges* (sources of widespread affliction).

13. **dilemma** Drug companies face an ethical *dilemma* (a situation requiring a choice between two equally unsatisfactory options) because they must choose between selling drugs cheaply in poor countries and not having enough money to develop new drugs and selling them at the market price in poor countries and thus have enough money to develop new drugs.

14. **jocular** *Jocular* (humorous) makes the best sense of the choices given because the comment is humorous in light of the fact that Sigmund Freud was the founder of the

field of psychoanalysis, which is to a large extent based on the view that the mind attaches a symbolic meaning to objects. "Does not always attach a symbolic meaning to objects" is a clue that Freud felt the mind generally attaches a symbolic meaning to objects.

15. **incarnations**   Venus has had many *incarnations* (bodily forms) in the Mediterranean world, but the one most commonly known there today is the goddess of love and beauty.

16. **implicated**   It is reasonable that a disease would usually be *implicated* (connected closely) as the cause of the body's inability to properly utilize ingested food and excessive excretion.

17. **an exotic**   Physicists assure laypeople that antimatter exists despite its being an "*exotic* (intriguingly unusual) and improbable substance."

18. **advent**   Communications satellites that allow line-of-sight transmissions use the very high-frequency segment of the radio spectrum. Thus, this segment of the spectrum has been increasingly used with the *advent* (coming) of such satellites.

19. **an attribute**   Superconductivity is an *attribute* (quality) that allows conductors to transmit electrical current very efficiently.

20. **solipsistic**   Peacock believed that the English romantic poets had "strayed too far from reality" and were creating their "own universe." *Solipsistic* (relating to the belief that the self is the only reality) is an appropriate word to describe such a universe.

21. **hampered**   In contrast to the planets, which are far from the Earth, the moon and the Earth are relatively near to each other. Thus, radio signals could travel from the Earth to the moon and vice versa with only a short delay. Radio communications would be little *hampered* (prevented from working freely).

22. **credibility**   Albert Einstein said he would not have lent his *credibility* (power of eliciting belief) to those in favor of building the atomic bomb if he had known at the time that the Germans would not develop one.

23. **disseminate**   The idea of the biosphere (living organisms and their environment) has helped to *disseminate* (spread) the idea of life on Earth as a fragile and interdependent system.

24. **Ambiguity**   *Ambiguity* (lack of clarity in meaning) is an inherent part of language. Despite this, however, writers should try to be as clear as language allows them to be. *Equivocation* (intentional use of vague language) makes some sense. However, this word can only be used to refer to a *person's* intentional use of vague language.

25. **inexorably**   Glaciers are melting "more rapidly than previously," so it makes sense that one is *inexorably* (in an unyielding manner) losing seven meters of its surface per year.

26. **aberrant**   Ice ages occur "regularly," so they are not *aberrant* (different from the normal).

27. **an ephemeral**   Scientists believe that antimatter is "very quickly destroyed by ordinary matter," so it makes sense that it has an *ephemeral* (short-lived) existence. *Precipitous* (hasty) is not a good choice because this word is only used to describe human conduct.

28. **utilitarian**   "Invaluable insight into the nature of life" implies "pure" knowledge as opposed to *utilitarian* (concerned with usefulness) knowledge, such as the knowledge of organic chemistry used to create products useful in everyday life.

29. **synthesize**   It is reasonable that chemists can *synthesize* (create by combining different parts) organic compounds from petroleum, which is composed of the remains of organisms.

30. **an intrinsic**   Animals eat plants, which become an *intrinsic* (inherent) part of the animals' tissue.

31. **enervated**   "But its [surrealism's] influence is still pervasive" contrasts with the idea that surrealism became *enervated* (weakened) fairly quickly.

32. **denotation**   The sentence contrasts the *connotations* (suggested meanings) of a word with its *denotation* (its direct, literal meaning).

33. **didactic**   The word "teach" in the sentence means that *didactic* (intended to instruct) is the best choice. Also, *didactic* contrasts with the phrase "merely entertain."

34. **a corpus**   The work of great poets is believed to create *a corpus* (a large collection of writings of a certain kind). "Oeuvre" is not a good choice because it means the lifework of one author.

35. **subtle**   The sentence states that some people are able to understand irony, whereas others cannot. It makes sense, therefore, that irony is *subtle* (not immediately obvious).

36. **nuances**   A writer who knows the *nuances* (shades of meaning) of similar words is able to choose the most appropriate word in each situation.

37. **induction**   *Induction* (deriving general principles from particular facts) was used by epidemiologists to establish that cigarette smoking causes lung cancer in smokers. Their induction used the fact that smokers have a higher rate of lung cancer to arrive at the general principle that smoking causes lung cancer.

38. **radical**   The word "revolutionary" indicates that the work of the romantic poets was a *radical* (extreme) challenge to the English poetic tradition.

39. **extrapolate**   It makes sense that science fiction would analyze "present trends" and *extrapolate* (estimate by projecting known information) them "into the future" to assess their "possible impact."

40. **husbanding**   Champions of the command economy contend that it can "effectively incorporate long-term strategies." One such long-term strategy is *husbanding* (managing carefully and thriftily) resources. "Utilization" is not as good an answer as "husbanding" because the latter better describes a strategy.

41. **autonomous**   The phrase "existing independently of its creator" signals that the text is regarded as *autonomous* (independent; not controlled by outside forces).

42. **clandestine**   Kidnapping and covert (secret) operations can accurately be described as *clandestine* (secretive).

43. **ratiocination**   It makes sense that human *ratiocination* (logical reasoning) is regarded as mainly an instrument to help human beings to live good lives.

44. **precludes**   The catch-22 described nearly *precludes* (makes it impossible) the work of modern composers from being heard publicly.

45. **circumscribed**   Everyone is a "prisoner" of his or her preconceptions and *circumscribed* (limited) experience.

46. **an incontrovertible**   Countries such as Sweden and Denmark are sometimes criticized for providing so many benefits for their citizens that they lose their incentive to work. However, it is an *incontrovertible* (indisputable) fact that such countries have some of the most productive economies in the world.

47. **sanguine**   *Sanguine* (cheerfully optimistic) provides the best contrast with the first part of the sentence ("Some…would"), which describes a pessimistic outlook in which an elite class exploits the labor of the world.

48. **premises**   The phrase "from which they are starting" indicates that the *premises* (propositions upon which arguments are based) writers start from are part of their frame of reference.

49. **undermining**   Historians believe that although Prohibition succeeded in significantly reducing the amount of alcohol consumed, other, negative, effects of Prohibition such as the *undermining* (weakening) of respect for law made it sensible to repeal it.

50. **zeitgeist**   An "almost unquestioning belief in science and ratiocination" is an important part of the modern *zeitgeist* (outlook characteristic of a period).

Text Completion Questions: Double Blank

> Fill in all of the blanks in the sentences by selecting one entry from the corresponding column of choices in the way that best completes the text. Answers that are not fully correct will not receive any credit.

1. Most people are generally (i) _____ to accept the assertion of an expert in a field; however, if the expert says something incorrect or ridiculous, his (ii) _____ will be undermined.

(i)	(ii)
loath	resolution
reluctant	credibility
predisposed	persona

2. The sun is surrounded by a powerful magnetic field, which, far from being of purely (i) _____ interest, has (ii) _____ effect on life on Earth in the form of its effect on radio communications.

(i)	(ii)
nebulous	an overweening
theoretical	a profound
utilitarian	an evanescent

3. The Hubble Space Telescope—in orbit around the Earth to offer observations in which the Earth's atmosphere does not (i) _____ light from celestial sources—has been (ii) _____ to astronomers; it is one of the finest astronomical instruments ever developed, expanding humanity's gaze into space tenfold.

(i)	(ii)
mitigate	a canard
attenuate	a sinecure
debilitate	a boon

4. Today's leading (i) _____ theory—the Big Bang Theory—states that the universe began as infinitely compressed and has been expanding ever since; the main competing hypothesis, the Steady State Theory, is no longer generally regarded as (ii) _____ .

(i)	(ii)
cosmological	tenable
metaphysical	ostensible
epistemological	mundane

5. A good habit for a writer is to read what he or she has written from a reader's perspective, and look for any language that might be (i) _____ or (ii) _____ and change it to make it clearer.

(i)	(ii)
surrealistic	plausible
definitive	equivocal
opaque	cogent

6. It is difficult to find exact synonyms for words because every word has its (i) _____ nuances and (ii) _____ .

(i)	(ii)
unique	connotations
orthodox	serendipity
polemical	nomenclature

7. One of the most perceptive and original science fiction novelists today is Kim Stanley Robinson, who in his Mars trilogy—*Red Mars, Blue Mars*, and *Green Mars*—uses humanity's settling of Mars to shed light on current political, social, economic, and religious issues on Earth through the (i) _____ of depicting (ii) _____ of human society that has the chance to begin history afresh without much of the "baggage" of the past.

(i)	(ii)
atavism	a dystopia
artifice	the bourgeoisie
duplicity	a microcosm

8. It is important to remember that authorities in the various fields of knowledge can be wrong; (i) _____ , their assertions should be examined (ii) _____ and not accepted uncritically.

(i)	(ii)
however	parenthetically
thus	objectively
nevertheless	oracularly

9. Astute governments promote policies which (i) _____ "virtuous circles" such as the following: good education produces a well-educated workforce, which results in higher productivity, which leads to greater economic growth, which results in higher tax revenues, which can be (ii) _____ .

(i)	(ii)
necessitate	used to reduce government deficits
promulgate	spent on even better education
create	spent on creating jobs to stimulate the economy

10. Universal peace and brotherhood is a (i) _____ that will probably (ii) _____ humanity, at least for the foreseeable future.

(i)	(ii)
specter	continue to elude
chimera	eventually lead to a united
panacea	polarize

11. In the debate about whether organized religion has done more good or more harm to humankind, it is often conceded, even by those who believe it has been, (i) _____ that it was (ii) _____ in the development of human values.

(i)	(ii)
on balance, detrimental,	superfluous
all factors considered, salutary,	a backward step
completely harmful	a necessary stage

12. The anthropologist (i) _____ his argument in which he contended that the species *Homo sapiens* originated one million years ago to discuss the (ii) _____ the existence of differing racial types in human history.

(i)	(ii)
digressed from	rationale for
prevaricated about	ideologies governing
acceded to	implications of

13. Reincarnation was a central (i) _____ of the ancient Greek religion Orphism, which taught that the main goal of life is to (ii) _____ oneself from the cycle of successive reincarnations.

(i)	(ii)
tenet	expiate
neologism	relegate
tautology	emancipate

14. A central hypothesis in the work of the French philosopher Jean Jacques Rousseau is that human beings are (i) _____ good but are often (ii) _____ by social forces.

(i)	(ii)
innately	deprecated
invariably	attenuated
inevitably	depraved

15. The hypothesis that money generally makes people happy has been (i) _____ by research demonstrating that people for whom (ii) _____ tend to have more anxiety, depression, and lower self-esteem than less ambitious people.

(i)	(ii)
bolstered	the premises of capitalism are abhorrent
corroborated	affluence is a high priority
undermined	personal wealth is of little consequence

16. A lasting (i) _____ of the Enlightenment is the concept of natural law, the belief that the world is governed by (ii) _____ principles that are part of the very nature of things and that can be understood by reason.

(i)	(ii)
artifact	ethical
testament	altruistic
legacy	meretricious

17. Advocates of capital punishment sometimes argue that although this form of punishment is (i) _____ wrong because it involves the taking of human life, it is (ii)_____ because it deters other people from killing.

(i)	(ii)
innately	sometimes unconscionable
ostensibly	always unethical
intrinsically	nevertheless justified

18. In debates about whether or not a particular war is morally justifiable, a common point of contention is whether the bad that will be prevented, (i) _____, outweighs the bad that will be (ii) _____ the war.

(i)	(ii)
or at least mitigated	obviated by
though not ameliorated	caused by
or at least proscribed	adumbrated by

19. During a debate, one may be tempted to (i) _____ evidence to (ii) _____ one's case, but it is better to be honest and objective.

(i)	(ii)
reify	buttress
embellish	misconstrue
invalidate	parody

20. The (i) _____ of European civilization in North America meant the demise of native American societies, which had (ii) _____ for centuries in the vast land.

(i)	(ii)
ascendancy	ossified
genesis	flourished
decadence	foundered

21. The French Revolution was (i) _____ event in Western history because feudalism, an institution that had developed in France over centuries, was (ii) _____ in the space of a few years.

(i)	(ii)
an impromptu	obliterated
an epic	manifested
an exemplary	revitalized

22. (i)_____ psychologists often draw (ii) _____ between the way a computer and the human brain process information.

(i)	(ii)
Humanistic	stratagems
Cognitive	analogies
Freudian	pastiches

23. According to the eminent nineteenth-century psychologist Sigmund Freud, some (i) _____ even in the happiest and best adjusted person, because there is a constant conflict between natural drives and what society (ii) _____.

(i)	(ii)
psychoses are rare	deems to be acceptable
neuroses are inevitable	proscribes
nescience is normal	censors

24. Slavery has been the norm in many societies throughout history, but in the modern world it has been (i) _____ , at least in its (ii) _____ forms, in nearly every part of the world.

(i)	(ii)
eradicated	embryonic
ameliorated	overt
emancipated	amorphous

25. In a speech to Congress in 1823, President Monroe outlined what came to be called the Monroe Doctrine, saying in part, "We owe it, therefore, to (i) _____ and to the (ii) _____ relations existing between the United States and those powers to declare that we should consider any attempt on their part to extend their system to any portion of this hemisphere as dangerous to our peace and safety."

(i)	(ii)
sophistry	amicable
pluralism	jaded
candor	temporal

26. The only war in American history in which (i) _____ran wild (and the United States acquired a colony, the Philippines) was the Spanish-American War of 1898, which was legitimized in the eyes of some by the (ii) _____ population of America and the supposed superiority of Euro-American civilization.

(i)	(ii)
hegemony	parochial
paternalism	chauvinistic
jingoism	burgeoning

27. In *A Study of History* the historian Arnold Toynbee's (i) _____ is that civilizations that receive challenges and meet them successfully succeed and flourish, whereas those that (ii) _____ .

(i)	(ii)
dilemma	do founder
thesis	do not languish
verisimilitude	do not prosper

28. Making illegal any activity that is popular and not overtly harmful (i) _____ a trade-off between the advantages gained and the disadvantages posed (ii) _____ a black market develops in the activity.

(i)	(ii)
impugns	if
entails	unless
abets	until

29. Determining whether a buyer purchased a good for its (i) _____ or because it shows his or her social status is a (ii) _____ matter.

(i)	(ii)
sentimental value	frivolous
extrinsic value	subjective
intrinsic merit	quixotic

30. Critics of consumerism contend that it leads to a situation in which experts dictate to the public what is worth paying for and introduces a mass of (i) _____ regulations that, ultimately, increases the cost to the consumer through higher priced products and increased taxes to support government (ii) _____ .

(i)	(ii)
convoluted	bureaucracy
jejune	fanaticism
tangential	malfeasance

31. The fact that social welfare programs existed only in (i) _____ form during the Great Depression exacerbated the effects of that depression because there was virtually no mechanism (ii) _____ sudden and pervasive unemployment.

(i)	(ii)
substantive	to fully understand
embryonic	for coping with
officious	to totally eliminate

32. Free trade is often praised as (i) _____ for developing countries' economic woes, but trade often also (ii) _____ a country's economy.

(i)	(ii)
a panacea	has an evanescent impact on
a debacle	has deleterious effects on
a euphemism	brings unexpected benefits to

33. (i) _____ leaders make appeals to both jingoism and (ii) _____ .

(i)	(ii)
Maverick	the courts
Fascist	xenophobia
Liberal	genocide

34. The nineteenth-century British (i) _____ Edmund Burke believed that change would inevitably continue, and even supported some gradual changes; however, he feared that the consequences of (ii) _____ altering the fundamental institutions of society could not be foreseen, and that such changes were, therefore, to be avoided whenever possible.

(i)	(ii)
partisan	radically
libertarian	preternaturally
conservative	purportedly

35. To the (i) _____ , the apparently innate tendency of human beings toward violence makes pacifism an appealing, but dangerously (ii) _____ , philosophy.

(i)	(ii)
pragmatist	ephemeral
nihilist	coercive
utopian	illusory

36. It is commonly believed that war is sometimes not only (i) _____ , but the only (ii) _____ moral choice between the evil of war and some greater evil.

(i)	(ii)
decisive	facile
draconian	viable
expedient	salient

37. The (i) _____ of political science are in philosophy, but today it is (ii) _____ study, utilizing the insights of history, sociology, economics, and other social sciences.

(i)	(ii)
posterity	a parochial
antecedents	an inter-disciplinary
fallacies	an empirical

38. Throughout American history, the (i) _____ tradition of the country being a sanctuary for foreigners seeking refuge from political or religious persecution has sometimes been offset by a tendency to regard refugees as bringing (ii) _____ into society, such as communism, socialism, and anarchism.

(i)	(ii)
abhorrent	European hegemony
nominal	undesirable ideologies
exemplary	illiterate miscreants

39. A presidential veto of a bill can be over-ridden by Congress; however, this requires a two-thirds vote in both houses of Congress, something that is extremely difficult for a bill's (i) _____, partially because even many in favor of it are afraid of (ii) _____ the president.

(i)	(ii)
supporters to lobby for	alienating
opponents to overcome	duping
proponents to achieve	mollifying

40. The psychology of Abraham Maslow is one of a number of schools of humanistic psychology, which take (i) _____ view of the human condition, placing more stress on the human being's potential to achieve fulfillment and less on (ii) _____ forces lurking in the recesses of the mind.

(i)	(ii)
a sanguine	sinister
a dogmatic	saccharine
a disinterested	scurrilous

41. Some critics of Freudian psychology regard it as a sort of (i) _____ religion, in which any threat to dogma is regarded as (ii) _____ and rejected, lest it undermine the entire "church."

(i)	(ii)
orthodox	fulsome
secular	politic
monolithic	heretical

42. It seems a reasonable contention that the social sciences have had a major impact on (i) _____, inclining contemporary legislators, jurists, and others involved in law toward placing a greater stress on social and economic (ii) _____ in crime than did their predecessors.

(i)	(ii)
jurisprudence	oracles
justice	determinants
meritocracy	proclivities

43. Minister Mentor Lee Kuan Yew of Singapore has argued that corporal punishment is a useful (i) _____ for a certain class of (ii) _____ criminal whose behavior is not much affected by the prospect of a fine or prison.

(i)	(ii)
deterrent	juvenile
placebo	reformed
subterfuge	incorrigible

44. Due process of law prevents government from (i) _____ people, and helps to ensure that they receive a fair and (ii) _____ trial.

(i)	(ii)
making facetious remarks about	dilatory
finding incriminating evidence against	impromptu
making spurious charges against	expeditious

45. Some legal scholars believe that law and morality are (i) _____, and thus law closely reflects a society's (ii) _____ .

(i)	(ii)
polar opposites	zeitgeist
synonymous	moral norms
inseparably linked	hedonistic values

46. (i) _____ is the study of the timing, location, and size of prehistoric earthquakes. It differs from (ii) _____ in its focus on the almost instantaneous deformation of landforms and sediments during individual earthquakes. This focus permits study of the distribution of earthquakes in space and over time periods of hundreds to tens of thousands of years.

(i)	(ii)
Geomorphology	geology
Paleoseismology	traditional science
Geophysics	other aspects of earthquake geology

47. (i) _____ as the philosopher Alfred North Whitehead remarked, "Western philosophy is a footnote to Plato," it could perhaps with (ii) _____ be said that Western literature is a footnote to the epic poems of Homer.

(i)	(ii)
Nevertheless,	equal validity
However,	less prevarication
If,	similar irony

48. The story in which the central character undertakes a heroic quest for something (i) _____, as Odysseus does in Homer's *Odyssey*, is a (ii) _____ one in world literature (a notable recent example is J.R.R. Tolkien's *The Lord of the Rings*).

(i)	(ii)
metaphorical	sectarian
exalted	recurrent
pristine	volatile

49. A plausible theory regarding human freedom is that the universe is (i) _____ so that human behavior is heavily influenced by external events, but (ii) _____ them.

(i)	(ii)
structured	rarely impinged on by
perpetuated	always determined by
polarized	not decisively affected by

50. Through (i) _____ efforts, scientists have (ii) _____ a compelling picture of a universe that is, in the words of one physicist, "not only strange, but stranger than we can imagine."

(i)	(ii)
draconian	built up
protean	nullified
Herculean	accrued

ANSWER KEY
Text Completion Questions: Double Blank

1. predisposed/credibility
2. theoretical/a profound
3. attenuate/a boon
4. cosmological/tenable
5. opaque/equivocal
6. unique/connotations
7. artifice/a microcosm
8. thus/objectively
9. create/spent on even better education
10. chimera/continue to elude
11. on balance, detrimental,/ a necessary stage
12. digressed from/implications of
13. tenet/emancipate
14. innately/depraved
15. undermined/affluence is a high priority
16. legacy/ethical
17. intrinsically/nevertheless justified
18. or at least mitigated/caused by
19. embellish/buttress
20. ascendancy/flourished
21. an epic/obliterated
22. Cognitive/analogies
23. neuroses are inevitable/deems to be acceptable
24. eradicated/overt
25. candor/amicable
26. jingoism/burgeoning
27. thesis/do not languish
28. entails/if
29. intrinsic merit/subjective
30. convoluted/bureaucracy
31. embryonic/for coping with
32. a panacea/has deleterious effects on
33. Fascist/xenophobia
34. conservative/radically
35. pragmatist/illusory
36. expedient/viable
37. antecedents/an inter-disciplinary
38. exemplary/undesirable ideologies
39. proponents to achieve/alienating
40. a sanguine/sinister
41. secular/heretical
42. jurisprudence/determinants
43. deterrent/incorrigible
44. making spurious charges against/ expeditious
45. inseparably linked/moral norms
46. Paleoseismology/other aspects of earthquake geology
47. If,/equal validity
48. exalted/recurrent
49. structured/not decisively affected by
50. Herculean/built up

ANSWER EXPLANATIONS

1. **predisposed/credibility**   Most people are *predisposed* (having a tendency) to accept assertions made by an expert; however, if the expert says something incorrect or ridiculous, his *credibility* (believability) will be weakened.

2. **theoretical/a profound**   The sun's magnetic field has not only a *theoretical* (abstract) interest but also a *profound* (far-reaching) effect on life because it affects radio communications.

3. **attenuate/a boon**   The Hubble Space Telescope offers observations in which the Earth's atmosphere does not *attenuate* (weaken) light from celestial sources and has been *a boon* (benefit bestowed) to astronomers because it has greatly increased their observational power.

4. **cosmological/tenable**   The Big Bang Theory is about how the universe began, so it is a *cosmological* (having to do with a theory about the origin of the universe) theory; since the Big Bang Theory is described as "today's leading…theory," it makes sense that the main competing theory is no longer regarded as *tenable* (reasonable).

5. **opaque/equivocal**   A writer can improve his or her writing by looking for language that might be *opaque* (not transparent) or *equivocal* (ambiguous) from a reader's point of view.

6. **unique/connotations**   It is difficult to find perfect synonyms for words because each word has *unique* (one of a kind) nuances and *connotations* (meanings suggested by words).

7. **artifice/a microcosm**   Robinson used the *artifice* (ingenious or artful device) of depicting *a microcosm* (a small system having analogies to a larger system) of human society.

8. **thus/objectively**   It follows from the statement that authorities can be wrong that *thus* their assertions should be examined *objectively* (being uninfluenced by emotions or personal prejudices).

9. **create/spent on even better education**   The sequence of events given in the sentence *create[s]* a virtuous circle, resulting in higher tax revenues that can be *spent on even better education*, completing the circle.

10. **chimera/continue to elude**   Universal peace and brotherhood can be described as a *chimera* (fanciful mental illusion) because it is unlikely to be attained in the foreseeable future and will *continue to elude* humanity.

11. **on balance, detrimental,/a necessary stage**   Even those who believe that organized religion has been *on balance, detrimental,* (all things considered, harmful) often admit that it was *a necessary stage* in the development of human values.

12. **digressed from/implications of**   The anthropologist *digressed from* (strayed from the main point of) his argument to discuss the *implications of* (things that are implied about) differing racial types.

13. **tenet/emancipate**   Reincarnation was a central *tenet* (doctrine) of Orphism, which taught that the main goal of life is to *emancipate* (free) oneself from the cycle of death and rebirth.

14. **innately/depraved**   Rousseau hypothesized that human beings are *innately* (in a way that is inborn) good but often are *depraved* (corrupted) by social forces.

15. **undermined/affluence is a high priority**   The hypothesis that money tends to make people happy has been *undermined* (weakened) by research showing that people for whom *affluence is a high priority* (wealth is very important) tend to exhibit more symptoms of unhappiness than less ambitious people.

16. **legacy/ethical**   A lasting *legacy* (something handed down from the past) of the Enlightenment is the idea of natural law, the belief that the world is governed by *ethical* (concerning moral standards) principles that are part of the very nature of things.

17. **intrinsically/nevertheless justified**   Advocates of capital punishment sometimes argue that it is *intrinsically* (inherently) wrong but is *nevertheless justified* because it deters people from killing. (i) "Innately" makes some sense, but it is not used to refer to human activities such as the imposition of punishment.

18. **or at least mitigated/caused by**   A common point of contention in debate about the moral justification for a particular war is whether the bad that will be prevented, *or at least mitigated* (or at least made less severe), outweighs the bad that will be *caused by* the war.

19. **embellish/buttress**   One may be tempted to *embellish* (make more attractive by adding details) evidence to *buttress* (reinforce) one's case.

20. **ascendancy/flourished**   The *ascendancy* (rise in power) of European civilization in North America resulted in the death of native American societies, which had *flourished* (thrived) for centuries. *Ascendancy* is a better choice than "genesis" (origin) because Europeans gained power over native societies.

21. **an epic/obliterated**   The French Revolution was an *epic* (surpassing the usual) event because feudalism, which had developed over centuries, was *obliterated* (completely destroyed) in a few years.

22. **Cognitive/analogies**   *Cognitive* (relating to mental processes by which knowledge is acquired) psychologists study human thought processes, so it makes sense that they would draw *analogies* (similarities) between information processing computers and the human brain.

23. **neuroses are inevitable/deems to be acceptable**   Freud believed that some *neuroses are inevitable* (mental or emotional disorders are inevitable) in everyone because there is in everyone conflict between natural drives and what society *deems to be acceptable*.

24. **eradicated/overt**   Slavery has been the norm in many societies in history, but in the modern world it has been *eradicated* (wiped out), at least in its *overt* (open and observable) forms.

25. **candor/amicable**   It makes sense that President Monroe would say that there should be *candor* (honesty of expression) in international relations and cite the *amicable* (friendly) relations between the United States and the other powers referred to.

26. **jingoism/burgeoning**   *Jingoism* (extreme support of one's country) ran wild during the Spanish-American War, which some people believed was made legitimate by America's *burgeoning* (flourishing) population.

27. **thesis/do not languish**   Toynbee's *thesis* (proposition put forward for consideration) is that civilizations that receive challenges and meet them successfully flourish whereas those that do not *languish* (become weak).

28. **entails/if**   Making a popular and not overtly harmful activity illegal *entails* (involves as a necessary result) a trade-off between the advantages gained and the disadvantages posed *if* a black market develops in the activity.

29. **intrinsic merit/subjective**   Determining whether a buyer purchased a good for its *intrinsic merit* (inherent merit) or because it shows his or her social status is a *subjective* (particular to a given person) matter.

30. **convoluted/bureaucracy**   Critics of consumerism argue that it introduces a mass of *convoluted* (complicated) regulations that eventually leads to higher cost to the consumer as a result of higher prices and increased taxes to support government *bureaucracy* (government administration).

31. **embryonic/for coping with**   The fact that social welfare programs existed only in *embryonic* (in early stages of development) form during the Great Depression exacerbated the effects of that depression because there was virtually no mechanism *for coping with* unemployment. It makes sense that a depression created unemployment and social welfare programs deal with unemployment and related issues.

32. **a panacea/has deleterious effects on**   The word "praised" signals that a positive word such as a *panacea* (cure-all) is appropriate. The word "but" signals a negative word such as "deleterious." Trade often also has *deleterious effects on* a country's economy.

33. **Fascist/xenophobia**   *Fascists* (persons who support Fascism) like Adolph Hitler made appeals to both jingoism (extreme support of one's country) and *xenophobia* (hatred of foreigners).

34. **conservative/radically**   *Conservative* (someone who opposes change) is the best choice because Burke is described as fearing "the consequences of *radically* (in an extreme manner) altering the fundamental institutions of society."

35. **pragmatist/illusory**   It makes sense that a *pragmatist* (person concerned with practicality) would consider pacifism (opposition to war or violence to resolve disputes) an *illusory* (based on an illusion) philosophy because of the innate (inborn) tendencies of human beings toward violence.

36. **expedient/viable**   It is commonly believed that war is sometimes not only *expedient* (suitable) but the only *viable* (practicable) moral choice between the evil of war and a greater evil.

37. **antecedents/an inter-disciplinary**   The words "but today" signal that the earlier part of the sentence is about the *antecedents* (things that come before something else) of political science. "But today" also suggests that in earlier years political science was relatively limited in the scope of fields it incorporated, whereas now it utilizes ideas from many fields, making it *inter-disciplinary* (involving two or more academic disciplines that are considered distinct).

38. **exemplary/undesirable ideologies**   The tradition of a country being a sanctuary for refugees can be described as *exemplary* (commendable). This "has sometimes been offset by a tendency to regard refugees as bringing *undesirable ideologies* (sets of undesirable political beliefs) into society."

39. **proponents to achieve/alienating**   It is difficult for a bill's *proponents to achieve* (supporters to attain) a two-thirds vote, partially because many members of Congress are afraid of *alienating* (estranging) the president.

40. **a sanguine/sinister**   "Placing more stress on the human being's potential to achieve fulfillment" suggests that Maslow's psychology is *sanguine* (optimistic), in contrast to psychologies that stress *sinister* (threatening evil) forces in the mind.

41. **secular/heretical**   Some critics see Freudian psychology as a sort of *secular* (not specifically pertaining to religion) religion that rejects any threat to its *dogma* (belief asserted on authority without evidence) as heretical (opposed to established teaching).

42. **jurisprudence/determinants**   "Legislators, jurists, and others involved in law" signals that *jurisprudence* (philosophy of law) is the best choice. It makes sense that the social sciences have encouraged those involved in law to place more stress on social and economic *determinants* (things that determine) in crime than did their predecessors.

43. **deterrent/incorrigible**   Lee has argued that corporal punishment is a useful *deterrent* (something that discourages) for a certain type of *incorrigible* (incapable of being reformed) criminal.

44. **making spurious charges against/expeditious**   Due process of law "ensure[s] that [people] receive a fair...trial," so it makes sense that it also prevents government from *making spurious* (false) *charges against* them. It also ensures that they receive an *expeditious* (done with speed and efficiency) trial.

45. **inseparably linked/moral norms**   Some legal scholars believe that law and morality are *inseparably linked* and that law therefore closely reflects a society's *moral norms* (moral standards considered typical for a group). "Zeitgeist" (the outlook characteristic of a period) makes some sense but *moral norms* is a better choice because it refers specifically to morality, whereas "zeitgeist" is more general.

46. **Paleoseismology/other aspects of earthquake geology** "The study of the timing, location, and size of prehistoric earthquakes" signals that *paleoseismology* is the correct answer. The meaning of "paleoseismology" can be inferred from a knowledge of the Greek root *paleo* (ancient) and the word "seismology" (the study of earthquakes). "Differs from" signals that paleoseismology is different from *other aspects of earthquake geology* because of its different focus.

47. **If,/equal validity** *If* Western philosophy is a footnote to Plato, it could perhaps with *equal validity* be said that Western literature is a footnote to the epic poems of Homer.

48. **exalted/recurrent** It makes sense that the object of a "heroic quest" would be something *exalted* (raised in rank or dignity). It also makes sense to describe this type of story as *recurrent* (occurring repeatedly) because a recent example is given.

49. **structured/not decisively affected by** A plausible (likely) theory about human freedom is that the universe is *structured* so that human behavior is heavily influenced by external events but *not decisively affected* by them. A clue to finding the correct answer is the contrast signaled by "heavily influenced" and "but."

50. **Herculean/built up** It makes sense that scientists have made *Herculean* (calling for great energy) efforts and as a result *built up* a compelling (demanding attention) picture of the universe.

Text Completion Questions: Triple Blank

Fill in all of the blanks in the sentences by selecting one entry from the corresponding column of choices in the way that best completes the text. Answers that are not fully correct will not receive any credit.

1. Although the (i) _____ breaks down if it is pushed too far, (ii) _____ comparison can be made between the solar system, on the macroscopic level, and an atom, on the microscopic level, in that they both have a central body containing most of the mass of the system, around which orbit numerous bodies of (iii) _____.

(i)	(ii)	(iii)
macrocosm	a credible	relatively small mass
analogy	a metaphysical	insignificant size
misnomer	an ostensible	great interest to scientists

2. The Renaissance can be viewed as (i) _____ to the Enlightenment, since (ii) _____ that (iii) _____ in the earlier period were fully developed in the later period.

(i)	(ii)	(iii)
a precursor	humanist ideas	had a major influence on thinking
an homage	incipient notions	had been nascent
anterior	seminal thinkers	had reached fruition

3. The following (i) _____, called Olber's paradox, long puzzled astronomers: If the universe is infinite in extent and age, and filled with stars, why is the sky dark at night? A plausible—but essentially incorrect—answer to Olber's paradox is that the expansion of the universe (ii) _____ light from stars. The fundamental answer to the puzzle is that the paradox is premised on the (iii) _____ notion that the universe is infinitely old, whereas in reality it was created in the Big Bang, and thus there is not sufficient time for the universe to be filled with light.

(i)	(ii)	(iii)
dilemma	increased	fallacious
conundrum	attenuated	incontrovertible
trope	subsumed	alluring

4. Since its (i) _____ , the Internet has (ii) _____ the exchange of information between people for both (iii) _____ purposes.

(i)	(ii)	(iii)
inception	sanctioned	innocuous and pragmatic
jubilee	facilitated	malign and benign
decline	proscribed	eclectic and humane

5. (i)_____ thinkers are often accused by more (ii)_____ thinkers of building castles in the air based more on lofty ideals and (iii) _____ than on a solid foundation in reality.

(i)	(ii)	(iii)
Sophomoric	prosaic	false ontology
Utopian	pragmatic	vicarious experience
Erudite	pedantic	wishful thinking

6. Belief may be distinguished from knowledge on the basis of the fact that knowledge is felt to be provable, certain or true, whereas a belief cannot be proven and is usually held in circumstances where it is not possible to be certain. An opinion is a (i) _____ belief based on available evidence—as more evidence becomes available an opinion may have to be changed to (ii) _____ . "Belief," "opinion," and "faith" are similar insofar as all are held with respect to that which is unproven, while "faith" has the additional (iii) _____ powers beyond human understanding.

(i)	(ii)	(iii)
specious	accommodate the evidence	need to affirm the existence of
provisional	confirm the evidence	implicit sense of trust in
temporary	extrapolate data from the evidence	burden of proving

7. The Nile Valley in Egypt (i) _____ alternating periods of flooding and aridity, but the ancient Egyptians built an irrigation and water control system to (ii) _____ the problems this caused. The Egyptian irrigation system enabled disastrous flooding to be circumvented and the water supply to be (iii) _____ in the dry season.

(i)	(ii)	(iii)
is inured to	pacify	obviated
is susceptible to	assuage	augmented
is culpable of	alleviate	palliated

8. A clear and (i) _____ argument is the first requirement of persuasive writing. To argue effectively, it is also important to (ii) _____ that may be raised against one's case, and (iii) _____ them in advance.

(i)	(ii)	(iii)
interesting	temper criticism	parody
cogent	anticipate objections	rebut
tautological	rationalize reasons	transcend

9. Many Westerners are inclined to view the shaman as a charlatan, but (i) _____ to the shaman can be found in Western society. One Western parallel to the shaman is the mystic, who undertakes the journey into the (ii) _____ of the soul where others fear to go. Another parallel to the shaman is the confessor, who allows God to act through him (iii) _____ a person's sins.

(i)	(ii)	(iii)
precursors	effulgent realm	to understand
objections	subterranean world	to decry
analogs	dystopia	to absolve

10. It has been argued that the United States learned the value of not (i) _____ the demands of aggressors (ii) _____ from the failure of the Munich Pact, and as a result in 1962 nearly (iii) _____ a nuclear war with the Soviet Union when it refused to acquiesce to the Soviet's placing nuclear missiles in Cuba.

(i)	(ii)	(iii)
acceding to	to a limited degree	prevented
admitting to	immediately	precipitated
ascribing to	*too* well	circumvented

11. In Newtonian physics, gravity is (i) _____ some sort of force that can act at a distance; (ii) _____, experimentalists have conducted rigorous and ingenious searches for gravity waves and particles, but they have (iii) _____ in finding them.

(i)	(ii)	(iii)
limited to	on the other hand	had little difficulty
predicated on	however	had scant success
hypostatized as	moreover	used obsolete techniques

12. The rare earth elements (REE) are essential for a diverse and expanding array of high-technology applications, which constitute an important part of the industrial economy of the United States. Long-term shortage or unavailability of REE would (i) _____ significant changes in many technological aspects of American society. Domestic REE sources, known and potential, may (ii) _____ become an increasingly (iii) _____ for scientists and policymakers in both the public and private sectors.

(i)	(ii)	(iii)
obviate	therefore	rare source
force	nevertheless	more costly supply of REE
presuppose	unexpectedly	important issue

13. "Rare" earth elements is an historical (i) _____; persistence of the term reflects unfamiliarity rather than true rarity. The more abundant REE are each similar in crustal concentration to commonplace industrial metals such as chromium, nickel, copper, zinc, molybdenum, tin, tungsten, or lead. Even the two least abundant REE (Tm, Lu) are nearly 200 times more common than gold. However, (ii) _____ ordinary base and precious metals, REE have very little tendency to become concentrated in (iii) _____ ore deposits. Consequently, most of the world's supply of REE comes from only a handful of sources.

(i)	(ii)	(iii)
malapropism	in contrast to	remote
neologism	like	primordial
misnomer	despite recent evidence,	exploitable

14. Some observers contend that poor countries are faced with (i) _____:
those that choose not to integrate themselves into the world economic system find it
difficult to advance enough technologically to be able to compete successfully in the
world market; those that do enter fully into the system are (ii) _____ the
bottom ranks of the world economic order, providing raw materials and cheap labor
for the (iii) _____ countries.

(i)	(ii)	(iii)
a double-bind	ostracized by	benighted
xenophobia	inured to	affluent
skepticism	relegated to	paternalistic

15. Some scientists are awed by the fact that carbon is (i) _____ in the universe
and at the same time is so suitable for forming the complex organic molecules that
are the basis of life; however, other scientists (ii) _____ such attitudes
as irrational because science can only explain *what* exists, not (iii) _____
it exists.

(i)	(ii)	(iii)
ubiquitous	acclaim	*when*
salient	disparage	*why*
obsequious	justify	*whether*

16. European colonial powers such as Britain and France used tariffs to control the
supply of raw materials *from* their colonies and of manufactured articles *to* their
colonies; the result of this was that other European countries (i) _____
tariffs (ii) _____ , so that tariffs (iii) _____ .

(i)	(ii)	(iii)
reduced	in retaliation	could be studied more easily
imposed	as an experiment	decreased significantly
flouted	judiciously	rose steadily

17. The philosopher Karl Popper held that it is not possible to conclusively prove but that
it is possible to (i) _____ a scientific hypothesis. His argument is founded
on the basic flaw underlying all (ii) _____ from which scientific principles
are derived: in Popper's words, "The logical situation is extremely simple. No number
of white swans can establish the theory that all swans are white: the first observation
of a black swan can (iii) _____ it."

(i)	(ii)	(iii)
qualify	inductive reasoning	validate
conclusively disprove	deductive reasoning	refute
tentatively corroborate	ratiocination	substantiate

18. By "flat" characters Forster means characters whose personalities are (i) _____ — that is, resistant to meaningful analysis of motivation and other aspects of their inner life. Perhaps the respect in which his (ii) _____ is held reflects (iii) _____, with its emphasis on what is regarded as the "inner," psychological states of individuals.

(i)	(ii)	(iii)
opaque	authority	a subliminal message
complex	typology	the modern ethos
ineffectual	parlance	an antiquated theory

19. Perhaps the second half of the twentieth century will be regarded in hindsight— from the perspective of some imagined (i) _____ —as the epoch in which high-tech developments in electronics and computing were the catalyst for an explosion in information technology that allowed human beings to create a global village in which information (ii) _____, allowing the emergence of (iii) _____ type of intelligence on the planet.

(i)	(ii)	(iii)
utopia	reached a critical mass	an atavistic
distant future	flowed freely	a radically different
omniscient observer	became abstruse	a preordained

20. The *Bhagavad Gita* is a (i) _____ story that most Hindus interpret as a synthesis of yoga philosophy (ii) _____ a method of purification and enlightenment leading to spiritual liberation by helping one to practice all the three main types of yoga in one's life. Some scholars regard the *Bhagavad Gita* as (iii) _____, a brilliant synthesis of many strands of Indian spiritual teaching.

(i)	(ii)	(iii)
didactic	adumbrating	syncretistic
sententious	prescribing	doctrinaire
scurrilous	proscribing	spurious

21. Since it originally meant the study of how to use language effectively, it is (i) _____ that the word "rhetoric" has come to have a (ii) _____ sense of language that is (iii) _____, pretentious, and insincere.

(i)	(ii)	(iii)
ironic	pejorative	honest
paradoxical	salient	ornate
enigmatic	definitive	direct

22. The sociologist Max Weber believed that the idea of the elect was the major reason capitalism arose in western Europe; Weber believed that with the rise of Calvinism people wanted to (i) _____ themselves and others that they were among the elect by (ii) _____ , and thus worked hard to achieve wealth, in (iii) _____.

(i)	(ii)	(iii)
admit to	renouncing lucre	an ever-changing scenario
demonstrate to	becoming affluent	a self-fulfilling prophecy
hide from	praying daily	contradistinction to fame

23. Irony is often used by (i) _____ to help it to maintain its superiority over those outside the group; however, in literature (as, notably, in the plays of George Bernard Shaw and Oscar Wilde) it is sometimes (ii) _____ the higher class, depicting their shallowness and (iii) _____ outlook.

(i)	(ii)	(iii)
an elite	opposed by	bourgeoisie
a cabal	turned against	liberal
a caucus	parodied by	humane

24. The student of religion should be aware of the tendency toward (i) _____, in which beliefs are explained as nothing but the result of external factors; (ii) _____, religious beliefs are often deeply held and, ultimately, perhaps even _____ to understanding from "outside."

(i)	(ii)	(iii)
recapitulation	despite this	opaque
reductionism	in fact	accessible
reification	in rare cases	confined

25. Sometimes principles are sacrificed to (i) _____, the process being (ii) _____ and given a (iii) _____ such as "an unfortunate necessity" or "a pragmatic decision."

(i)	(ii)	(iii)
ideals	understood	misnomer
the gods	rationalized	euphemism
expediency	recognized	platitude

26. Scholars are sometimes tempted into (i) _____ to discuss (ii) _____ areas of interest to them, but which are regarded by most readers as a (iii) _____ display of erudition.

(i)	(ii)	(iii)
"monetizing" their discoveries	peripheral	pedantic
digressions off the main topic	posterior	quintessential
exploiting their graduate students	moribund	protean

27. Explosive volcanic eruptions that destroy vegetation and deposit volcanic rocks and ash over wide areas create conditions that (i) _____ increased rates of surface runoff during rainstorms, dramatically increase the availability of loose debris that can be eroded and transported into river valleys, and typically result in persistent airborne "ashy" conditions due to wind and human activities. The destruction of vegetation combined with deposition of ash on hill slopes reduces the amount of water that normally soaks into the ground or is transpired by plants. The increased overland flow of water erodes rock debris from hill slopes and carries it into river valleys. There, sediment can accumulate and change (ii) _____ of river valleys. The net effect of such changes to watersheds is that post-eruption stream velocities and peak discharges during rainstorms are temporarily much higher than during pre-eruption conditions. Streams typically respond more quickly to a given amount of rainfall and produce higher flows as rainfall is quickly flushed through a (iii) _____.

(i)	(ii)	(iii)
prevent	regular gestation period	watershed
promote	normal hydrology	river valley
exacerbate	general morphology	stream

28. If it is true that all human beings (i) _____ language acquisition, then it follows that all languages, no matter what their superficial differences, share a number of basic features. (ii) _____ and other evidence, it has been proposed that there exist "linguistic universals"—features common to all human languages—(iii) _____.

(i)	(ii)	(iii)
vary in their talent for	On the basis of this	consistent with the culture of the people who speak them
share an innate need for	Despite this	depending on the ability of the people speaking them
are equipped with identical faculties for	Disregarding this	irrespective of period or place

29. In Greek mythology Daedalus represents (i) _____ craftsmanship and innovation, building the labyrinth, and then escaping from it when King Minos refused to allow him to leave. His son Icarus, who flew too close to the sun and melted his wings, has become a sort of (ii) _____ those who strive to innovate, (iii) _____.

(i)	(ii)	(iii)
disrespect for	patron saint of	even at the risk of failure
the zenith of	figure of ridicule for	ignoring the minuscule chance of death
the nadir of	critic of	taking into account the inevitability of failure

30. The driving force behind the atomic bomb—J. Robert Oppenheimer, the director of the Manhattan Project—was (i) _____ diametrically opposed forces: the beauty of his research (what he called the "sweet" technical solutions to problems his team encountered) and his misgivings about the uses to which his work might one day be put. Edward Teller, one of the scientists instrumental in creating the first hydrogen bomb, had, in contrast to Oppenheimer, no (ii) _____ about his work, believing, as a (iii) _____ anti-Communist, that it would be an unmitigated disaster if totalitarian regimes were to possess such weapons before the United States did.

(i)	(ii)	(iii)
skeptical about	epistemological uncertainty	former
torn between	moral qualms	fervent
proud of	certainty	tepid

31. A negative aspect of the increased dominance of Big Business in the United States is that political (i) _____ might come to center on economic matters, ignoring the larger requirements of (ii) _____ society. Such a society would have lost its perspective, seeing what should be a means to an end—business—as an end in itself; this might lead to excessive competitiveness, individualism, materialism, and (iii) _____ in society.

(i)	(ii)	(iii)
parlance	civil	impassivity
discourse	partisan	cupidity
bombast	sectarian	narcissism

32. A (i) _____ piece of expository prose requires few (ii) _____ indicators that a transition is being made to another topic; (iii) _____ , the transitions are made as an integral part of the discourse.

(i)	(ii)	(iii)
truly creative	explicit	on the other hand
logically coherent	subliminal	rather
mundane	nominal	in the final analysis

33. The dogma of the Roman Catholic Church is that free will and predestination, while (i) _____ contradictory, can be (ii) _____ by God who "moves" the soul according to its nature. Some theologians contend that the Roman Catholic Church's doctrine on predestination is predicated on the logical fallacy of begging the question, since, if a soul has a particular nature, its future is necessarily (iii) _____ .

(i)	(ii)	(iii)
somewhat	determined	indeterminate
undoubtedly	abrogated	predestined
ostensibly	reconciled	doomed

34. Breeding populations of California gulls in San Francisco Bay have increased 37 fold over the past two decades from less than 1,000 breeding birds in 1982 to more than 37,000 in 2007. Their (i) _____ increase in the bay may be (ii) _____ their use of landfills and other (iii) _____ sources of food.

(i)	(ii)	(iii)
exponential	as important as	unadulterated
putative	closely related to	exigent
complicit	complemented by	anthropogenic

35. Considering the (i) _____ the world's leading (ii) _____ that there will be a vastly greater number of natural calamities (such as hurricanes and floods) during the first several decades of the twenty-first century, some experts recommend that more developing countries should do what Bangladesh has done—build into their development plans strategies to (iii) _____ the impact of such disasters on development.

(i)	(ii)	(iii)
prowess of	meteorologists	ameliorate
obeisance to	technocrats	attenuate
consensus of	taxonomists	comprehend

36. Several geographers and historians have speculated that temperate climates foster the (i) _____ of civilizations, but that after a civilization has developed past the (i) _____ stage, it is more likely to flourish in (iii) _____ because challenges are needed that must be overcome for further progress to occur.

(i)	(ii)	(iii)
maturation	nomadic	a relatively inhospitable climate
genesis	nascent	an idyllic environment
demise	embryonic	a pastoral area

37. Proponents of (i) _____ in democracies often justify this extreme (ii) _____ of individual rights on the grounds that, although it is wrong to violate people's rights in this manner, there is sometimes no other realistic way to (iii) _____, and thus the ends justify the means.

(i)	(ii)	(iii)
conscription	qualification	raise an army to defend the country
authoritarianism	circumscription	govern a nation
covert surveillance of citizens	sanctioning	ensure a meritocratic society

38. Scientists (i) _____ disposition (ii) _____ the impact of human activities on climate has been greatly mitigated—perhaps even counterbalanced—by the natural trend over the past several centuries toward much cooler weather. This optimistic conclusion seems unrealistic to other scientists, who find it difficult to believe either that the greenhouse effect could be (iii) _____, or that such a fortunate combination of events is likely.

(i)	(ii)	(iii)
of a sanguine	fear that	inimical
with a skeptical	realize that	innocuous
with a histrionic	conjecture that	ineluctable

39. An example of "speculative history" is (i) _____ that during World War II the Germans developed the atomic bomb before the Allies, and used it to intimidate the Allies into surrender. Some historians argue that such exercises in "speculative history"—even if based on reasonable (ii) _____ from existing trends—are merely meaningless (iii) _____, while others believe that they can add to our understanding of history.

(i)	(ii)	(iii)
postulating	abstractions	solecisms
lamenting	reifications	conjectures
verifying	extrapolations	heuristics

40. With the inception in the 1950s of nuclear reactors able to power electrical generators, there (i) _____ a virtually unlimited supply of cheap power that would usher in an age of universal prosperity. In (ii) _____, such predictions were naive in that they neglected to consider some technical realities that make power generators incorporating nuclear reactors more expensive to build and operate than conventional oil or coal fuelled generators, such as disposal of waste products and the need for (iii) _____ in monitoring them.

(i)	(ii)	(iii)
were predictions of a future with	the past	extreme vigilance
was skepticism about the possibility of	the long run	naive optimism
was no longer a reason for	hindsight	pusillanimous engineers

41. If by science we (i) _____ a systematic study of phenomena, we would be (ii) _____ that history fulfills the (iii) _____ necessary to be considered a science.

(i)	(ii)	(iii)
hypothesize	inclined to say	goal
validate	unable to understand	criterion
mean	interested in the idea	objective

42. Antibiotics first came into widespread use in World War II, (i) _____ the detrimental effects of that war on human life. They work on the principle that they harm (ii) _____ but are (iii) _____ to humans.

(i)	(ii)	(iii)
temporizing	pathogens	innocuous
subsuming	fauna	inimical
alleviating	morphology	toxic

43. Though their critics (i) _____ them as (ii) _____ dreamers, some people contend that a new (iii) _____ is forming that sees the world as one enlightened, planetary civilization.

(i)	(ii)	(iii)
lampoon	quixotic	epiphany
invoke	flamboyant	milieu
relish	irascible	zeitgeist

44. The specter of Malthusianism—the ideology that (i) _____ that population will inevitably outrun food supplies—has, at least for the present, been (ii) _____ by (iii) _____ food production and better birth control, but whether it will triumph in the long run remains to be seen.

(i)	(ii)	(iii)
postulates	stymied	decreasing
stipulates	obviated	burgeoning
necessitates	assuaged	chronic

45. It is (i) _____ that communism and fascism, two systems of government which in many ways are (ii) _____ , lying at opposite poles of the political spectrum, have turned out (iii) _____ to be such similar totalitarian systems.

(i)	(ii)	(iii)
a hypothesis	unimpeachable	in practice
a paradox	antithetical	in theory
an archetype	incontrovertible	in the abstract

46. It is often resistance movements—groups of people opposed to the (i) _____ of colonial or other (ii) _____ regimes—that use guerilla tactics (iii) _____ conducting conventional war in which they would be at a disadvantage.

(i)	(ii)	(iii)
dissolution	monolithic	when
imposition	paternalistic	in the hope of
abolition	repressive	rather than

47. Anglo-American (i) _____ is imbued with an overriding concern for natural law—with its emphasis on (ii) _____ individual rights—because its critical period of development was the Enlightenment and subsequent times when this concern (iii) _____ .

(i)	(ii)	(iii)
legislation	inviolable	provoked heated debate
jurisprudence	anachronistic	was immaterial
litigation	metaphysical	predominated

48. Some political scientists have (i) _____ of what they see as the "imperial Presidency" that runs roughshod over the judicial branch and legislative branch; (ii)_____ others in the field see such dominance as the only (iii)_____ way that the institution of the presidency can meet the demands placed upon it in the modern world.

(i)	(ii)	(iii)
applauded the demise	indeed,	nefarious
assailed the apotheosis	nevertheless,	unimpeachable
lamented the emergence	however,	feasible

49. Perhaps people might take some (i) _____ in the knowledge that, as the sun expands to many times its present size and increases its heat emission dramatically— causing devastation on Earth—it will also shrink continuously, losing mass until its (ii) _____. As the sun nears the end of its life, its (iii) _____ in mass will mean that the planets—though lifeless at that time—will probably escape obliteration because the sun will exert less gravitational pull, and so the planets will move to more remote orbits.

(i)	(ii)	(iii)
solace	parity	diminution
stature	demise	accretion
camaraderie	metamorphosis	senescence

50. The (i) _____ student of literature is aware that terms used in literary criticism are (ii) _____ in that their meanings are ever shifting depending on the (iii) _____of the writer using them and the nature of the work under discussion.

(i)	(ii)	(iii)
cynical	completely arbitrary	academic status
craven	notoriously plastic	clique
sagacious	static	premises

ANSWER KEY
Text Completion Questions: Triple Blank

1. analogy/a credible/relatively small mass
2. a precursor/humanist ideas/had been nascent
3. conundrum/attenuated/fallacious
4. inception/facilitated/malign and benign
5. Utopian/pragmatic/wishful thinking
6. provisional/accommodate the evidence/implicit sense of trust in
7. is susceptible to/alleviate/augmented
8. cogent/anticipate objections/rebut
9. analogs/subterranean world/ to absolve
10. acceding to/*too* well/precipitated
11. predicated on/however/had scant success
12. force/therefore/important issue
13. misnomer/in contrast to/exploitable
14. a double-bind/relegated to/affluent
15. ubiquitous/disparage/*why*
16. imposed/in retaliation/rose steadily
17. conclusively disprove/inductive reasoning/refute
18. opaque/typology/the modern ethos
19. distant future/reached a critical mass/a radically different
20. didactic/prescribing/syncretistic
21. ironic/pejorative/ornate
22. demonstrate to/becoming affluent/ a self-fulfilling prophecy
23. an elite/turned against/bourgeoisie
24. reductionism/in fact/opaque
25. expediency/rationalized/ euphemism
26. digressions off the main topic/ peripheral/pedantic
27. promote/normal hydrology/ watershed
28. are equipped with identical faculties for/On the basis of this/irrespective of period or place
29. the zenith of/patron saint of/even at the risk of failure
30. torn between/moral qualms/fervent
31. discourse/civil/cupidity
32. logically coherent/explicit/rather
33. ostensibly/reconciled/predestined
34. exponential/closely related to/ anthropogenic
35. consensus of/meteorologists/ ameliorate
36. genesis/embryonic/a relatively inhospitable climate
37. conscription/circumscription/raise an army to defend the country
38. of a sanguine/conjecture that/ innocuous
39. postulating/extrapolations/ conjectures
40. were predictions of a future with/ hindsight/extreme vigilance
41. mean/inclined to say/criterion
42. alleviating/pathogens/innocuous
43. lampoon/quixotic/zeitgeist
44. postulates/stymied/burgeoning
45. a paradox/antithetical/in practice
46. imposition/repressive/rather than
47. jurisprudence/inviolable/ predominated
48. lamented the emergence/however,/ feasible
49. solace/demise/diminution
50. sagacious/notoriously plastic/ premises

ANSWER EXPLANATIONS

1. **analogy/a credible/relatively small mass**   An *analogy* (similarity) is made between a solar system and an atom. The comparison is *credible* (believable) because of the fairly close similarities between a solar system and an atom. A solar system and an atom both have a central body containing "most of the mass of the system" and numerous small bodies of *relatively small mass.*

2. **a precursor/humanist ideas/had been nascent**   The comparison between what occurred in "the earlier period" and "the later period" signals that the Renaissance was *a precursor* (forerunner) to the Enlightenment, since *humanist ideas* (a system of ideas relating to human beings, emphasizing their value and de-emphasizing belief in God) that *had been nascent* (coming into existence) in the Renaissance were developed fully in the Enlightenment. (ii) "incipient notions" makes sense by itself but does not make sense with any of the choices for (iii).

3. **conundrum/attenuated/fallacious**   Olber's paradox is best described as a *conundrum* (a puzzle) because common sense says that an infinitely old and large universe would fill the night sky with light. It seems reasonable that the expansion of the universe *attenuated* (weakened) light from stars because it appears to explain why the sky is dark at night. "Whereas in reality" signals a contrast, so *fallacious* (false) is the correct choice for (iii).

4. **inception/facilitated/malign and benign**   Since its *inception* (beginning) the Internet has *facilitated* (made less difficult) the exchange of information between people. *Malign and benign* (evil and harmless) is the best choice because it is the only pair of words that are contrasting.

5. **Utopian/pragmatic/wishful thinking**   *Utopian* (referring to a utopia, that is, a perfect place) is the best choice because thinkers are described as "building castles in the air." These thinkers are contrasted with more *pragmatic* (practical) thinkers. Utopian thinkers can be described as basing their plans on *wishful thinking* because these plans are unrealistic.

6. **provisional/accommodate the evidence/implicit sense of trust in**   An opinion is a *provisional* (provided for the time being) belief "based on available evidence." When "more evidence becomes available" the opinion may need to be changed to *accommodate the evidence* (allow for the evidence). Like "belief" and "opinion," "faith" refers to an idea that is unproven, but "faith" also has the *implicit sense of trust in* (meaning of trust in something understood but not stated) powers beyond human understanding.

7. **is susceptible to/alleviate/augmented**   Alternating periods of flooding and aridity prompted the ancient Egyptians to build an irrigation and water control system, so it makes sense that the Nile Valley *is susceptible to* such conditions. It also makes sense that they built such a system to *alleviate* (improve partially) the problems caused by these periods. The irrigation system *augmented* (made greater) the normal water supply in the dry season.

8. **cogent/anticipate objections/rebut**   It makes sense that a clear and *cogent* (logically compelling) argument is the first requirement of persuasive writing. It also makes

sense that an effective argument is able to *anticipate objections* (consider in advance) that may be raised to counter the argument and to *rebut* (refute) them. (ii) *Temper criticism* makes sense in context, but it does not make sense with any of the choices for (iii).

9. **analogs/subterranean world/to absolve**   *Analogs* (things that are comparable to other things) to the shaman (a person who acts as intermediary between the natural and supernatural worlds)—such as the mystic (a person who undergoes profound spiritual experiences), who undertakes the journey into the *subterranean world* (hidden world) of the soul—can be found in Western society. Note that the word "subterranean" is used figuratively. Like the shaman, the confessor allows God to act through him to *absolve* (forgive) a person's sins.

10. **acceding to/*too* well/precipitated**   It has been argued that the United States learned the value of not *acceding to* (agreeing to) the demands of aggressors *too well*, as a result of which it nearly *precipitated* (caused to happen) a nuclear war. "Refused to acquiesce" is a clue to the correct answers because it contrasts with (i) *acceding to*.

11. **predicated on/however/had scant success**   Gravity is *predicated on* (based on) a force that can act at a distance. *However*, experimentalists have searched for gravity waves and particles but have *had scant success*.

12. **force/therefore/important issue**   Long-term shortage or unavailability of REE would *force* significant changes in American technology because REE play an important part in America's industrial economy. *Therefore*, (as a result of this importance) domestic REE sources may become an increasingly *important issue*.

13. **misnomer/in contrast to/exploitable**   *Misnomer* (incorrect name) is the best choice because the sentence says "the term ['rare'] reflects unfamiliarity rather than true rarity." The difference between REE and ordinary base and precious metals is described, so *in contrast to* is the best choice. The clue to (iii) is "Consequently, most of the world's supply of REE comes from only a handful of sources." This is because REE do not tend to become concentrated in *exploitable* (able to be used to the greatest possible advantage) ore deposits.

14. **a double-bind/relegated to/affluent**   The situation described in the sentence is *a double-bind* (a situation in which a choice must be made between equally unsatisfactory alternatives) because poor countries are faced with equally unsatisfactory choices. Poor countries that do not become a part of the world economic system are *relegated to* (consigned to an inferior position) the bottom ranks of the world economic order, providing raw materials and labor for the *affluent* (rich) countries.

15. **ubiquitous/disparage/*why***   It makes sense that some scientists would be awed by the fact that carbon is *ubiquitous* (widespread) and thus suitable for forming complex organic molecules that life is based on. The word "however" signals the contrasting attitude of other scientists who *disparage* (belittle) such attitudes as irrational because they believe that the role of science is to explain what exists, not *why* it exists.

16. **imposed/in retaliation/rose steadily**   European colonial powers like Britain and France used tariffs to gain economic advantage. Other European countries *imposed*

(forced upon) tariffs *in retaliation,* resulting in a situation in which tariffs *rose steadily.*

17. **conclusively disprove/inductive reasoning/refute**   *Conclusively disprove* contrasts with "conclusively prove." The hypothesis that all swans are white because all observed swans are white is *inductive reasoning* (related to the process of deriving general principles from particular facts). Popper's argument is that the first observation of a black swan can *refute* (disprove) the hypothesis that all swans are white.

18. **opaque/typology/the modern ethos**   *Opaque* (not transparent) describes characters whose personalities are "resistant to meaningful analysis of motivation and other aspects of their inner life." *Typology* (a theory of types) refers to Forster's categorization of characters, in which "flat" characters are one type. *The modern ethos* (beliefs of a group) emphasizes the "inner, psychological states of individuals."

19. **distant future/reached a critical mass/a radically different**   "Hindsight" is a clue to "from the perspective of some imagined *distant future.*" "An explosion in information technology" is a clue that information *reached a critical mass.* It makes sense that a critical mass of information might explode, creating *a radically different* (extremely different) type of intelligence.

20. **didactic/prescribing/syncretistic**   The *Bhagavad Gita* teaches spiritual practices, so it is *didactic* (intended to instruct), *prescribing* (ordering the use of) a method of purification and enlightenment. "A brilliant synthesis of many strands of Indian spiritual teaching" signals that the *Bhagavad Gita* might be *syncretistic* (composed of differing systems of belief).

21. **ironic/pejorative/ornate**   It is *ironic* (related to an incongruity between what might be expected and what occurs) that the word "rhetoric" first referred to the study of how to use language effectively but has now come to have a *pejorative* (having bad connotations) "sense of language that is *ornate* (elaborately ornamented), pretentious, and insincere." A clue that both (ii) and (iii) require a word with a negative sense is that the sentence contrasts the original, positive use of the word "rhetoric" with the newer, negative use of the word.

22. **demonstrate to/becoming affluent/a self-fulfilling prophecy**   Good clues to the correct answers are "capitalism" and "worked hard to achieve wealth." Weber believed that Calvinism encouraged people to *demonstrate to* themselves and others that they were among the elect by becoming *affluent* (rich). This process can be described as *a self-fulfilling prophecy* because by working to prove that they had been chosen by God to be wealthy they became wealthy.

23. **an elite/turned against/bourgeoisie**   "Its superiority over those outside the group" signals that *an elite* (select group of people) is the correct answer. "However" signals that irony can be *turned against* "the higher class." It makes sense that writers using irony to portray the higher class would regard members of that class as *bourgeoisie* (middle class).

24. **reductionism/in fact/opaque**   "Explained as nothing but" signals that *reductionism* (attempt to explain complex phenomena by simple principles) is being discussed. *In*

fact is the best choice because it helps connect the further point being made about religious belief to the earlier point. "Ultimately" signals that in the final analysis religious beliefs may be *opaque* (not transparent) to understanding from "outside"— that is, not subject to objective analysis.

25. **expediency/rationalized/euphemism** "Unfortunate necessity" and "pragmatic decision" suggest the sentence is saying that principles are sometimes sacrificed to *expediency* (self-serving methods), the process being *rationalized* (provided with self-satisfying but incorrect reasons) and given a *euphemism* (use of inoffensive language in place of unpleasant language) to avoid facing the fact that principles have been sacrificed.

26. **digressions off the main topic/peripheral/pedantic** Scholars are sometimes tempted into *digressions* (deviations) off the main topic to discuss *peripheral* (of minor importance) areas of interest to them but that are regarded by most readers as a *pedantic* (showing off learning) display of erudition (deep, wide learning).

27. **promote/normal hydrology/watershed** It makes sense that the destruction of vegetation and deposition of volcanic rock and ash over large areas would *promote* increased rates of runoff. The "increased overland flow of water…carries [rock debris] into river valleys," resulting in an accumulation of sediment that changes the *normal hydrology* (the occurrence, distribution, and movement of water on, in, and above the earth) of river valleys. During rainstorms after volcanic eruptions, therefore, rainfall is more quickly flushed through a *watershed* (the region draining into a river, river system, or other body of water). A clue to the correct answer to (iii) is "the net effect of such changes to watersheds …."

28. **are equipped with identical faculties for/On the basis of this/irrespective of period or place** If it is true that all human beings *are equipped with identical faculties for* acquiring language, then it is also true that all languages share some basic features. "*On the basis of this* and other evidence it has been proposed that there are 'language universals,' which are shared by all human languages *irrespective of period or place*. (i) Share an innate need for makes some sense, but (ii) *are equipped with identical faculties* is the better answer because if people have identical abilities for acquiring language then it is likely that all human languages share common features. (iii*) Irrespective of period or place* is the best choice because "linguistic universals" suggest that there are common features of human language that remain constant regardless of period or place.

29. **the zenith of/patron saint of/even at the risk of failure** In building the labyrinth and escaping from it, Daedalus represents *the zenith of* (highest point) craftsmanship and innovation. Icarus has become a sort of *patron saint of* (saint who is regarded as the intercessor and advocate in heaven for someone) people who strive to innovate, *even at the risk of failure*.

30. **torn between/moral qualms/fervent** "Diametrically opposed forces" signals an opposition indicating that *torn between* is the correct answer. Oppenheimer is described as having "misgivings about the uses to which his work might one day be put," whereas Teller, "in contrast to Oppenheimer," had no *moral qualms* (uneasy

feelings about the rightness of an action) because he was a *fervent* (full of strong emotion) anti-Communist.

31. **discourse/civil/cupidity**   Political *discourse* (verbal expression) might come to center on economic matters, ignoring the larger requirements of *civil* (relating to citizens) society. Such a business-oriented society might see an increase in *cupidity* (greed).

32. **logically coherent/explicit/rather**   If a piece of expository prose is *logically coherent* (intelligible) it requires a few *explicit* (very clear) indicators of transition from one topic to another topic; *rather*, the transitions are an integral part of the discourse.

33. **ostensibly/reconciled/predestined**   The dogma (system of principles or tenets) of the Roman Catholic Church is that free will and predestination are *ostensibly* (apparently) contradictory. However, it believes that this apparent contradiction can be *reconciled* (made consistent) by God. Some theologians believe that this doctrine is false because logically if a soul has a particular nature, its future is necessarily *predestined* (decided in advance).

34. **exponential/closely related to/anthropogenic**   There has been an *exponential* (very great) increase in breeding populations of California gulls. This great increase may be *closely related to* the use the gulls make of landfills and other *anthropogenic* (caused by humans) sources of food. "Landfills and other" signals that the sources of food are related to human activity, providing a clue to the meaning of the word "anthropogenic."

35. **consensus of/meteorologists/ameliorate**   The *consensus of* (general agreement of) the world's leading *meteorologists* (scientists who study the weather) is that the number of natural calamities will greatly increase. As a result, some experts recommend that more developing countries include in their development plans strategies to *ameliorate* (make better) the impact of such disasters on development. It makes sense that the effects of disasters can only be ameliorated, not completely eliminated.

36. **genesis/embryonic/a relatively inhospitable climate**   Several geographers and historians have speculated that temperate climates promote the *genesis* (beginning) of civilizations, but that after a civilization has developed past the *embryonic* (in early stages of development) stage it is more likely to develop further in a *relatively inhospitable climate*. "Challenges are needed that must be overcome for progress to occur" signals that less than ideal conditions, such as a *relatively inhospitable climate*, is the correct answer.

37. **conscription/circumscription/raise an army to defend the country**   "Extreme *circumscription* (limiting) of individual rights" makes good sense because *conscription* (compulsory enrollment for service) is such an extreme restriction of individual rights. (i) "covert surveillance of citizens" makes sense but is not correct because none of the choices for (iii) make sense with this answer. (iii) *Raise an army to defend the country* makes sense because the main purpose of conscription is to raise an army for national defense.

38. **of a sanguine /conjecture that/innocuous**   Scientists of a *sanguine* (optimistic) disposition *conjecture that* (speculate) the impact of human activities on climate has been mitigated by the trend toward cooler weather. The correct answer to (i) of a sanguine disposition is signaled by "This optimistic conclusion." Other scientists find it difficult to believe that the greenhouse effect could be *innocuous* (harmless).

39. **postulating/extrapolations/conjectures**   An example of speculative history is *postulating* (presupposing) that the Germans developed the atomic bomb before the Allies. Some historians argue that such exercises—even if based on reasonable *extrapolations* (estimates made by projecting known information) from existing trends—are meaningless *conjectures* (speculations).

40. **were predictions of a future with/hindsight/extreme vigilance**   "Would usher in" signals the correct answer for (i) *were predictions of a future with*. In (ii) *hindsight* (perception of events after they happen) is correct because the sentence describes limitations of nuclear reactors that were discovered after optimistic predictions were made about them. One of the limitations of nuclear reactors is the need for *extreme vigilance* (watchfulness) in monitoring them.

41. **mean/inclined to say/criterion**   If by science we (i) *mean* a systematic study of phenomena, we would be (ii) *inclined to say* that history fulfills the (iii) *criterion* (standard used in judging) necessary to be considered a science.

42. **alleviating/pathogens/innocuous**   It makes sense that antibiotics played a part in *alleviating* (improving partially) the harmful effects of war on human life. Antibiotics work on the principle that they harm *pathogens* (agents that cause disease) but are *innocuous* (harmless) to human beings.

43. **lampoon/quixotic/zeitgeist**   The word "dreamers" signals that the people referred to are unrealistic, so (ii) *quixotic* (overly idealistic) is the correct answer. It makes sense that "their critics" would (i) *lampoon* (mock harshly) these people for believing that a new (iii) *zeitgeist* (the outlook characteristic of a period) is forming.

44. **postulates/stymied/burgeoning**   It makes sense that an ideology *postulates* (presupposes) something occurring. The ideology of Malthusianism has been *stymied* (thwarted) by *burgeoning* (growing) food production and better birth control.

45. **a paradox/antithetical/in practice**   Clues to the correct answers are "lying at opposite poles" and "similar." Communism and fascism are in many ways (ii) *antithetical* (contrasting) because they are at opposite ends of the political spectrum. (iii) *In practice*, however, they are similar totalitarian (related to a system of government in which one political group maintains complete control) political systems.

46. **imposition/repressive/rather than**   It is reasonable that resistance movements would be opposed to the *imposition* (the act of forcing upon) of colonial or other *repressive* (tending to repress rights) regimes. Such groups often use guerilla tactics *rather than* conducting conventional war because using guerilla tactics gives them an advantage over their enemies.

47. **jurisprudence/inviolable/predominated**   All the choices make some sense for (i); however, *jurisprudence* (philosophy of law) is the best choice because the sentence deals with a topic in the philosophy of law. It makes sense that Anglo-American jurisprudence is greatly concerned with *inviolable* (safe from assault) human rights because this concern *predominated* (prevailed) during the Enlightenment and subsequently.

48. **lamented the emergence /however, /feasible**   "Runs roughshod" suggests that some political scientists see the "imperial presidency" negatively, so it makes sense that they have (i) *lamented the emergence* (regretted the emergence) of this type of presidency. (ii) *However,* (in contrast to this view) other political scientists believe that such a strong presidency is the only (iii) *feasible* (possible) way that the institution can properly perform its function.

49. **solace/demise/diminution**   Some people might take some *solace* (consolation) in the fact that the sun will eventually shrink and die. (ii) *Demise* (death) is signaled by "nears the end of its life." (iii) *Diminution* (lessening) is signaled by "losing mass."

50. **sagacious/notoriously plastic/premises**   The *sagacious* (wise) student of literature is aware that terms used in literary criticism are *notoriously plastic* (well-known for being able to be shaped). The correct answer to (ii) *notoriously plastic* is signaled by "ever shifting." The meanings of literary terms shift according to the *premises* (propositions upon which an argument is based) of the writer using them.

Reading Comprehension Questions

Read the passages below, and then answer the questions that follow them based on the information in the passages themselves and in any introductory material or notes. The correct answer may be either stated or merely suggested in the passage.

PASSAGE 1

Indian religion is commonly regarded as the offspring of an Aryan religion, brought into India by invaders from the north and modified by contact with Dravidian civilization. The materials at our disposal hardly permit us to take any other point of view, for the literature of the Vedic Aryans is relatively ancient and full and we have no information about the old Dravidians comparable with it. But were our knowledge less one-sided, we might see that it would be more correct to describe Indian religion as Dravidian religion stimulated and modified by the ideas of Aryan invaders. For the greatest deities of Hinduism, Siva, Krishna, Râma, Durgâ and some of its most essential doctrines such as metempsychosis and divine incarnations, are either totally unknown to the Veda or obscurely adumbrated in it. The chief characteristics of mature Indian religion are characteristics of an area, not of a race, and they are not the characteristics of religion in Persia, Greece or other Aryan lands.

Select one answer choice for the following question.

1. It can be inferred that "the Veda" mentioned in the passage is
   - (A) the oldest sacred writings of Dravidian civilization.
   - (B) a holy book mainly devoted to the worship of the great deities of Hinduism such as Krishna, Shiva, and Rama.
   - (C) the oldest sacred writings of Hinduism.
   - (D) the holy book of an ancient Aryan religion before that religion was brought to India.
   - (E) a religious book describing abstruse doctrines such as metempsychosis and divine incarnation.

*Note: Some passages in this chapter use terminology that is not commonly used today but that was acceptable when it was written.

2. Based on the information in the passage, which of the following are true?
   (A) The author is almost certain that nearly all of the important features of Indian religion originated in India rather than being brought there.
   (B) Dravidian civilization probably developed the idea of divine incarnation.
   (C) Aryan invaders probably brought with them the deities that later became the great deities of Hindu belief.

PASSAGE 2

Global change phenomena such as climate warming, permafrost thaw, wildfires, and drought are affecting terrestrial ecosystem biogeochemistry, particularly in northern latitudes, but also in the continental U.S. Soil microbial communities are critical to
Line the carbon biogeochemistry of ecosystems; for they decompose as much carbon
(5) as is annually photosynthesized by plants. There is strong evidence that variation in the composition of the below ground microbial community affects the way in which ecosystems function, and this can affect regional to global biogeochemistry. Particular functional groups of microorganisms, such as decomposer fungi, have a disproportionate effect on elemental cycles. For example, in northern latitude soils,
(10) climate warming is accelerating permafrost thaw and wildfire intensity, altering the abundance of soil decomposers which has direct effect on rates of biogeochemical processes. This and other types of microbial community information can be used by the next generation of mechanistic microbial-based C cycling models. A next step will be to merge bioinformatics with geoinformatics that can be used to build
(15) a spatially explicit map of microbial biogeography that is linked to environmental and process data. Such a map has many uses beyond understanding ecological principles that structure community composition and diversity. Such spatially explicit information can potentially be used for assessing how global change will affect microbial communities and the biogeochemical processes within specific regions.

1. It can be inferred that one of the substances primarily involved in elemental cycles mentioned in the passage is
   (A) soil microbes
   (B) water
   (C) heat
   (D) carbon
   (E) decomposer fungi

2. The primary purpose of this passage is

   (A) to call for a major reduction in human activities that affect soil microbial communities

   (B) to articulate what is known about the effects of global change phenomena on ecosystems, particularly those involving soil microbial communities, and to show how further research can add to our understanding of how global change will affect microbial communities in different areas

   (C) to explain how particular groups of microorganisms such as decomposer fungi now have an effect on the carbon cycle far greater than they did before climate warming occurred

   (D) to show how scientists are moving toward an understanding of global change phenomena that will not be reliant on regional variations in such effects

   (E) to focus on the effects of climate warming on the ecology of soil microbial communities in the northern latitudes to show how what happens in one region affects what happens around the globe

---

> **Consider each of the three choices separately and select all that apply.**

3. Based on the information in the passage, which of the following are true?

   (A) The amount of carbon released by soil microbial communities is approximately equal to the amount of carbon photosynthesized by plants.

   (B) Scientists have an excellent understanding of the effect of global change phenomena on soil microbial communities in every region of the globe.

   (C) There is no evidence that climate warming will accelerate the rate at which soil decomposition releases carbon.

PASSAGE 3

Dr. Proudie may well be said to have been a fortunate man, for he was not born to wealth, and he is now Bishop of Barchester; nevertheless, he has his cares. He has a large family, of whom the three eldest are daughters, now all grown up and fit for
Line fashionable life, and he has a wife. It is not my intention to breathe a word against
(5) the character of Mrs. Proudie, but still I cannot think that with all her virtues she adds much to her husband's happiness. The truth is that in matters domestic she rules supreme over her titular lord, and rules with a rod of iron. Nor is this all. Things domestic Dr. Proudie might have abandoned to her, if not voluntarily, yet willingly. But Mrs. Proudie is not satisfied with such home dominion, and stretches her power
(10) over all his movements, and will not even abstain from things spiritual. In fact, the bishop is hen-pecked.

> **Select one answer choice for the following questions.**

1. The word "titular" as it is used in the passage most nearly means
    (A) sycophantic
    (B) spiritual
    (C) docile
    (D) high-ranking
    (E) in name only.

> **Identify the sentence by writing its first three words and its last three words on the line below.**

Select the sentence in which an assertion is made and then undercut.

2. _____

PASSSAGE 4

The relative merit and importance of different periods of a literature should be determined by the relative degrees of spirituality which these different periods exhibit.
The intellectual power of two or more periods, as exhibited in their literatures, may
Line show no marked difference, while the spiritual vitality of these same periods may
(5) very distinctly differ. And if it be admitted that literature proper is the product of
co-operative intellect and spirit (the latter being always an indispensable factor,
though there can be no high order of literature that is not strongly articulated, that
is not well freighted, with thought), it follows that the periods of a literature should
be determined by the ebb and flow of spiritual life which they severally register,
(10) rather than by any other considerations. There are periods which are characterized
by a "blindness of heart," an inactive, quiescent condition of the spirit, by which the
intellect is more or less divorced from the essential, the eternal, and it directs itself
to the shows of things. Such periods may embody in their literatures a large amount
of thought,—thought which is conversant with the externality of things; but that of
(15) itself will not constitute a noble literature, however perfect the forms in which it may
be embodied, and the general sense of the civilized world, independently of any
theories of literature, will not regard such a literature as noble. It is made up of what
must be, in time, superseded; it has not a sufficiently large element of the essential,
the eternal, which can be reached only through the assimilating life of the spirit. The
(20) spirit may be so "cabined, cribbed, confined" as not to come to any consciousness of
itself; or it may be so set free as to go forth and recognize its kinship, respond to the
spiritual world outside of itself, and, by so responding, *know* what merely intellectual
philosophers call the *unknowable*.

1. Which of the following sequences best characterizes the general structure of
   this passage?
   (A) Statement of a premise; questioning of validity of the premise; assertion;
       explanation of assertion
   (B) Assertion; statement of a premise and what follows from it and the preceding
       assertion; explanation
   (C) Assertion; statement of a premise; explanation of premise; examples from
       literature
   (D) Generalization; examination of the generalization; statement of a premise;
       conclusion
   (E) Examination of two competing philosophies of aesthetics; statement of a
       premise and its consequences; explanation

2. Based on the information in the passage, the author would most likely agree that
   literature of a high quality
   (A) is amoral
   (B) is based on the values of Judeo-Christian civilization
   (C) is concerned primarily with the ancient Greek ideals of nobility and heroism
   (D) reflects the zeitgeist of the time in which it is written
   (E) is almost entirely free from the influence of the attitudes and values of the time
       in which it is written

3. Based on the information in the passage, which of the following would the author
   be likely to believe is true?
   (A) The literature of a period can be considered excellent as long as it is original and
       makes people think.
   (B) Literature of the highest order need not have any real intellectual merit as long
       as it is profoundly spiritual.
   (C) The primary importance of literature lies in the part it plays in spiritual life.

4. Which of the following is/are reasonable criticism/s of the argument made in
   the passage?
   (A) Definitions of key terms, such as "spirituality," are not provided.
   (B) Examples are not given to illustrate the assertions made.
   (C) It is illogical.

PASSAGE 5

It goes without saying that you will not write a good novel unless you possess the sense of reality; but it will be difficult to give you a recipe for calling that sense into being. Humanity is immense and reality has myriad forms; the most one can affirm
Line is that some of the flowers of fiction have the odor of it, and others have not; as for
(5) telling you in advance how your nosegay should be composed, that is another affair. It is equally excellent and inconclusive to say that one must write from experience; to our supposititious aspirant such a declaration might savor of mockery. What kind of experience is intended, and where does it begin and end? Experience is never limited and it is never complete; it is an immense sensibility, a kind of huge spider-
(10) web, of the finest silken threads, suspended in the chamber of consciousness and catching every air-borne particle in its tissue. It is the very atmosphere of the mind; and when the mind is imaginative—much more when it happens to be that of a man of genius—it takes to itself the faintest hints of life, it converts the very pulses of the air into revelations.

Select one answer choice for the following question.

1. Which of the following is not used in this passage?
   (A) Metaphor
   (B) Assertion of a proposition
   (C) Rhetorical question
   (D) Parody
   (E) Simile

Consider each of the three choices separately and select all that apply.

2. Based on the information in the passage, which of the following statements would the author be likely to agree with?
   (A) To be a good novelist a person must understand and appreciate reality.
   (B) An aspiring novelist must carefully follow the advice of renowned writers as to what types of experience he or she should seek.
   (C) A novelist with a great imagination is able to transform what appears to be limited experience into true art.

PASSAGE 6

Populations of certain Northern sea otters have experienced recent declines. Suggested causes for these declines are complex and have been attributed to a variety of ecological or anthropogenic pressures. Major disasters such as oil spills are usually
Line noted for their sudden dramatic impact on marine and coastal species. The acute
(5) effects of a spill are evaluated by mortality estimations, clinical evaluation, and necropsy examinations. The long-term effects of these tragedies are more difficult to document, and studies often are restricted to demographic modeling, estimations of reproductive efficiency, or time-differential, age-specific survival rates. While several recent studies have eloquently shown that many species face long term oil-related
(10) effects after a spill, biological markers that identify oil-induced sublethal pathology in susceptible species are urgently needed. The goal of the proposed study is to identify specific, sensitive genetic markers that signify persistent pathological and physiological injury associated with either acute or chronic hydrocarbon exposure.

Crude petroleum oil has multiple aromatic and aliphatic hydrocarbon constitu-
(15) ents, and the toxic effects of exposure and ingestion understandably can be diverse and extensive within the body. Under these circumstances, the molecular investigation of subtle alterations of expressed genes indicative of multiple physiological processes at the cellular level is particularly useful. Further, samples required for molecular investigations are minimally invasive or stressful to the subject animals.
(20) Gene expression technologies have the exciting potential of providing methods for monitoring the long-term effects of oil exposure in federally listed, free-ranging sea otters. An added benefit is that these methods may elucidate the mechanisms by which oil can deleteriously affect an individual sea otter over a long period, and thereby aid in the design of therapeutic and preventative strategies to treat and pro-
(25) tect susceptible individuals and populations at risk from oil exposure.

Select one answer choice for the following questions.

---

1. The word "chronic" as it is used in the first paragraph most nearly means
   (A) severe
   (B) recurring periodically but in a mild form
   (C) continuing over a fairly long period of time
   (D) confined to certain areas
   (E) cumulative

2. If the study proposed in this passage is carried out successfully, which of the following would be least likely to occur?
   (A) The rate of decline in Northern sea otter populations would decrease.
   (B) Scientists would gain a better understanding of the effects of hydrocarbon ingestion and exposure on sea otters.
   (C) Populations of sea otters would decline by a relatively small but significant amount due to injuries sustained during the collection of samples from the animals for molecular analysis.
   (D) Scientists would devise more effective means to protect sea otters from the effects of oil spills.
   (E) Scientists would better understand why some species of sea otters are more susceptible to the effects of exposure to oil than others.

Consider each of the three choices separately and select all that apply.

---

3. Based on the information in the passage, which of the following is/are true?
   (A) Scientists know more about the short-term effects of oil spills on marine life than they do about the long-term effects of oil spills on marine life.
   (B) An oil-induced pathology in a Northern sea otter is regrettable, but it would have no effect on the number of sea otters in an area unless the pathology was lethal.
   (C) Scientists have concluded that major oil spills are the only major cause of the decline in certain species of Northern sea otters.

PASSAGE 7

Pidgins and creoles are the outcome of the need of people not sharing a language to communicate but differ from national and international languages in that a pidgin does not begin as an already existing language or dialect selected to serve this
Line purpose; it is rather a particular combination of two languages. Loreto Todd has the
(5) following to say about pidgins and creoles:

> A pidgin is a marginal language which arises to fulfill certain restricted communication needs among people who have no common language. In the initial stages of contact the communication is often limited to transactions where a detailed exchange of ideas is not required and where a small vocabulary, drawn almost exclusively from one language,
> (10) suffices. The syntactic structure of the pidgin is less complex and less flexible than the structures of the languages that were in contact, and though many pidgin features clearly reflect usages in the contact languages others are unique to the pidgin.

> A creole arises when a pidgin becomes the mother tongue of a speech community. The simple structure that characterized the pidgin is carried over into the
> (15) creole but since a creole, as a mother tongue, must be capable of expressing the whole range of human experience, the lexicon is expanded, and frequently a more elaborate syntactic system evolves.

Since creoles are often not regarded as "real" languages and consequently considered as inferior, it is worth noting that, for example, both French and English may be
(20) the outcome of pidgins—in the first case through contact between native Gauls and
occupying Romans, and in the second through contact between the native Anglo-
Saxons and the Danes who settled on the east coast of England.

Select one answer choice for the following question.

1. Based on the information in the passage, it is reasonable to infer that many pidgins
developed
(A) as a result of the efforts of a colonial power to impose a simple language on a
population in order to control them.
(B) to allow the exchange of religious and philosophic ideas.
(C) in order to facilitate trade.
(D) as simplified forms of creoles.
(E) as mother tongues.

Consider each of the three choices separately and select all that apply.

2. Based on the information in the passage, which of the following is/are true?
(A) A creole always has a more complex syntax than the pidgin from which it
originated.
(B) Pidgins develop as a way to facilitate communication among groups who do
not speak a common language.
(C) It is possible that English is a creole.

PASSAGE 8

Many bacteria that live and bring about chemical changes in acid drainage environments are known as lithotrophs ("rock-eaters"). These microbes utilize just a few
inorganic compounds or elements for energy or growth. Iron-oxidizing bacteria
Line obtain energy by oxidizing ferrous iron (Fe^{2+}) to ferric iron (Fe^{3+}). The best-known
(5)   lithotrophic iron oxidizer, *Acidithiobacillus ferrooxidans*, thrives in acidic (low pH)
environments. Bacteria that use organic compounds for energy or growth are known
as heterotrophs ("diverse eaters"). Important heterotrophs are sulfate reducers that
use sulfate (SO_4^{2-}), rather than oxygen as most bacteria do, to aid their decomposition of organic matter. The end product of this decomposition, sulfide (S_2), is pro-
(10) duced almost exclusively by sulfate-reducing bacteria. Sulfide reacts to form HS(g)
(hydrogen sulfide gas), the compound that produces the odor of rotten eggs. The
best-known sulfate-reducing bacteria are in the genus *Desulfovibrio*, but many other
sulfate reducers are present in nature.

Bacterial processes involving iron and sulfate can be especially important in depo-
(15)   sitional sites such as wetlands that receive acid drainage. Sulfate is present in high
concentration in acid drainage because of the oxidation of sulfide minerals. High
sulfate and abundant organic matter promote sulfate-reducer growth (which in turn
supports near-neutral pH values). Sulfate reduction permits chemically reducing
conditions to develop and persist in water-saturated, oxygen-poor portions of the
(20)   sediment. Other areas of the sediment, such as areas at or near the surface, remain
oxygenated. Thus, wetlands can have chemically reducing and chemically oxidizing
zones in close proximity. In general, reducing conditions tend to immobilize metals
and prevent them from moving in the surface-water/ground-water system, whereas
oxidizing conditions tend to mobilize metals and allow them to move in the surface-
(25)   water/ground-water system. The mobility of metals is important because metals
usually are the source of toxicity in acid drainage.

Consider each of the three choices separately and select all that apply.

1. Based on the information in the passage, which of the following are not true?
    (A) All bacteria that decompose organic matter use oxygen in the process.
    (B) *Desulfovibrio* thrive in oxygen-rich areas of depositional sites.
    (C) Some bacteria use only inorganic compounds or elements for energy.

2. Based on the information in the passage, which of the following are true?
    (A) *Desulfovibrio* feeds primarily on sulfate.
    (B) Raising the pH of a wetland area near an abandoned iron mine would be likely
        to slow the rate at which *Acidithiobacillus ferrooxidans* oxidizes ferrous iron.
    (C) It is possible that *Desulfovibrio* and similar bacteria play a significant role in
        reducing the level of toxicity in wetlands receiving acid drainage.

PASSAGE 9

Moral questions immediately present themselves as questions whose solution cannot wait for sensible proof. A moral question is a question not of what sensibly exists,
but of what is good, or would be good if it did exist. Science can tell us what exists;
Line   but to compare the *worths*, both of what exists and of what does not exist, we must
(5)   consult not science, but what Pascal calls our heart. Science herself consults her
heart when she lays it down that the infinite ascertainment of fact and correction
of false belief are the supreme goods for man. Challenge the statement, and science
can only repeat it oracularly, or else prove it by showing that such ascertainment
and correction bring man all sorts of other goods which man's heart in turn declares.
(10)   The question of having moral beliefs at all or not having them is decided by our will.
Are our moral preferences true or false, or are they only odd biological phenomena,
making things good or bad for *us*, but in themselves indifferent? How can your pure

intellect decide? If your heart does not *want* a world of moral reality, your head will assuredly never make you believe in one. Skepticism, indeed, will satisfy the head's play-instincts much better than any rigorous idealism can. Some men (even at the student age) are so naturally cool-hearted that the moralistic hypothesis never has for them any pungent life, and in their supercilious presence the hot young moralist always feels strangely ill at ease. The appearance knowingness is on their side, of naïveté and gullibility on his. Yet, in the inarticulate heart of him, he clings to it that he is not a dupe, and that there is a realm in which all their wit and intellectual superiority is no better than the cunning of a fox. Moral skepticism can no more be refuted or proved by logic than intellectual skepticism can. When we stick to it that there *is* truth (be it of either kind), we do so with our whole nature, and resolve to stand or fall by the results. The skeptic with his whole nature adopts the doubting attitude; but which of us is the wiser, Omniscience only knows.

Select one answer choice for the following questions.

1. If it is true that human moral preferences are "odd biological phenomena," which of the following is most likely to be true?
   (A) A world of moral reality exists.
   (B) A world of moral reality does not exist.
   (C) With sufficient effort each person is capable of understanding the world of morality that definitely exists.
   (D) The objective truth about morality can be found by consulting our hearts.
   (E) Human behavior is not governed by scientific laws.

2. Which of the following most accurately expresses the view of the author of this passage?
   (A) It can be scientifically proven that moral truth exists.
   (B) There is no way to either prove or disprove the existence of absolute truth.
   (C) Moral truth does not exist.
   (D) Logic and science will one day be able to prove that moral beliefs are illusory.
   (E) Skepticism is the only reasonable attitude to adopt toward the question of whether moral truth exists.

3. The meaning of the word "sensible" as it is used in the passage most nearly means
   (A) based on sound reason and judgment
   (B) conscious
   (C) absolute
   (D) able to be perceived by the senses
   (E) rigorous

PASSAGE 10

Let us suppose that I am looking at a star, Sirius say, on a dark night. If physics is to be believed, light waves which started to travel from Sirius many years ago reach (after a specified time which astronomers calculate) the earth, impinge upon my
Line retinas and cause me to say that I am seeing Sirius. Now the Sirius about which they
(5) convey information to me is the Sirius which existed at the time when they started. This Sirius, may, however, no longer exist; it may have disappeared in the interim. To say that one can see what no longer exists is absurd. It follows that, whatever it is that I am seeing, it is not Sirius. What in fact, I do see is a yellow patch of a particular size, shape and intensity. I infer that this yellow patch had an origin (with which it is con-
(10) nected by a continuous chain of physical events) several years ago and many million miles away. But this inference may be mistaken; the origin of the yellow patch, which I call a star, may be a blow on the nose, or a lamp hanging on the mast of a ship.

Nor is this the only inference involved. It is true that I *think* I am seeing a yellow patch, but am I really justified in holding this belief? So far as physics and physiol-
(15) ogy are concerned, all that we are entitled to say is that the optic nerve is being stimulated in a certain way, as a result of which certain events are being caused in the brain. Are we really justified in saying any more than this? Possibly we are—the question is really a philosophical one and this is not the place to offer an opinion upon the issues raised—but it is important to realize that once again an inference
(20) is involved, and once again the inference may be mistaken. Directly we go beyond the bare statement "the optic nerve is being stimulated in such and such a way" and conclude from this fact "therefore I am seeing an object of such and such a charac- ter," we are drawing an inference and are liable to fall into error. What, then, if the physicist and physiologist are right, we in fact know are certain events taking place
(25) in our own brains. The outside world is not itself known; its existence is merely an inference due to the fact that we think these events must have a cause.

If we accept the teaching of physics and physiology, what we know in perception are not the movements of matter, but certain events in ourselves connected with those movements; not objects external to ourselves, but the effects of the impact of
(30) light-rays and other forms of energy proceeding from these objects upon our bodies . . . What, then, is left in the world outside us? We cannot tell . . .

Consider each of the three choices separately and select all that apply.

1. Based on what he says in the passage, which of the following would the author be most likely to agree with?
   (A) All of a person's knowledge of the outside world is based on inference.
   (B) It has been demonstrated that the world outside our brains does not exist.
   (C) To gain knowledge we must carefully consider the justification for inferences we make.

2. Assuming that the star Sirius does exist at this moment and that the laws of physics are correct, which of the following would, according to the author, be true?

(A) An observer on Earth looking at it at this moment would actually be seeing it.

(B) An observer on Earth looking at it at this moment would not actually be seeing it.

(C) There is no way to know whether or not an observer on Earth looking at it at this moment would actually be seeing it.

3. Which of the following statements would, according to the author, involve making an assumption (or assumptions)?

(A) When a person hears the sound of a baby crying it is actually being produced by a baby.

(B) The laws of optics as outlined by modern physics are true.

(C) The physical reality we call the world exists only in the human mind.

PASSAGE 11

Language as the term will be used here refers to a uniquely human mode of communicating and organizing one's perceptions of the world. It has been demonstrated that the signaling systems used by animals often referred to as "language" differ
Line from human language in one crucially important respect. The signs animals use to
(5) communicate are limited in number and the messages which can be communicated using these signs are similarly limited. This is not true of human language. Any human being (who is not suffering from brain damage and is at a certain period of his life exposed to an environment where a language is spoken) will acquire language and will be able to produce and understand an unlimited number of meaningful
(10) utterances, the great majority of which he has never heard before. Human language is therefore "creative" in a way that systems of animal communication are not, and for this reason in particular human language has come to be regarded as a defining ability which distinguishes man from all other species. (It has been suggested that we should speak of "homo loquens" rather than of "homo sapiens.")
(15)   It was asserted above that all human beings are born with the ability to acquire language given exposure to an environment where a language is spoken. Three points arise from this. Firstly, language is a social activity, and the acquisition of language can be seen as part of the process of "socialization." Secondly, the ability to acquire language is species-specific and innate (i.e., genetically transmitted from
(20) one generation to the next), which is to say that all human beings are "programmed" to acquire language in much the same way that they are programmed to walk—at a particular stage of their development. Thirdly, a distinction has been made implicitly between the ability to speak language and the ability to speak a particular language. Human beings are equipped with the ability to acquire the former. Any human
(25) being, given the exposure at the age during which language is acquired, can learn to speak any language. There is no evidence to suggest that people of a particular racial type, say, are more able to acquire certain languages than others or than people of different racial types. Those differences in ability to speak or learn a language result from other factors.

1. Which of the following statements would the author not be likely to agree with?
   (A) Although human language allows greater scope for expression than does animal language, they are fundamentally the same.
   (B) A racially Chinese child raised in a Chinese-speaking family will learn to speak Chinese with less effort than would a Caucasian child adopted at an early age and raised by that Chinese-speaking family.
   (C) It is more difficult for a child to learn a tone-based language such as Cantonese than languages not based on tone, such as English.

PASSAGE 12

While the Oriental had been compelled by Rome to draw his political frontier at the Euphrates, and had failed so far to cross the river-line, he had maintained his cultural independence within sight of the Mediterranean. In the hill country of Judah, overlooking the high road between Antioch and Alexandria, the two chief foci of Hellenism in the east which the Macedonians had founded, and which had grown to maturity under the aegis of Rome, there dwelt a little Semitic community which had defied all efforts of Greek or Roman to assimilate it, and had finally given birth to a world religion about the time that a Roman punitive expedition razed its holy city of Jerusalem to the ground. Christianity was charged with an incalculable force, which shot like an electric current from one end of the Roman Empire to the other. The highly-organized society of its adherents measured its strength in several sharp conflicts with the Imperial administration, from which it emerged victorious, and it was proclaimed the official religious organization of the Empire by the very emperor that founded Constantinople.

The established Christian Church took the best energies of Hellenism into its service. The Greek intellectuals ceased to become lecturers and professors, to find a more human and practical career in the bishop's office. The Nicene Creed, drafted by an "ecumenical" conference of bishops under the auspices of Constantine himself, was the last notable formulation of ancient Greek philosophy. The cathedral of Aya Sophia, with which Justinian adorned Constantinople, was the last original creation of ancient Greek art. The same Justinian closed the University of Athens, which had educated the world for nine hundred years and more, since Plato founded his college in the Academy. Six recalcitrant professors went into exile for their spiritual freedom, but they found the devout Zoroastrianism of the Persian court as unsympathetic as the devout Christianity of the Roman. Their humiliating return and recantation broke the "Golden Chain" of Hellenic thought forever.

Hellenism was thus expiring from its own inanition, when the inevitable avalanche overwhelmed it from without. In the seventh century A.D. there was another religious eruption in the Semitic world, this time in the heart of Arabia, where

(30) Hellenism had hardly penetrated, and under the impetus of Islam the Asian burst his bounds again after a thousand years. Syria was reft away from the Empire, and Egypt, and North Africa as far as the Atlantic, and their political severance meant their cultural loss to Greek civilization. Between the Koran and Hellenism no fusion was possible. Christianity had taken Hellenism captive, but Islam gave it no quarter, and the (35) priceless library of Alexandria is said to have been condemned by the caliph's order to feed the furnaces of the public baths.

Select one answer choice for the following questions.

1. The focus of the passage is on
   (A) Christianity's rise to become a world religion
   (B) the pervasive cultural influence of Hellenism
   (C) Asian cultural influence on Europe that led to the decline of Rome
   (D) the decline of Hellenism
   (E) Islam's incompatibility with Hellenism

2. The word "inanition" as it is used in the third paragraph most nearly means
   (A) energy
   (B) exhaustion
   (C) internal contradictions
   (D) soullessness
   (E) rigidity

Consider each of the three choices separately and select all that apply.

3. According to the passage, which of the following are true?
   (A) Christianity had its origins in Asia.
   (B) Islam made better use of Hellenic culture for its own purposes than did Christianity.
   (C) Zoroastrianism became a popular religion among Greek intellectuals throughout the Mediterranean world as the influence of Hellenic culture receded.

The distinction between pleasure and the sense of beauty has sometimes been said to consist in the unselfishness of aesthetic satisfaction. In other pleasures, it is said, we gratify our senses and passions; in the contemplation of beauty we are raised
Line above ourselves, the passions are silenced and we are happy in the recognition of a
(5) good that we do not seek to possess. The painter does not look at a spring of water with the eyes of a thirsty man, nor at a beautiful woman with those of a satyr. The difference lies, it is urged, in the impersonality of the enjoyment. But this distinction is one of intensity and delicacy, not of nature, and it seems satisfactory only to the least aesthetic minds.

(10)   In the second place, the supposed disinterestedness of aesthetic delights is not truly fundamental. Appreciation of a picture is not identical with the desire to buy it, but it is, or ought to be, closely related and preliminary to that desire to buy it. The beauties of nature and of the plastic arts are not consumed by being enjoyed; they retain all the efficacy to impress a second beholder. But this circumstance is
(15) accidental, and those aesthetic objects which depend upon change and are exhausted in time, as are all performances, are things the enjoyment of which is an object of rivalry and is coveted as much as any other pleasure. And even plastic beauties can often not be enjoyed except by a few, on account of the necessity of travel or other difficulties of access, and then this aesthetic enjoyment is as selfishly pursued
(20) as the rest.

The truth which the theory is trying to state seems rather to be that when we seek aesthetic pleasures we have no further pleasure in mind; that we do not mix up the satisfactions of vanity and proprietorship with the delight of contemplation. This is true, but it is true at bottom of all pursuits and enjoyments. Every real pleasure is
(25) in one sense disinterested. It is not sought with ulterior motives, and what fills the mind is no calculation, but the image of an object or event, suffused with emotion. A sophisticated consciousness may often take the idea of self as the touchstone of its inclinations; but this self, for the gratification and aggrandizement of which a man may live, is itself only a complex of aims and memories, which once had their direct
(30) objects, in which he had taken a spontaneous and unselfish interest. The gratifications which, merged together, make the selfishness are each of them ingenuous, and no more selfish than the most altruistic, impersonal emotion. The content of selfishness is a mass of unselfishness. There is no reference to the nominal essence called oneself either in one's appetites or in one's natural affections; yet a man absorbed in
(35) his meat and drink, in his houses and lands, in his children and dogs, is called selfish because these interests, although natural and instinctive in him, are not shared by others. The unselfish man is he whose nature has a more universal direction, whose interests are more widely diffused.

1. Which of the following best describes the structure of the argument in the passage?
   (A) Description of a commonly held view of the relationship between beauty and pleasure; critique and refinement of this view; outlining of a comprehensive theory of aesthetics; application of this theory of aesthetics to another issue in philosophy, the status of the notion of the "self"
   (B) Discussion of the relationship between pleasure and the sense of beauty; analysis of the proposition that pleasure derived from beauty is necessarily disinterested; presentation of author's own theory of aesthetic appreciation; analysis of the idea of selfishness; conclusion
   (C) Description of one view of aesthetic satisfaction; argument against this view; description of a refined version of the refuted view of aesthetic satisfaction; argument against this refined view
   (D) Introduction to the topic of aesthetics; analysis of examples to illustrate the relationship between pleasure and beauty; comparison and analysis of higher as opposed to lower aesthetic pleasures; discussion of the relation of aesthetics to broader philosophical issues; conclusion
   (E) Outline of an aesthetic theory; analysis of examples of aesthetic appreciation in light of this theory; discussion of the notion of selfishness in relation to aesthetic pleasure; discussion of the implications of the author's aesthetic theory in relation to notions of the "self"

2. The word "nominal" as it is used in the passage most nearly means
   (A) difficult to define
   (B) ephemeral
   (C) illusory
   (D) being something in name only
   (E) fundamental

3. Based on the information in this passage, which of the following would the author agree with?
   (A) The varying capacities of people to appreciate beauty are illusory.
   (B) Art is "pure" insofar as it transcends nature and human emotion.
   (C) There is no more reason to call a man selfish who is enjoying a delicious meal than one who is enjoying looking at an artistic masterpiece.

Select the sentence in the passage that could most accurately be described as paradoxical.

4. _____

PASSAGE 14

So far scientists have not found a way to determine the exact age of the Earth directly
from Earth rocks because Earth's oldest rocks have been recycled and destroyed by
the process of plate tectonics. If there are any of Earth's primordial rocks left in their
Line original state, they have not yet been found. Nevertheless, scientists have been able
(5) to determine the probable age of the Solar System and to calculate an age for the
Earth by assuming that the Earth and the rest of the solid bodies in the Solar System
formed at the same time and are, therefore, of the same age.

The ages of Earth and Moon rocks and of meteorites are measured by the decay of
long-lived radioactive isotopes of elements that occur naturally in rocks and miner-
(10) als and that decay with half lives of 700 million to more than 100 billion years to stable isotopes of other elements. These dating techniques, which are firmly grounded
in physics and are known collectively as radiometric dating, are used to measure
the last time that the rock being dated was either melted or disturbed sufficiently to
rehomogenize its radioactive elements.

(15) Ancient rocks exceeding 3.5 billion years in age are found on all of Earth's conti-
nents. The oldest rocks on Earth found so far are the Acasta Gneisses in northwestern
Canada near Great Slave Lake (4.03 billion years) and the Isua Supracrustal rocks in
West Greenland (3.7 to 3.8 billion years), but well-studied rocks nearly as old are also
found in the Minnesota River Valley and northern Michigan (3.4–3.7 billion years),
(20) in Swaziland (3.4–3.5 billion years), and in Western Australia (3.4–3.6 billion years).
These ancient rocks have been dated by a number of radiometric dating methods
and the consistency of the results gives scientists confidence that the ages are correct
to within a few percent. An interesting feature of these ancient rocks is that they are
not from any sort of "primordial crust" but are lava flows and sediments deposited
(25) in shallow water, an indication that Earth history began well before these rocks were
deposited. In Western Australia, single zircon crystals found in younger sedimentary
rocks have radiometric ages of as much as 4.3 billion years, making these tiny crystals the oldest materials to be found on Earth so far. The source rocks for these zircon
crystals have not yet been found. The ages measured for Earth's oldest rocks and
(30) oldest crystals show that the Earth is at least 4.3 billion years in age but do not reveal
the exact age of Earth's formation. The best age for the Earth (4.54 billion years)
is based on old, presumed single-stage leads coupled with the Pb ratios in troilite
from iron meteorites, specifically the Canyon Diablo meteorite. In addition, mineral
grains (zircon) with U-Pb ages of 4.4 billion years have recently been reported from
(35) sedimentary rocks in west-central Australia. The Moon is a more primitive planet
than Earth because it has not been disturbed by plate tectonics; thus, some of its
more ancient rocks are more plentiful. Only a small number of rocks were returned
to Earth by the six Apollo and three Luna missions. These rocks vary greatly in age,
a reflection of their different ages of formation and their subsequent histories. The
(40) oldest dated moon rocks, however, have ages between 4.4 and 4.5 billion years and
provide a minimum age for the formation of our nearest planetary neighbor. Thousands of meteorites, which are fragments of asteroids that fall to Earth, have been
recovered. These primitive objects provide the best ages for the time of formation

of the Solar System. There are more than 70 meteorites, of different types, whose
(45) ages have been measured using radiometric dating techniques. The results show
that the meteorites, and therefore the Solar System, formed between 4.53 and 4.58
billion years ago. The best age for the Earth comes not from dating individual rocks
but by considering the Earth and meteorites as part of the same evolving system in
which the isotopic composition of lead, specifically the ratio of lead-207 to lead-206
(50) changes over time owing to the decay of radioactive uranium-235 and uranium-238,
respectively. Scientists have used this approach to determine the time required for
the isotopes in the Earth's oldest lead ores, of which there are only a few, to evolve
from their primordial composition, as measured in uranium-free phases of iron
meteorites, to their compositions at the time these lead ores separated from their
(55) mantle reservoirs. These calculations result in an age for the Earth and meteorites,
and hence the Solar System, of 4.54 billion years with an uncertainty of less than
1 percent. To be precise, this age represents the last time that lead isotopes were
homogeneous throughout the inner Solar System and the time that lead and ura-
nium was incorporated into the solid bodies of the Solar System. The age of 4.54
(60) billion years found for the Solar System and Earth is consistent with current calculations of 11 to 13 billion years for the age of the Milky Way Galaxy (based on the stage
of evolution of globular cluster stars) and the age of 10 to 15 billion years for the age
of the Universe (based on the recession of distant galaxies).

Select one answer choice for the following questions.

1. Why do meteorites provide better evidence for the age of the Solar System than does
the Earth?
   (A) They come from a wide variety of sources, thus providing a more accurate
   measure of the ages of the various objects in the Solar System.
   (B) Meteorites were formed in the initial stages of the creation of the Solar System,
   whereas the Earth was formed subsequently.
   (C) Meteorites, fragments of asteroids that fall to Earth, are closer in composition
   to the Sun, the first body to form in the early Solar System.
   (D) They are in essentially the same condition as when they were formed, whereas
   the Earth has undergone great changes.
   (E) They broke off from the Moon billions of years ago, before the formation of
   the Earth.

2. The main purpose of the first paragraph is
   (A) to examine carefully the assumption that the Earth and the other solid bodies
   in the Solar System were formed at the same time.
   (B) to introduce the main topic—determining the age of the Earth.
   (C) to summarize the main points of the passage.
   (D) to explain why scientists have been unable to determine the precise age of the
   Earth directly from Earth rocks.
   (E) to explain to the reader the close correspondence between the findings of
   geology and astronomy.

3. Which of the following discoveries would call into question the conclusions about the age of the Earth discussed in the passage?
   (A) The discovery of rocks on Earth 4.5 billion years old
   (B) The discovery of rocks on Earth significantly older than 4.6 billion years
   (C) The discovery on the Moon of rocks 4.51 billion years old
   (D) Improvements in radiometric dating techniques that increase accuracy of results by 20 percent
   (E) The discovery that a great many Earth rocks have been melted or disturbed so that their radioactive elements were rehomogenized

4. The word "primitive" is used twice in the third paragraph. Its meaning in context in both cases is
   (A) rudimentary
   (B) old
   (C) unsophisticated
   (D) close to its original condition
   (E) lifeless

Consider each of the three choices separately and select all that apply.

5. Based on the information in the passage, which of the following is true?
   (A) The Moon, unlike the Earth, did not undergo plate tectonics.
   (B) There is good scientific evidence that the Earth is older than the Moon.
   (C) Scientists have proven that Earth's oldest rocks in their original form no longer exist.

PASSAGE 15

The ever-increasing prosification of poetry assures prospective students that they needn't employ meter or rhyme or cadence or figurative language, or any of the devices, for that matter, in a standard poet's dictionary; that the drabbest encyclo-
Line pedia prose, even technical jargon, can be hailed as "poetry" of the highest order. It's
(5) the profession's way of redefining the art downward to accommodate its talent pool.
       "Defictionalization" of poetry is another disturbing trend. In this case, the profession hitches its star to a legitimate revolution, but does so in a robotic way.
       In the '50s and '60s "Beat" and "Confessional" poets found the High Modernist Mode—with its masks, personae and characters, and emphasis on irony, paradox,
(10) ambiguity, and allusion—stifling. They wanted to talk about the vital details of their biographies, including hitherto taboo subjects like sexuality and mental instability. They wanted poetry to be more expressive, more directly and intimately connected to the lives they were living, including their socio-political dimensions. As in all valid aesthetic revolutions, new subject matter demanded new form. Readers were not

(15) only fascinated by the diverse lives revealed by Ginsberg, Kerouac, Lowell, Plath, and Sexton, but by the new poetics each developed to make his or her life sing with a fresh and authoritative voice.

We should keep in mind that the Beats and Confessionals had no more aversion to embellishing their lives with fiction in the interest of poetic truth than they had (20) to arranging syllables to make their lines musical in ways clearly distinct from prose. The father figure in Sylvia Plath's "Daddy" is a mythic creation that bears only a tenuous relation to the professor of entomology who died when Plath was eight years old.

While artistically-shaped biographical material can be compelling, much of the poetry coming from the profession that purports to tell "the truth" about the poet's (25) life is anecdotal, over-literal, and trivial. Senior poets who have written well in the past seem particularly susceptible to believing that the most banal details of their lives are so inherently fascinating that they need add little or nothing in the way of fiction to command the attention of readers. Because ordinary readers continue to want lively stories and interesting characters (that is what draws them to (30) novels, television, and the movies) defictionalization is one more way the profession limits poetry to those who read not so much for pleasure as to keep an eye on the competition.

Take "Happiness" (from *Sun Under Wood*) by Robert Hass. The poem offers readers an ordinary day in the life of the poet. Yesterday, the speaker and his wife "saw (35) a pair of red foxes across the creek." This morning, when "she went into the gazebo with her black pen and yellow pad" he "drove into town to drink tea in the cafe and write notes in a journal." On the way he observes "a small flock of tundra swans . . . feeding on new grass." In closing, he turns the page of his journal and (after jotting down the poem's title) reminisces about how he and his wife "lay in bed kissing" that (40) morning, their eyes "squinched up like bats." Evidently, Hass assumes that readers will find these details fascinating. Too often, the focus on literal truth presents us not with the essence or core of the poet's being, but with the patio furniture of his or her life.

Prosification and defictionalization frequently converge in writing that succeeds (45) neither as poetry nor fiction—its virtue amounting to little more than the fact that it's easy to write for professionals and amateurs alike. James Tate's "The Diagnosis" (*Best American Poetry: 2001*) exemplifies what happens when poets embrace fiction half-heartedly. It is a "prose poem," in which an attempt to write fiction fizzles, leaving us with something partial and abortive. In clean (though undistinguished) prose, (50) Tate tells us about a man who fails to keep from his wife the fact that he is dying. Tate's solitary paragraph reads like the opening of a short story or novel; it is a snippet of fiction that leaves us wondering why the writer didn't finish what appears to be the beginning paragraph of a longer piece. Work that is too short, anecdotal, or unrealized to be published as fiction routinely appears as "poetry" or "prose poems" (55) in today's literary journals.

1. What is the main reason the author discusses Beat and Confessional poets?
    (A) To contrast them with the High Modernist poets in order to show their overall superiority
    (B) To show how poetry began to move in what the author considers the wrong direction during the 1950s and 1960s
    (C) To illustrate an extreme example of the trend toward defictionalization
    (D) To explain how the roots of contemporary poetry are in these movements of the 1950s and 1960s
    (E) To show that defictionalization of poetry does not necessarily produce trivial verse

2. Based on the information in this passage, which of the following statements would the author be likely to agree with?
    (A) Good poets sometimes don't tell the literal truth about their lives in their poetry.
    (B) The Beat and Confessional poets of the 1950s and 1960s made no use of traditional poetic techniques.
    (C) The more literal detail a poet gives about his or her life in a poem the better that poem will be.

3. Which of the following statements would the author of this extract be likely to disagree with?
    (A) Most contemporary poets make regular and effective use of traditional poetic techniques.
    (B) Contemporary poetry too often describes superficial reality.
    (C) Posterity will judge the present era as one of the golden ages of poetry.

Select the sentence that gives an explanation for the fact that the audience for contemporary poetry is circumscribed.

4. _____

PASSAGE 16

The high cosmic abundance of oxygen, the relatively high condensation temperature of water ice, and favorable thermochemical equilibrium behavior at low temperatures conspire to guarantee that water ice is a key component in the assembly of solid bodies in the solar system at and beyond Jupiter's distance from the sun. From the measured mass and radii of the regular satellites of Jupiter and Saturn and models of satellite interior structure it can be determined that Ganymede, Callisto, and Titan are each approximately 40% water ice in bulk composition with the remainder predominately silicate rock though the internal distribution of these components is not fully known. Europa has a higher bulk density indicating that water ice on its surface is a relatively thin veneer. Saturn's satellites Mimas, Enceladus, Tethys, Dione, Rhea, and Iapetus have lower densities indicating bulk compositions with 60% or more water ice.

Infrared spectra, particularly in the 1–3 micrometer wavelength range, are the primary data from which the presence and physical state of water ice on the surface of these satellites can be deduced. Relatively strong absorption bands occur in water ice at 3.0, 2.0, and 1.5 μm with weaker bands falling at 1.25 and 1.04 μm. The identification of these bands in spectra of Europa and Ganymede was the first evidence for the presence of water ice on these bodies. These bands have since been observed in Callisto and in Saturn's moderate-sized satellites. Saturn's large satellite Titan represents a special case because of its dense atmosphere and haze that make spectroscopic observations of its surface extremely difficult. Despite these barriers, however, isolate spectrophotometric measurements of Titan's surface and evidence for inhomogeneous reflactance of the surface suggest the possible presence of water ice on the surface of Titan.

All of these satellites are tidally locked to their parent planet and therefore rotate with a period equal to the period of their revolution. Variations in the reflectance as a function of orbital position (and therefore longitude) are observed for virtually all of these satellites indicating the presence of a non-ice component on the surfaces of these objects. Resolved images from spacecraft flybys and HST show numerous albedo features that similarly necessitate the presence of non-water-ice components on the surface. From cosmochemical* considerations it can be argued that silicate minerals should be present on the surfaces of these objects. Infrared spectra at wavelengths of 3 μm and longer suggest that, indeed, silicate minerals such as olivine may be present on the surfaces of Callisto and Ganymede. All the icy satellites exhibit a strong absorption at ultraviolet wavelengths that is not attributable to water ice. Several possible sources for this absorption have been proposed including silicate minerals and iron-bearing minerals, but no firm identification has been made.

Environmental factors play an important role in altering the composition of satellite surfaces. Jupiter's and Saturn's satellites (except Iapetus and sometimes Titan) orbit within their parent planet's magnetosphere so that their surfaces are subject to large fluxes of high energy ions trapped in the magnetic fields. The principle consequence of this irradiation appears to be the buildup of oxygen in the surface ice

*Another name for cosmochemistry is "chemical cosmology."

which is manifested in a number of observables including UV and IR absorption by sulfur dioxide ice on Europa and Callisto, molecular oxygen and ozone trapped in
(45) the surface ice of Ganymede, possible IR absorption by carbon dioxide ice in Jupiter's satellites, indirect evidence for molecular oxygen atmospheres around Europa and Ganymede, and UV absorption by ozone trapped in the surface ice of Rhea and Dione. Micrometeorite gardening of the surface may also play a role particularly for Iapetus and Callisto. The most conspicuous inhomogeneity in either satellite sys-
(50) tem, the hemispheric dichotomy present on Iapetus, remains unexplained despite many attempts to do so.

Consider each of the three choices separately and select all that apply.

1. Based on the information in this passage, which of the following is true?
   (A) Jupiter's regular satellites are made up of a higher percentage of water ice than Saturn's satellites.
   (B) Spectroscopic observation is the main method that scientists have used to determine the make-up of the surfaces of most of the major satellites of Jupiter and Saturn.
   (C) Scientists are quite sure that Titan, unlike the other satellites of Jupiter, does not have water ice on its surface because of its dense and relatively warm atmosphere.

2. Based on the information in this passage, which of the following is true?
   (A) It would be reasonable to hypothesize that the main satellites of Uranus, the next planet after Saturn, are made up of a significant amount of water ice.
   (B) Information about the composition of the regular satellites of Jupiter and Saturn gathered from spacecraft flybys and information gathered from spectroscopic measurements have been largely contradictory.
   (C) There is good evidence that the amount of oxygen in the surface ice of most of the regular satellites of Jupiter and Saturn is significantly influenced by the powerful magnetospheres of these planets.

Select one answer choice for the following question.

3. Based on the information in the passage, it is most reasonable to hypothesize that the inhomogeneity between the hemispheres of Iapetus is caused by
   (A) the fact that it is tidally locked to Saturn
   (B) the fact that far more micrometeorites have impacted on one hemisphere than the other
   (C) the fact that Saturn's magnetosphere is stronger in one of its hemispheres rather than on the other
   (D) the higher surface reflectance of one hemisphere as compared with the other hemisphere
   (E) The greater percentage of water ice in the surface composition of one hemisphere as compared to the other hemisphere

4. Scientists believe that the surface composition of most of the regular satellites of Jupiter and Saturn is affected by all of the following except
   (A) micrometeorites
   (B) the high cosmic abundance of oxygen
   (C) the magnetospheres of Jupiter and Saturn
   (D) dense atmospheres
   (E) the relatively high condensation temperature of water ice

> **Identify the sentence by writing its first three words and its last three words on the line below.**

Select the sentence that suggests a hypothesis about the composition of the surfaces of the regular satellites of Jupiter and Saturn based on what is known about the formation of the solar system.

5. _____

PASSAGE 17

Feminist criticism comes in many forms, and feminist critics have a variety of goals. Some have been interested in rediscovering the works of women writers overlooked by a masculine-dominated culture. Others have revisited books by male authors
Line and reviewed them from a woman's point of view to understand how they both
(5) reflect and shape the attitudes that have held women back. A number of contemporary feminists have turned to topics as various as women in postcolonial societies, women's autobiographical writings, lesbians and literature, womanliness as masquerade, and the role of film and other popular media in the construction of the feminine gender. Until a few years ago, however, feminist thought tended to
(10) be classified not according to topic but, rather, according to country of origin. This practice reflected the fact that, during the 1970s and early 1980s, French, American, and British feminists wrote from somewhat different perspectives. French feminists tended to focus their attention on language, analyzing the ways in which meaning is produced. They concluded that language as we commonly think of it is a decid-
(15) edly male realm. Drawing on the ideas of the psychoanalytic philosopher Jacques Lacan, they reminded us that language is a realm of public discourse. A child enters the linguistic realm just as it comes to grasp its separateness from its mother, just about the time that boys identify with their father, the family representative of culture. The language learned reflects a binary logic that opposes such terms as active/
(20) passive, masculine/feminine, sun/moon, father/mother, head/heart, son/daughter, intelligent/sensitive, brother/sister, form/matter, phallus/vagina, reason/emotion. Because this logic tends to group with masculinity such qualities as light, thought, and activity, French feminists said that the structure of language is phallocentric: it privileges the phallus and, more generally, masculinity by associating them with

(25) things and values more appreciated by the (masculine-dominated) culture. More-over, French feminists suggested, "masculine desire dominates speech and posits woman as an idealized fantasy-fulfillment of the incurable emotional lack caused by separation from the mother."

(30) French feminists associated language with separation from the mother. Its distinctions, they argued, represent the world from the male point of view. Language systematically forces women to choose: either they can imagine and represent themselves as men imagine and represent them (in which case they may speak, but will speak as men) or they can choose "silence," becoming in the process "the invisible and unheard sex."

(35) But some influential French feminists maintained that language only *seems* to give women such a narrow range of choices. There is another possibility, namely, that women can develop a *feminine* language. In various ways, early French feminists such as Annie Leclerc, Xaviere Gauthier, and Marguerite Curas suggested that there is something that may be called *l'ecriture feminine*: women's writing. More

(40) recently, Julia Kristeva has said that feminine language is "semiotic," not "symbolic." Rather than rigidly opposing and ranking elements of reality, rather than symbolizing one thing but not another in terms of a third, feminine language is rhythmic and unifying. If from the male perspective it seems fluid to the point of being chaotic, that is a fault of the male perspective.

(45) According to Kristeva, feminine language is derived from the pre-oedipal period of fusion between mother and child. Associated with the maternal, feminine language is not only a threat to culture, which is patriarchal, but also a medium through which women may be creative in new ways. But Kristeva paired her central, liberating claim—that truly feminist innovation in all fields requires an understanding of

(50) the relation between maternity and feminine creation—with a warning. A feminist language that refuses to participate in "masculine" discourse, that places its future entirely in a feminine, semiotic discourse, risks being politically marginalized by men. That is to say, it risks being relegated to the outskirts (pun intended) of what is considered socially and politically significant.

Select one answer choice for the following question.

1. Which of the following would be the most appropriate title for this extract?
   (A) Feminist Literary Criticism
   (B) Feminism and Psychoanalytic Thought
   (C) French Feminist Literary Criticism
   (D) Feminist Language in Patriarchal Society
   (E) Masculine Oppression, Feminine Liberation

2. Which of the following are implicitly assumed in the theories of the French feminists described in the passage?

   (A) Language has a decisive role in determining how human beings think.

   (B) The premises of psychoanalytic thought are fundamentally sound.

   (C) Psychoanalysis is suspect because it is the product of patriarchal nineteenth-century European culture.

3. If Julia Kristeva's beliefs about language are correct and are understood by a large number of women who agree with these beliefs, which of the following is the most likely?

   (A) Men will become increasingly feminine in their thinking and approach to the arts.

   (B) Psychoanalytic thought will undergo a revolution, changing its focus from phallocentrism to an emphasis on the pre-oedipal period of fusion between mother and child.

   (C) An increasing number of women will pioneer new movements in the arts.

PASSAGE 18

The outer continental shelf reefs of the Northeastern Gulf of Mexico (NEGOM) are home to many large and well-known species, particularly the seabasses *Serranida*, *Carangidae*, and *Lutjanidae*. However, lesser-known small serranids and species
Line of several other families are numerically dominant on NEGOM deep-reef biotopes.
(5) Of the small serranids inhabiting NEGOM shelf-edge deep reefs (60–120 m), two anthiine planktivores, the roughtongue bass, *Pronotogrammus martinicensis*, and the red barbier, *Hemanthias vivanus*, are dominant. A third serranid, the tattler, *Serranus phoebe*, and a damselfish, the yellowtail reef-fish, *Chromis enchrysurus*, are also abundant on the NEGOM outer continental shelf reefs. Together, these four
(10) species are of great ecological importance to the deep reef ecosystem, consuming much of the available biomass of plankton and small mobile epibenthos, and in turn forming a substantial portion of the forage base of larger piscivores.

   Pronotogrammus martinicensis, *H. vivanus*, and *C. enchrysurus* feed mostly on small zooplankton such as copepods and amphipods. In contrast, *S. phoebe* feeds
(15) on a variety of small epibenthis crustaceans and small fishes. All four species are important prey items for larger reef and pelagic predators. Stomach content analyses have revealed that *P. martinicensis* and *H. vivanus* are preyed upon by commercially important species, including red snapper (*Lutjanus campechanus*) and grouper (*Mycteroperca* spp. and *Epinephelus* spp.). In addition to their ecological impor-
(20) tance, *P. martinicensis*, *H. vivanus*, and other small deep-reef species are collected by a small but profitable deep-water marine ornamental fishery.

(25)   Knowledge of the life history of these forage species is not only crucial to ensuring healthy populations of the individual prey species, but is also important to the multi-species management of the larger, more economically-important fishery species. Currently, most fisheries are managed from a single-species approach based solely on abundance and age/size structure. Trophic interactions and fluctuations in prey

(30) density are not included in management analyses. However, recent studies indicate a multi-species approach may better explain population dynamics and spatial shifts in abundance. For example, when herring stocks in the Gulf of Maine collapsed during the 1970s, humpback whale numbers also diminished locally as these predators relocated to areas of higher prey abundance. Some reef-associated predators, how-

(35) ever, may exhibit little emigration from their home reefs making them less likely to relocate in the event of prey shortage. As a result, knowledge of the biology of prey populations such a *P. martinicensis*, *H. vivanus*, and *S. phoebe*, as well as the factors influencing abundance and distribution of these species, is useful to the successful management of the larger predators.

(40)   Despite the ecological and economic importance of small serranid forage species, comprehensive information concerning their life history remains scarce. Individuals of *P. martinicensis* and *H. vivanus* begin their life as a female, then change into a male at the onset of some biological or sociological cue. This sequence of sexual change is termed protogynous hermaphrodism. *Serranus phoebe* has been identified

(45) as a simultaneous hermaphrodite, with gonads containing simultaneously active male and female gonad tissue. In each of these three species, however, a detailed description of reproductive biology has not been generated. Neither has the age-structure or size-structure for any of these species been described.

         These fishes form a substantial portion of the forage base of economically

(50) important resource species, including snappers and groupers. Thus, knowledge of their longevity, age structure, and age at first reproduction is critically important to understanding the ecology, productivity, and repopulation potential of the food base of deep reef ecosystems in the NEGOM. This knowledge may prove valuable in assessing current and future anthropogenic impacts upon deep reef ecosystems

(55) due to harvest of both forage base species and their larger predators, and/or due to habitat disturbance from hydrocarbon exploration and development, or other human enterprises.

Select one answer choice for the following questions.

---

1. According to the passage which of the following is not true?
    (A) The life history of small serranid forage species is not well understood.
    (B) The red snapper preys on the red barbier.
    (C) The management of most fisheries is based on observation of only one species of fish.
    (D) All predators of reef-dwelling fish relocate to areas where prey is more abundant when prey becomes insufficient in a particular area.
    (E) Small serranid forage fish are sometimes preyed on by fish from the open sea.

2. Based on the information in the passage, which of the following statements would the author be likely to agree with?
   - (A) Scientific research on the roughtongue bass, the red barbier, the tattler, and the yellow tail-reef fish is important because the knowledge gained will allow better management of fisheries in NEGOM.
   - (B) Scientific research on the roughtongue bass, the red barbier, the tattler, and the yellow tail-reef fish is important because the knowledge gained will help in evaluating the effects of human activity on deep reef ecosystems.
   - (C) Scientific research on the roughtongue bass, the red barbier, the tattler, and the yellow tail-reef fish is important because it may provide evidence that over-harvesting of the large piscivores in NEGOM is causing changes in the life histories of the small serranid forage species.

PASSAGE 19

The Arctic could potentially alter the Earth's climate by becoming a possible source of global atmospheric carbon dioxide. The arctic now traps or absorbs up to 25 percent of this gas but climate change could alter that amount.

Line The Arctic has been a carbon sink since the end of the last Ice Age, which has
(5) recently accounted for between zero and 25 percent, or up to about 800 million metric tons, of the global carbon sink. On average, the Arctic accounts for 10–15 percent of the Earth's carbon sink. But the rapid rate of climate change in the Arctic—about twice that of lower latitudes—could eliminate the sink and instead, possibly make the Arctic a source of carbon dioxide.

(10) Carbon generally enters the oceans and land masses of the Arctic from the atmosphere and largely accumulates in permafrost, the frozen layer of soil underneath the land's surface. Unlike active soils, permafrost does not decompose its carbon; thus, the carbon becomes trapped in the frozen soil. Cold conditions at the surface have also slowed the rate of organic matter decomposition, allowing Arctic carbon
(15) accumulation to exceed its release.

But recent warming trends could change this balance. Warmer temperatures can accelerate the rate of surface organic matter decomposition, releasing more carbon dioxide into the atmosphere. Of greater concern is that the permafrost has begun to thaw, exposing previously frozen soil to decomposition and erosion. These changes
(20) could reverse the historical role of the Arctic as a sink for carbon dioxide. In the short term, warming temperatures could release more Arctic carbon to the atmosphere, and with permafrost thawing, there will be more available carbon to release.

On the scale of a few decades, the thawing permafrost could also result in a more waterlogged Arctic, a situation that could encourage the activity of methane-
(25) producing organisms. Currently, the Arctic is a substantial source of methane to the atmosphere: as much as 50 million metric tons of methane are released per year, in comparison to the 400 million metric tons of carbon dioxide the Arctic stores yearly.

But methane is a very potent greenhouse gas—about 23 times more effective at trapping heat than carbon dioxide on a 100-year time scale. If the release of Arctic
(30) methane accelerates, global warming could increase at much faster rates. Scientists don't understand methane very well, and its releases to the atmosphere are more episodic than the exchanges of carbon dioxide with the atmosphere. It is important to pay attention to methane dynamics because of methane's substantial potential to accelerate global warming.

(35)   But uncertainties still abound about the response of the Arctic system to climate change. For example, global warming may produce longer growing seasons that promote plant photosynthesis, which removes carbon dioxide from the atmosphere. Also, the expansion of shrubs in tundra and the movement of tree line northward could sequester more carbon in vegetation. However, increasingly dry conditions
(40) may counteract and overcome these effects. Similarly, dry conditions can lead to increased fire prevalence, releasing even more carbon.

Select one answer choice for the following questions.

1. Based on the information in the passage, which of the following would not be likely to increase the amount of carbon dioxide in the Earth's atmosphere?
    (A) An increased rate of decomposition of surface organic matter in the Arctic
    (B) Thawing of the Arctic permafrost
    (C) An increase in the rate of release of Arctic methane
    (D) Longer growing seasons in the Arctic
    (E) An increased number of fires in the Arctic

2. Based on the information in the passage, how likely is it that the Arctic will become a significant source of global atmospheric carbon dioxide?
    (A) Certain
    (B) Nearly certain
    (C) Very likely
    (D) Fairly likely
    (E) Unlikely

Consider each of the three choices separately and select all that apply.

3. Which statements would the author be likely to agree with?
    (A) Scientists do not fully understand the dynamic interactions that lead to climate change.
    (B) Most of the carbon stored in the Arctic is in permafrost.
    (C) As more shrubs grow in the tundra as a result of warming trends, it is likely that more carbon dioxide will be released into the atmosphere, resulting in further warming.

Identify the sentence by writing its first three words and its last three words on the line below.

Select the sentence in which the author speculates that possible factors offsetting the increase in atmospheric carbon dioxide in the Arctic will be outweighed by other factors.

4. _____

PASSAGE 20

If then we consider, on the one hand, all the essential similarity of man's chief wants everywhere and at all times, and on the other hand, the great disparity between the means he has adopted to satisfy them in different ages, we shall perhaps be inclined

Line to conclude that the movement of man's higher cognitive processes, so far as we
(5) can trace it, has on the whole been from magic through religion to science. In magic man depends on his own strength to meet the difficulties and dangers that assail him on every side. He believes in a certain established order of nature on which he can surely count, and which he can manipulate for his own ends. When he discovers his mistake, when he recognizes sadly that both the order of nature which he

(10) had assumed and the control which he had believed himself to exercise over it were purely chimerical, he ceases to rely on his own intelligence and his own unaided efforts, and throws himself humbly on the mercy of certain great invisible beings behind the veil of nature, to whom he now ascribes all those far-reaching powers which he once arrogated to himself. Thus in the acuter minds magic is gradually

(15) superseded by religion, which explains the succession of natural phenomena as regulated by the will, the passion, or the caprice of spiritual beings like man in kind, though vastly superior to him in power.

But as time goes on this explanation in its turn proves to be unsatisfactory. For it assumes that the succession of natural events is not determined by immutable laws,

(20) but is to some extent variable and irregular, and this assumption is validated by closer observation. On the contrary, the more we scrutinize that succession the more we are struck by the rigid uniformity, the punctual precision with which, wherever we can follow them, the operations of nature are carried on. Every great advance in knowledge has extended the sphere of order and correspondingly circumscribed

(25) the sphere of apparent disorder in the world, till now we are ready to anticipate that even in regions where chance and confusion appear still to be predominant, a fuller knowledge would everywhere reduce the seeming chaos to order. Thus minds of the greatest acuity, still pressing forward to a deeper solution of the mysteries of the universe, come to reject the religious theory of nature as inadequate, and to revert in

(30) a measure to the older standpoint of magic by postulating explicitly, what in magic had only been implicitly assumed, to wit, an inflexible regularity in the order of natural events, which, if carefully observed, enables us to foresee their course with

certainty and to act accordingly. In short, religion, regarded as an explanation of nature, is displaced by science.

(35)　　But while science has this much in common with magic that both rest on a faith in order as the underlying principle of all things, the order upon which magic is predicated differs widely from that which forms the basis of science. The difference flows naturally from the different modes in which the two orders have been reached. For whereas the order on which magic reckons is merely an extension, by false analogy,
(40) of the order in which ideas present themselves to our minds, the order laid down by science is derived from patient and meticulous observation of the phenomena themselves. The abundance, the solidity, and the splendor of the results already achieved by science are well fitted to inspire us to take a sanguine view of the soundness of its method. Here at last, after groping about in the dark for countless ages, man has
(45) hit upon a clue to the labyrinth, a golden key that opens many locks in the treasury of nature. It is probably not too much to say that the hope of progress—moral and intellectual as well as material—in the future is bound up with the fortunes of science, and that anything that impedes scientific discovery is a wrong to humanity.

　　Yet the history of thought should warn us against concluding that because the
(50) scientific theory of the world is the best that has yet been formulated, it is necessarily complete and final. We must remember that at bottom the generalizations of science or, in common parlance, the laws of nature are merely hypotheses devised to explain that ever-shifting phantasmagoria of thought which we dignify with the high-sounding names of the world and the universe. In the last analysis magic, reli-
(55) gion, and science are nothing but theories of thought; and as science has supplanted its predecessors, so it may subsequently be itself superseded by some more perfect hypothesis, perhaps by some radically different way of looking at the phenomena— of registering the shadows on the screen—of which we in this generation can form no idea. The advance of knowledge is an infinite progression towards a goal that
(60) forever recedes.

Select one answer choice for the following questions.

1. The word "chimerical" as it is used in the first paragraph most nearly means
   (A) solipsistic
   (B) deterministic
   (C) apocryphal
   (D) illusory
   (E) fortuitous

2. Which of the following ideas is not discussed, either directly or indirectly, in the passage?
   (A) Anthropomorphism
   (B) Teleology
   (C) Magic
   (D) Nature
   (E) Progress

3. What is the most likely reason that in the final paragraph the author uses the phrase "of registering the shadows on the screen"?
   (A) To reinforce the point that the search for truth is wholly illusory
   (B) To show through a metaphor that reality is, in the final analysis, like a shadow projected on a screen
   (C) To illustrate his point that some "radically different way of looking at the phenomena" may one day be developed
   (D) To remind us that any interpretation of the world is dependent on the thought processes used to arrive at that interpretation
   (E) To remind us that like shadows on a screen, human understanding and memory are ephemeral

4. What is the most probable reason that in the final paragraph the author uses the phrase "more perfect"?
   (A) To reinforce the idea that a hypothesis, although it may be considered perfect at a particular time, can never truly be perfect
   (B) To show that although science is a perfect system of thought, it will be steadily refined in the future to account for phenomena as yet unimagined
   (C) To convince us that science is a perfect hypothesis to explain the world because nothing can be "more perfect" than perfect
   (D) To convey through the use of sarcasm that although future generations may think that they have developed a better theory than science to explain the world, in reality they will be deceiving themselves
   (E) To show that intellectual progress is a chimerical dream because human beings are bound up in space and time and therefore in no position to objectively determine which way of interpreting the world corresponds with reality

> **Consider each of the three choices separately and select all that apply.**

5. Which of the following would the author be likely to agree with?
   (A) There is no doubt that human beings, through the application of science, will one day come to understand everything.
   (B) Science is, at least up to the present, humanity's greatest intellectual achievement.
   (C) Magic and science see an identical order in nature.

> **Identify the sentence by writing its first three words and its last three words on the line below.**

Select the sentence that contrasts the way in which magic, on the one hand, and science, on the other hand, have discovered what they believe to be regularities in nature.

6. _____

ANSWER KEY
Reading Comprehension

Passage 1
1. C
2. B

Passage 2
1. D
2. B
3. A

Passage 3
1. E
2. "It is not . . . her husband's happiness."

Passage 4
1. B
2. D
3. C
4. A, B

Passage 5
1. D
2. A, C

Passage 6
1. C
2. C
3. A

Passage 7
1. C
2. B, C

Passage 8
1. A, B
2. B, C

Passage 9
1. B
2. B
3. D

Passage 10
1. A, C
2. B
3. A, B, C

Passage 11
1. A, B, C

Passage 12
1. D
2. B
3. A

Passage 13
1. C
2. D
3. C
4. "The content of . . . mass of unselfishness."

Passage 14
1. D
2. C
3. B
4. D
5. A

Passage 15
1. E
2. A
3. A, C
4. "Because ordinary readers . . . on the competition."

Passage 16
1. B
2. A, C
3. A
4. D
5. "From cosmochemical considerations . . . of these objects."

Passage 17
1. C
2. A, B
3. C

Passage 18
1. D
2. A, B

Passage 19
1. D
2. D
3. A, B
4. "However, increasingly dry . . . overcome these effects."

Passage 20
1. D
2. B
3. D
4. A
5. B
6. "For whereas the . . . the phenomena themselves."

ANSWER EXPLANATIONS

Passage 1

1. **(C)**   The author believes that the foundation of Indian religion was Dravidian but that there is not much information available about the old Dravidians comparable to what is available about the Vedic Aryans. He believes that "the literature of the Vedic Aryans is relatively ancient and full." He also says that many of the essential features of Hinduism "are . . . totally unknown to the Veda." On the basis of this information, the other choices can be eliminated. It is reasonable that the Veda is the oldest sacred writing of Hinduism because hardly any of the literature of the Dravidians has survived.

2. **(B)**   The author says that some of the "most essential doctrines such as metempsychosis and divine incarnations" of Hinduism have little importance in the Veda, which was the ancient sacred writing of the Aryans. Thus, it can be concluded that the idea of divine incarnation developed in Dravidian civilization.

    (A)   The author says "But were our knowledge less one-sided, we might see that it would be more correct to describe Indian religion as Dravidian religion stimulated and modified by the ideas of the Aryan invaders." The author is speculating and is certainly not almost certain.

    (C)   The author says that "the greatest deities of Hinduism . . . are either totally unknown to the Veda or obscurely adumbrated by it."

Passage 2

1. **(D)**   "Particular functional groups of microorganisms . . . have a disproportionate effect on elemental cycles." From this information we can deduce that elemental cycles are such phenomena as the water cycle and the carbon cycle, in which fundamental elements or molecules are, in effect, recycled. Since one of the major concerns described in the passage is the effects of increased amounts of carbon being released, it is reasonable to conclude that carbon is one of the important substances involved in elemental cycles.

2. **(B)**   This is a balanced summary of the passage.

    (A)   The passage offers an analysis of the situation; there is no suggestion that human activities affecting soil microbial communities should be reduced.

    (C)   This describes only one aspect of the larger issue of the impact of global change phenomena on terrestrial ecosystem biogeochemistry.

    (D)   This describes only one aspect of the larger issue of the impact of global change phenomena on ecosystems.

    (E)   The ecology of soil microbial communities in northern latitudes is discussed as an example, not to show how what happens in one region affects what happens in other regions.

3. **(A)**   It is stated that "Soil microbial communities . . . decompose as much carbon as is annually photosynthesized by plants."

    (B)   It can be deduced that scientists do not have an excellent understanding of the effect of global change phenomena on microbial soil communities in every region of the globe from the fact that the author concludes, "Such spatially explicit information can potentially be used for assessing how global change will affect microbial communities and the biogeochemical processes within specific regions."

(C) The author says, "Climate warming is accelerating permafrost thawing and wildfire intensity, altering the abundance of soil decomposers which has direct effect on rates of biogeochemical processes."

Passage 3

1. **(E)** The main meanings of "titular" are "relating to a title" and "in name only." In context "in name only" makes the better sense because Dr. Proudie is described as being ruled over by Mrs. Proudie.

2. **"It is not . . . her husband's happiness."** "It is not my intention to breathe a word against the character of Mrs. Proudie, but still I cannot think that with all her virtues she adds much to her husband's happiness." The narrator says he does not intend to say anything bad about Mrs. Proudie's character and then says that she does not contribute to her husband's happiness.

Passage 4

1. **(B)** The author *asserts* that the merit of different periods of literature should be determined by how spiritual they are. The author then states a *premise*, saying that if we admit the preceding assertion and that literature is produced by "intellect and spirit," it follows that "the periods of literature should be determined by the ebb and flow of spiritual life which they generally register." Finally, the author *explains* how in some periods literature does not contain much of a spiritual element.

2. **(D)** It can be inferred that the author believes that literature reflects the zeitgeist of its time by the fact that he says "the periods of literature should be determined by the ebb and flow of spiritual life which they severally register." A major underlying assumption is that literature reflects the thinking of its time.

3. **(C)** The main concern of the passage is the place of spirituality in literature. The author believes that the merit of literature lies mainly in its spirituality. We can thus infer that the author believes that the primary importance of literature is the part it plays in the spiritual life of a people.

   (A) This excludes the element of spirituality that the author believes is fundamental to good literature.

   (B) The author says that "there can be no high order of literature that is not strongly articulated, that is not well freighted, with thought."

4. **(A)** Nowhere in the passage does the author elaborate on what is meant by "spirituality" and related terms. Since these are central to the argument, it is reasonable to expect them to be defined.

   (B) No examples from literature are provided to support and illustrate the argument.

   (C) The author states the premise of the argument clearly and argues logically from the premise. Although the argument arguably has flaws—such as lack of exemplification and questioning of the premise—it is fundamentally logical.

Passage 5

1. **(D)**   Parody (imitating a characteristic style of writing for comic effect) is not used in this passage.

   (A)   A metaphor is a figure of speech in which a word or phrase that refers to one thing is applied to another in an implicit comparison. Several metaphors are used. For example: "Some of the flowers of fiction have the odor of it."

   (B)   The author asserts several propositions.

   (C)   Two rhetorical questions are asked: "What kind of experience is intended, and where does it begin and end?"

   (E)   A simile is a figure of speech in which two basically unlike things are compared. The author uses a simile: "Experience is . . . a kind of huge spider-web."

2. **(A)**   It is clearly stated in that a person must "possess the sense of reality."

   (C)   The author says that "Experience . . . is an immense sensibility . . . It is the very atmosphere of the mind; and when the mind is imaginative . . . it takes to itself the faintest hints of life, it converts the very pulses of the air into revelations."

   (B)   The author says "but it will be difficult to give you a recipe for calling that sense into being." He also says "as for telling you . . . how your nosegay should be composed, that is another affair."

Passage 6

1. **(C)**   "Chronic" in context means "lasting for a long period of time."

2. **(C)**   The author says "Further, samples required for molecular investigations are minimally invasive or stressful to the subject animals."

3. **(A)**   The author says, "The acute effects of a spill are evaluated by mortality estimations, clinical evaluations, and necropsy examinations." (The word "acute" in this context means "brief and severe.") This strongly suggests that scientists gain a lot of information about the effects of oil spills on marine life by these means. The author says also "the long-term effects of these tragedies are more difficult to document."

Passage 7

1. **(C)**   The selection states that a pidgin "arises to fulfill certain *restricted communication needs* among people who have no common language" (my italics). It is reasonable to infer that there were many cases where two peoples wishing to trade did not share a common language, and so a pidgin developed. Also, trade normally does not require a fully developed language.

   (A)   There is nothing to suggest that pidgins are imposed on one people by another.

   (B)   This is possible. However, since a pidgin meets "restricted communication needs" it make less sense that a pidgin develops to exchange abstract, complex ideas than it develops to facilitate trade, which requires more concrete and practical communication.

   (D)   There is nothing to suggest that pidgins develop from simplified creoles.

   (E)   It is stated that "a pidgin does not begin as an already existing language," and that "a mother tongue . . . must be capable of expressing the whole range of human experience." A pidgin would not develop to be a mother tongue because a mother tongue is an already existing language that is able to express the range of human experience. Also, it is stated that "A creole arises when a pidgin becomes the mother tongue of a speech community."

2. **(B)**   This is stated in the second paragraph: "A pidgin is a marginal language which arises to fulfill certain restricted communication needs among people who have no common language."

    (C)   It is stated that "both French and English may be the outcome of pidgins." The author believes that English may be a creole that developed from a pidgin spoken by "native Anglo-Saxons and the Danes who settled on the east coast of England."

    (A)   It is stated that "frequently a more elaborate syntactic system evolves."

Passage 8

1. **(A)**   The author says, "Important heterotrophs are sulfate reducers that use sulfate (SO_4^{2-}), rather than oxygen as most bacteria do, to aid their decomposition of organic matter.

    (B)   It is stated that *Desulfovibrio* is a sulfate-reducing bacteria, which do not use oxygen to aid their decomposition of organic matter. Therefore, *Desulfovibrio* would not thrive in an oxygen-rich area.

    (C)   It is stated that "These microbes [lithotrophs] utilize just a few inorganic compounds or elements for energy or growth."

2. **(B)**   It is stated that "*Acidithiobacillus ferroxidans* . . . thrives in acidic (low pH) environments." Raising the pH of a wetland area would therefore be likely to slow the rate at which *Acidithiobacillus ferroxidans* oxidizes ferrous iron.

    (C)   In the final paragraph the author states that "Bacterial processes involving iron and sulfate can be especially important in depositional sites such as wetlands that receive acid drainage. . . . High sulfate and abundant organic matter promote sulfate-reducer growth. . . . Sulfate reduction permits chemically reducing conditions to develop and persist . . . . In general, reducing conditions tend to immobilize metals and prevent them from moving in the surface-ground-water system. . . . The mobility of metals is important because metals are usually the source of toxicity in acid drainage."

    (A)   *Desulfovibrio* is a sulfate-reducing heterotroph, which uses organic compounds for growth and energy.

Passage 9

1. **(B)**   In posing the question "Are our moral preferences true or false, or are they only odd biological phenomena, making things good or bad for us, but in themselves indifferent?" the author suggests that either our moral beliefs are a result of the existence of a world of morality or they are a result of biology. If moral preferences are "odd biological phenomena," then it follows that they are not the result of the existence of a world of morality. It is thus likely that a world of morality does not exist.

2. **(B)**   The main point of the passage is that our beliefs are to a large extent determined by our feelings, or what the author calls our "will." He says, "Moral skepticism can no more be refuted or proved by logic than intellectual skepticism can. When we stick to

it that there is truth . . . ,we do so with our whole nature, and resolve to stand or fall by the results. The skeptic with this whole nature adopts the doubting attitude, but which of us is the wiser, Omniscience only knows."

3. **(D)** In the sentence following the one in which the word "sensible" is used the author says, "A moral question is a question not of what sensibly exists, but what is good or would be good if it did exist." This shows that he is using "sensible" to refer to the ability of something to be perceived by the senses.

Passage 10

1. **(A)** The author stresses throughout the passage that our knowledge of the world is based on inference. Specifically, he says, "What, then, if the physicist and physiologist are right, we in fact know are certain events taking place in our own brains. The outside world is not itself known; its existence is merely an inference due to the fact that we think these events must have a cause."
(C) The author emphasizes that our knowledge is dependent on inference and that these inferences may be mistaken. It is reasonable to conclude from this that the author would agree that to gain knowledge—that is, truths about the world—we must carefully consider if the inferences we make are justified.
 (B) According to the author, we cannot be certain of the existence of a world outside our brains. However, it does not follow from this that it has been demonstrated that a world outside our brains does not exist.

2. **(B)** An observer would not actually be seeing it because it takes time for light to travel to the observer.
 (A) An observer would not be seeing it because, as stated above, light takes a certain amount of time to travel through space.
 (C) The author stresses that we must be careful in making inferences, but he does not say that we cannot know anything.

3. **(A, B, C)** All of the statements are based on assumptions.

Passage 11

1. **(A)** The author regards language as "a uniquely human mode of communicating and organizing one's perceptions of the world."
(B) The author says, "There is no evidence to suggest that people of a particular racial type, say, are more able to acquire certain languages than others or than people of different racial types."
(C) The author says, "There is no evidence to suggest that people of a particular racial type, say, are more able to acquire certain languages than others or than people of different racial types."

Passage 12

1. **(D)** The author's main concern is to describe Hellenism's decline. He describes the development of Christianity and its use of Greek culture and expertise, as well as the effect of the rise of Islam on the Greek world, in order to show how this decline occurred.

2. **(B)**   Earlier in the passage the author described how Hellenism was declining, citing, among other things, "the last notable formulation of Greek philosophy" and "the last original creation of ancient Greek art." Thus, it makes sense that he uses the word "inanition" to describe Hellenism's exhaustion.

3. **(A)**   The author says, "While the Oriental had been compelled by Rome to draw his political frontier at the Euphrates . . . he had maintained his cultural independence within sight of the Mediterranean" and then describes "a little Semitic community" in the area that gave birth to Christianity.

Passage 13

1. **(C)**   The author begins by describing a view of aesthetic satisfaction. He then argues against this view, saying, "But this distinction is one of intensity and delicacy, not of nature" and "the supposed disinterestedness of aesthetic delights is not truly fundamental." Next, the author gives a more sophisticated version of the view of aesthetic satisfaction that he has refuted: "The truth which . . . delight of contemplation." Finally, he argues against this refined view.

2. **(D)**   "Nominal" in this context means "being something in name only."

3. **(C)**   The author's argument is that the common distinction between selfish and unselfish pleasures is incorrect. Thus, he would agree with the statement.

4. **"The content of . . . mass of unselfishness."** The statement that selfishness is made up of unselfishness is paradoxical—that is, seemingly contradictory but possibly true.

Passage 14

1. **(D)**   The author says meteorites "provide the best ages for the time of formation of the Solar System." This is because they are "primitive" objects; that is, they haven't changed much since they were created. The Earth, by contrast, has undergone major changes as a result of plate tectonics, making it difficult to find rocks in "their original state" (lines 3–4).

2. **(C)**   In the first paragraph it is stated that because the Earth has undergone plate tectonics it is difficult to determine the Earth's age from Earth rocks. However, scientists have used other means to calculate the probable age of the Solar System and the Earth. The rest of the passage explains how scientists have used various dating techniques on different substances to arrive at these ages.

3. **(B)**   The author says, "The results [of measurements of the ages of meteorites] show that the meteorites, and therefore the Solar System, formed between 4.53 and 4.58 billion years ago." It is also stated that the ages of the solid bodies in the Solar System are the same. Therefore, finding rocks on Earth significantly older than 4.5 billion years old would cast doubt on the validity of the conclusions reached that the Earth is between 4.53 and 4.58 billion years old, that it is the same age as the other bodies in the Solar System, and that the bodies in the Solar System formed at the same time.

4. **(D)**   In both contexts "primitive" means "close to its original condition." The Moon is described as "primitive" because unlike the Earth it has not undergone plate tectonics. We can infer that meteorites are described as "primitive" because, like the Moon, they have not undergone any major changes since their creation.

5. **(A)** The author says that "the Earth's oldest rocks have been recycled and destroyed by the process of plate tectonics" (lines 2–3) but that "The Moon . . . has not been disturbed by plate tectonics" (lines 35–36).

   (B) The oldest moon rocks available for study are 4.5 billion years old, whereas the Earth is believed to be 4.58 billion years old. However, there could very possibly be older moon rocks not yet found.

   (C) The author says, "If there are any of Earth's primordial rocks left in their original state, they have not yet been found." The fact that such rocks have not been found does not prove that they do not exist.

Passage 15

1. **(E)** The author says that "'defictionalization'" is another disturbing trend" in poetry. The "legitimate revolution" he refers to is the change in poetry created by the Beat and Confessional poets described in paragraphs 3 and 4. The author says that these poets made use of defictionalization to produce very good poetry.

2. **(A)** After expressing his admiration for the poetry of the Beat and Confessional poets the author says, "We should keep in mind that the Beats and Confessionals had no . . . aversion to embellishing their lives with fiction in the interest of poetic truth."

   (B) Although the Beats and Confessionals used defictionalization, which is a nontraditional technique, extensively, they "had no . . . aversion to arranging syllables to make their lines musical in ways clearly distinct from prose," which is a traditional technique.

   (C) The author says that the Beats and Confessionals "embellish[ed] their lives with fiction" to create excellent poetry. However, he says, "much of the poetry coming from the profession that purports to tell 'the truth' about the poet's life is anecdotal, over-literal, and trivial." Literal biographical detail, the author is saying, can be an ingredient of good poetry, but it must be used well.

3. **(A)** The author describes a major trend in contemporary poetry toward both prosification and "defictionalization." Traditional poetry makes little use of these.

   (C) The author would not be likely to agree that this is a golden age of poetry in light of his severe criticism of the poetry it has produced.

   (B) The author gives examples of how contemporary poetry frequently describes superficial reality. He describes this: "Too often, the focus on literal truth presents us not with the essence or core of the poet's being, but with the patio furniture of his or her life" (lines 41–43).

4. **"Because ordinary readers . . . on the competition."** The author is saying that the extensive use of defictionalization by contemporary poets limits the appeal of their poetry because ordinary readers don't like poetry that uses it.

Passage 16

1. **(B)** "Infrared spectra, particularly in the 1–3 micrometer wavelength range, are the primary data from which the presence and physical state of water ice on the surface of these satellites can be deduced" (lines 13–15).

2. **(A)** The author says that a number of factors "guarantee that water ice is a key component in the assembly of solid bodies in the solar system at and beyond Jupiter's distance from the sun" (lines 3–4).

   (C) In paragraph 4 the author describes how most of the regular satellites of Jupiter and Saturn "are subject to large fluxes of high energy ions trapped in the magnetic fields" generated by the magnetosphere of their parent planet. He says that "the principle consequence of this irradiation appears to be the buildup of oxygen in the surface ice" and then gives evidence for this.

3. **(A)** The author says that "the hemispheric dichotomy present on Iapetus . . . remains unexplained" (line 50). There is no evidence presented for (B), (D), and (E), and (C) is not possible because Iapetus does not orbit within the magnetosphere of its parent planet, Saturn. All the satellites are tidally locked to their parent planet and thus rotate with a period equal to the period of their revolution. We can infer from this that only one hemisphere of a satellite faces the parent planet. From this it is reasonable to hypothesize that this in some way causes an inhomogeneity between the hemispheres, perhaps because there is stronger gravitational force exerted on one hemisphere than on the other.

4. **(D)** All of the factors are cited as affecting the surface composition of the regular satellites except dense atmospheres.

5. **"From cosmochemical considerations . . . of these objects."** It can be inferred that "Cosmochemical considerations" refers to what is known about the origin of the solar system, especially its chemical composition. The note says that cosmochemistry is also called "chemical cosmology," so it can be inferred that the field studies the origin and development of substances of the universe, including the solar system.

Passage 17

1. **(C)** The focus of the passage is French feminist literary criticism.

   (A) The first part of the passage briefly discusses feminist literary criticism in general, but most of the passage is about French feminist literary criticism.

   (B) Psychoanalytic thought figures prominently in the passage because French feminists used the ideas of a psychoanalytic philosopher. However, it is not the focus, and neither is the more general topic of its relationship to feminism.

   (D) The "possibility" of a "feminine language" is discussed, but this is not the focus.

   (E) This is too general. The passage focuses on the views of French literary critics about how language shapes people's thinking.

2. **(A)** All of the thinkers described appear to believe that language has a central role in determining how we think about the world because they argue that language is a "male realm" and "reflects a binary logic" that imposes this way of thought on people from childhood.

   (B) The writers base much of their thinking on the ideas of a psychoanalytic philosopher, so it makes sense that they believe the premises of psychoanalytic thought are sound.

   (C) As stated above, the writers base many of their ideas on psychoanalysis, so it is unlikely that they think it is "suspect."

3. **(C)** Julia Kristova believes that "feminine language . . . is a medium through which women may be creative in new ways." and that if they understand "the relation between maternity and feminine creation" there will be "truly feminist innovation in all fields."

   (A)   There is nothing in the passage to suggest this.

   (B)   There is nothing in the passage to suggest that psychoanalytic thought is phallocentric, so this choice can be eliminated. However, it is conceivable that psychoanalytic thought will come to focus more on the pre-oedipal period as women innovate in various fields with their newly discovered creativity.

Passage 18

1. **(D)** The passage says, "Some reef-associated predators, however, may exhibit little emigration from their home reefs making them less likely to relocate in the event of prey shortage."

2. **(A)** "Knowledge of the life history of these forage species is . . . important to the multi-species management of the larger, more economically important fishery species" (lines 25–27).

   (B)   "This knowledge [of their longevity, age structure, and age at first reproduction] may prove valuable in assessing current and future anthropogenic impacts upon deep reef ecosystems due to harvest of both forage base species and their larger predators, and/or due to habitat disturbance from hydrocarbon exploration and development, or other human enterprises."

Passage 19

1. **(D)** "For example, global warming may produce longer growing seasons that promote plant photosynthesis, which removes carbon dioxide from the atmosphere" (lines 36–37).

2. **(D)** The author describes a number of trends and processes affecting the Arctic system that seem likely to cause the Arctic to become a significant source of global atmospheric carbon dioxide. However, the author repeatedly uses the word "could" and several times the words "possible" and "if" in describing the likelihood of these processes occurring. Also, in the final paragraph the author says, "But uncertainties still abound about the responses of the Arctic system to climate change" (lines 35–36). The author then describes processes that could significantly mitigate the effects of warming on the Arctic. On balance, therefore, it seems fairly likely that the Arctic will become a significant source of global atmospheric carbon dioxide.

3. **(A)** The author describes a number of complex, interacting processes and, as noted in Question 2 above, expresses considerable uncertainty about what their effect will be on climate. Good examples of this complexity are the interacting processes, possibly counter-balancing, described in the final paragraph.

   (B)   The author says, "Carbon . . . largely accumulates in permafrost" (lines 10–11).

   (C)   The author says, "the expansion of shrubs in tundra . . . could sequester more carbon in vegetation" (lines 38–39).

4. **"However, increasingly dry . . . overcome these effects."** Drier conditions might cancel out the effects of increased plant photosynthesis, expansion of shrubs in tundra, and movement of treeline northward because the increase in plant growth would be negated.

Passage 20

1. **(D)** In the sentence in which "chimerical" is used, "When he discovers his mistake" signals that man realizes that the order in nature and his control over it did not exist in reality, but rather in his mind. Thus, they can be described as "illusory."

2. **(B)** The author is concerned with the ways in which human beings understand the world. Teleology—belief in a purposeful development toward an end—is not discussed.

   (A) Anthropomorphism—attributing human characteristics to non-human things—is indirectly referred to in the discussion of those who believe in religion. These people believe that nature is "regulated by the will, the passion, or the caprice of spiritual beings like man in kind" (lines 16–17).

   (C) Magic is one of the major topics discussed.

   (D) Nature is referred to often because the author is concerned with how human beings interpret nature.

   (E) The author is concerned with the progress human beings have made in understanding nature and, more generally, the world.

3. **(D)** The author is discussing the idea that magic, religion, and science are "nothing but theories of thought." "Some radically different way of looking at the phenomena" is another way of interpreting the world, which cannot be known directly.

4. **(A)** The author says that we should not conclude that "because the scientific theory of the world is the best that has yet been formulated, it is necessarily complete and final" (lines 49–51). Science may appear to us today to be a perfect theory, yet it may in the future be replaced by a theory that is even better.

5. **(B)** Referring to science the author says "Here at last, after groping about in the dark for countless ages, man has hit upon a clue to the labyrinth, a golden key that opens many locks in the treasury of nature . . . the hope of progress—moral and intellectual as well as material—in the future is bound up with the fortunes of science . . . " (lines 44–48).

   (A) The author says, "The advance of knowledge is an infinite progression towards a goal that forever recedes" (lines 59–60).

   (C) The author says, "the order upon which magic is predicated differs widely from that which forms the basis of science" (lines 36–37).

6. **"For whereas the . . . the phenomena themselves."** The author is explaining how the order on which science is based is different from the order on which magic is based. This sentence explains that this difference arises from a fundamental difference in the way in which magic and science explain the order of nature.

Practice Test 1

ANSWER SHEET
Practice Test 1

SECTION 1

1. (A) (B) (C) (D) (E) (F)
2. (A) (B) (C) (D) (E) (F)
3. (A) (B) (C) (D) (E) (F)
4. (A) (B) (C) (D) (E) (F)
5. _____
6. _____
7. (i) _____
   (ii) _____
8. (i) _____
   (ii) _____

9. (i) _____
   (ii) _____
10. (i) _____
    (ii) _____
    (iii) _____
11. (i) _____
    (ii) _____
    (iii) _____
12. (i) _____
    (ii) _____
    (iii) _____

13. (A) (B) (C) (D) (E)
14. (A) (B) (C) (D) (E)
15. (A) (B) (C)
16. (A) (B) (C) (D) (E)
17. (A) (B) (C) (D) (E)
18. (A) (B) (C) (D) (E)
19. (A) (B) (C) (D) (E)
20. _____
    _____

SECTION 2

1. (A) (B) (C) (D) (E) (F)
2. (A) (B) (C) (D) (E) (F)
3. _____
4. _____
5. (i) _____
   (ii) _____
6. (i) _____
   (ii) _____
7. (i) _____
   (ii) _____

8. (i) _____
   (ii) _____
   (iii) _____
9. (i) _____
   (ii) _____
   (iii) _____
10. (i) _____
    (ii) _____
    (iii) _____

11. (A) (B) (C)
12. (A) (B) (C) (D) (E)
13. (A) (B) (C) (D) (E)
14. (A) (B) (C)
15. (A) (B) (C)
16. (A) (B) (C) (D) (E)
17. (A) (B) (C) (D) (E)
18. (A) (B) (C) (D) (E)
19. (A) (B) (C) (D) (E)
20. (A) (B) (C)

SECTION 1

Time: 30 minutes
20 questions

> Choose the best answer to each of the following questions in this section.

> Fill in the blank in each sentence by selecting two answer choices that fit the overall meaning of the sentence and produce completed sentences that are equivalent in meaning.

1. The _____ of the *Foundation* novels by the noted science-fiction writer Isaac Asimov is that historians and psychologists succeed in finding laws that can successfully predict—based on collective human behavior—the broad outlines of future events.
   - (A) premise
   - (B) verisimilitude
   - (C) postulate
   - (D) paradox
   - (E) incongruity
   - (F) implication

2. Although it is loathsome to some people, slang often expresses ideas with great directness, avoiding the _____ of more refined language.
   - (A) circumlocution
   - (B) syntax
   - (C) ornateness
   - (D) obfuscation
   - (E) periphrasis
   - (F) opprobrium

3. To its _____, the weaknesses of metaphysics are mitigated by its lofty goal of trying to achieve a comprehensive and accurate picture of reality.
   - (A) detractors
   - (B) mentors
   - (C) sophists
   - (D) proponents
   - (E) advocates
   - (F) opponents

4. One of the greatest hoaxes in the history of science was perpetrated by the Indian paleontologist Dr. Chandra Gupta, who fabricated entirely _____ evidence for fossils throughout his career.

    (A) counterfeit
    (B) feckless
    (C) refractory
    (D) plausible
    (E) circumstantial
    (F) spurious

> **Fill in all of the blanks in the sentences by selecting one entry from the corresponding column of choices in the way that best completes the text.**

5. In the Middle Ages, Europeans placed the holy city of Jerusalem at the center of maps, reflecting the prevailing _____ of the era.

iniquity
parsimony
anthropocentrism
cosmology
proximity

6. The ancient Greek philosopher Socrates displayed great _____ in accepting his sentence of death for corrupting the morals of Athenian youth and for advocating religious heresies; he resisted efforts to save his life and willingly drank the cup of poison given him.

elation
stoicism
elitism
erudition
skepticism

7. The origin of the word "barbarian" reflects the (i) _____ of the ancient Greeks; its (ii) _____ is that it comes (through Latin and French words) from the Greek word *barbaros*, meaning "non-Greek, foreign."

(i)	(ii)
ignorance	idiom
ethnocentrism	genesis
hegemony	etymology

8. Some people argue that the increased gap between rich and poor is caused (i) _____, which tends to favor those who are already wealthy because they have knowledge, skills, and access to information that the poor do not have; from the above perspective, the world is (ii) _____ into two groups, one able to exploit the system to its advantage, the other forced to suffer the negative effects of the new economic order.

(i)	(ii)
entirely by the bourgeoisie	truncated
partly by globalization	polarized
to a significant degree by demography	desiccated

9. Geologists believe that ice ages are caused by small changes in the Earth's orbit around the sun and by changes in the Earth's tilt on its axis which—though not (i) _____—have a considerable (ii) _____ effect.

(i)	(ii)
precise	cumulative
of great magnitude	correlative
observable	retroactive

10. In some ways, fascism can be viewed as (i) _____ social contract: The individual (ii) _____ nearly all his or her political identity and (iii) _____ to the state.

(i)	(ii)	(iii)
an arbitrary	cedes	machinations
an altruistic	ascribes	autonomy
the ultimate	denies	ascendancy

11. In considering whether to (i) _____ mergers of large corporations, governments now must consider the impact of such mergers on a country's international competitiveness; for example, the United States has allowed the mergers of (ii) _____ such as Lockheed and Boeing in the aerospace industry in the belief that European consortiums, backed by government funding, could pose a threat to American (iii) _____ in that industry.

(i)	(ii)	(iii)
encourage	behemoths	chauvinism
prevent	offshoots	preeminence
investigate	mavericks	sovereignty

12. (i) _____ are fond of arguing that technology in itself is neither good nor bad, but rather that it must be judged on the use to which it is put; some commentators, however, regard computers as a unique case within the area of technology because of their (ii) _____ influence that divorces computer users from reality and causes the users to become dependent on them. A rebuttal by proponents of computers of the argument that computers are (iii) _____ is that such misgivings are based on Luddite arguments that have no place in a world in which progress is so dependent on computers.

(i)	(ii)	(iii)
Technophiles	insidious	ostensibly malevolent
Libertarians	intangible	interminably bad
Neophytes	benign	inherently evil

> **Read the passages below, and then answer the questions that follow them based on the information in the passages themselves and in any introductory material or notes. The correct answer may be stated or merely suggested in the passages.**

"Yearning" is the word that best describes a common psychological state shared by many of us, cutting across boundaries of race, class, gender, and sexual practice. Specifically in relation to the postmodernist deconstruction of "master" narratives, the yearning that wells in the hearts and minds of those whom such narratives have silenced is the longing for critical voice. It is no accident that "rap" has usurped the primary position of R&B music among young black folks as the most desired sound, or that it began as a form of "testimony" for the underclass. It has enabled underclass black youth to develop a critical voice, as a group of young black men told me, a "common literacy." Rap projects a critical voice, explaining, demanding, urging.

(10) Working with this insight in his essay "Putting the Pop Back into Postmodernism," Lawrence Grossberg comments: The postmodern sensibility appropriates practices as boasts that announce their own—and consequently our own—existence, like a rap song boasting of the imaginary (or real—it makes no difference) accomplishments of the rapper. They offer forms of empowerment not only in the face of nihil-

(15) ism but precisely through the forms of nihilism itself: an empowering nihilism, a moment of positivity through the production and structuring of affective relations. Considering that it is as a subject that one comes to voice, then the postmodernist focus on the critique of identity appears, at first glance, to threaten and close down the possibility that this discourse and practice will allow those who have suffered

(20) the crippling effects of colonization and domination to gain or regain a hearing. Even if this sense of threat and the fear it evokes are based on a misunderstanding of the postmodernist political project, they nevertheless shape responses. It never surprises me when black folk respond to the critique of essentialism, especially when it denies the validity of identity politics, by saying "yeah, it's easy to give up identity,

(25) when you got one." Though an apt and oftentimes appropriate comeback, this does not really intervene in the discourse in a way that alters and transforms. We should indeed be suspicious of postmodern critiques of the "subject" when they surface at a historical moment when many subjugated people feel themselves coming to voice for the first time.

Select one answer choice for the following questions.

13. What is the most likely reason that the author believes "We should indeed be suspicious of postmodern critiques of the 'subject' when they surface at a historical moment when many subjugated people feel themselves coming to voice for the first time"?
    (A) Such critiques are based on the false premise that colonization and domination of the underclass will continue if identity politics are not accepted.
    (B) The postmodern political project is widely misunderstood by subjugated people and therefore we should not trust the motivation for it.
    (C) It is likely that critiques of essentialism have been embraced by "black folk" as a result of their misunderstanding of the political motivation behind it.
    (D) It is probable that such critiques are the result of the coming to voice of those whom the postmodernist deconstruction of "master" narratives have silenced for so long.
    (E) There is a good chance that one of the reasons for such critiques is a desire on the part of those with power to deny those without power the opportunity to express themselves.

14. The author's attitude toward postmodernism can most accurately be described as
    (A) wholly critical
    (B) patronizing
    (C) largely approving
    (D) unreservedly approving
    (E) skeptical

Less certain than why and when we became naked is how hominids evolved bare flesh. The genetic evidence for the evolution of nakedness has been difficult to locate because many genes contribute to the appearance and function of our skin.
Line Nevertheless, hints have emerged from large-scale comparisons of the sequences
(5) of DNA "code letters," or nucleotides, in the entire genomes of different organisms. Comparison of the human and chimp genomes reveals that one of the most significant differences between chimp DNA and our own lies in the genes that code for proteins that control properties of the skin. The human versions of some of those genes encode proteins that help to make our skin particularly waterproof and
(10) scuff-resistant—critical properties, given the absence of protective fur. This finding implies that the advent of those gene variants contributed to the origin of nakedness by mitigating its consequences.

The outstanding barrier capabilities of our skin arise from the structure and makeup of its outermost layer, the stratum corneum (SC) of the epidermis. The SC
(15) has what has been described as a bricks-and-mortar composition. In this arrangement, multiple layers of flattened dead cells called corneocytes, which contain the protein keratin and other substances, are the bricks; ultrathin layers of lipids surrounding each of the corneocytes make up the mortar. Most of the genes that direct the development of the SC are ancient, and their sequences are highly conserved
(20) among vertebrates. That the genes undergirding the human SC are so distinctive signifies, therefore, that the advent of those genes was important to survival. These genes encode the production of a unique combination of proteins that occur only in the epidermis, including novel types of keratin and involucrin. A number of laboratories are currently attempting to unravel the precise mechanisms responsible for
(25) regulating the manufacture of these proteins.

Other researchers are looking at the evolution of keratins in body hair, with the aim of determining the mechanisms responsible for the sparseness and fineness of body hair on the surface of human skin. To that end, Roland Moll of Philipps University in Marburg, Germany, and his colleagues have shown that the keratins
(30) present in human body hair are extremely fragile, which is why these hairs break so easily compared with those of other animals. This finding, detailed in a paper Moll published in 2008, suggests that human hair keratins were not as important to survival as the hair keratins of other primates were over the course of evolution and thus became weak.

Consider each of the three choices separately and select all that apply.

15. Which of the following are true about human skin?
    (A) It is impervious to water.
    (B) Some of the genes that direct the development of the stratum corneum of the epidermis in humans evolved relatively recently.
    (C) Body hair on humans is generally sparse but very strong.

16. According to the article, scientists believe that
    (A) humans lost most of their body hair because human skin evolved to become so waterproof and scuff-resistant that hair was no longer needed to protect it
    (B) it is likely that as humans evolved bare flesh the skin became more waterproof and scuff-resistant, helping to counteract the negative effects of having bare flesh
    (C) all vertebrates possess genes for the distinctive human-type stratum corneum that become active when a species evolves the trait of bare flesh
    (D) human hair is as strong as that of other primates
    (E) the DNA of chimps and humans is the same in all respects except for important differences in the genes that control skin properties

     During the Restoration period, and later, spiritual life was at its very lowest ebb. I mean, spiritual life as exhibited in the poetic and dramatic literature of the time, whose poisoned fountainhead was the dissolute court of Charles II. All the slops of
Line that court went into the drama, all the "sentina reipublicae," the bilge water of the
(5) ship of state. The age, as Emerson says, had no live, distinct, actuating convictions. It was in even worse than a negative condition. As represented by its drama and poetry, it may almost be said to have repudiated the moral sentiment. A spiritual disease affected the upper classes, which continued down into the reign of the Georges. There appears to have been but little belief in the impulse which the heart imparts
(10) to the intellect, or that the latter draws greatness from the inspiration of the former. It can be said, emphatically, that in the time of Charles II there was no open vision. And yet that besotted, that spiritually dark age, which was afflicted with pneumato-phobia*, flattered itself that there had never been an age so flooded with light. The great age of Elizabeth, in which the human faculties, in their whole range, both intel-
(15) lectual and spiritual, reached such a degree of expansion as they had never before reached in the history of the world,—that great age, the age of Spenser, Sidney, Mar-lowe, Shakespeare, Bacon, Raleigh, Hooker, Ben Jonson, Beaumont, Fletcher, Chap-man, Dekker, Ford, Herbert, Heywood, Massinger,—that great age was regarded by the men of the Restoration period as barbarous in comparison with their own. But
(20) beneath all, still lay the restorative elements of the English character, which were to reassert themselves and usher in a new era of literary productiveness, the greatest since the Elizabethan age, and embodying the highest ideals of life to which the race has yet attained.

*Pneumatophobia is an intense fear of incorporeal beings such as ghosts.

17. Which of the following is not an underlying assumption made by the author of this passage?

(A) Literature, at its best, is one of humanity's greatest achievements.

(B) The King of England has a major effect on the literature of the country.

(C) The spirituality of a people is reflected in its literature.

(D) It is possible to meaningfully generalize the attitudes and values of the people of a particular period.

(E) Once the literature of a people has declined, it can never recover its greatness.

In the Vedic hymns there survives the record of a religion remarkably like the Greek in spirit, but less dramatic and articulate in form. The gods of the Vedas are unmistakably natural elements. Vulcan is there nothing but fire, Jupiter nothing but the
Line sky. This patriarchal people, fresh from the highlands, had not yet been infected
(5) with the manias and diseases of the jungle. It lived simply, rationally, piously, loving all natural joys and delighted with all the instruments of a rude but pure civilization. It saluted without servility the forces of nature which ministered to its needs. It burst into song in the presence of the magnificent panorama spread out before it—day-sky and night-sky, dawn and gloaming, clouds, thunder and rain, rivers,
(10) cattle and horses, grain, fruit, fire, and wine. Nor were the social sanctities neglected. Commemoration was made of the stages of mortal life, of the bonds of love and kinship, of peace, of battle, and of mourning for the dead. By a very intelligible figure and analogy the winds became shepherds, the clouds flocks, the day a conqueror, the dawn a maid, the night a wise sibyl and mysterious consort of heaven. These
(15) personifications were tentative and vague, and the consequent mythology was a system of rhetoric rather than of theology. The various gods had interchangeable attributes, and, by a voluntary confusion, quite in the manner of later Hindu poetry, each became on occasion any or all of the others. Here the Indian pantheistic vertigo begins to appear. Many dark superstitions, no doubt, bubbled up in the torrent
(20) of that plastic reverie; for this people, clean and natural as on the whole it appears, cannot have been without a long and ignoble ancestry. The Greeks themselves, heirs to kindred general traditions, retained some childish and obscene practices in their worship. But such hobgoblins naturally vanish under a clear and beneficent sun and are scattered by healthy mountain breezes. A cheerful people knows how to
(25) take them lightly, play with them, laugh at them, and turn them again into figures of speech. Among the early speakers of Sanskrit, even more than among the Greeks, the national religion seems to have been nothing but a poetic naturalism. Such a mythology, however, is exceedingly plastic and unstable. If the poet is observant and renews his impressions, his myths will become more and more accurate descriptions
(30) of the facts, and his hypotheses about phenomena will tend to be expressed more

and more in terms of the phenomena themselves; that is, will tend to become scientific. If, on the contrary and as usually happens, the inner suggestions and fertility of his fables absorb his interest, and he neglects to consult his external perceptions any further, or even forgets that any such perceptions originally inspired the myth, (35) he will tend to become a dramatic poet, guided henceforth in his fictions only by his knowledge and love of human life.

> **Select one answer choice for the following questions.**

18. What is the meaning of the phrase "a system of rhetoric" as it is used in the first paragraph?
    (A) A comprehensive and well-ordered set of beliefs about God's relationship to man and nature
    (B) An organized set of images and other literary devices that allows meaning to be communicated
    (C) A set of beliefs about gods that take on different characteristics depending on the season and mood of the people
    (D) A system of mythology that acknowledges that god can never be fully understood by the human mind
    (E) A logically structured set of assertions about the preternatural origins of natural phenomena

19. Which of the following statements most accurately describes the author's attitude toward Vedic religion and civilization?
    (A) Unreserved admiration for a religion that represents the zenith of human spiritual attainment
    (B) Admiration for Vedic religion and civilization's dignity and exuberant celebration of life and nature, coupled with an admission of its limitations
    (C) Condemnation of Vedic religion and civilization as having a primitive, superstitious belief system, together with admiration for its powerful song and poetry
    (D) Admiration for the power of the poetry of Vedic religion and civilization but contempt for its inability to understand nature objectively
    (E) Amused dismissal of Vedic religion and civilization as mythologically based, pantheistic, often superstitious, and logically incoherent

> **Identify the sentence by writing its first three words and last three words on the line below.**

Select the sentence that describes Vedic culture as relatively undeveloped.

20. _____

SECTION 2

Time: 30 minutes
20 questions

> Choose the best answer to each of the following questions in this section.

> Fill in the blank in each sentence by selecting two answer choices that fit the overall meaning of the sentence and produce completed sentences that are equivalent in meaning.

1. The phrase "catch-22" originated in Joseph Heller's novel *Catch-22,* in which a soldier asks to be relieved from combat and is given the _____ explanation that the criterion for being relieved of duty is being insane, and that since he is asking to not be involved in the insanity of war he must be sane, and therefore cannot be relieved based on insanity.
   - (A) officious
   - (B) complicated
   - (C) cursory
   - (D) bizarre
   - (E) convoluted
   - (F) bureaucratic

2. It generally becomes tedious when a writer deviates from the main topic to make many _____ remarks to discuss secondary issues.
   - (A) pejorative
   - (B) parenthetical
   - (C) subsidiary
   - (D) disinterested
   - (E) pedantic
   - (F) qualifying

> Fill in all of the blanks in the sentences by selecting one entry from the corresponding column of choices in the way that best completes the text.

3. Law, as it has been established in democratic societies, is one of the most noble and impressive _____ created by humanity, protecting individuals through an open and equitable process that does not terrorize them or deprive them of their rights.

abstractions
purports
juggernauts
edifices
exigencies

4. Absolute zero is _____ state in which there is no movement of molecules.

an intrinsic
a prostrate
a pristine
a multifarious
a quiescent

5. Generally, traditional societies tend to be more socially stratified than modern ones because the latter are much more (i) _____ and (ii) _____.

(i)	(ii)
cosmopolitan	exploitative
egalitarian	homogeneous
elitist	meritocratic

6. Scientific and technical terms have become (i) _____ , and so a great deal of scientific (ii) _____ has passed into everyday language (*feedback, fine tune,* and *filter,* for example).

(i)	(ii)
redoubtable	banter
elusive	jargon
ubiquitous	doggerel

7. Malay was the (i) _____ of the Malay Peninsula for centuries, but it is in many parts of that region being superseded in that role by a European (ii) _____ , English.

(i)	(ii)
lexicon	parvenu
lingua franca	interloper
maverick	dilettante

8. Positions on (i) _____ issues are often polarized, each side (ii) _____ the other side's argument to a (iii) _____.

(i)	(ii)	(iii)
social	relegating	colorful travesty of the truth
regional	refuting	black and white caricature
contentious	reducing	parody

9. If a nation is defined as a people sharing the same language and broadly the same culture, and a state as any geographical area under the (i) _____ of one central government, then (ii) _____ the people of one nation may inhabit more than one state and the population in one state may belong to more than one nation. In this view the nation-state is to be defined as a political, geographical, and cultural entity where nation and state (iii) _____.

(i)	(ii)	(iii)
aegis	it is possible that	conflict
sovereignty	it is not true that	are coterminous
influence	it follows that	are synonymous

10. The mind has a tendency to (i) _____ abstractions, so that one might envision the ego existing somewhere physically in the brain, but Freud (ii) _____ such a physical structure: rather, he (iii) _____.

(i)	(ii)	(iii)
create	did not posit	believed that it is illusory
hypostatize	did not preclude	theorized that it is autonomous
incorporate	did not abjure	regarded it as a process

> Read the passages below, and then answer the questions that follow them based on the information in the passages themselves and in any introductory material or notes. The correct answer may be stated or merely suggested in the passages.

A large number of variables and different combinations of these variables determine whether a sedimentary basin contains microbial methane, natural gas, crude oil, tars, or no petroleum. Not all basins have organic-rich sediment layers deposited
Line during their subsidence history. As a result, these basins will contain no appreciable
(5) quantities of petroleum regardless of how deep the basin subsides. Other basins that do have an organic-rich rock layer may not have been buried to sufficient depths to generate natural gas or crude oil through thermal maturation, but may contain microbial methane accumulations. An organic-rich rock layer in some basins may thermally mature to generate mostly natural gas because of the dominance of higher
(10) plant debris contribution to its organic matter. Conversely, an organic-rich rock layer in other basins may thermally mature to generate mostly crude oil because of the dominance of lower plant debris contributing to its organic matter. More than one organic-rich rock layer may be deposited in the burial history of some basins with all, one, or none subsiding deep enough to thermally mature to generate petro-
(15) leum. In other basins that have an organic-rich rock layer and sufficient burial to generate petroleum, the lack or scarcity of seals and reservoirs to collect generated petroleum may result in natural gas losses to the atmosphere or large degraded oil and tar deposits at or near the basin surface.

11. Which of the following statements are true?

    (A) If more than one organic-rich layer is deposited in a sedimentary basin, at least one of them is likely to contain substantial amounts of petroleum.

    (B) Depth is a major determinant of whether an organic-rich rock layer contains natural gas.

    (C) A sedimentary basin that contains substantial amounts of natural gas is certain to also have a roughly equal amount of crude oil.

Buddhism arising out of Brahmanism suggests a comparison with Christianity arising out of Judaism, but the comparison breaks down in most points of detail. But there is one real resemblance, namely that Buddhism and Christianity have both
Line   won their greatest triumphs outside the land of their birth. The flowers of the mind,
(5)   if they can be transplanted at all, often flourish with special vigor on alien soil. Witness the triumphs of Islam in the hands of the Turks and Mughals, the progress of Nestorianism in Central Asia, and the spread of Manichaeism in both the East and West outside the limits of Persia. Even so Lamaism in Tibet and Amidism in Japan, though scholars may regard them as singular perversions, have more vitality than
(10)   any branch of Buddhism which has existed in India since the seventh century. But even here the parallel with Christian sects is imperfect. It would be more complete if Palestine had been the center from which different phases of Christianity radiated during some twelve centuries, for this is the relation between Indian and foreign Buddhism. Lamaism is not the teaching of the Buddha travestied by Tibetans but
(15)   a late form of Indian Buddhism modified there in some external features (such as ecclesiastical organization and art) but not differing greatly in doctrine from Bengali Buddhism of the eleventh century. And even Amidism appears to have originated not in the Far East but in Gandhara and the adjacent lands. Thus the many varieties of Buddhism now existing are due partly to local color but even more to the work-
(20)   ings of the restless Hindu mind which during many centuries after the Christian era continued to invent for it novelties in metaphysics and mythology.

12. The author uses the example of Islam to show that
    (A) religions originating in Judaism maintain more of the central beliefs of their mother religion than did religions originating in Brahmanism
    (B) religions that developed from Judaism spread more rapidly than did religions that developed from Brahmanism
    (C) Islam was unique among world religions in being able to flourish in an alien environment
    (D) Islam, like Christianity, differs greatly from Buddhism in all its many forms
    (E) religious belief systems often develop more robustly outside the land of their origin than in the land of their origin

13. Based on the information in the passage, it is reasonable to infer that the author believes that
    (A) Brahmanism produced such diverse offspring in the form of varieties of Buddhism that their common origin can hardly be recognized
    (B) a religion can be debased yet still possess more vigor than its parent religion
    (C) Buddhism and Judaism share central doctrines that make them clearly distinguishable from Brahmanism
    (D) Lamaism in Tibet originated from an early form of Brahmanism
    (E) Manichaeism had a greater influence on Brahmanical beliefs than it did on Christian beliefs

Aesthetic feeling, in different people, may make up a different fraction of life and vary greatly in volume. The more nearly insensible a man is the more incompetent he becomes to proclaim the values which sensibility might have. To beauty men
Line are habitually insensible, even while they are awake and rationally active. Tomes of
(5) aesthetic criticism hang on a few moments of real delight and intuition. It is in rare and scattered instants that beauty smiles even on her adorers, who are reduced for habitual comfort to remembering her past favors. An aesthetic glow may pervade experience, but that circumstance is seldom remarked; it figures only as an influence working subterraneously on thoughts and judgments which in themselves
(10) take a cognitive or practical direction. Only when the aesthetic ingredient becomes predominant do we exclaim, how beautiful! Ordinarily the pleasures which formal perception gives remain an undistinguished part of our comfort or curiosity.

Taste is formed in those moments when aesthetic emotion is massive and distinct; preferences then grown conscious, judgments then put into words will rever-
(15) berate through calmer hours; they will constitute prejudices, habits of apperception, secret standards for all other beauties. A period of life in which such intuitions have been frequent may amass tastes and ideals sufficient for the rest of our days. Youth

in these matters governs maturity, and while men may develop their early impressions more systematically and find confirmations of them in various quarters, they
(20) will seldom look at the world afresh or use new categories in deciphering it. Half our
standards come from our first masters, and the other half from our first loves. Never
being so deeply stirred again, we remain persuaded that no objects save those we
then discovered can have a true sublimity. These high-water marks of aesthetic life
may easily be reached under tutelage. It may be some eloquent appreciations read
(25) in a book, or some preference expressed by a gifted friend, that may have revealed
unsuspected beauties in art or nature; and then, since our own perception was
vicarious and obviously inferior in volume to that which our mentor possessed, we
shall take his judgments for our criterion, since they were the source and exemplar
of all our own. Thus the volume and intensity of some appreciations, especially
(30) when nothing of the kind has preceded, makes them authoritative over our subsequent judgments. On those warm moments hang all our cold systematic opinions;
and while the latter fill our days and shape our careers it is only the former that are
crucial and alive.

Consider each of the three choices separately and select all that apply.

14. Which of the following statements would the author be likely to agree with?
    (A) People are seldom truly aware of the beauty around them.
    (B) A person's ability to appreciate new forms of art tends to decline as he or she
        grows older.
    (C) A person must learn to appreciate beauty solely by himself or herself.

15. Which of the following statements would the author be likely to disagree with?
    (A) Art critics, unlike music critics, rely for their judgment to a large extent on taste
        developed in youth.
    (B) All forms of natural beauty, unlike artistic beauty, can be easily appreciated by
        everyone.
    (C) People vary in their ability to appreciate beauty.

Toxins released by bacteria are only one source of the illnesses they produce. Some of the symptoms of bacterial infections arise directly from the bugs' tactics for staying alive. Because many pathogens produce a similar array of symptoms—diarrhea,
Line fever, and so forth—it may seem logical to think that they cause disease in similar
(5) ways, too. Although many pathogens do act on some of the same fundamental elements of cellular machinery, such as certain proteins that make up the cell's internal skeleton, the microbes use surprisingly diverse and complex methods to attack.

The first step in any bacterial assault, for instance, is attachment to the host's cells. A disease-causing strain of *Escherichia coli*, known as enterohemorrhagic *E.*
(10) *coli* 0157, has perhaps the most remarkable method of locking itself onto a host cell. People typically pick up this pathogen by eating tainted food; once inside the gastrointestinal tract, 0157 attaches to the intestinal wall and produces a toxin that induces bloody diarrhea. At one time, scientists thought that this virulent form of *E. coli*, like all other adherent pathogens, latched onto a receptor molecule already
(15) present on the host's intestinal cells. More recent work has shown, though, that 0157 actually makes its own receptor and delivers it into the cell through a specialized device known as a type 3 secretion system, or T3SS for short. (Secretion systems have historically been named based on the order of their discovery.)

The bacterium's T3SS injects a molecule called Tir, along with 40 or more other
(20) "effector" proteins directly into the membrane of the host cell and then locks one of its own surface molecules onto Tir. But that is only its first step in taking over the cell. Tir and some of the other injected effectors also induce the host cell's internal skeleton to behave abnormally. A key cytoskeletal building block, actin, interacts with the bacterial proteins and begins forming polymers that push on the cell membrane
(25) from the inside until it forms a pedestal. The *E. coli* remains outside the cell, securely anchored to its new throne, while the effectors and toxins it has injected into the cell do their dirty work. The exact function of these striking pedestals remains unknown, but investigators have demonstrated that they are central to the bacterium's ability to cause disease.

(30) Another potentially lethal pathogen, *Helicobacter pylori*, attaches itself to the epithelial cells lining the stomach, then begins customizing its environment to promote its own survival. *H. pylori* releases an enzyme called urease that locally counters the stomach's high acidity, which normally kills most bacteria. Not all strains cause disease, but those that do can generate gastric ulcers and even stomach cancer—mak-
(35) ing it the only bacterium known to cause cancer. The pathogenic strains produce a type 4 secretion system that injects an effector protein called CagA. The protein's exact purpose is unclear, but recent work suggests that it can induce stomach epithelial cells to display more of the receptors to which *H. pylori* attaches. The effector may also directly alter the stomach cells' internal signaling in a way that makes them
(40) elongate, scatter and ultimately die, contributing to ulcer formation.

E. coli 0157 and *H. pylori* bacteria do not need to enter cells to cause disease, but *Salmonella* species, which are closely related to *E. coli* and cause diarrhea in more than a billion people worldwide every year, do penetrate cell walls. Indeed, to thrive, *Salmonella* bacteria have to pass into and through epithelial cells that line the intes-
(45) tine. This invasion begins when the bacteria use a T3SS variant known as *Salmonella*

pathogenicity island 1 (SPI-1) to inject epithelial cells with effectors that reorganize actin polymerization in a way that produces "ruffles" in the cell membrane—similar to *E. coli's* pedestal. The ruffle structures reach up and around a bacterium attached to the outside of the cell membrane, causing the cell to literally drag the microbe

(50) inside. Molecules injected through SPI-1 also induce the diarrhea characteristic of these infections, but the *Salmonella* bacteria do not stop there.

Macrophages and other cells belonging to what is called the innate arm of the immune system, such as neutrophils and dendritic cells, normally ingest and destroy ("phagocytose") any invaders. These phagocytes engulf bacteria and sequester them

(45) in membrane-bound vacuoles where killing molecules destroy the captives. But *Salmonella* species penetrate the intestinal lining by passing from epithelial cells to immune cells waiting on the other side. Once inside the phagocytic vacuole, the bacteria deploy a second T3SS, called SPI-2, which releases effector proteins that convert the vacuole into a safe haven where *Salmonella* can multiply. The proteins

(60) cause this switch from death chamber to sanctuary by altering the vacuole membrane so that the killing molecules cannot get in.

The SPI-2 system is critical to the success of *Salmonella typhi*, the strain that causes typhoid fever. By allowing the microbes to survive inside the phagocytic cells, which travel within the body via the bloodstream and lymphatic system, SPI-2

(65) enables the organisms to reach and replicate in tissues far beyond the intestine, such as the liver and spleen.

Select one answer choice for the following questions.

16. The word "pathogens" as it is used in the first paragraph most nearly means
    (A) bacterial infections
    (B) bacteria
    (C) substances that cause the body to mimic the symptoms of a disease
    (D) microorganisms that prey on larger host organisms
    (E) agents that cause disease

17. Which of the following needs support by more evidence before it can be accepted as scientific fact?
    (A) *Helicobacter pylori* can cause stomach cancer.
    (B) Enterohemorrhagic *E. coli* 0157 is often spread to humans in food.
    (C) *Salmonella* bacteria neutralize phagocytes by a complex process that involves altering the vacuoles created by phagocytes.
    (D) The CagA protein causes stomach epithelial cells to display more receptors to which *Helicobacter pylori* attaches.
    (E) Bacteria produce illness in a variety of ways.

18. To which of the following phenomena described in the passage could the adjective "ironic" best be applied?
    (A) Phagocytes sequester bacteria and vacuoles and kill them with their molecules.
    (B) In order to thrive, *Salmonella* bacteria have to pass into and through epithelial walls lining the human intestine.
    (C) *Salmonella typhi* can spread through the body by using the body's immune system.
    (D) Many of the symptoms produced by bacterial infections arise directly as a result of the bacteria's tactics for staying alive.
    (E) *E. coli* 0157 and *Helicobacter pylori* do not enter healthy cells to cause disease yet are still able to disrupt the functioning of such healthy cells.

19. Which of the following would be the most suitable title for this passage?
    (A) Bacterial Pathogens in Human Beings
    (B) Biochemical Strategies by which Bacteria Attach Themselves to Host Cells
    (C) Breaking and Entering: The Art of Bacterial Warfare
    (D) Major Bacterial Diseases in Humans and Their Causes
    (E) Commonalities in Enterohemorrhagic *E. coli* 0157, *Helicobacter Pylori*, and *Salmonella typhi*

Consider each of the three choices separately and select all that apply.

20. According to the information in the passage, which of the following are not true?
    (A) All bacteria must enter cells in order to cause disease.
    (B) *E. coli* 0157 uses receptor molecules in its host's cells as a means to pass its own molecules into the host.
    (C) All bacteria are killed by acid in the human stomach.

ANSWER KEY
Practice Test 1

Section 1

1. A, C
2. A, E
3. D, E
4. A, F
5. cosmology
6. stoicism
7. ethnocentrism/etymology
8. partly by globalization/ polarized
9. of great magnitude/cumulative
10. the ultimate/cedes/autonomy
11. prevent/behemoths/ preeminence
12. Technophiles/insidious/ inherently evil
13. E
14. C
15. A, B
16. B
17. E
18. B
19. B
20. "It lived simply . . . but pure civilization."

Section 2

1. B, E
2. B, F
3. edifices
4. a quiescent
5. egalitarian/meritocratic
6. ubiquitous/jargon
7. lingua franca/interloper
8. contentious/reducing/black and white caricature
9. sovereignty/it follows that/ are coterminous
10. hypostatize/did not posit/ regarded it as a process
11. B
12. E
13. B
14. A, B
15. A, B
16. E
17. D
18. C
19. C
20. A, B, C

SCORING GUIDE

CORRECT ANSWERS	SCORE
1–6	VERY POOR
7–12	POOR
13–18	BELOW AVERAGE
19–24	AVERAGE
25–30	GOOD
31–36	VERY GOOD
37–40	EXCELLENT

ANSWER EXPLANATIONS

Section 1

1. **(A), (C)** The *premise* (a proposition upon which an argument is based) of the *Foundation* novels is that laws are found that can predict future events. *Postulate* (a principle provisionally adopted as a basis for argument) has the same meaning as premise in context.

2. **(A), (E)** "Great directness" signals that more refined language leads to *circumlocution* (indirect way of saying something). *Periphrasis* (the use of circumlocution) has the same meaning in context.

3. **(D), (E)** It makes sense that the *proponents* (people who argue for something) of metaphysics (speculative philosophy about the nature of reality) believe that its weaknesses are mitigated by its lofty goal. *Advocates* (people who plead for) has the meaning as proponents in context.

4. **(A), (F)** "Hoaxes" and "fabricated" signal that the evidence was *counterfeit*. *Spurious* (counterfeit) has the same meaning in context.

5. **cosmology** "At the center of maps" signals that the *cosmology* (a system of beliefs that seeks to describe or explain the origin and structure of the universe) of an era is being referred to. *Anthropocentrism* (regarding humans as the center of the universe) makes some sense because Jerusalem was placed at the center of maps. However, this is not as good a choice as *cosmology* because the focus of the sentence is on the religious world view of Europeans in the Middle Ages, not on their emphasis on human beings.

6. **stoicism** Socrates "resisted efforts to save his life" and "willingly drank the cup of poison," so he showed great *stoicism* (indifference to pleasure or pain).

7. **ethnocentrism/etymology** The Greek word *barbaros* means "foreign," so the origin of the word "barbarian" reflects the *ethnocentrism* (attitude that one's group is superior) of the ancient Greeks. *Etymology* (origin and history of a word) is a better choice than *genesis* (origin) because *etymology* is more specific.

8. **partly by globalization/polarized**   It is reasonable that the increased gap between rich and poor is caused *partly by globalization* because globalization might favor those people who have better access to knowledge than those who do not have such access, thus increasing the gap further. The existence of this gap suggests that the world is *polarized* (concentrated around two conflicting positions) into two groups.

9. **of great magnitude/cumulative**   Geologists believe that the "small changes" in the Earth's movement and position are not *of great magnitude* (extent) but never the less have a considerable *cumulative* (increasing by successive addition) effect.

10. **the ultimate/cedes/autonomy**   In the social contract described the individual *cedes* (surrenders possession of something) most of his or her political identity and *autonomy* (freedom) to the state, making it the *ultimate* (representing the greatest possible development) social contract. "Social contract" refers to the idea that society and government function as a result of implicit agreements between them and individuals.

11. **prevent/behemoths/preeminence**   Governments often *prevent* mergers of certain large corporations to prevent monopolies from forming. However, they must also consider whether preventing large mergers could lead to a loss of international competitiveness. The United States government, for example, allowed the merger of *behemoths* (things that are large and powerful) such as Boeing and Lockheed because they believed that European consortiums posed a threat to American *preeminence* (condition of being superior to all others) in the aerospace industry.

12. **Technophiles/insidious/inherently evil**   *Technophiles* (people who are enthusiastic about technology) like to argue that technology must be judged on the use to which it is put. Some people, however, regard computers as a unique technology because of their *insidious* (causing harm in a way that is not apparent) influence on people who use them. Proponents of computers defend them, saying that they are not *inherently* (in a way that exists as an essential characteristic) *evil* but rather play a main role in progress.

13. **(E)**   Earlier the author said, "Considering that it as a subject that one comes to voice, then the postmodernist focus on the critique of identity appears, at first glance, to threaten and close down the possibility that this discourse and practice will allow those who have suffered the crippling effects of colonization and domination to gain or regain a hearing" (lines 17–20). Thus, it is reasonable to infer that the author believes that we should be suspicious of critiques of the "subject" at this time because it is possible that such critiques are at least partially motivated by a desire by the powerful to deny power to the powerless.

14. **(C)**   The author generally approves of postmodernism. For example, she says that "they [practices the postmodern sensibility appropriates] offer forms of empowerment . . ., a moment of positivity through the production and structuring of affective relations." She believes that it is understandable that the underclass are suspicious of the motivation behind the postmodern political project, but she suggests that she believes such suspicions are essentially based on a "misunderstanding of the postmodernist political project."

15. **(A)** The author says, "proteins...help to make our skin particularly waterproof" (line 9).

(B) The author says, "The human versions of some of these genes [that code for proteins that control properties of the skin] encode proteins that help to make our skin particularly waterproof and scuff-resistant" (lines 8–10), and describes these genes as "gene variants" (line 11). She says that although "most of the genes that direct the development of the SC are ancient" (lines 18–19), "the genes undergirding the human SC are . . . distinctive" (line 20). It is reasonable to infer from this that the genes evolved relatively recently because humans evolved bare skin relatively recently.

  (C)   The author says that body hair on the surface of human skin is sparse and fine. However, she says also that it is weak: "[Scientists] have shown that keratins present in human body hair are extremely fragile, which is why these hairs break so easily compared with those of other animals" (lines 29–31).

16. **(B)** The author says, "The human [as opposed to chimp] versions of some of [the genes that code for proteins that control properties of the skin] encode proteins that help to make our skin particularly waterproof and scuff-resistant—critical properties, given the absence of protective fur. This finding implies that the advent of those gene variants contributed to the origin of nakedness by mitigating its consequences" (lines 8–12).

17. **(E)** We can infer that the author does not assume that the literature of people cannot recover its greatness after it has declined because he says, "But beneath all, still lay the restorative elements of the English character, which were to reassert themselves and usher in a new era of literary productiveness, the greatest since the Elizabethan age, and embodying the highest ideals of life to which the race has yet attained" (lines 19–23).

18. **(B)** The author describes how Vedic civilization personified natural elements, creating a mythology. He believes that the main importance of the mythology was the central role it played in the art and ceremonies of the Vedic people, providing "a system of rhetoric"—an organized set of images that allows meaning to be communicated. Although this system had similarities to theology—an organized body of beliefs about God and humanity's relationship to God—it was too vague and changeable to be called a theology.

19. **(B)** The author expresses considerable admiration for Vedic civilization: "It lived simply, rationally, piously, loving all natural joys and delighted with all the instruments of a rude but pure civilization. It saluted without servility the forces of nature" (lines 5–7). However, he also believes that Vedic religion was "less . . . articulate" (line 2) than Greek religion and susceptible to "dark superstitions" (line 19). He also believes that the literature of Vedic civilization failed, like that of most literatures, to develop in a more objective, "scientific" direction.

20. **"It lived simply . . . but pure civilization."** The word "rude" in this context means "undeveloped."

Section 2

1. **(B), (E)** The explanation the soldier is given is most appropriately described as *convoluted* (complicated). *Complicated* has the same meaning in context.

2. **(B), (F)** When a writer goes off the main topic to make *parenthetical* (clarifying or qualifying) remarks, it often becomes tedious. *Qualifying* (limiting) is the closest in meaning to *parenthetical* in this context because it makes sense that a writer would make qualifying remarks parenthetically about his or her major points.

3. **edifices** Law can be described as one of the *edifices* (large abstract structures) created by humanity because it is made of many ideas built up over a long period of time.

4. **a quiescent** *A quiescent* (inactive) state is signaled by "no movement of molecules."

5. **egalitarian/meritocratic** Traditional societies are more socially stratified (arranged into layers) than modern societies because modern societies are more *egalitarian* (characterized by belief in equal right for all people) and *meritocratic* (based on achievement).

6. **ubiquitous/jargon** "A great deal of" signals that scientific terms have been *ubiquitous* (widespread). *Jargon* (specialized language) refers to such scientific terms.

7. **lingua franca/interloper** Malay is a language, so it could have been a *lingua franca* (a language used for communication among peoples speaking different languages). "Superseded" signals that an *interloper* (trespasser) has replaced Malay as the lingua franca.

8. **contentious/reducing/black and white caricature** It makes sense that positions would be polarized (tending toward opposite extremes) on *contentious* (causing quarrels) issues, each side *reducing* the argument of the other to a *black and white caricature* (exaggerated *portrait*). *Black and white caricature* is the best choice with *reducing* because a caricature reduces, or simplifies, complexity.

9. **sovereignty/it follows that/are coterminous** *Sovereignty* (supremacy of authority) makes sense because of the phrase "one central government." Aegis (protection) and influence make some sense but do not make sense with the choices for the other blanks. If a nation and state are defined as stated *it follows that* the people of one nation may inhabit more than one state and the population in one state may belong to one nation. A nation-state, therefore, would be defined in terms of both its geography and its cultural composition, meaning that nation and state *are coterminous* (having the same boundaries).

10. **hypostatize/did not posit/regarded it as a process** "Existing physically in the brain" signals that *hypostatize* (ascribe physical existence to) is the best choice. "But" signals a contrast, so *did not posit* (propose as an explanation) makes sense. "Rather" indicates an alternative, and the best alternative to "physical structure" is *regarded it as a process* because the composition of the ego is under discussion, not whether it is autonomous or not or whether it is illusory or not.

11. **(B)** "Other basins that do have an organic-rich rock layer may not have been buried to sufficient depths to generate natural gas" (lines 5–7).

   (A) "More than one organic-rich rock layer my be deposited in the burial history of some basins with all, one, or none subsiding deep enough to thermally mature to generate petroleum" (lines 12–15).

   (C) "An organic-rich rock layer in some basins may thermally mature to generate mostly natural gas" (lines 8–9). It can be inferred that a basin containing substantial amounts of natural gas is not certain to also contain a roughly equal amount of crude oil because in some cases there is mostly natural gas.

12. **(E)** The author says, "The flowers of the mind, if they can be transplanted at all, often flourish with special vigor on alien soil" (lines 4–5). He then cites several examples to support this statement, including Islam: "Witness the triumphs of Islam in the hands of the Turks and Mughals" (lines 5–6).

13. **(B)** Lamaism is an example of this. The author says, "Lamaism in Tibet and Amidism in Japan, though scholars may regard them as singular perversions, have more vitality than any brand of Buddhism which has existed in India since the seventh century" and "Lamaism is not the teaching of the Buddha travestied by Tibetans but a late form of Indian Buddhism" (lines 8–10 and 14–15).

14. **(A)** The author says, "To beauty men are habitually insensible" (lines 3–4).

   (B) The author says, "Youth in these matters governs maturity, and . . . men . . . will seldom look at the world afresh or use new categories in deciphering it" (lines 17–20).

   (C) The author says, "These high-water marks of aesthetic life may easily be reached under tutelage."

15. **(A)** The author does not discuss art critics or music critics. However, it is likely that he would believe that art critics and music critics, like other people, rely for their judgment to a large extent on taste developed in youth. This can be inferred from several statements: (1) "Youth in these matters governs maturity, and . . . men . . . will seldom look at the world afresh or use new categories in deciphering it" (lines 17–20); (2) "Half our standards come from our first masters, and the other half from our first loves"; (3) "On those warm moments hang all our cold systematic opinions" (line 31).

   (B) This is neither stated nor implied. The author does not distinguish between the ability to appreciate natural and artistic beauty. In lines 24–26, he says, "some . . . appreciations . . . or . . . preference . . . may have revealed unsuspected beauties in art or nature," which shows that he does not make a distinction between the ability to appreciate art and the ability to appreciate nature. Also, there is nothing to suggest that the author believes that any form of beauty can be easily appreciated by anyone.

   (C) The author says "Aesthetic feeling, in different people, may make up a different fraction of life and vary greatly in volume" (lines 1–2).

16. **(E)** Pathogens are agents that cause disease. In the sentence in which the word "pathogens" is used, "cause disease in similar ways" provides a good clue to its meaning.

17. **(D)** "The protein's [CagA's] exact purpose is unclear, but recent work suggests that it can induce stomach epithelial cells to display more receptors to which *H. pylori* attaches" (lines 36–38).

18. **(C)** This can be described as ironic because *Salmonella typhi* spreads through the body by making use of the very system designed to destroy it. It is ironic because there is an incongruity between what is expected—bacteria attack cells in the body, trying to destroy them—and what actually happens—bacteria make use of cells designed to destroy them to multiply safely inside the body.

19. **(C)** "Breaking and Entering: The Art of Bacterial Warfare" is the best title for the passage because "The Art of Bacterial Warfare" aptly describes the focus of the passage—the tactics used by bacteria to attack cells in the body—while "Breaking and Entering" colorfully describes the fact that the bacteria described break into, and some actually enter, healthy cells.

      (A) This is too general. The passage deals with how certain bacteria attack human cells.

      (B) This is too specific. How bacteria attach themselves to host cells is only one aspect of a larger topic.

      (D) The focus is not on diseases.

      (E) The focus is not on what these bacteria have in common.

20. **(A)** "*E. coli* 0157 and *H. pylori* bacteria do not need to enter cells to cause disease" (line 41).

      (B) "At one time, scientists thought that this virulent form of *E. coli* . . . latched onto receptor molecules already present on the host's intestinal cells . . . [but] 0157 actually makes its own receptor and delivers it into the cell" (lines 13–16).

      (C) The fact that all bacteria are not killed by acid in the human stomach can be inferred from "*H. pylori* releases an enzyme called urease that locally counters the stomach's high acidity, which normally kills most bacteria" (lines 32–33).

Practice Test 2

ANSWER SHEET
Practice Test 2

SECTION 1

1. Ⓐ Ⓑ Ⓒ Ⓓ Ⓔ Ⓕ
2. Ⓐ Ⓑ Ⓒ Ⓓ Ⓔ Ⓕ
3. _____
4. _____
5. _____
6. (i) _____
   (ii) _____
7. (i) _____
   (ii) _____
8. (i) _____
   (ii) _____

9. (i) _____
   (ii) _____
   (iii) _____
10. (i) _____
    (ii) _____
    (iii) _____
11. (i) _____
    (ii) _____
    (iii) _____

12. Ⓐ Ⓑ Ⓒ
13. Ⓐ Ⓑ Ⓒ Ⓓ Ⓔ
14. Ⓐ Ⓑ Ⓒ Ⓓ Ⓔ
15. Ⓐ Ⓑ Ⓒ
16. Ⓐ Ⓑ Ⓒ Ⓓ Ⓔ
17. Ⓐ Ⓑ Ⓒ
18. Ⓐ Ⓑ Ⓒ Ⓓ Ⓔ
19. Ⓐ Ⓑ Ⓒ Ⓓ Ⓔ
20. Ⓐ Ⓑ Ⓒ Ⓓ Ⓔ

SECTION 2

1. Ⓐ Ⓑ Ⓒ Ⓓ Ⓔ Ⓕ
2. Ⓐ Ⓑ Ⓒ Ⓓ Ⓔ Ⓕ
3. Ⓐ Ⓑ Ⓒ Ⓓ Ⓔ Ⓕ
4. Ⓐ Ⓑ Ⓒ Ⓓ Ⓔ Ⓕ
5. _____
6. _____
7. (i) _____
   (ii) _____

8. (i) _____
   (ii) _____
9. (i) _____
   (ii) _____
   (iii) _____
10. (i) _____
    (ii) _____
    (iii) _____

11. Ⓐ Ⓑ Ⓒ
12. Ⓐ Ⓑ Ⓒ Ⓓ Ⓔ
13. Ⓐ Ⓑ Ⓒ Ⓓ Ⓔ
14. Ⓐ Ⓑ Ⓒ
15. Ⓐ Ⓑ Ⓒ
16. Ⓐ Ⓑ Ⓒ Ⓓ Ⓔ
17. Ⓐ Ⓑ Ⓒ
18. Ⓐ Ⓑ Ⓒ Ⓓ Ⓔ
19. Ⓐ Ⓑ Ⓒ Ⓓ Ⓔ
20. Ⓐ Ⓑ Ⓒ Ⓓ Ⓔ

SECTION 1

Time: 30 minutes
20 questions

Choose the best answer to each of the following questions in this section.

Fill in the blank in each sentence by selecting <u>two</u> answer choices that fit the overall meaning of the sentence and produce completed sentences that are equivalent in meaning.

---

1. In a cross-cultural study of four hundred pre-industrial societies, social scientist James W. Prescott found that in societies in which little affection is shown to infants, there is a _____ of institutions devoted to organized religion and social hierarchy.
    (A) miscellany
    (B) deluge
    (C) preponderance
    (D) plethora
    (E) shortage
    (F) majority

2. A simplistic _____ of idealism is to assert that because physical reality appears solid and "real" to the senses, no other substances exist.
    (A) refutation
    (B) censure
    (C) antithesis
    (D) equivocation
    (E) rebuttal
    (F) summary

Fill in all of the blanks in the sentences by selecting one entry from the corresponding column of choices in the way that best completes the text.

---

3. Dr. Jack Kevorkian became a subject of controversy in the 1990s by assisting terminally ill people to commit suicide in contravention of Michigan statutes _____ such actions.

justifying
proscribing
presaging
abjuring
substantiating

4. Like most movements in art, surrealism became _____ fairly quickly, but its influence is still pervasive.

atavistic
insolvent
rarefied
enervated
rococo

5. Many contemporary thinkers argue that the theory of evolution solved the philosophical problem of _____—that nature seems to possess inherent goals toward which life moves—by establishing that there is no such purpose, rather merely continuous adaptation by organisms to their habitat.

ontology
eugenics
teleology
speciation
reification

6. In the debate in America concerning whether guns should be more strictly controlled, it has been asserted that comparisons between America and other Western developed countries are (i) _____ because they do not take into consideration the cultural context of American history and values such as the frontier tradition and the (ii) _____ reliance of isolated farmers on guns.

(i)	(ii)
ephemeral	legitimate
dubious	sporadic
invidious	anachronistic

7. The Permanent Court of International Justice ((i) _____called the "World Court") is one of the primary bodies rendering judgments on international law, (ii) _____ disputes between countries in such areas as refugees, resources, and national borders.

(i)	(ii)
euphemistically	facilitating
pedantically	absolving
colloquially	adjudicating

8. Some critics argue that it is a writer's responsibility to (i) _____ the values of society, and that literature that does not do so is (ii) _____ and irresponsible.

(i)	(ii)
inculcate in readers	stupefying
ignore	fulsome
parody	self-indulgent

9. Early Chinese works (i) _____ during the performance of ancestral rites, the ghosts are to be represented by people known as the personators of the dead who are supposed to receive the offerings and be their mouthpieces. (ii) _____ , in the popular view, frequently occurs in India, China, Japan, and Indo-China and is one of the many factors which have contributed to the idea of (iii) _____ .

(i)	(ii)	(iii)
proscribe that	Ritual sacrifice	theism
prescribe that	Obsequies for the dead	incarnation
speculate that	Possession by spirits	reification

10. As does every human endeavor, philosophy involves (i) _____; thus when a philosopher with a different point of view presents a (ii) _____ argument against the view of another philosopher, the latter often gives it only (iii) _____ .

(i)	(ii)	(iii)
cognition	tenuous	superficial criticism
human feelings such as pride	derivative	grudging admiration
collective effort	reasonable	unfeigned praise

11. Stock market (i) _____ are sometimes (ii) _____ , dispensing (iii) _____ advice such as, "The company's shares are likely to rise in the long run, but in the short term there is uncertainty which could affect the long-term prospects of the stock."

(i)	(ii)	(iii)
progenitors	described as Delphic oracles	spurious
prognosticators	portrayed as iconoclasts	apposite
champions	lampooned as plutocrats	enigmatic

*First we must realize that no such institution as the Negro church could rear itself without definite historical foundations. These foundations we can find if we remem-
Line ber that the social history of the Negro did not start in America. He was brought from
(5) a definite social environment—the polygamous clan life under the headship of the chief and the potent influence of the priest. His religion was nature-worship, with profound belief in invisible surrounding influences, good and bad, and his worship was through incantation and sacrifice. The first rude change in this life was the slave ship and the West Indian sugar-fields. The plantation organization replaced the
(10) clan and tribe, and the white master replaced the chief with far greater and more despotic powers. Forced and long-continued toil became the rule of life, the old ties of blood relationship and kinship disappeared, and instead of the family appeared a new polygamy and polyandry, which, in some cases, almost reached promiscuity. It was a terrific social revolution, and yet some traces were retained of the former
(15) group life, and the chief remaining institution was the Priest or Medicine-man. He early appeared on the plantation and found his function as the healer of the sick, the interpreter of the Unknown, the comforter of the sorrowing, the supernatural avenger of wrong, and the one who rudely but picturesquely expressed the longing, disappointment, and resentment of a stolen and oppressed people. Thus, as bard,
(20) physician, judge, and priest, within the narrow limits allowed by the slave system, rose the Negro preacher, and under him the first church was not at first by any means Christian nor definitely organized; rather it was an adaptation and mingling of heathen rites among the members of each plantation, and roughly designated as Voodooism. Association with the masters, missionary effort and motives of expedi-
(25) ency gave these rites an early veneer of Christianity, and after the lapse of many generations the Negro church became Christian.

12. Based on the information in the passage, which of the following would the author be likely to agree with?
    (A) The religious practices of members of plantations brought from Africa were identical.
    (B) The family was the central institution of the society of the Negroes brought from Africa to be slaves.
    (C) One of the factors that encouraged the early church of the Negroes on the plantation to take on a facade of Christianity was to make it more acceptable to the white master of the plantation.

*Note that this passage uses some terminology that is not commonly used today but that was acceptable when it was written (from *The Souls of Black Folk* by W.E.B. Du Bois, 1903).

Egyptian painters laid on broad, flat, uniform washes of color; they did not paint in our sense of the term; they illuminated. Just as in drawing they reduced everything to lines, and almost wholly suppressed the internal modeling, so in adding color they still further simplified their subject by merging all varieties of tone, and all play of light and shadow, in one uniform tint. Egyptian painting is never quite true, and never quite false. Without pretending to the faithful imitation of nature, it approaches nature as nearly as it may; sometimes understating, sometimes exaggerating, sometimes substituting ideal or conventional renderings for strict realities. Water, for instance, is always represented by a flat tint of blue, or by blue covered with zigzag lines in black. The buff and bluish hues of the vulture are translated into bright red and vivid blue. The flesh-tints of men are of a dark reddish brown, and the flesh-tints of women are pale yellow. The colors assigned to each animate and inanimate object were taught in the schools, and their use handed on unchanged from generation to generation. Now and then it happened that a painter more daring than his contemporaries ventured to break with tradition. In the Sixth Dynasty tombs at Deir el Gebrawî, there are instances where the flesh tint of the women is that normally devoted to the depiction of men. At Sakkarah, under the Fifth Dynasty, and at Abû Simbel, under the Nineteenth Dynasty, we find men with skins as yellow as those of the women; while in the tombs of Thebes and Abydos, about the time of Thothmes IV. and Horemheb, there occur figures with flesh-tints of rose-color.

It must not, however, be supposed that the effect produced by this artificial system was grating or discordant. Even in works of small size, such as illuminated manuscripts of *The Book of the Dead*, or the decoration of mummy-cases and funerary coffers, there is both sweetness and harmony of color. The most brilliant hues are boldly placed side by side, yet with full knowledge of the relations subsisting between these hues, and of the phenomena which must necessarily result from such relations. They neither jar together, nor war with each other, nor extinguish each other. On the contrary, each maintains its own value, and all, by mere juxtaposition, give rise to the half-tones which harmonize them.

Select one answer choice for the following questions.

13. The meaning of the word "conventional" as it is used in the first paragraph is most nearly
    (A) artificial
    (B) conformist
    (C) unoriginal
    (D) established by usage
    (E) stereotyped

14. Based on the information in the passage, which of the following techniques would an ancient Egyptian painter have been least likely to use?
    (A) Understatement
    (B) Conventions
    (C) Contrast
    (D) Exaggeration
    (E) Perspective

Consider each of the three choices separately and select all that apply.

15. Based on the information in the passage, which of the following would the author be likely to agree with?
    (A) Knowledge of the conventions of ancient Egyptian art would very probably enhance a person's aesthetic appreciation of it.
    (B) Ancient Egyptian art was handicapped by adherence to conventions passed down from generation to generation.
    (C) Painters of ancient Egypt played a major role in the development of chiaroscuro, the technique of depicting light and dark tones to create an illusion of depth and modeling.

Viewed from a cosmic perspective, Earth is a dry planet yet its oceans are enriched in deuterium by a large factor relative to nebular hydrogen. The question of exogenous delivery of organics and water to Earth and other young planets is of critical
Line importance for understanding planetary systems, and for assessing the prospects for
(5) existence of Earth-like exo-planets. Icy bodies today reside in two distinct reservoirs, the OC and the KB region (divided into the classical KB, the scattered disk, and the detached or extended disk populations). Comets injected into the inner planetary system are classified dynamically as isotropic (LPC or HTC) or ecliptic (Centaur-type, Encke-type, of JFC). Ecliptic comets come from the KB reservoir while the
(10) isotropic comets come from the Oort cloud.

All except Centaur-type comets have the potential of becoming sufficiently bright to obtain sensitive detection of their volatile fraction through high-resolution NIR spectra. Strong gradients in temperature and chemistry in the proto-planetary disk, coupled with dynamical dispersion of an outer disk of icy planetesimals, imply that
(15) comets from the formative phase of the Solar System should have diverse composition. The "Nice" model predicts that comets formed in (and ejected from) the giant-planets' feeding zones probably entered the outer disk, whose subsequent disruption contributed some of the mass impacting Earth during the late heavy bombardment. Comets formed in the outer proto-planetary disk entered both the
(20) Kuiper disk and the OC, though likely in different proportions. However, recent dynamical studies suggest that many Oort cloud comets may have been captured from sibling stars in the Sun's birth cluster, posing additional questions regarding diversity among comets in that reservoir. While orbital parameters can indicate the cosmic storage reservoir for a given comet, identifying its region of origin depends
(25) on quantitative knowledge of its components—dust and ice. The so-called parent volatiles provide the preferred metrics for building taxonomy for cometary ices, but

until recently they were difficult to measure. Secondary (or even tertiary) free radicals are more easily detected and so form the basis of extensive taxonomies that have provided valuable insights. However, these derivative species can have multiple ori-
(30) gins, and these are sometimes poorly constrained, complicating their interpretation. Taxonomies based on native species (parent volatiles) are now beginning to emerge.

Select one answer choice for the following question.

16. The "Nice" model referred to in the passage is most likely
    (A) a theory about the composition of comets in the Oort cloud
    (B) a theory about the origin of the gassy giant planets, such as Jupiter and Saturn
    (C) a theory about the origin of the objects that impacted Earth during the late heavy bombardment
    (D) a theory of the evolution of the Solar System
    (E) a leading hypothesis about how comets disrupted the outer proto-planetary disc, leading to the late heavy bombardment

---

Consider each of the three choices separately and select all that apply.

17. Based on the information in the passage, which of the following is true?
    (A) Astronomers need only to know a comet's orbital parameters to determine its area of origin.
    (B) Based on what scientists now know, it is probable that a significant amount of Earth's water is from comets that impacted on its surface.
    (C) Nearly all of the comets in the Solar System originated well after the Solar System formed.

If poetry in its higher reaches is more philosophical than history, because it presents the memorable types of men and things apart from unmeaning circumstances, so in its primary substance and texture poetry is more philosophical than prose because
Line it is nearer to our immediate experience. Poetry breaks up the trite conceptions des-
(5) ignated by current words into the sensuous qualities out of which those conceptions were originally put together. We name what we conceive and believe in, not what we see; things, not images; souls, not voices and silhouettes. This naming, with the whole education of the senses which it accompanies, subserves the uses of life; in order to thread our way through the labyrinth of objects which assault us, we must make a
(10) great selection in our sensuous experience; half of what we see and hear we must pass over as insignificant, while we piece out the other half with such an ideal comple-ment as is necessary to turn it into a fixed and well-ordered conception of the world. This labor of perception and understanding, this spelling of the material meaning of experience, is enshrined in our workaday language and ideas; ideas which are literally
(15) poetic in the sense that they are "made" (for every conception in an adult mind is a fiction), but which are at the same time prosaic because they are made economically, by abstraction, and for use.

When the child of poetic genius, who has learned this intellectual and utilitarian language in the cradle, goes afield and gathers for himself the aspects of nature, he
(20) begins to encumber his mind with the many living impressions which the intellect rejected, and which the language of the intellect can hardly convey; he labors with his nameless burden of perception, and wastes himself in aimless impulses of emotion and reverie, until finally the method of some art offers a vent to his inspiration, or to such part of it as can survive the test of time and the discipline of expression.

(25) The poet retains by nature the innocence of the eye, or recovers it easily; he disintegrates the fictions of common perception into their sensuous elements, gathers these together again into chance groups as the accidents of his environment or the affinities of his temperament may conjoin them; and this wealth of sensation and this freedom of fancy, which make an extraordinary ferment in his ignorant heart,
(30) presently bubble over into some kind of utterance.

The fullness and sensuousness of such effusions bring them nearer to our actual perceptions than common discourse could come; yet they may easily seem remote, overloaded, and obscure to those accustomed to think entirely in symbols, and never to be interrupted in the algebraic rapidity of their thinking by a moment's pause and
(35) examination of heart, nor ever to plunge for a moment into that torrent of sensation and imagery over which the bridge of prosaic associations habitually carries us safe and dry to some conventional act. How slight that bridge commonly is, how much an affair of trestle and wire, we can hardly conceive until we have trained ourselves to an extreme sharpness of introspection. But psychologists have discovered, what
(40) laymen generally will confess, that we hurry by the procession of our mental images as we do by the traffic of the street, intent on business, gladly forgetting the noise and movement of the scene, and looking only for the corner we would turn or the door we would enter. Yet in our alertest moment the depths of the soul are still dreaming; the real world stands drawn in bare outline against a background of chaos and unrest.
(45) Our logical thoughts dominate experience only as the parallels and meridians make a checkerboard of the sea. They guide our voyage without controlling the waves, which toss forever in spite of our ability to ride over them to our chosen ends. Sanity is a madness put to good uses; waking life is a dream controlled.

Out of the neglected riches of this dream the poet fetches his wares. He dips into
(50) the chaos that underlies the rational shell of the world and brings up some superfluous image, some emotion dropped by the way, and reattaches it to the present object; he reinstates things unnecessary, he emphasizes things ignored, he paints in again into the landscape the tints which the intellect has allowed to fade from it. If he seems sometimes to obscure a fact, it is only because he is restoring an experi-
(55) ence. The first element which the intellect rejects in forming its ideas of things is the emotion which accompanies the perception; and this emotion is the first thing the poet restores. He stops at the image, because he stops to enjoy. He wanders into the bypaths of association because the bypaths are delightful. The love of beauty which made him give measure and cadence to his words, the love of harmony which made
(60) him rhyme them, reappear in his imagination and make him select there also the material that is itself beautiful, or capable of assuming beautiful forms. The link that binds together the ideas, sometimes so wide apart, which his wit assimilates, is most often the link of emotion; they have in common some element of beauty or of horror.

18. The word "philosophical" is used twice in the first paragraph. In each case, its meaning in context is most nearly
    (A) abstract
    (B) reflective
    (C) logical
    (D) capable of arriving at the truth
    (E) incapable of being conclusively proven

19. The most likely reason that the author uses the metaphor of a bridge is to
    (A) dramatically illustrate that the only way in which the truth can be described is through images
    (B) show that imagery can not convey "philosophical" truth
    (C) show that metaphor is the predominant way in which words are created
    (D) make vivid the idea that the language used in everyday life helps people to avoid the turmoil of sensations and images that lie just below the conscious mind
    (E) make clear the idea that our conscious thoughts travel across a vast unexplored sea of churning feelings and images

20. According to the author of this passage, one of the important roles of the poet is to
    (A) enable us to put a name to vague feelings and ideas so that we can better order our world
    (B) help us to experience things directly, unmediated by the intellect
    (C) descend into the part of the mind that is in most people unconscious to bring up important memories
    (D) encourage people to leave behind "the rational shell of the world" in order to appreciate beauty
    (E) help us to formulate our own original images out of our experience

Time: 30 minutes
   20 questions

> Choose the best answer to each of the following questions in this section.

> Fill in the blank in each sentence by selecting <u>two</u> answer choices that fit the overall meaning of the sentence and produce completed sentences that are equivalent in meaning.

1. Because of the vast potential energy available from controlled fusion, scientists have worked hard to make the dream a reality; however, thus far experimenters have succeeded only in producing _____ controlled fusion reactions lasting about one second.
   (A) arbitrary
   (B) illusory
   (C) transient
   (D) ordinary
   (E) anomalous
   (F) short-lived

2. Advances in technology are often purported to indicate progress, but it is possible that some of these advances are actually _____ to the overall improvement of human well-being.
   (A) due
   (B) harmful
   (C) tangential
   (D) extraneous
   (E) inimical
   (F) inured

3. Within an infinitesimal amount of time after its creation, the universe was filled with a _____ of microscopic particles of matter.
   (A) pastiche
   (B) maelstrom
   (C) mélange
   (D) modicum
   (E) surfeit
   (F) mixture

4. Evidence is mounting that although planets might be relatively abundant, it may be rare to find non-gaseous planets in an orbit that is not highly _____ , making it difficult for stable conditions to arise suitable for the advent of life.

(A) idiosyncratic
(B) irregular
(C) precarious
(D) eccentric
(E) elusive
(F) unstable

Fill in all of the blanks in the sentences by selecting one entry from the corresponding column of choices in the way that best completes the text.

---

5. While it is true that some jargon is unnecessary, much of it is used legitimately by experts, especially in _____ fields.

pedantic
esoteric
substantive
prosaic
problematic

6. The advantage of a satellite in a geostationary orbit is that it is always available to receive and transmit, unlike other satellites that periodically "disappear" over the horizon, _____ their signal; such twenty-four-hour availability greatly facilitates communication.

truncating
mitigating
refracting
occluding
enhancing

7. Proponents of expeditions to other solar systems contend that they are (i) _____ because large vessels would contain (ii) _____ that would closely mimic life on Earth, so that the astronauts would be comfortable even if the mission lasted several human generations.

(i)	(ii)
viable	thespians
unrealistic	a microcosm
subversive	an anachronism

8. Consumer advocates often criticize advertising for promoting demand for products that people do not truly need, and for (i) _____ making an objective assessment of the (ii) _____ of products.

(i)	(ii)
distracting consumers from	ephemeral nature
aggrandizing themselves by	Machiavellian market
maligning others by	intrinsic worth

9. In the United States, much of the debate about abortion has (i) _____ into two positions, one camp arguing that it is (ii) _____ and the other asserting a woman's (iii) _____ to make decisions affecting her life.

(i)	(ii)	(iii)
reified	fatuous to support abortion,	whimsical need
crystallized	immoral to kill a fetus,	inviolable right
polarized	an obligation to support abortion,	volition

10. Since cognitive (i) _____ (a condition of conflict between belief and action) produces anxiety, there is a tendency to avoid it by methods such as (ii) _____, which allow one to at least (iii) _____ the effect of the conflict on one's psyche.

(i)	(ii)	(iii)
pathology	antipathy	expiate
discrepancy	rationalization	remedy
dissonance	dissembling	mitigate

Read the passages below, and then answer the questions that follow them based on the information in the passages themselves and in any introductory material or notes. The correct answer may be stated or merely suggested in the passages.

The global average sea level rose between 0.1 m and 0.2 m during the twentieth century and it is projected to rise by another 0.09 m to 0.88 m between 1990 and 2100. But regional specificities must also be taken into account. On the one hand, in the
Line Mediterranean, the increase of sea levels is moderated by the declining freshwater
(5) input (with the decrease of average precipitations) and subsequent seawater density increase. But on the other hand, deltas, islands, coastal wetlands and estuaries are among the most threatened coastal environments in Europe. Also the tidal range is an important factor, with projected sensitivity to a given sea-level rise reaching maximum values in areas with a small tidal range. The Mediterranean is typically an
(10) area of limited tidal range, which suggests that its vulnerability to sea-level rise will be exacerbated.

11. According to the information in the passage, which of the following are true?
    (A) Tides in the Mediterranean generally vary little from high to low tide.
    (B) Changes in average annual precipitation in an area have a negligible effect on sea level.
    (C) Global average sea level might increase less between 1990 and 2100 than it did in the twentieth century.

Great powers and empires are, I would suggest, complex systems, made up of a very large number of interacting components that are asymmetrically organized, which means their construction more resembles a termite hill than an Egyptian pyramid.
Line They operate somewhere between order and disorder—on "the edge of chaos," in
(5) the phrase of the computer scientist Christopher Langton. Such systems can appear to operate quite stably for some time; they seem to be in equilibrium but are, in fact, constantly adapting. But there comes a moment when complex systems "go critical." A very small trigger can set off a "phase transition" from a benign equilibrium to a crisis—a single grain of sand causes a whole pile to collapse, or a butterfly flaps its
(10) wings in the Amazon and brings about a hurricane in southeastern England.

Not long after such crises happen, historians arrive on the scene. They are the scholars who specialize in the study of "fat tail" events—the low-frequency, high-impact moments that inhabit the tails of probability distributions, such as wars, revolutions, financial crashes, and imperial collapses. But historians often misun-
(15) derstand complexity in decoding these events. They are trained to explain calamity in terms of long-term causes, often dating back decades. This is what Nassim Taleb rightly condemned in *The Black Swan* as "the narrative fallacy": the construction of psychologically satisfying stories on the principle of *post hoc, ergo propter hoc*.

Drawing casual inferences about causation is an age-old habit. Take World War I.
(20) A huge war breaks out in the summer of 1914, to the great surprise of nearly everyone. Before long, historians have devised a story line commensurate with the disaster: a treaty governing the neutrality of Belgium that was signed in 1839, the waning of Ottoman power in the Balkans dating back to the 1870s, and malevolent Germans and the navy they began building in 1897. A contemporary version of this fallacy
(25) traces the 9/11 attacks back to the Egyptian government's 1966 execution of Sayyid Qutb, the Islamist writer who inspired the Muslim Brotherhood. Most recently, the financial crisis that began in 2007 has been attributed to measures of financial deregulation taken in the United States in the 1980s.

In reality, the proximate triggers of a crisis are often sufficient to explain the
(30) sudden shift from a good equilibrium to a bad mess. Thus, World War I was actually caused by a series of diplomatic miscalculations in the summer of 1914, the real origins of 9/11 lie in the politics of Saudi Arabia in the 1990s, and the financial crisis was principally due to errors in monetary policy by the U.S. Federal Reserve

and to China's rapid accumulation of dollar reserves after 2001. Most of the fat-tail
(35) phenomena that historians study are not the climaxes of prolonged and deterministic story lines; instead, they represent perturbations, and sometimes the complete
breakdowns, of complex systems.

Select one answer choice for the following questions.

12. The fact that historians have not been able to accurately predict the collapse of
empires (such as the Soviet Union) suggests that
(A) the author is correct in saying that historians tend to identify calamities after
they occur and then retrospectively provide causal explanations for them
(B) the author is correct in his view that historians fail to understand that empires
are complex and that the reasons for their collapse lie quite far in the past
(C) historians have not gathered enough information about empires to be able to
predict their future accurately
(D) the concept of empire is so vague that empires cannot be studied scientifically
(E) historians fail to understand that every empire is by definition in a period of
"phase transitions"

13. *Post hoc, ergo propter hoc* as it is used in line 18 most nearly means
(A) after a certain period of time, therefore because of that period of time
(B) after one event, therefore because of another event
(C) after this, therefore because of this
(D) small causes in the past, therefore great calamities in the present
(E) true in the past, therefore proven even more to be true in the present

---

Consider each of the three choices separately and select all that apply.

14. The author feels that historians
(A) have a tendency to believe that the causes of calamities are in the fairly
distant past
(B) generally feel a need to construct a story that explains how a calamity occurred
as the outcome of a series of events
(C) tend to view empires as complex systems operating "between order and
disorder"

15. Based on the information in the passage, which of the following statements would the author be likely to agree with?
    (A) An event that precedes another event in time does not necessarily cause the event.
    (B) Nearly every historical calamity can be explained as the result of one major event in the quite distant past.
    (C) The causes of major events are often to be found in events that cause an imbalance in a system in equilibrium.

Linguistics may be defined as the scientific study of language. There are many reasons for studying language. For some, language has an intrinsic interest, and different language systems, their history and relationships may be found worth
Line investigating in themselves. Another reason for studying human language—one
(5) which has gained prominence in the last 40 years or so through the work of Noam Chomsky—follows from human beings' innate capacity to acquire language. That is, language reflects mind: by investigating the organization and use of language systems we can gain some understanding of something basic in human nature, in particular regarding human cognitive ability.
(10)   Linguistic determinism refers to the proposition that, if human language reflects the structure of the human mind and all languages share the same basic properties, it follows that human language by its very nature determines how we perceive and organize our experience of the world, and in so doing imposes restrictions on the ways in which we can conceive "reality." In this view language does not reflect
(15) the nature of reality "as it is," but rather our conception of reality, all human beings having been born with an innate capacity to organize the world in a particular way (and that way alone).
     The term linguistic relativity refers to the view that not only does human language in general impose these mental limitations, but that particular languages
(20) impose their own specific limitations. A language, it has been said, is an implicit philosophy of the world, and to speak a particular language is to subscribe to the philosophy it embodies.

Select one answer choice for the following question.

16. Linguistic determinism would most likely be of interest to
    (A) a sophist
    (B) a theologian
    (C) an epistemologist
    (D) a philologist
    (E) a pantheist

17. A person who believes that linguistic relativity is true would probably also believe that
    (A) linguistic determinism is true
    (B) some languages are more sophisticated than others
    (C) the nature of a language greatly affects how a person using that language thinks

An "ideal" cinder cone forms when eruption occurs on flat ground. From deep within the Earth, magma charged with gas (like a carbonated drink) rises through a vertical pipe-shaped conduit and erupts as a fountain of frothy lava that may spray
Line as high as 2,000 feet into the air. As an individual blob of this frothy molten rock flies
(5) through the air, it cools quickly enough to solidify before falling back to Earth. Many gas bubbles remain trapped in the fragments. If small, these fragments of rock are called "cinders," and if larger, "bombs." As eruption continues, cinders accumulate to form a conical hill. Periodically, the flanks of the growing hill may become so steep that lobes and sheets of cinders slide downward. When lava fountaining ends, a sym-
(10) metrical cone-shaped hill, commonly indented by a summit crater, has been added to the landscape. Internally, the cone is a pile of loose cinders in layers that dip away from the volcano's vent in all directions.

During the waning stage of an ideal cinder-cone eruption, the magma has lost most of its gas content. This gas-depleted magma does not fountain but oozes qui-
(15) etly into the crater or beneath the base of the cone as lava. Because it contains so few gas bubbles, the molten lava is denser than the bubble-rich cinders. Thus, it burrows out along the bottom of the cinder cone, lifting the less-dense cinders like a cork on water, and advances outward, creating a lava flow around the cone's base. When the eruption ends, a symmetrical cone of cinders sits at the center of a surrounding pad
(20) of lava.

Field studies conducted by U.S. Geological Survey and Northern Arizona University scientists suggest that Red Mountain grew on a nearly flat surface that may have sloped gently to the north. However, little else about this volcano mimics the features of an ideal cinder cone. When viewed from above, Red Mountain is a U-shaped
(25) landform open to the west, rather than a symmetrical cone. The base of the U is a curving ridge that forms the highest part of the mountain. The nearly half-mile-long arms of the U slope down to the west and merge with the gently rolling surface of the Red Mountain lava flow.

By carefully measuring the orientation of cinder layers over all parts of Red
(30) Mountain, geologists have mapped a radial pattern of layers, dipping away from the middle of the U in all directions. At the amphitheater, all the exposed layers dip uniformly to the northeast. This pattern indicates that the vent is somewhere in the middle of the U and not at the amphitheater.

The shape of Red Mountain and its overall pattern of cinder layers raises the
(35) question of why a symmetrical cone was not created around the vent at the center
of the U. Three possible explanations are:

- If the lava-fountaining phase of eruption occurred during a time of sustained wind
blowing from west to east, most cinders could have been blown eastward creating
the asymmetrical shape of Red Mountain. However, eruptions of the type that
(40) built Red Mountain usually last several years to a decade or longer, and it seems
unlikely that a westerly wind could have persisted for such a period of time.
- Perhaps the conduit through which magma rose to the surface was inclined eastward enough to give the same effect as a westerly wind, but this seems unlikely
because the driving force for rising magma is the buoyancy of very hot volcanic
(45) gases. Like a cork released in water, such gases tend to rise vertically rather than
follow an inclined path.
- The most likely possibility is that the waning-stage lava flow of the Red Mountain
eruption rafted the western section of the cinder cone away, like wood on flowing
water. When gas-poor molten lava burrows its way outward beneath a cinder cone,
(50) it may either leave the cone undisturbed or carry pieces piggyback, literally float-
ing pieces on the surface of the denser lava.

Many examples of both situations are known worldwide; a spectacular example of
rafting is found at Sunset Crater National Monument, northeast of Flagstaff. At Red
Mountain, geologists have discovered several outcrops of layered cinder deposits,
(55) some of which are hundreds of feet wide and tens of feet thick, at the top of the lava
flow. Typically, these "floaters" form hills on the surface of an otherwise fairly flat
flow. Apparently, molten lava oozed out beneath the west base of Red Mountain and
rafted away much of that side of the cinder cone, creating its U shape.

Select one answer choice for the following questions.

---

18. The word "ideal" as it is used in the first paragraph most nearly means
    (A) perfect
    (B) symmetrical
    (C) created as a result of theorized stages of development
    (D) able to exist for millions of years with little change
    (E) existing only in a Platonic realm of ideal forms

19. The hypotheses and supporting evidence put forward to explain why a symmetrical cone was not created around the vent at the center of the U that forms Red Mountain could most accurately be described as
    (A) unconvincing
    (B) almost completely persuasive
    (C) not tenable because based on evidence not applicable to the case of the Red Mountain cinder cone
    (D) ingenious but almost entirely speculative
    (E) reasonably convincing but based to some extent on conjecture and on comparisons with similar phenomenon

20. The author of the passage is most likely
    (A) a university geology professor writing in a general geology journal
    (B) a graduate student summarizing a research paper she wrote for a graduate level geology seminar
    (C) a volcanologist writing in a specialist volcanology journal
    (D) a professional geologist writing in a magazine aimed at interested laypersons
    (E) a layperson who has studied the literature on cinder cones and who has reached a conclusion about how Red Mountain formed

ANSWER KEY
Practice Test 2

Section 1

1. C, F
2. A, E
3. proscribing
4. enervated
5. teleology
6. dubious/legitimate
7. colloquially/adjudicating
8. inculcate in readers/
   self-indulgent
9. prescribe that/Possession by
   spirits/incarnation
10. human feelings such as pride/
    reasonable/grudging admiration
11. prognosticators/described as
    Delphic oracles/enigmatic
12. C
13. D
14. E
15. A
16. D
17. B
18. D
19. D
20. B

Section 2

1. C, F
2. B, E
3. C, F
4. B, D
5. esoteric
6. occluding
7. viable/a microcosm
8. distracting consumers from/
   intrinsic worth
9. polarized/immoral to kill a
   fetus,/inviolable right
10. dissonance/rationalization/
    mitigate
11. A, C
12. A
13. C
14. A, B
15. A, C
16. C
17. A, C
18. C
19. E
20. D

SCORING GUIDE

CORRECT ANSWERS	SCORE
1–6	VERY POOR
7–12	POOR
13–18	BELOW AVERAGE
19–24	AVERAGE
25–30	GOOD
31–36	VERY GOOD
37–40	EXCELLENT

ANSWER EXPLANATIONS

Section 1

1. **(C), (F)** *Preponderance* (majority in number) and *majority* are synonymous in context and make good sense in the sentence. The sentence refers to a study that showed a correlation between affection shown to infants and the existence of certain institutions.

2. **(A), (E)** "Physical reality appears solid and 'real'" signals that *refutation* (disproof of opponent's argument) of idealism is referred to. In context *rebuttal* (response with contrary evidence) is nearly synonymous with *refutation*.

3. **proscribing** Dr. Kevorkian "became a subject of controversy," so it makes sense that his actions were "in contravention" of statutes *proscribing* (outlawing) such actions.

4. **enervated** "But its influence is still pervasive" signals a contrast, so *enervated* (weakened) is the best choice.

5. **teleology** The clause "that nature seems to possess inherent goals toward which life moves" provides a definition of the word *teleology*.

6. **dubious/legitimate** The sentence refers to factors affecting America that make comparisons of its situation with those of other Western developed countries *dubious* (doubtful). The *legitimate* (reasonable) reliance of isolated farmers on guns is one of these factors.

7. **colloquially/adjudicating** The Permanent Court of International Justice is *colloquially* (in a way that is typical of informal speech) called the "World Court." "Rendering judgments on international law" signals that this involves *adjudicating* (studying and settling a dispute) disputes between countries.

8. **inculcate in readers/self-indulgent** "Responsibility" signals that *inculcate* (impress in the mind) *in readers* is the best choice. "Does not do so" signals that *self-indulgent* (related to excessive gratification of desires) is the best choice.

9. **prescribe that/Possession by spirits/incarnation** Early Chinese works *prescribe that* (set down as a guide that) ghosts are to be represented by "personators" of the

dead. It makes sense that belief in *possession by spirits* contributed to the idea of *incarnation* (act of assuming a human body and nature) because both involve a spirit inhabiting a body.

10. **human feelings such as pride/reasonable/grudging admiration**   Philosophy involves *human feelings such as pride*. When one philosopher presents another philosopher with a *reasonable* argument against that philosopher's own view, the latter often is only *grudging admiration* because, although he knows it has merit, his feelings about himself are involved.

11. **prognosticators/described as Delphic oracles/enigmatic**   Stock market *prognosticators* (people who make a prediction through use of present conditions as a guide) are sometimes *described as Delphic oracles* (in Greek mythology, the oracle of Apollo at Delphi; an oracle is a person who foresees the future and gives advice), dispensing *enigmatic* (deeply puzzling) advice. The Delphic oracle was known for giving advice that could not be clearly interpreted.

12. **(C)**   The author says, "Association with the masters, missionary effort and motives of expediency gave these rites an early veneer of Christianity" (lines 24–25). It can be inferred that "motives of expediency" refers to the fact that people involved with the early church were motivated to some degree by a desire to make the white plantation master happy by introducing into their church some superficial elements of his religion, Christianity. In context, "veneer" and "facade" are synonyms.

    (A)   The author says, "the first church was . . . an adaptation and mingling of heathen rites among the members of each plantation" (lines 21–24). This shows that religious practices differed.

    (B)   The author says, "He [the Negro] was brought from a definite social environment—the polygamous clan life under the leadership of the chief and the potent influence of the priest" (lines 4–6). Also, he says "the old ties of blood relationship and kinship disappeared, and instead of the family appeared a new polygamy and polyandry" (lines 11–13).

13. **(D)**   The word "conventional" is used in this sentence: "Without pretending . . . strict realities" (lines 6–8). In context "conventional" means established by usage. "Conventional" is used here to describe renderings that do not follow "strict realities," so we can infer that they are created by painters over time and come to be understood and accepted.

14. **(E)**   Perspective is not mentioned, whereas the author describes the use of the other technique by Egyptian painters.

15. **(A)**   The author describes a number of conventions used by Egyptian painters, so it would be difficult for a person not familiar with these conventions to appreciate the beauty of Egyptian painting.

    (B)   After describing how artistic conventions were passed down from generation to generation, the author says, "It must not, however, be supposed that the effect produced by this artificial system was grating or discordant" (lines 21–22). The author then goes on to describe the positive qualities of Egyptian painting. There is no suggestion that artists were handicapped by the convention.

    (C)   There is nothing in the passage to suggest this.

16. **(D)** "The 'Nice' model predicts that comets formed in (and ejected from) the giant-planets' feeding zones probably entered the outer disk, whose subsequent disruption contributed some of the mass impacting Earth during the late heavy bombardment" (lines 16–19). It can be inferred that the "Nice" model is a theory about the evolution of the Solar System by the fact that it makes predictions about how various bodies in the Solar System originated and their subsequent history. The author is discussing what is known and theorized about the origin and history of comets, so it makes sense that he would refer to a model used by scientists to predict the behavior of objects in the Solar System. Choices A and E are too specific for this purpose, and choices B and C are not directly relevant to the main topic, comets.

17. **(B)** "The 'Nice' model predicts that comets . . . probably entered the outer disk, whose subsequent disruption contributed some of the mass impacting Earth during the late heavy bombardment" (lines 16–19). It can be inferred that "the late heavy bombardment" refers to a period when many objects such as comets hit the Earth. Since comets are made up of a great deal of water, it makes sense that a significant amount of Earth's water is from comets.

    (A) "While orbital parameters can indicate the cosmic storage reservoir for a given comet, identifying its region of origin depends on quantitative knowledge of its components"(lines 23–25).

    (C) The author is concerned with "comets from the formative phase of the Solar System" (line 15), which signals that a significant number (and perhaps a large number) of comets originated early in the formation of the Solar System. Also, the author says, "many Oort cloud comets may have been captured from sibling stars in the Sun's birth cluster" (lines 21–22), which suggests that a lot of comets originated fairly early in the formation of the Solar System.

18. **(D)** The author says that "poetry in its higher reaches is more philosophical than history . . . because it presents the memorable types of men and things apart from unmeaning circumstances" (lines 1–2). This suggests that the author believes poetry is better able than history to arrive at the truth about people and things because it portrays them in an ideal form that has general applicability rather then being tied to particular conditions or situations. Also, he says, "poetry is more philosophical than prose because it is nearer to our immediate experience" (lines 3–4). He then goes on to explain how poetry helps us to come closer to our immediate experience that abstract thought and ordinary language separate us from. In this sense poetry helps us arrive at the truth.

19. **(D)** The author says, "The fullness and . . . some conventional art" (lines 31–37). The author uses the metaphor of a bridge to illustrate the idea that people who think mostly in symbols rely on those symbols and what they normally associate with them to avoid thinking about the chaos of sensation and images that lies just below conscious logical thought.

20. **(B)** Throughout the passage, the author stresses that abstract thought separates us from immediate experience and that poetry brings us close to immediate experience. The author says that the poet "disintegrates the fictions of common perception into their sensuous elements" (lines 25–26) and that "the fullness and sensuousness of

such effusions [i.e., poetry] bring them nearer to our actual perception than common discourse could come" (lines 31–32).

(C)   The author does say that the poet uses the "neglected riches" (line 49) of the mind's images. However, this does not mean that he believes that the poet goes into the unconscious mind. Also, the author's concern is not with memories but with images and emotions.

Section 2

1. **(C), (F)**   "However" signals that scientists have not succeeded in making long-lasting fusion reactions. They have produced only *transient* (short-lived) reactions. *Short-lived* is synonymous with *transient* in context.

2. **(B), (E)**   "But" signals a contrast with "progress," so it makes sense that some of the advances purported (claimed) to bring overall progress are really *harmful* to human well-being. *Inimical* (harmful) is synonymous with *harmful* in context.

3. **(C), (F)**   *Modicum* (limited quantity) makes sense, but there is no other similar word. The same is true of *surfeit*. *Mélange* (mixture) and *mixture* are synonymous in context and make good sense in the sentence.

4. **(B), (D)**   "Making it difficult for stable conditions to arise" signals that the orbits are highly *irregular*. *Eccentric* (irregular) has the same meaning as *irregular* in context. Non-gaseous planets in an orbit that is fairly regular ("not highly eccentric") may be rare, leading to the conclusion that conditions suitable for the advent of life may not be easily created.

5. **esoteric**   "Used legitimately by experts" signals that jargon can be used in *esoteric* (known only to a few) fields.

6. **occluding**   Satellites not in geostationary orbit "disappear" over the horizon at times, *occluding* (blocking) their signal.

7. **viable/a microcosm**   It is reasonable that proponents of expeditions to other solar systems would argue that they are *viable* (practicable). The reason they give is that vessels would contain *a microcosm* (small world) so that astronauts would be comfortable on very long journeys.

8. **distracting consumers from/intrinsic worth**   Advertising is criticized for promoting demand for unneeded products, so it makes sense that it would also be criticized for *distracting consumers from* making an objective assessment of the *intrinsic worth* (inherent value) of products.

9. **polarized/immoral to kill a fetus,/inviolable right**   "Two positions" signals that *polarized* (tending toward opposite extremes) is the best choice. *Immoral to kill a fetus* and *inviolable right* (right that is safe from violation) are the only two choices that constitute positions at two extremes.

10. **dissonance/rationalization/mitigate**   A condition of conflict between belief and action" defines cognitive *dissonance* (conflict). *Rationalization* (act of providing self-satisfying but incorrect reasons for something) is a better choice than "dissembling" because rationalization can *mitigate* (make less severe) the effect of the conflict on a person's psyche.

11. **(A)** "The Mediterranean is typically an area of limited tidal range" (lines 9–10). This means that there is generally relatively little variation between water height at low tide and water height at high tide in the Mediterranean area.

(C) The author says, "the global average sea level rose between 0.1 meter and 0.2 meter during the twentieth century and it is projected to rise by another 0.09 meter to 0.88 meter between 1990 and 2100."

(B) "In the Mediterranean, the increase of sea levels is moderated by the declining freshwater input (with the decrease of average precipitations)" (lines 3–5). This shows that precipitation has a significant effect on sea levels.

12. **(A)** One of the author's main contentions is that "[historians] are trained to explain calamity in terms of long-term causes" (lines 15–16). He says they often draw "casual inferences about causation" (line 19) and "[devise] a story line commensurate with the disaster" (lines 21–22). The author believes that empires are "complex systems" (line 1) that operate "on the edge of chaos" (line 4), so it makes sense that historians have not been able to predict their collapse because they do not concentrate on studying such systems, looking for indications that they have "gone critical."

13. **(C)** The author describes the "narrative fallacy" of "[constructing] psychologically satisfying stories on the principle" (lines 17–18). Immediately after this he says, "Drawing casual inferences about causation is an age-old habit" (line 19). We can infer that the principle states that an event following another event in time is necessarily caused by that other event.

14. **(A)** The author says, "[Historians] are trained to explain calamity in terms of long-term causes, often dating back decades" (lines 15–16). He then gives two examples of historians explaining calamities as a result of events in the fairly distant past.

(B) In addition to what he says about historians mentioned in choice A, the author says they "[construct] psychologically satisfying stories on the principle of *post hoc, ergo propter hoc*" (line 18) and "[devise] a story line commensurate with the disaster" (lines 21–22).

(C) There is nothing in the passage to suggest that the author believes historians view empires as complex systems. Indeed, most of what he says suggests that they do not take this view.

15. **(A)** The author says, "This is what Nassim Taleb rightly condemned…as 'the narrative fallacy': the construction of psychologically satisfying stories on the principle of *post hoc; ergo propter hoc*" (lines 16–18).

(C) The author says, "the proximate triggers of a crisis are often sufficient to explain the sudden shift from a good equilibrium to a bad mess" (lines 29–30).

16. **(C)** The author says that linguistic determinism is the idea that language "determines how we perceive and organize our experience of the world" (lines 12–13) and "does not reflect the nature of reality 'as it is,' but rather our conception of reality" (lines 14–15). Since an epistemologist studies the origin and nature of knowledge, he or she would be interested in linguistic determinism because it is an idea about how human beings come to have notions about the nature of reality that we call knowledge. Choices (A), (B), (D), and (E) all might have some interest in linguistic determinism, but it would probably not be central to their investigations or theorizing.

17. **(A)** A person who believes that linguistic relativity is true would almost certainly also believe that linguistic determinism is true because linguistic relativity is the idea that language determines how we think, an idea that is also part of the notion of linguistic relativity.

   (C) The author says that according to linguistic relativity "a language . . . is an implicit philosophy of the world, and to speak a particular language is to subscribe to the philosophy it embodies" (lines 20–22).

    (B) There is nothing in the passage to suggest this.

18. **(C)** The author is describing how a cinder cone is created, going through stages of development theorized by scientists.

19. **(E)** The hypothesis is based on quite well understood phenomena and is a reasonable conjecture to explain why a symmetrical cone was not created around the vent at the center of the U. Also, similar processes have been observed elsewhere.

20. **(D)** The passage is written in an authoritative but not overly technical manner, so it is likely that it was written by a professional geologist writing for interested laypersons. Clues that the author is not writing for other scientists are that some terms and phenomena are explained (an example of this is "like a carbonated drink" (line 2) and the technical terms for certain things are given, notably "cinders" and "bombs."

   (E) This makes some sense but is not as good of a choice as D) because a layperson would be unlikely to demonstrate such familiarity with the complexities and underlying principles of the phenomena described.

   (A), (B), and (C) are unlikely because the article is not highly technical and explains certain things that would not have to be explained to a geologist, to a graduate student in geology, or to a volcanologist.

GRE Dictionary

The following is a list of words that are likely to appear on the GRE. Refer to this list when you encounter a word whose meaning you do not know. The list can also be used as the foundation of a vocabulary study program.

The meanings given are the ones most likely to apply in the case of the GRE. You should consult a good dictionary if you need a fuller definition of a word.

Some frequently used terms, such as "quantum leap," have been included, as well as some common foreign words and phrases that are often used in academic writing.

A

abandon N. total lack of inhibition
The normally conservative executive danced with *abandon* at the party.

abase V. to humble, disgrace
The commoner *abased* himself before his king.

abash V. embarrass
Grace was *abashed* by all the fuss her family made about her birthday.

abatement N. decrease, reduction
We were relieved at the *abatement* of the hurricane.

abdicate V. to give up a position, right, or power
The aging king *abdicated* in favor of his son.

aberrant ADJ. deviating from what is normal
The student's behavior was considered *aberrant*.

aberration N. something different from the usual or normal
Getting a "D" was an *aberration* for the normally excellent student.

abet V. to aid, act as an accomplice
Mr. Harris said that he refuses to *abet* the misconduct of his colleagues.

abeyance N. temporary suppression or suspension
Hold your judgment in *abeyance* until we have all the facts of the case.

abhor V. to loathe, detest
Tim *abhors* the idea of killing animals.

abhorrent ADJ. disgusting, repellent, loathsome
The group's values are considered *abhorrent* by most people.

abject ADJ. miserable, pitiful
The peasants live in *abject* poverty.

abjure V. to reject, abandon formally
The president *abjured* any wrongdoing by members of his administration.

ablution N. act of cleansing
"You'd better shorten your morning *ablutions* or you'll be late for school," Clara's mom said.

abnegation N. self-denial
The religion encourages its followers to practice *abnegation* periodically.

abolitionist N. one who opposes the practice of slavery
Abolitionists in the northern states of the United States helped rid that country of slavery.

abomination N. abhorrence; a cause of disgust
Torture is regarded as an *abomination*.

aboriginal ADJ. being the first of its kind in a region
The *aboriginal* people of Australia traditionally hold a nighttime festival called a "corroboree."

abortive ADJ. interrupted while incomplete
Scientists studied the *abortive* flight of the rocket to determine what had gone wrong.

abrade V. to wear off or down by scraping or rubbing
Millions of years of erosion had *abraded* the hillside.

abridge V. to condense, shorten
The long novel was *abridged* to make it easier for people to read.

abrogate V. to abolish or invalidate by authority
The president has the power to *abrogate* the agreement by executive order.

abscission N. act of cutting; natural separation of a leaf or other part of a plant
The botanist is studying the process of *abscission* in the Norway maple.

abscond V. to depart secretly
The treasurer *absconded* with the funds.

absolutism N. a form of government in which all power is vested in a single authority
Moral *absolutism* holds that there are absolute moral standards by which moral questions can be judged.

absolve V. to forgive, free from blame
The priest *absolved* the woman's sins.

abstemious ADJ. moderate in appetite
Be an *abstemious* eater if you want to be thin.

abstinence N. the giving up of certain pleasures
The priest urged the man to practice sexual *abstinence*.

abstract ADJ. theoretical; not concrete
The plan is fine in the *abstract*; the problem will be carrying it out in reality.

abstract N. statement that summarizes the important points of a text
John wrote an *abstract* of Professor Mill's study of green algae.

abstraction N. act or result of considering something independently of its qualities

It's wise to not use too many *abstractions* like "freedom" and "goodness" in your writing without defining them.

abstruse ADJ. difficult to comprehend
The mathematical equation was so *abstruse* no one in the class could understand it.

abysmal ADJ. very bad
Amanda's performance on the test was so *abysmal* that she dropped the subject.

academic ADJ. having no practical purpose, theoretical
Researchers argue that the discovery will be of more than *academic* interest.

accede V. to express approval; agree to
"If I *accede* to your request for a favor, the other employees will be angry with me," the boss said.

accessible ADJ. attainable, available; approachable
Students like teachers who are *accessible* so they can ask them questions.

accessory N. attachment, ornament; accomplice, partner
Liz was named as an *accessory* because she drove the car to the scene of the crime.

acclaim N. loud applause, approval
The novelist won *acclaim* for her portrayal of life in ancient Rome.

accolade N. praise, distinction
The highest *accolade* a teacher can win is the appreciation of his students.

accommodate V. to allow for, bring into harmony
The teacher organizes his class so that the abilities and interests of each student are *accommodated*.

accordance N. agreement
Since we are in *accordance* on this issue, we can move on to the next item for discussion.

accost V. to approach and speak to someone
She doesn't like being *accosted* by strangers on the street.

accretion N. growth in size or increase in amount
The steady *accretion* in the federal budget is a concern to many citizens.

accrue V. to accumulate, grow by additions
Compound interest helps your savings to *accrue* quickly.

acculturation N. adoption of the cultural patterns of another group
The process of *acculturation* is usually easier for young immigrants than for old immigrants.

acerbic ADJ. bitter, sharp in taste or temper
Late night talk show hosts often make *acerbic* comments about current events.

acidulous ADJ. sour in taste or manner; sharp; caustic
His *acidulous* criticism of the novel was labeled as unfair by other critics.

acknowledge V. recognize; admit
I was forced to *acknowledge* that he was a better tennis player after he beat me three times in a row.

acme N. highest point; summit; zenith
John considered winning the Pulitzer Prize to be the *acme* of his career in journalism.

acoustics N. scientific study of sound; the total effect of a sound
The orchestra refused to play in the hall because of its poor *acoustics*.

acquiesce V. to agree without protesting
The people *acquiesced* to the dictator's demands.

acquiescent ADJ. disposed or willing to agree without protesting
Management was *acquiescent* to the workers' demands.

acquittal N. release from blame
The jury voted for *acquittal* after concluding that the woman was innocent of the crime.

acrid ADJ. harsh, bitter
The lemon left an *acrid* taste in my mouth.

acrimonious ADJ. disposed to bitterness and animosity
The dispute was *acrimonious*.

acrimony N. bitterness, animosity
The fight for the presidential nomination caused *acrimony* within the political party.

acronym N. a word formed from the initial letters of a name or series of words
Some *acronyms*—such as "radar"—are so common that we tend to forget that they are *acronyms*.

acuity N. sharpness
Some people are born with excellent visual *acuity*.

acumen N. sharpness of insight
Some people believe that business *acumen* can only be learned in the "school of hard knocks."

acute ADJ. sharp, pointed
Jill has an *acute* sense of taste.

adage N. old saying or proverb
Everyone has heard the *adage* "Haste makes waste."

adamant ADJ. uncompromising, unyielding
The prime minister is *adamant* that she will not resign.

adapt V. to accommodate, adjust
Life on earth frequently must *adapt* to changing climatic conditions.

adduce V. to cite as an example as a means of proof
The lawyer *adduced* his client's good standing in the community as evidence of her good character.

adhere V. to cling or follow without deviation
Some people criticize schools because they encourage students to *adhere* unthinkingly to rules.

adherent N. follower
A debate broke out between groups of the religious leader's *adherents* with different views.

ad hoc ADJ. for the present purpose only
An *ad hoc* committee was formed by the school to investigate the growing problem of student lateness to class.

ad hominem ADJ. appealing to prejudice or passions; attacking one's adversary rather than his or her argument
The debate moderator warned participants that she would not tolerate *ad hominem* arguments.

ad infinitum ADV. forever; without limit
Mathematicians believe that pi represented as a decimal continues *ad infinitum*.

adjacent ADJ. next to
My office is *adjacent* to a supermarket.

adjudicate V. to study and settle a dispute
The chief umpire was called in to *adjudicate* the dispute during the baseball game.

adjunct N. something added, attached, or joined
The army officer was assigned as an *adjunct* to advise the civilian government agency.

admonish V. to caution or reprimand
Children who misbehave in public should be *admonished* by their parents.

admonition N. mild reproof
The student received an *admonition* for being a few minutes late to class.

ad nauseum ADV. to a disgusting or ridiculous degree
The issue has been debated *ad nauseum*.

adobe ADJ. relating to sun-dried brick of clay and straw
The *adobe* houses in that area were built over 300 years ago.

adroit ADJ. skillful
With an *adroit* move, the wrestler pinned his opponent.

adulation N. high praise
The writer won *adulation* for his masterly biography of George Washington.

adulterate V. to corrupt or make impure
Be careful not to drink water that has been *adulterated*.

adumbrate V. to sketch in a shadowy way; foreshadow
The theory was *adumbrated* in his early work, but only now he has clearly outlined it.

advent N. coming or arrival
The *advent* of football season is greeted with enthusiasm by football fans.

adventitious ADJ. added from without
The architect confirmed that the house was Colonial, without *adventitious* later additions.

adversarial ADJ. antagonistic; competitive
I would prefer that we have a cooperative relationship rather than an *adversarial* one.

adverse ADJ. unfavorable, unlucky, harmful
The investigators gave an *adverse* report on the governor's conduct.

advocate V. to speak or write in favor of something
The speaker *advocated* better funding of public education.

advocate N. person who pleads for
Many scientists are *advocates* for increased spending on basic scientific research.

aegis N. protection; sponsorship; shield
Negotiations are being conducted under the *aegis* of the United Nations.

aerial ADJ. having to do with the air
Aerial warfare was a major factor in determining the outcome of World War II.

aerie N. nook or nest built high in the air
The eagle kept her young safe in an *aerie* on the mountain.

aerodynamic ADJ. relating to objects moving through the air
Engineers who design cars take into consideration *aerodynamic* factors.

aesthetic ADJ. pertaining to beauty or art
The town council banned billboards for *aesthetic* reasons.

aesthetic N. guiding principle in art
Every new movement in the arts has its own *aesthetic*.

affable ADJ. pleasant to speak to; approachable
The affable teacher is popular with students and fellow teachers.

affectation N. artificial behavior to impress others
Tom's *affectation* is that he adopts a high-class English accent.

affected ADJ. pretentious, phony
His fake-sounding accent made him seem *affected*.

affective ADJ. relating to the emotions
In life, *affective* skills are often as important as intellectual skills.

affinity N. fondness, liking; similarity
The young people's *affinity* for each other was so strong that they spent nearly all their free time together.

affirm V. to make a positive assertion; confirm
The new citizens *affirmed* their loyalty to the country.

affirmation N. confirmation; positive assertion
The couple made an *affirmation* of their love for one another.

afflatus N. creative impulse; divine inspiration
The novelist at the writing workshop says that it is better to start writing than to wait for divine *afflatus* because that may never arrive.

affluent ADJ. rich; abundant
Affluent people and poor people often live in different areas of a town.

affront N. personal offense, insult
The president of the company regards the criticism of his employees as an *affront*.

aficionado N. an enthusiastic admirer
A wine *aficionado*, Bob can tell how good a wine is with one sip.

a fortiori ADV. for a still stronger reason
"But I do not feel that I and my fellow citizens have a religious duty to sacrifice our lives in war on behalf of our own state, and, *a fortiori*, I do not feel that we have an obligation or a right to kill and maim citizens of other states or to devastate their land." (Arnold Toynbee)

agenda N. plan, schedule
The *agenda* for the meeting says that lunch is at 12:30 P.M.

aggrandize V. to make larger or greater
During the nineteenth century many Americans wanted the country to do things to *aggrandize* itself.

aggregate ADJ. relating to a collective mass or sum; relating to a total
The *aggregate* wealth of a country includes public as well as private possessions and resources.

aggrieve V. to afflict; to distress
I am *aggrieved* by your refusal to apologize for your misconduct

agile ADJ. well-coordinated, nimble
Gymnasts should be very *agile*.

agitation N. commotion, excitement; uneasiness
The nightly bombings were causing *agitation* in the children.

agnostic N. one who doubts that people can know god
Many scientists are *agnostics*.

agnostic ADJ. non-committal
Larry is *agnostic* on the question of whether war is ever justified.

agrarian ADJ. relating to the land and its cultivation
The country has a predominantly *agrarian* economy.

alacrity N. cheerful willingness, eagerness; speed
We were happy when the clerk replaced the faulty cartridge with *alacrity*.

albedo N. the proportion of incident radiation reflected by a surface
Fresh snow has a very high *albedo*.

albeit CONJ. even though; notwithstanding; although
There is sufficient food, *albeit* at high prices.

alchemical ADJ. seemingly magical process of change
Psychologists say that love produces *alchemical* changes in personality.

alchemy N. medieval chemical philosophy based on changing metal into gold; seemingly magical process of change
Alchemy was the forerunner of the modern science of chemistry.

algorithm N. a problem-solving procedure
The intelligence officers are trying to find the correct *algorithm* to break the enemy code.

alias N. assumed name
Many actors use *aliases* or change their name legally.

alien N. person not included in a group; outsider
It took the *alien* several years to adjust to his new country.

alien ADJ. strange
The astronauts stepped onto the *alien* surface of Mars.

alienated ADJ. distanced, estranged
His extreme policies have created a large group of *alienated* voters.

alienation N. being separated; feeling of detachment from the world or society
Alienation is a major problem in large, modern societies.

aligned ADJ. precisely adjusted; committed to one side
During the Cold War many countries were *aligned* to either the Soviet Union or the United States.

allay V. to lessen, ease, or soothe
The call from her friend *allayed* the mother's fear about her daughter's safety.

allegiance N. loyalty
He pledged his *allegiance* to his new country.

allegorical ADJ. characteristic of symbolic representation
Allegorical stories are not nearly as popular now as they were in the Middle Ages.

allegory N. symbolic representation
In literature a voyage is often used as an *allegory* for the journey through life.

alleviate V. to relieve, improve partially
Coffee was used by the Aztecs to *alleviate* the effects of illness.

alliteration N. repetition of the beginning sounds of words
The phrase "the great and the good" uses *alliteration*.

allocation N. allowance, portion
The political party disputed its *allocation* of votes in the national assembly.

alloy N. a combination; a mixture of two or more metals
Steel is an *alloy* of iron, carbon, and other substances.

allude V. to make an indirect reference to
Don't *allude* to something in your writing unless you're confidant your readers will be familiar with it.

allure N. the power to entice by charm
Vickie bought a new dress to add to her *allure*.

alluring ADJ. enticing
The child found the chocolate too *alluring* to resist.

allusion N. indirect reference
His *allusion* to an earlier character in his work was understood by readers familiar with his earlier books.

alluvial ADJ. relating to *alluvium*, that is, sediment that is deposited by flowing water
Farmers like the area's rich *alluvial* soil.

aloof ADJ. detached, indifferent
The new student remained *aloof* from the other students.

altercation N. noisy dispute
The *altercation* became so serious that someone called the police.

alter ego N. a second self; a perfect substitute or deputy

The president's chief adviser acts as his *alter ego* during his absence.

altruism N. unselfish generosity

Altruism motivated the student to volunteer in the shelter for homeless people.

altruistic ADJ. unselfishly generous

Few people act from entirely *altruistic* motives.

amalgam N. mixture, combination

The artist drew a sketch of the suspect that was an *amalgam* of the facial characteristics reported by witnesses.

amalgamate V. combine in a homogenous whole

The three schools decided to *amalgamate* because of declining enrollments.

ambidextrous ADJ. able to use both hands well

The *ambidextrous* painter worked equally well with each of his hands.

ambience N. the special mood or atmosphere created by a particular environment

The restaurant's romantic *ambience* makes it popular with young couples.

ambiguity N. lack of clarity in meaning

Avoid *ambiguity* in your essays.

ambiguous ADJ. unclear or doubtful in meaning

Please clarify your *ambiguous* statement.

ambit N. sphere or scope

The court ruled that the case was not within the *ambit* of state law.

ambivalence N. the state of having conflicting emotional attitudes

Gail's *ambivalence* toward Ray has prevented her from accepting a date with him.

ambivalent ADJ. exhibiting or feeling conflicting emotional attitudes

Hillary is *ambivalent* about dating Tim.

ambrosia N. something delicious; the food of the gods

To some people raw oysters are *ambrosia*.

ameliorate V. to improve; make better

Congress passed legislation to *ameliorate* the effects of poor nutrition among poor children.

amenable ADJ. agreeable, cooperative; suited

I am *amenable* to your plan to start a new school.

amend V. to correct flaws; to improve

After the bill was *amended*, it was passed unanimously.

amenity N. something that increases comfort

Modern navy vessels have *amenities* onboard that sailors of 300 years ago could only dream of.

amiable ADJ. friendly and agreeable; good-natured

We met some *amiable* people in the train and had a pleasant conversation.

amicable ADJ. friendly, agreeable

After the war the two countries restored *amicable* relations.

amity N. friendship

Amity between nations is one of the goals of the United Nations.

amoral ADJ. neither moral nor immoral; not caring about right and wrong

Many people believe that science is *amoral* in that it can be used for good or for bad.

amorous ADJ. showing love

Ray's *amorous* intentions toward Jessica were evident from the roses in his hand.

amorphous ADJ. lacking definite form

My ideas tend to be *amorphous* until I write them down; then they begin to take shape.

amphitheater N. an area for spectacles; a level area surrounded by upward sloping ground

We all crowded into the *amphitheater* to hear the famous writer's lecture.

ample ADJ. abundant, plentiful

There is *ample* food in the world for everyone; the problem is distributing it equitably.

amulet N. ornament worn as a charm against evil spirits

Joe's birthstone is emerald, a piece of which he wears around his neck as an *amulet*.

anachronism N. something out of the proper time

Movie producers have to be careful not to accidentally allow *anachronisms* to appear in movies about the past.

anachronistic ADJ. containing an error in the date of an event

This historical novel, set in 1550, contains *anachronistic* references to events that didn't occur until the nineteenth century.

analgesic N. medication that reduces or eliminates pain
Aspirin is one of the best all-around *analgesics*.

analog N. something that is comparable to something else
A computer is an analog of the human brain.

analogous ADJ. comparable
If we compare a book to a person's life, then each of its pages can be regarded as *analogous* to a period in the person's life.

analogy N. similarity
An *analogy* can be made between the capacity of a car engine and a person's capacity for thinking.

anarchic ADJ. lawless
After the revolution the country was *anarchic*.

anarchist N. one who does not believe in government
The *anarchist* attacked the government as an infringement of individual freedom.

anarchy N. absence of government; state of disorder
The ruler warned of *anarchy* if the rebellion continued.

anathema N. ban, curse; something shunned
Guys who don't shower regularly are *anathema* to most girls.

ancillary ADJ. accessory, subordinate
The armed forces have many *ancillary* units that support the main fighting forces.

androgynous ADJ. having both female and male characteristics
The film portrays the aliens as *androgynous*.

android N. a self-operating machine made from biological materials to resemble a human
The country's military plans to use *androids* as soldiers in the next war.

anecdote N. short account of an event
The teacher told an amusing *anecdote* to break the monotony of the lesson.

angst N. a feeling of anxiety or apprehension
The counselor dismissed the student's anxiety as "teenage *angst*."

angular ADJ. characterized by sharp angles
Belinda thinks her features are too *angular*, so she uses makeup to make them appear more rounded.

animadvert V. to comment critically
The travel writer *animadverts* against nearly every country he visits.

animation N. enthusiasm; excitement
The speaker's *animation* was infectious; members of the audience got to their feet and began to cheer.

animism N. the belief in the existence of individual spirits that inhabit natural objects
Native American religion is sometimes wrongly dismissed as "simple *animism*."

animosity N. hatred, hostility
As the campaign increased in intensity, so also did the *animosity* between the two main candidates.

animus N. ill will
The biographer's *animus* toward her subject is obvious.

annex V. to add or join to
Great powers often increase their territory by *annexing* smaller neighboring countries.

annihilate V. to destroy completely
The asteroid threatens to *annihilate* the earth.

annihilation N. complete destruction
The asteroid's impact with the earth caused the *annihilation* of life on the planet.

annotate V. to add notes or commentary
The English professor *annotated* Shakespeare's *King Lear*.

annul V. to cancel, nullify, or declare void
The marriage was *annulled* by order of the judge.

anodyne N. something that calms or soothes pain
I applied an anodyne to my burn to relieve the pain.

anomalous ADJ. deviating from or inconsistent with the common order, form, or rule; irregular; abnormal
Some scientists speculate that life is *anomalous* in the universe.

anomaly N. irregularity; deviation from the norm
There was an *anomaly* in the data, so the experiment was repeated.

anomie N. alienation and purposelessness as a result of a lack of values or ideals

The premise of the sociological study is that *anomie* is the underlying cause of crime.

anonymity N. the state of being unknown
The philanthropist prefers *anonymity*.

anonymous ADJ. having no name
The *anonymous* donor gave no hint of his identity.

antagonism N. hostility; opposition
There is considerable *antagonism* to the new idea.

antagonistic ADJ. hostile; opposed
The rivals for the big promotion became *antagonistic* toward each other.

antebellum ADJ. before or existing before the war, especially the American Civil War
The historian specializes in the *antebellum* period in American history.

antecedent N. something that comes before something else
An *antecedent* of the automobile was the horse-drawn carriage.

antedate V. precede in time
The invention of the automobile *antedates* the invention of the airplane.

antediluvian ADJ. prehistoric
Scientists have pieced together a fascinating picture of human life in *antediluvian* times.

anterior ADJ. preceding, previous
The prosecutor asked the witness to recall all the events *anterior* to the crime.

anthology N. collection of literary works
This *anthology* contains the best stories published in America this year.

anthropocentrism N. regarding man as the center of the universe
It is hard to imagine *anthropocentrism* surviving human contact with a vastly superior alien civilization.

anthropogenic ADJ. caused by humans
The government is working to reduce the amount of *anthropogenic* pollution.

anthropoid ADJ. resembling a human
The cartoon features *anthropoid* mice.

anthropology N. the scientific study of the origin, behavior, and development of humans

The study of social organization and kinship is a central focus of *anthropology*.

anthropomorphic ADJ. attributing human qualities to non-humans
This *anthropomorphic* cartoon features talking trees and thinking flowers.

anthropomorphize V. to attribute human qualities to non-humans
The poet *anthropomorphized* the sea, calling it "the brooding ocean."

antipathy N. dislike, hostility
Antipathy toward strangers seems to be inborn in human beings.

antipodes N. any two places on opposite sides of the earth
New York City and Singapore are nearly *antipodes*.

antiquated ADJ. too old to be fashionable; outmoded
The tenant asked his landlord to modernize the apartment's *antiquated* electrical system.

antiquity N. ancient times
Athens was one of the great centers of classical *antiquity*.

antithesis N. contrast; the opposite of
Could good exist without its *antithesis*, evil?

antithetical ADJ. contrasting; opposite
Our views are so *antithetical* I feel that we should simply agree to disagree.

apartheid N. an official policy of racial segregation formerly practiced in South Africa against non-whites; segregation
Apartheid was abolished in South Africa in 1991.

apathetic ADJ. lacking feeling or emotion
Voters are unusually *apathetic* this year; fewer than half are planning to vote.

apathy N. indifference
Apathy was high in the election because there was no major controversy or issue to arouse voter interest.

apex N. the highest point
Scientists believe that humanity is the *apex* reached by evolution on earth.

aphasia N. loss of the ability to articulate ideas or comprehend language, resulting from brain damage

The speech therapist is working with a patient suffering from *aphasia*.

aphelion N. point in a planet's orbit furthest from the sun
At *aphelion*, Pluto is so far from the sun that it is barely in the solar system.

aphorism N. short pithy statement
On his desk was a sign with the *aphorism*, "If you can't stand the heat, get out of the kitchen."

aphrodisiac N. substance arousing or intensifying sexual desire
The Romans worshipped the apple as an *aphrodisiac*.

aplomb N. self-confident assurance
Movie audiences admire how James Bond keeps his *aplomb* in every situation.

apocalyptic ADJ. portending devastation or doom
Many religions contain beliefs in a period of time marked by *apocalyptic* events.

apocryphal ADJ. not genuine, fictional
Historians regard the story of George Washington and the cherry tree as *apocryphal*.

apogee N. the point in an orbit most distant from the body being orbited
When the spacecraft reached its *apogee* in its orbit around the earth it fired rockets that would send it to Mars.

apologia N. a formal defense or justification
Critics see his work as an *apologia* for elitism.

apologist N. a person who defends or justifies a cause
The economist Milton Friedman was a leading *apologist* for capitalism.

apoplexy N. sudden impairment of neurological function; a fit of extreme anger
The man had a fit of *apoplexy* after hearing the news.

apostate N. one who renounces a religious faith
Jim became an *apostate* from his faith when he decided he did no longer believe in its central beliefs.

apothegm N. terse, witty saying
Most people have heard the apothegm from *Romeo and Juliet*, "He stumbles who runs fast."

apotheosis N. glorification; glorified ideal
The hero was regarded as the *apotheosis* of courage.

apparent ADJ. readily seen; easily understood
The truth of the saying "life is tough" became *apparent* to Bob when he embarked on his first job search.

appease V. to calm, pacify, placate
To *appease* workers angry at having their pay cut, the company increased their health benefit.

appellation N. name
Rulers often assign themselves *appellations* such as "The Great" and "The Magnificent."

apperception N. conscious perception with full awareness; the process of understanding by which newly observed qualities of an object are related to past experience
"The art of watching has become mere skill at rapid *apperception* and understanding of continuously changing visual images. The younger generation has acquired this cinematic perception to an amazing degree." (John Huizinga)

apposite ADJ. strikingly appropriate and relevant
The talk show host has a gift for making *apposite* comments on what her guests say.

apprehend V. to understand; know; dread
To the best of our knowledge, only human beings are able to *apprehend* the laws of nature.

apprehensive ADJ. fearful about the future
Rapid changes tend to make people *apprehensive*.

apprise V. to inform
The president asked to be kept *apprised* of the situation on the Korean peninsula.

approbation N. praise, approval
The young governor had received nothing but *approbation* in the early part of her presidential campaign.

appropriate V. to take possession for one's own use
The army *appropriated* the trucks during the emergency.

a priori ADJ. from a general law to a particular instance; valid independently of observation; formed or conceived beforehand
The judge reminded the jury not to reach any

a priori conclusions about the guilt or innocence of the accused.

apropos ADJ. relevant
When you write an essay, try to make all of your points *apropos* to the subject you're discussing.

apt ADJ. precisely suitable
An *apt* quotation can improve a piece of writing.

aptitude N. a natural or acquired talent or ability; intelligence
Aptitude for mathematics is to a significant degree inherited.

arabesque N. ornate design featuring intertwined curves; a ballet position in which one leg is extended in back while the other supports the weight of the body
Arabesques have a central role in Islamic art.

arable ADJ. suitable for cultivation
Countries such as Japan and South Korea are handicapped by not having much *arable* land.

arbitrary ADJ. unreasonable; randomly selected; determined by whim
The appeals court ruled that the judge's decision had been *arbitrary* and overturned it.

arbitrator N. a person chosen to settle an issue in dispute between parties
The union and the company agreed on an *arbitrator* to settle their dispute.

arboreal ADJ. relating to trees; living in trees
Scientists say that the distant ancestors of human beings were small *arboreal* creatures.

arcana N. secrets; mysteries
A great deal of *arcana* is represented in the symbolism of tarot cards.

arcane ADJ. secret, obscure; known only to a few
For most of us the *arcane* workings of a computer are "invisible."

archaic ADJ. antiquated; out of date
Morse code is an *archaic* form of communication, but it still plays a role in emergency communications.

archeology N. the study of material evidence of past human life
Archeology has discovered that the Egyptian pyramids were built by about 20,000 people working in teams.

archetypal ADJ. characteristic of an original model after which others are patterned
Sherlock Holmes is the *archetypal* private detective.

archetype N. original model after which others are patterned
Sherlock Holmes is the *archetype* for many other intellectual sleuths.

archipelago N. large group of islands
Indonesia is a nation in the Malay *archipelago* consisting of over 13,000 islands.

archive N. place or collection containing records of historical interest
The file room of a local newspaper is usually an excellent *archive* of the town's history.

ardent ADJ. passionate, enthusiastic, fervent
Charlie is a devoted Yankee fan, while his wife is an equally *ardent* Red Sox fan.

ardor N. great emotion or passion
Although Sue and Ted had been married for twenty years, their *ardor* for each other was undiminished.

arduous ADJ. extremely difficult; laborious
We made the *arduous* drive across Australia.

argot N. a specialized vocabulary used by a group
Some of the *argot* of the hippies of the 1960s—"rip-off," for example—has passed into general usage.

arid ADJ. extremely dry
Death Valley is extremely hot and *arid*, so make sure you have plenty of water before you drive across it.

aristocracy N. hereditary ruling class; government by the elite
Some people compare families like the Kennedys and Bushes to *aristocracies*.

arraign V. to call to court to answer an indictment
The defendant was *arraigned* on a charge of fraud.

array N. an impressive display of persons or objects
The *array* of important officials at the governor's inauguration was impressive.

arrogance N. pride; haughtiness
The new president felt he had to guard against the *arrogance* that can come with winning an election.

arrogate V. to claim or seize without justification
They believe that the federal government has *arrogated* powers to itself not specified in the Constitution.

arrogation N. the act of claiming or seizing without justification
The treaty forbids the *arrogation* of territory by any of the countries.

arsenal N. ammunition storehouse; storehouse
The *arsenal* is closely guarded to prevent enemy forces from capturing it.

articulate ADJ. distinct; effective
One of the best ways to become an *articulate* writer is to read good prose.

articulate V. to speak clearly and distinctly; to express in coherent verbal form
Please *articulate* your position so that we can understand it clearly.

artifact N. item made by human craft
Archeologists have found *artifacts* on the site, proving human settlement prior to 1200 BCE.

artifice N. stratagem; trickery; ingenious or artful device
James used clever *artifice* to defeat his opponent in the chess game.

artisan N. a skilled manual worker; a craftsperson
The *artisans* formed a co-operative to sell their work.

artless ADJ. guileless; natural
The salesperson's boss was amazed by the success of her *artless* employee.

ascend V. to rise or climb
Hugh *ascended* to the position of mayor.

ascendancy N. state of rising; power
The *ascendancy* of China is worrying many leaders in Japan.

ascendant ADJ. rising; moving upward
The Eagles are an *ascendant* football team this year.

ascertain V. to determine; make certain
Engineers are studying the site of the building collapse to *ascertain* its cause.

ascertainment N. the act of determining or making certain
The *ascertainment* of truth is the goal of science.

ascetic ADJ. self-denying; austere
Ralph enjoys a yearly retreat during which he lives the *ascetic* life of a monk.

asceticism N. self-denial; austerity
The nun practices *asceticism*.

ascribable ADJ. attributable to
His illness is *ascribable* to overwork.

ascribe V. to attribute to
The motives a person *ascribes* to others often tell a lot about his or her own motives.

askew ADJ. crooked; tilted
We realized that a break-in had occurred when we noticed several things *askew*.

asperity N. severity; irritability; harshness of manner
The accused person asked the witness with some *asperity* why she was lying.

aspersion N. slander; false rumor
Negative political campaigns cast *aspersions* on opponents, hoping that voters find them believable.

aspirant N. person who aspires to honors, high position, etc.
"There is no road to wealth so easy and respectable as that of matrimony; that is, of course, provided that the *aspirant* declines the slow course of honest work." (Anthony Trollope)

aspiration N. desire to achieve
The student's *aspiration* is to be a teacher.

aspire V. to have great hopes, to aim at a goal
The author *aspires* to be one of America's great writers.

assail V. to attack
The liberal politician *assailed* his opponent's voting record as too conservative.

assay V. to subject a substance to chemical analysis to determine the strength and quality of its components; to examine by trial or experiment
The ore was sent to the lab to be *assayed*.

assent V. to express agreement
I *assented* to my wife's plan to enlarge the guest room.

assert V. to declare to be true; maintain
If you *assert* an opinion, you should be prepared to back it up with a logical argument.

assertion N. act of declaring to be true
The debater cleverly refuted the *assertion* put forward by the opposition.

assess V. to estimate; evaluate
Stan's house was *assessed* to be worth $260,000.

assessment N. estimation; evaluation
The congressional committee's *assessment* is that there is too much wastage in the program.

assiduous ADJ. diligent, hard-working
The novelist did *assiduous* research before writing his book.

assignation N. appointment for lovers' meeting
The couple chose Lover's Lane for their *assignation*.

assimilate V. to blend in
The new immigrants were *assimilated* into society.

assimilation N. blending in
In sociology, *assimilation* refers to the process by which a minority group adopts the lifestyles and attitudes of the majority.

assonance N. resemblance in sound
Here's an example of *assonance* from a poem by W.B. Yeats: "that dolphin-torn, that gong-tormented sea."

assuage V. to make less severe
A piece of fruit should *assuage* my hunger until dinner.

astringent ADJ. harsh, severe
The teacher was well-known for his *astringent* remarks about students who handed homework in late.

astronomical ADJ. immense
The number of cells in the human body is *astronomical*.

astute ADJ. shrewd; wise
Psychologists say that females tend to be more *astute* judges of other peoples' motives than males.

asylum N. place of refuge or shelter
Before World War II many Europeans found *asylum* in America.

asymmetrical ADJ. not corresponding in size, shape, etc.
The sides of the human face are not perfectly *asymmetrical*.

asymmetry N. lack of balance or symmetry
There is *asymmetry* between the two sides of the human brain.

atavism N. in biology, the reappearance of a characteristic in an organism after several generations of absence; individual or part that exhibits the reappearance of a characteristic after a period of absence; return of a trait after a period of absence
An example of an *atavism* in humans is the appearance of a vestigial tail on a baby.

atheist N. person who does not believe in the existence of God
Some *atheists* object to the words "in God we trust" on coins.

atone V. to make amends for a wrong
To *atone* for drawing graffiti on the wall, Tom spent an hour every day this week cleaning up the school grounds.

atrocious ADJ. shockingly bad
The student's writing is so *atrocious* I wonder how he made it to high school.

atrocity N. appalling or *atrocious* condition, quality, or behavior
The atrocity was committed by armed troops against unarmed civilians.

atrophy V. to waste away
Astronauts on long space voyages do special exercises to prevent their muscles from *atrophying*.

attenuate V. to weaken
Advanced technology in modern radios is able to amplify even signals that have been greatly *attenuated*.

attest V. to testify, bear witness
As her tutor, I can *attest* to the hard work Julie did to improve her GRE score.

attribute N. essential quality
Charles has all the *attributes* needed for success except one—a willingness to work hard.

attribute V. ascribe; explain
Max *attributes* his success to his acting ability, but many people believe it has more to do with his good looks.

au courant ADJ. up-to-date; informed on current affairs

Debra reads a weekly news magazine to stay *au courant.*

audacious ADJ. bold, daring
The senator proposed an *audacious* plan to give every American adequate health care.

audible ADJ. capable of being heard
Sounds below a frequency of 20 hertz are not *audible* to the human ear.

augment V. to make greater
The buildup of naval forces in the Mediterranean was *augmented* by the arrival of more aircraft carriers.

augur V. to predict, especially from omens
The rise in the stock market *augurs* well for the economy.

augury N. prophecy, prediction of events
The famous economists gave their *augury* of economic conditions in the coming year.

august ADJ. dignified, awe-inspiring
The inauguration of a president is an *august* affair, with pomp and ceremony.

auspices N. protection; support; patronage
The class is conducted under the *auspices* of the university.

auspicious ADJ. promising
Hindus believe that certain times of the day are more *auspicious* than others.

austere ADJ. stern; unadorned
The writer concentrates best in *austere* surroundings.

austerity N. sternness; condition of having no adornment
The president asked the nation to endure a period of economic *austerity.*

authoritarian ADJ. favoring or exercising total control
Her father is *authoritarian* in his approach to raising children.

autism N. a psychiatric disorder characterized by serious impairments in communication and social interaction
Recent research on the brain has helped scientists to understand the causes of *autism.*

autocracy N. government by a single person who has unlimited power

The rebels formed a committee to challenge the *autocracy.*

autocratic ADJ. dictatorial
It is difficult to establish democratic government in countries that have known only generations of *autocratic* rule.

autonomous ADJ. self-governing; independent
Australians voted to not become an *autonomous* nation but rather remain to some degree under British rule.

autonomy N. self-government, independence
The British colony gained *autonomy* in 1965.

autopsy N. examination of a dead body to determine the cause of death
The law normally requires an *autopsy* if there is a suspicion of foul play in someone's death.

auxiliary ADJ. supplementary
We were glad our boat was equipped with an *auxiliary* engine after the main engine broke down.

avant-garde ADJ. relating to a group active in the invention of new techniques
I enjoy watching *avant-garde* performances because they stimulate me to think in new ways.

avant-garde N. a group active in the invention of new techniques
The *avant-garde* in our town organized a display of their art that many people found difficult to appreciate.

avarice N. greed
Traditionally, doctors are supposed to practice medicine to ease human suffering, not out of *avarice.*

avatar N. the descent to earth of a Hindu deity in human or animal form
Hindus believe that Krishna was an *avatar.*

avenge V. to take revenge
Adam vowed to *avenge* the death of his wife at the hands of terrorists.

aver V. to affirm; declare to be true
The accuracy of the testimony was *averred* by several witnesses.

aversion N. intense dislike
An *aversion* to snakes is universal in human beings.

avert v. to turn away; prevent
To avert a head-on collision, the driver swerved off the road.

aviary N. enclosure for birds
Several of the neighborhood cats have begun to hang around my backyard aviary.

avid ADJ. having keen interest
Bill is an *avid* stamp collector.

avocation N. secondary occupation
Sometimes an *avocation* can be turned into a person's main source of income.

avow v. to state openly
The position he now *avows* contradicts his earlier statements on the issue.

avuncular ADJ. like an uncle, benevolent and tolerant
The first graders all love the *avuncular* principal.

awry ADJ. crooked; askew
Jill knew something was *awry* when she walked into the office in the morning and found that her desk had been removed.

axiom N. premise; postulate; widely accepted principle
An *axiom* cited by many writers is that you should write what you know about.

axiomatic ADJ. taken for granted
The principle that every person has rights is regarded as *axiomatic* by most people.

B

bacchanalian ADJ. pertaining to riotous or drunken festivity
The secretive club's *bacchanalian* celebrations have attracted the interest of the local authorities.

baleful ADJ. harmful
Some people believe that the moon can exert a *baleful* influence on people.

balk v. to refuse
The student *balked* when the teacher asked him to rewrite his essay.

ballad N. folk song, narrative poem
The performer sang a *ballad* telling the story of a runaway slave.

banal ADJ. commonplace; trite
Many comedies employ the same *banal* situations.

bane N. something causing death or destruction
Weapons of mass destruction are one of the great *banes* of the modern world.

banter N. playful conversation
"OK, cut the *banter* and get back to work," the foreman shouted to the workers as their break was ending.

barbarous ADJ. uncivilized; lacking refinement
War sometimes shows that human beings are capable of *barbarous* behavior.

bard N. poet
Many famous *bards* have been Poet Laureates of Britain.

baroque ADJ. highly ornate
The hotel where I stayed in Paris was too *baroque* for my taste; I prefer a simple style.

bastion N. fortification
Many people regard Australia as a *bastion* of democracy.

bawdy ADJ. obscene
Daniel Defoe's *Moll Flanders* is a *bawdy* eighteenth-century novel.

bedevil v. plague; annoy; spoil
The new car model was *bedeviled* by so many problems that the manufacturer withdrew it from production.

bedizen v. to dress in a showy, vulgar manner
The old actress was *bedizened* with costume jewelry.

beguile v. to deceive, mislead; to charm or delight
We were so *beguiled* by the car's appearance that we neglected to consider whether it was really suitable.

behaviorism N. a school of psychology that studies only observable and measurable behavior
Psychologists who subscribe to the tenets of *behaviorism* believe that behavior can be explained without recourse to hypothetical constructs such as mind.

behemoth N. huge creature; anything very large and powerful
Modern aircraft carriers are *behemoths* with a crew the size of a small town.

belabor v. to insist repeatedly; harp on
The English teacher *belabored* the point that students must write in full sentences.

belated ADJ. late
I sent my wife a *belated* birthday card.

beleaguer v. to harass
The army, *beleaguered* by enemy troops, was forced to surrender.

belie v. to misrepresent
Jim's tough appearance *belies* his soft heart.

belittle v. to disparage; make effort
Joe's efforts to get a perfect GRE score were *belittled*, but no one was laughing when he got a perfect score.

bellicosity N. condition of being warlike or aggressive
The increased *bellicosity* of nations in the region worried experts at the United Nations.

belligerence N. hostility, tendency to fight
The student's *belligerence* was always getting him into fights.

bemuse v. to confuse
The class was *bemused* by the new teacher's vague directions.

benefactor N. patron; one who helps others
Judy discovered that a wealthy *benefactor* was going to pay for her college education.

beneficent ADJ. kindly; doing good
The billionaire is admired for his *beneficent* charitable contributions.

benevolent ADJ. generous; charitable
The *benevolent* billionaire donated half of his fortune to charity.

benighted ADJ. unenlightened
The poor *benighted* country had little success in its efforts to develop.

benign ADJ. harmless, kind
Shari was relieved when the doctor said her tumor was *benign*.

bequeath v. to hand down
Mr. Ford will *bequeath* all of his possessions to his wife.

berate v. to scold
The teacher *berated* the student for not handing in her homework in time.

beseech v. to beg, plead
The hostage *beseeched* his captors to release him.

bestial adj. beastly
Many *bestial* acts were committed during the war.

bestow v. to give as a gift
It is customary to *bestow* gifts on family and friends at Christmas.

bête noir N. something especially dreaded or hated
The novelist described mathematics as the *bête noir* of his childhood years.

betoken v. to indicate, signify
A wedding ring *betokens* the union of two people in marriage.

bevy N. group
A *bevy* of cheerleaders gathered around the quarterback after the football game.

bias N. prejudice
A teacher should treat students without *bias*.

bibliophile N. book lover
The *bibliophile* has a collection of over 20,000 books.

bicameral ADJ. composed of two legislative branches
The U.S. Congress is a *bicameral* body consisting of the Senate and the House of Representatives.

bifurcate v. to divide into two parts
Let's *bifurcate* this apple so we can share it evenly.

bigotry N. intolerance
One definition of education is the process of losing our *bigotry* and becoming more accepting of others and their views.

bilateral ADJ. two-sided
The two countries have started *bilateral* talks about the dispute.

binary ADJ. relating to something made of or based on two things or parts
A *binary* star is a system of two stars that revolve about their common center of mass.

biomass N. the amount of living matter in a unit area of a habitat; plant materials and animal waste used especially as a source of fuel
Biomass is derived from five sources: garbage, waste, wood, landfill gases, and alcohol fuels.

bipartisan ADJ. supported by two political parties
The president is working to build *bipartisan* support for the plan.

biped N. two-footed animal
Human beings are *bipeds*.

bivouac N. a temporary encampment
The major ordered the battalion to make a *bivouac* in the park.

bizarre ADJ. strikingly unusual; fantastic
Dreams sometimes have *bizarre* events that could not occur in reality.

blandishment N. flattery
The retired couple couldn't resist the *blandishments* of the glossy travel brochure.

blasé ADJ. bored because of frequent indulgence; unconcerned
The veteran movie stuntman has became *blasé* about his work.

blasphemy N. profanity, irreverence
The suggestion that schools be abolished was considered *blasphemy* by the teacher's union.

blatant ADJ. glaring, obvious
First, eliminate *blatant* errors from your writing; then, worry about the small ones.

bleak ADJ. cheerless; unlikely to be favorable
People with little education often face a *bleak* future.

blight N. affliction
Researchers are studying the causes of the potato *blight*.

blithe ADJ. joyful, cheerful; carefree
In her youth Karen was a *blithe* spirit, but as she grew older she became more serious.

blitzkrieg N. a swift, sudden military offensive, usually by combined air and mobile land forces
Careful planning must be done to launch a successful *blitzkrieg*.

bludgeon V. to hit
The referee stopped the bout after one boxer began to *bludgeon* his opponent mercilessly.

bohemian ADJ. unconventional in an artistic way
The *bohemian* area of the tour attracted many artists, writers, and musicians.

boisterous ADJ. rowdy, unrestrained
The Red Sox fans became *boisterous* after their team won the World Series.

bolster V. to give a boost to; prop up; support
Many famous men were *bolstered* in their careers by the support of their wives.

bombastic ADJ. pompous; using inflated language
The audience was bored by the long, *bombastic* speech.

bona fide ADJ. good faith, sincere, authentic
"I expect each of you to make a *bona fide* effort in this class," the teacher told the class.

bonanza N. large amount
The oil company spent years drilling for oil, hoping to find a *bonanza*—a lost store of crude oil.

bonhomie N. atmosphere of good cheer
Dad and Mom like dinner to be filled with *bonhomie*.

boon N. blessing
Summer vacation is an extra week long this year—what a *boon*!

boorish ADJ. rude; insensitive
Everyone avoids the *boorish* guy.

botanist N. scientist who studies plants
The *botanist* discovered a plant with the power to relieve pain.

bountiful ADJ. plentiful
The *bountiful* harvest means that we'll have plenty to eat this year.

bourgeois ADJ. typical of the middle class
The artist denounced his critics as *bourgeois* fools.

bourgeoisie N. the middle class
Television generally reflects the tastes of the *bourgeoisie*.

bovine ADJ. cow-like
Asked to describe the students walking slowly to the auditorium the English teacher said, "*Bovine.*"

Brahmanism N. Hinduism, the religious beliefs and practices of ancient India as reflected in the Vedas
The scholar is studying monistic tendencies in the *Rigveda*, one of *Brahminism's* sacred books.

Brahmin N. a member of a cultural and social elite
The poet T.S. Eliot was a member of a well-known family of Boston *Brahmins*, the Eliots.

brazen ADJ. bold, shameless
The *brazen* girl locked her parents out of the house after being scolded for lying.

breach N. violation
"One more *breach* of school rules and you're out of here," the principal told the student.

brigand N. outlaw
Some *brigands* like Jesse James are romanticized in books and films.

broach V. to mention for the first time
Jason decided that he would *broach* the subject of marriage to his girlfriend over dinner.

bromide N. a commonplace remark; a platitude
The politician's speech is filled with *bromides*.

brusque ADJ. abrupt in manner
Although Professor Robinson is *brusque* with students, he always has their best interest at heart.

bucolic ADJ. characteristic of the countryside; rustic; pastoral
The inn's *bucolic* setting makes it a popular weekend retreat for city people.

buffoon N. clown
Why is it that every class in school has a *buffoon*?

bulwark N. something serving as a defense
U.S. military bases in South Korea are *bulwarks* against invasion by North Korea.

bureaucracy N. government administration; management marked by diffused authority and inflexibility
Modern democracies require vast *bureaucracies* to carry out the many functions of government.

bureaucratic ADJ. rigidly devoted to the details of administrative procedure
Fed up with *bureaucratic* delays, the customer sent an e-mail to the president of the company.

burgeon V. to flourish, grow
China's *burgeoning* population is putting severe strain on its natural resources.

burly ADJ. brawny, husky
The *burly* bouncer threw Billy out of the club for starting a fight.

burnish V. to polish
The soldier proudly *burnished* his medals.

bustle N. commotion
Raised on a farm, Jim isn't used to the *bustle* of a big city.

buttress V. to reinforce, support
This argument needs to be *buttressed* with additional evidence.

C

cabal N. small group of people united secretly to promote their interests
The reporter discovered a *cabal* working to overthrow the government.

cache N. hiding place; something hidden
The rebel army had a *cache* of weapons in a cave.

cachet N. superior status; prestige
Dr. Lee thinks that the *cachet* of a Lexus is worth the expense.

cacophony N. jarring, unpleasant noise
There was a *cacophony* as each member of the rock band tuned his instrument at full volume.

cadence N. balanced, rhythmic flow; the measure or beat of movement
Although she couldn't understand the language, the visitor enjoyed listening to its *cadence*.

cadge V. to beg or get by begging
Why is that rich guy always trying to *cadge* a meal?

cajole V. to flatter, coax, persuade
The teacher *cajoled* the lazy student into completing his assignment.

calamitous ADJ. disastrous, catastrophic
Scientists believe that the effect of pollution on the environment will be *calamitous*.

calculated ADJ. deliberately planned
The advertisement was *calculated* to create a demand for the new product.

callous ADJ. thick-skinned, insensitive
The *callous* boys laughed at the miserable beggar.

callow ADJ. immature
Though still a *callow* youth, Steven thought he had the answer to just about every question.

calumny N. false and malicious accusation, slander
The political candidate used *calumny* to tarnish his opponent's reputation.

camaraderie N. good will and rapport among friends
There's a great *camaraderie* in Ms. Smith's class.

canard N. false, deliberately misleading rumor or story
The comedian likes to repeat the old *canard* that New Jersey is a cultural desert.

candid ADJ. honest in expression
The musician asked the teacher for a *candid* evaluation of her performance.

candor N. honesty of expression
The judge asked for *candor* from the witness.

canny ADJ. intelligent
The *canny* pitcher constantly varies his pitches so batters don't know what type of pitch they'll get.

canon N. an established principle; standard for judging; an authoritative list
The *canons* of artistic taste vary from era to era.

canonize V. to declare a person a saint, raise to highest honors
Saints are *canonized* only after a thorough investigation of their lives.

cant N. insincere talk; language of a particular group
After the editor removed the *cant* from the senator's speech, little was left.

cantankerous ADJ. irritable; ill-humored
The old man became *cantankerous* after becoming ill.

canvas V. to examine thoroughly; conduct a poll
The new company *canvassed* the town to find out how much demand there was for its products.

capacious ADJ. large, roomy
The couple moved into a *capacious* house after they had children.

capitulate V. to surrender
Surrounded by enemy forces, the general *capitulated* to the surrender terms of the enemy commander.

capricious ADJ. impulsive and unpredictable
This *capricious* weather makes it difficult to plan what to wear.

captious ADJ. faultfinding; intended to entrap, as in argument
The lawyer objected to the prosecutor's *captious* questioning of the witness.

carcinogen N. a substance or agent that causes cancer
Scientists have identified thousands of *carcinogens*.

cardinal ADJ. of foremost importance
The professor told her students, "For me, intellectual honesty is the *cardinal* virtue."

cardiologist N. doctor who treats diseases of the heart
The *cardiologist* detected an irregular heartbeat when he examined the patient.

caricature N. exaggerated portrait
This book contains *caricatures* of leading politicians.

carnal ADJ. of the flesh
Many modern films appeal to people's *carnal* desires.

carping V. constantly complaining or being naggingly critical
The student is tired of her English teacher *carping* about her grammar mistakes.

carte blanche N. unrestricted power
The recording studio gave the rock band *carte blanche* to create the best record they could.

cartography N. science of making maps
Advances in *cartography* have given us accurate maps.

Casanova N. a man who is amorously attentive to women; a promiscuous man
Ted's getting a reputation as a real *Casanova*.

caste N. any of the hereditary social classes of India; social stratification
Caste has existed in India from the beginning of that society.

castigate V. to punish, chastise, criticize
The bank manager *castigated* the teller for cashing a bad check.

casuistry N. false or excessively subtle reasoning
The judge accused the lawyer of *casuistry* when she offered ten meanings of the word "is."

cataclysm N. a violent upheaval that causes great destruction and change
A collision of the Earth with another planet would cause a *cataclysm*.

catalyst N. something causing change
The journalist's well-researched articles were a *catalyst* for reform in government.

catastrophe N. a great calamity
The government set up a department to deal with *catastrophes* such as large earthquakes.

categorical ADJ. absolute, without exception
"My answer is *categorical*: no exception will be made."

catharsis N. purification, cleansing
To some people that movie is shallowly sentimental, while to others it produces a *catharsis*.

cathartic ADJ. relating to purification or cleansing
Many people found the movie *cathartic*.

catholic ADJ. universal, comprehensive
The United Nations seeks to be a *catholic* organization, embracing all the peoples of the world.

caucus N. smaller group within an organization
Ten members of the political party formed a *caucus* to discuss policy changes.

causal ADJ. involving a cause
The study established a *causal* relationship between smoking and heart disease.

causality N. cause-and-effect relationship
It is often difficult to prove *causality* in scientific experiments.

causation N. the causing of an effect; the relation of cause and effect
"Correlation does not imply *causation*" is a phrase used in science and statistics to emphasize that correlation between two variables does not automatically imply that one causes the other.

causative ADJ. functioning as a cause
The scientist is trying to identify the *causative* agent in the process.

cause célèbre N. any controversy that attracts great public attention
The Dreyfus affair was a *cause célèbre* in France in the late nineteenth century.

caustic ADJ. sarcastically biting; burning
The teacher made a *caustic* comment about the student's poor writing.

cavalier ADJ. carefree, happy; showing offhand disregard; dismissive
His *cavalier* approach annoys me; I prefer a systematic and careful approach.

caveat N. a warning; a qualification or explanation
The experienced businessman added several important *caveats* to the contract.

cavort V. to frolic
The young couple *cavorted* on the beach all afternoon.

cede V. to surrender possession of something
This court ruling means he will have to *cede* his house to the person who sued him.

celestial ADJ. concerning the sky or heaven; sublime
Even as a child the astronomer loved to look at *celestial* objects.

celibate ADJ. abstaining from sexual intercourse; unmarried
The monk took a vow to remain *celibate* for his entire life.

censorious ADJ. severely critical
The investigating committee's report was *censorious*, condemning government inaction on the environment.

censure V. to blame; criticize
The Senate voted to *censure* one of its members for unethical conduct.

centrifugal ADJ. moving away from a center
When a car is turning a corner, its occupants experience *centrifugal* force as a force pushing them in the opposite direction to which the car is turning.

centripetal ADJ. moving or directed toward the center
Centripetal force pulls an object toward the center of a circular path.

cerebral ADJ. intellectually sophisticated
Joe's interests tend toward *cerebral* subjects such as literature and science.

certitude N. assurance, certainty
According to some philosophers, *certitude* is never possible because our knowledge of the world is limited.

cessation N. halt
The *cessation* of work at the construction site brought welcome relief from the noise.

chagrin N. shame, embarrassment
To his *chagrin*, John realized he had forgotten to say thank you to the man that saved his life.

chalice N. cup
The winner of the golf tournament receives a silver *chalice*.

champion V. to defend or support
The union *champions* the rights of workers.

charisma N. personal magnetism or charm
The president's charisma helps him to gain support for his policies.

charismatic ADJ. relating to personal magnetism or charm
The *charismatic* leader was re-elected in a landslide.

charlatan N. fake
The licensing of medical practitioners by the state helps protect the public from *charlatans*.

chary ADJ. wrathful, cautious
Children are generally taught to be *chary* of strangers.

chaste ADJ. not having experienced sexual intercourse; morally pure in thought and conduct
Young people in the country are expected to remain *chaste* until marriage.

chastise V. to punish, scold
The boss *chastised* the worker for her bad performance.

chauvinism N. fanatical patriotism; prejudiced belief in the superiority of a certain group
The dictator made an appeal to *chauvinism*.

chauvinistic ADJ. relating to fanatical patriotism or prejudiced belief in the superiority of a group
Each of the three candidates tried to appear more *chauvinistic* than the other.

cherubic ADJ. sweet, innocent, resembling an angel
The artist is famous for her paintings of *cherubic* infants.

chicanery N. trickery, fraud
The political party used *chicanery* to ensure their candidate's election.

chide V. to scold
The teacher *chided* the student for being late to class.

chimera N. something that is fantastic; fanciful mental illusion
Tim's goal of becoming a movie star is a *chimera*.

chimerical ADJ. fantastic; highly imaginative
The fantasy writer populates her novel with *chimerical* creatures.

chivalry N. the qualities idealized by knighthood such as bravery and gallantry toward women
Chivalry is still alive in practices such as men holding doors open for women.

choleric ADJ. short-tempered
Ralph's *choleric* disposition is always getting him into disputes.

chromatic ADJ. relating to color
Astronomers call the haze of color surrounding bright objects in a telescope "*chromatic* aberration."

chronic ADJ. habitual, repetitive; constant
Earl takes medicine to relieve his *chronic* back pain.

chronicle N. record of historical events
The book is a *chronicle* of our town's past.

chronicle V. to record historical events
Historians work to *chronicle* historical events.

churlish ADJ. rude; boorish
The hotel guest apologized for his *churlish* behavior.

cipher N. secret code
The intelligence service broke the enemy's *cipher*.

cipher N. non-entity; worthless person or thing
Barely anyone notices the *cipher* who works in our office.

circuitous ADJ. roundabout
Sometimes I take a *circuitous* route home from work because of the great views.

circumlocution N. indirect way of saying something
Tired of the speaker's *circumlocution*, someone shouted, "Just tell us what you really think."

circumscribe V. to limit narrowly; restrict
The educator believes that a child's reading should not be *circumscribed*.

circumscription N. the act of limiting or confining
The participants agree to a *circumscription* of the scope of the debate.

circumspect ADJ. cautious, wary
Hillary has adopted a *circumspect* approach after agreeing with every proposal without a protest.

circumvent V. to avoid by clever maneuvering
Some people like to confront problems, whereas others prefer to *circumvent* them.

citadel N. fortress
Rather than attack the *citadel*, the general decided to lay siege to it.

civil ADJ. polite; relating to citizens
Jim is a gentleman known for his *civil* behavior.

civility N. courtesy, politeness
Many people have complained about the lack of *civility* in political debate today.

clairvoyant ADJ. able to predict the future, psychic
The economist's predictions were so accurate that some people said she must be *clairvoyant*.

clamber V. to climb by crawling
The children *clambered* into their bunk beds.

clamor N. noisy outcry
The public *clamor* following the train crash resulted in an official investigation into the accident.

clamor V. cry out noisily
The public *clamored* for an investigation into the cause of the accident.

clandestine ADJ. secretive
The lovers arranged a *clandestine* meeting.

claustrophobia N. fear of small confined places
The astronauts in the small spaceship complained of *claustrophobia*.

clemency N. leniency
The prisoner appealed to the warden for *clemency*.

cliché N. an overused expression or idea
"As American as apple pie" may be a *cliché*, but that doesn't stop a lot of people from saying it.

clique N. a small, exclusive group
Unable to gain admission to any of the *cliques* in school, Richard decided to start his own clique.

cloister V. to confine, seclude
The writer *cloistered* herself in a cabin in the mountains for a week to finish her book.

coagulate V. thicken; congeal
Aspirin makes human blood *coagulate* less readily.

coalesce V. to cause to become one
The class *coalesced* as the year went on.

coalition N. an alliance
A *coalition* of nations combined their forces to defeat the aggressor.

coda N. concluding part of literary or musical composition; something that summarizes or concludes
The novel's *coda* suggests several ways to interpret the work.

codification N. systematization
Codification of the state's laws was completed in 1886.

codify V. to systematize
The state's laws were *codified* in 1824.

coercion N. use of force
The bully didn't get what he wanted by using threats, so he resorted to *coercion*.

coerce V. to persuade someone to do something by using threats or force
The student was *coerced* to attend detention.

coercive ADJ. characterized by force
The police used *coercive* measures to control the riot.

cogent ADJ. convincing; logically compelling
His *cogent* argument convinced me that he was right.

cogitate V. to think carefully; ponder
I have finished *cogitating* about her proposal, and I have reached a decision.

cognate ADJ. related, similar
The French word "amour" and the English word "amorous" are *cognate*.

cognate N. word related to one in another language
The English word "is" and the Latin word "est" are *cognates*.

cognition N. mental process by which knowledge is acquired
During *cognition* there is increased activity in certain parts of the brain.

cognitive ADJ. involving or relating to cognition
Brad took a course in *cognitive* psychology.

cognizant ADJ. informed; conscious; aware
I am *cognizant* of your problem, but you'll have to solve it yourself.

cognomen N. a surname; a nickname
The two-hundred-pound football tackle is known by his *cognomen* "Little John."

coherent ADJ. intelligible, understandable; sticking together
The essay is admirably logical and *coherent*.

coherence N. condition of being intelligible and understandable
Coherence is considered a major virtue in modern expository writing.

cohesion N. the act or process of sticking together
Crime tends to rise when there is poor social *cohesion*.

cohesive ADJ. well-integrated; unified
Let's have a party to make our class more *cohesive*.

collaborate V. to work together
Before you *collaborate* with someone, it's a good idea to find out whether that person is a good worker.

collaborative ADJ. relating to or characteristic of working together
The book is a *collaborative* effort.

collage N. artistic composition of materials pasted over a surface; an assemblage of diverse elements
The artist's *collage* was made out of materials he had collected in China.

collateral ADJ. accompanying or concomitant
During war, *collateral* damage to civilian areas is sometimes difficult to avoid.

colloquial ADJ. typical of informal speech
Colloquial expressions are ordinarily acceptable in informal speech but not in formal speech.

colloquy N. dialogue, conversation
The university sponsored a *colloquy* on social problems.

collude V. to make a secret agreement for deceitful purposes
The two companies were accused of *colluding* to raise prices.

collusion N. secret agreement between two or more parties for a fraudulent or illegal purpose
Investigators suspect the mayor of *collusion* to commit fraud.

colossal ADJ. huge
The sun produces a *colossal* amount of heat.

combustible ADJ. easily burned
The campers searched for *combustible* material to build a fire.

commendable ADJ. praiseworthy
The student made a *commendable* effort to improve his performance.

commensurate ADJ. proportional
Punishment should be *commensurate* with the crime.

commiseration N. expression of pity
Immediately after the disaster rescue workers had little time for *commiseration*.

commodious ADJ. spacious, roomy
His promotion to vice-president meant that Stan would move to a *commodious* new office.

commodity N. something that can be turned to commercial advantage
Information is increasingly becoming a *commodity*.

commune V. to be very sensitive and receptive to something
The poet went for a walk in the mountains to *commune* with nature.

communicable ADJ. transmittable
The school was closed because of a severe outbreak of a *communicable* disease.

compelling ADJ. having a powerful effect; demanding attention
The evidence was so *compelling* that the judge ordered the prisoner to be released.

compendium N. a brief, comprehensive summary
The history professor gave the class a *compendium* of European history she had written.

complacent ADJ. self-satisfied
The coach was concerned that his team would become *complacent* after winning ten straight games.

complaisant ADJ. overly polite; willing to please; obliging
The novel is mainly about a woman and her *complaisant* husband.

complement N. something that completes or makes up a whole
The football team's good running game is a *complement* to its excellent passing game.

compliant ADJ. yielding
The legislature was *compliant*, giving into all of the president's demands.

complicity N. partnership in wrongdoing
The suspect denied *complicity* in the crime.

composure N. mental calmness
Good leaders are able to keep their *composure* during a crisis.

comprehensive ADJ. thorough, conclusive
The new president of the company ordered a *comprehensive* review of marketing strategies.

compulsive ADJ. obsessive
Adrian is a *compulsive* gambler.

compunction N. uneasiness caused by guilt
The judge had no *compunction* at sentencing the murderer to life imprisonment.

concave ADJ. curving inward
The lens is *concave*.

concede V. to yield, admit
Though far behind in the election tally, the candidate refused to *concede*.

conception N. something conceived in the mind
The artist tried to capture his *conception* in pen and ink.

conceptualize V. to envision, imagine
The chemistry teacher made a model of the compound to help her students *conceptualize* it.

conciliatory ADJ. overcoming distrust or hostility
Ben felt bad about starting the argument with Sue and talked to her in a *conciliatory* way.

concise ADJ. brief and compact
The new dictionary is a *concise* version of the full-length one.

conclusive ADJ. decisive; ending all controversy
The study provides *conclusive* evidence for the theory.

concoct V. to invent
The teacher waited to see what excuse Billy would *concoct* for not doing his assignment.

concomitant ADJ. existing concurrently
The increase in poverty led to a *concomitant* increase in crime.

concord N. harmony; agreement
After so much bitter dispute, the senators were happy to discuss an issue on which there was *concord*.

concordance N. agreement; concord
The nation signed a *concordance* agreeing to cultural exchanges with its neighbor.

concur V. to agree
A majority of the committee *concurs* with the proposal.

condescend V. to bestow courtesy with a superior air
The queen *condescended* to allow commoners to visit the palace.

condone V. to overlook voluntarily; forgive
The teacher *condoned* the student's poor behavior because she knew that he had serious family problems.

conduit N. a pipe or channel for conveying fluids; conveyor of information
The embassy is a *conduit* for confidential information about the country.

conflagration N. big fire
After the oil refinery was bombed, there was a *conflagration*.

confluence N. meeting place, meeting of two streams
Our plan is to paddle our canoes to the *confluence* of this stream and Otter Creek.

conformity N. harmony; agreement
We were surprised to find *conformity* in views on the controversial issue.

confound V. to baffle, perplex; mix up
The weakest hitter on the team *confounded* everyone by going on a 30-game hitting streak.

congenial ADJ. similar in tastes and habits; friendly; suited to
The *congenial* host greeted us at the door.

congenital ADJ. existing at or before birth
No one trusts Jim because he has a reputation as a *congenital* liar.

conglomerate N. group of varied things
The painting uses a *conglomerate* of colors.

conglomeration N. an accumulation of diverse things
The firm grew into a *conglomeration* as it acquired different types of businesses.

congress N. formal meeting
The student leaders met at a national *congress*.

congruent ADJ. corresponding
The two triangles are *congruent*.

conjecture N. speculation, prediction; conclusion reached without proof
There has been a lot of *conjecture* about the existence of ghosts, but little proof.

conjugal ADJ. pertaining to marriage agreement
Conjugal visits were denied to all inmates after the prison riots.

conjunction N. a simultaneous occurrence; a combination
An exact *conjunction* of Jupiter and Venus at 15 degrees Aquarius will occur on August 20.

conjure V. to evoke a spirit; bring to mind
The spiritualist claims to be able to *conjure* spirits.

connivance N. act of conspiring or scheming
The crime could only have been committed with the *connivance* of employees of the company.

connoisseur N. a person with refined taste
The art *connoisseur* was asked to judge the art contest.

connotation N. a meaning suggested by a word or thing
The word "lady" has acquired unfavorable *connotations* for many people.

connote V. to suggest or imply in addition to literal meaning
Good writers consider what words *connote* to readers.

consanguinity N. relationship by blood or by a common ancestor; close connection
The woman is seeking a divorce on grounds of *consanguinity*.

conscientious ADJ. careful and thorough; governed by conscience
Airplane mechanics should be *conscientious* in doing their job because lives depend on them.

conscript N. a person compulsorily enrolled for service
Modern nations sometimes enroll men as *conscripts* in the army if there aren't enough volunteers available.

conscript V. to enroll for service
Bud was *conscripted* and sent to fight overseas.

consecrate V. to declare sacred
The church was *consecrated* by the bishop.

consensus N. general agreement
There is a *consensus* among political scientists that the best system of government is democracy.

conservative ADJ. favoring traditional values; tending to oppose change
The Republican Party tends to be more *conservative* on social issues than the Democratic Party.

conservative N. someone who favors traditional values; one who opposes change
The congressman is a *conservative* on economic matters but a liberal on social issues.

consign V. to entrust; commit irrevocably
My wife *consigned* my five-year-old sweatshirt to the garbage.

consolidate V. to combine; form into one system
The prime minister *consolidated* his power by appointing new ministers.

consonance N. something consistent with; in agreement with something else
Our actions should have *consonance* with our values.

consonant ADJ. consistent with, in agreement with
Ideally, our actions are *consonant* with our values.

consortium N. an association formed for joint venture
The three companies formed a *consortium* to build the new plane.

conspicuous ADJ. very noticeable, striking
Beth's orange hair makes her *conspicuous*.

constituency N. body of voters of the residents of a district represented by an elected official
The senator's *constituency* is very varied.

constituent N. part; citizen, voter
The senator visits her *constituents* regularly.

constraint N. something that forces or restrains
Teenagers often complain about the *constraints* placed on them.

construe V. to explain or interpret
The odd message could be *construed* in different ways.

consummate ADJ. accomplished, complete
A *consummate* pianist, Jan has performed all over the world.

consummate V. to complete, fulfill
The merger of the two companies was *consummated* last month.

contagion N. a contagious disease
Health officials worked to stop the spread of the *contagion*.

contemporary ADJ. belonging to the same period of time; current, modern
The club holds discussions of *contemporary* affairs.

contemptuous ADJ. manifesting or feeling contempt; scornful
The novelist is *contemptuous* of the work of other writers.

contend V. to battle, compete; assert
Harry plans to *contend* for the middle weight boxing title.

contention N. assertion; controversy
There is some truth in your *contention*.

contentious ADJ. quarrelsome; causing quarrels
The Vietnam War was a *contentious* issue in the 1960s and early 1970s.

context N. part of a text that surrounds a particular word or passage; circumstances of an event
If you don't know a word, try looking for clues to its meaning from its *context*.

contiguous ADJ. touching; neighboring; connecting without a break
The United States and Canada are *contiguous* countries.

continence N. self-control
Continence is a virtue that he aspires to.

contingent ADJ. dependent on conditions not yet established
The sale of the house is *contingent* on the prospective buyer selling her house.

contract V. to compress or shrink; affected by
The economy *contracted* two percent last year.

contravene V. to contradict, deny, act contrary to; violate
Anyone who *contravenes* school regulations will be punished.

contrite ADJ. very sorrowful for a wrong
The daughter looked so *contrite* her mother forgave her.

contrivance N. something invented or fabricated
The time machine is a *contrivance* that is popular in science fiction.

contrived ADJ. artificial; not spontaneous
The plot of this novel is rather *contrived*.

controversial ADJ. marked by controversy
The poll measures public opinion on *controversial* issues.

contumacious ADJ. disobedient; rebellious
The king has grown weary of his contumacious subjects.

conundrum N. riddle, puzzle with no solution
The *conundrum* has baffled scientists for centuries.

convalesce V. to return to health after illness; recuperate
Joan is *convalescing* after having major surgery.

convene V. to meet, come together
The student council president *convened* the first meeting of the year.

convention N. an accepted technique or device; practice widely observed in a group
The *conventions* of English spelling are difficult to master.

conventional ADJ. customary, commonplace
Bob holds *conventional* views on most issues.

convex ADJ. curved outward
The image of an object reflected by a *convex* mirror is upright and reduced in size.

conviction N. a fixed belief
Julie's *conviction* is that more should be done to help the poor.

conviviality N. sociable state or condition
Everyone praised the *conviviality* of the hosts.

convoke V. to call together
The national association *convoked* a meeting of all its local chapters.

convoluted ADJ. twisted, complicated
The plot of this book is so *convoluted* I can no longer follow it.

copious ADJ. abundant, plentiful
The teacher provided *copious* notes for her students.

coquette N. woman who flirts
Shirley enjoys acting in plays in which she is a *coquette*.

cordial ADJ. warm and sincere
The two nations enjoy *cordial* relations.

cornucopia N. horn overflowing with fruit and grain; state of abundance
A modern university is a *cornucopia* of knowledge.

corollary N. a proposition that follows logically from one already proven; a natural consequence
The mathematician proved the *corollary* of the theorem.

corporal ADJ. relating to the body
Corporal punishment has been outlawed in many countries.

corporeal ADJ. concerned with the body; tangible, material
The scholar, concerned mainly with the life of the mind, had little interest in *corporeal* concerns.

corpulence N. condition of being excessively fat
Corpulence is becoming increasingly common in the United States.

corpus N. a large collection of writings on a specific subject or of a specific kind
The scholar searched the Shakespeare *corpus* for the reference.

correlation N. mutual relationship
The scientist proved a strong *correlation* between exercise and health.

correlative ADJ. corresponding; related
As knowledge progresses, let's hope for a *correlative* increase in wisdom.

corroborate V. to support the correctness of; make more certain
The prosecutor asked her assistant to *corroborate* the testimony before indicting the suspect.

corrugated ADJ. wrinkled; ridged
The roofs of the houses are made of *corrugated* metal.

cosmetic ADJ. relating to beauty; affecting only the surface
There are only *cosmetic* differences between the two candidates.

cosmology N. a system of beliefs that seeks to describe or explain the origin and structure of the universe; the branch of science dealing with the large-scale structure, origins, and development of the universe
Cosmology has been greatly aided by the development of powerful telescopes.

cosmopolitan ADJ. sophisticated, free of local prejudices
The ambassador is the most *cosmopolitan* woman I know.

cosmos N. physical universe regarded as a totality
Astronomers believe that the laws of nature are the same throughout the *cosmos*.

cosset V. to pamper
The rich man *cosseted* his only child.

coterie N. small group of persons with a similar interest
The *coterie* of poets met regularly to read and discuss their poems.

coterminous ADJ. having common boundaries; contiguous; coextensive in scope or time
In a democracy the interests of the people should be *coterminous* with those of the state.

countenance N. facial expression
Her *countenance* showed her emotions clearly.

countenance V. to favor, support
The principal *countenanced* greater involvement of the student council in running the school.

countermand V. to annul, cancel
The commander *countermanded* his earlier order.

countervailing ADJ. counteracting
The three branches of the U.S. federal government are designed to act as *countervailing* centers of power.

coup N. a brilliantly executed stratagem; coup d'état
Winning the contract to supply jet fighters to the air force was a *coup* for the company.

coup de grâce N. a finishing blow; a decisive stroke
The general delivered the *coup de grâce*, killing the enemy commander.

coup d'état N. the sudden overthrow of a government by a group of people in positions of authority
The *coup d'état* was led by a group of air force officers.

coven N. group of witches
A local legend says a *coven* meets here every Halloween.

covert ADJ. hidden, secret
James Bond specializes in *covert* operations.

covet V. to desire something owned by another
Cathy *covets* the latest model cell phone that Mona just got.

coy ADJ. shy and flirtatious
Sheila finds that being *coy* attracts boys.

cozen V. to mislead by trick or fraud; deceive
The conman *cozened* Rick into investing in a fraudulent scheme.

crass ADJ. crude, unrefined
Susan had trouble forgiving Burt for his *crass* behavior at her graduation party.

craven ADJ. cowardly
The soldier's *craven* act was condemned by his commanding officer.

credence N. acceptance of something as true
I can't give any *credence* to your ridiculous claims.

credible ADJ. believable, plausible
Your story is *credible*, but I'll need more evidence before I believe it without question.

credo N. statement of belief or principle; creed
The party issued its *credo*.

credulity N. belief on slight evidence; naiveté; gullibility
The advertising campaign was based largely on the public's *credulity*.

credulous ADJ. gullible, trusting
The *credulous* customer accepted the claim that the skin cream would make her wrinkles disappear.

creed N. statement of belief or principle
The new church outlined its *creed*.

creole N. a mother tongue formed from the contact of two languages through an earlier pidgin stage; a person of mixed European and black descent; a white descendent of French settlers in some parts of the southern United States
Most English *creoles* were formed in English colonies, following the great expansion of British naval military power and trade in the seventeenth, eighteenth, and nineteenth centuries.

crescendo N. gradual increase in volume of sound
The cheering reached a *crescendo*.

criteria N. standards used in judging
The college's *criteria* for assessing applicants are clear to everyone.

critique N. a critical commentary
The teacher asked her students to write a *critique* of the poem.

cryptic ADJ. puzzling
The reporters tried to figure out the president's *cryptic* comment.

crystallize V. to give definite form to
Our plans are beginning to *crystallize*.

cuisine N. style of cooking
Mediterranean *cuisine* is becoming very popular.

culinary ADJ. related to cooking
Jean decided to enroll in *culinary* school.

culmination N. climax
The big Christmas party was the *culmination* of a two week celebration.

culpable ADJ. guilty
The teacher questioned the two boys to see which of them was *culpable* of the offense.

cult N. a religious sect considered by many to be extremist or false
John surprised his friends when he joined a *cult*.

cupidity N. greed

The investor had already made five million dollars, but *cupidity* made him want more.

curator N. caretaker of an exhibition

The *curator* is planning for an exhibition of Native American art.

curmudgeon N. cranky person

The old *curmudgeon's* favorite pastime is writing letters to the newspaper complaining about young people.

cursory ADJ. done with little attention to detail

Mechanics only had time for a *cursory* inspection of the aircraft.

curt ADJ. abrupt

John answered his boss's question with a *curt* "no" and walked out the door.

curtail V. to cut short

The baseball game was *curtailed* after five extra innings due to darkness.

cynical ADJ. skeptical or distrustful of human motives

Luke refused to become *cynical*, even after years of having his honesty taken advantage of.

cynosure N. object of common interest; guide

The builders turned that eyesore of a dilapidated building into a *cynosure*.

D

dais N. raised platform for guests of honor

The governor and his cabinet were seated on the *dais* ready to take questions from the press.

daunting ADJ. discouraging

Coach Jones began the *daunting* job of turning a losing football program into a winning one.

dearth N. scarcity

There is a *dearth* of girls wanting to try out for the basketball team.

debacle N. a crushing defeat

Our football team suffered a *debacle* last week—an 81–0 loss.

debauchery N. corruption

The writer lived a life of *debauchery* until he was thirty years old.

debilitate V. to weaken

The Supreme Court justice has been *debilitated* by illness.

debunk V. to discredit

The theory has been *debunked* by modern science.

decadence N. a process or period of deterioration or decline

The historian believes that moral *decadence* is an indicator of a civilization's imminent collapse.

decapitate V. to behead

The soldier was *decapitated* in the battle.

decathlon N. athletic contest with ten events

Jim's weakest event in the *decathlon* is the 1500 meter race.

deciduous ADJ. falling off or shedding at a particular season or stage of growth

Mrs. Miller's yard has a mix of *deciduous* and evergreen trees.

decimate V. to kill a large part of a group; destroy

The city was *decimated* by intensive bombing.

decipher V. to interpret; decode

The student found the teacher's comments on the test paper difficult to *decipher*.

decisively adv. determinedly

The major powers acted *decisively* to end the conflict.

declivity N. downward slope

The steep *declivity* allowed the cyclist to coast for a long time.

deconstructionism N. a philosophical movement and theory of literary criticism that holds that words only refer to other words and tries to demonstrate that statements about a text undermine their own meaning

The distinguished literary critic J. Hillis Miller was heavily influenced by *deconstructionism*.

decorous ADJ. proper, tasteful

Decorous behavior is expected in a five-star hotel.

decorum N. proper behavior

It is wise to conduct yourself with *decorum* at a job interview.

decry V. to condemn openly

The president *decried* the opposition party's tactic of blocking every proposal he put forward.

deduce v. to draw a conclusion by reason
I *deduce* from your appearance that you've just woken up.

deduction N. the drawing of a conclusion by reason
Based on your appearance, my *deduction* is that you just woke up.

deface v. to mar the external appearance
Vandals *defaced* the statue.

de facto ADV. in fact; actual; existing whether rightfully or not
The elections are considered by some to be a *de facto* referendum on democracy in the country.

defamation N. the act of slandering or injuring another's reputation or character
The movie star sued the newspaper for *defamation*.

defamatory ADJ. slanderous, injurious to the reputation
The writer was sued for making *defamatory* remarks in his book.

defer v. to postpone
The executive officer *deferred* her decision until she could gather more information.

deference N. respect; regard for another's wish
In most cultures children are expected to show deference to their elders.

defile v. to dirty; disgrace
The lawyer's name was *defiled* by the charge of corruption.

definitive ADJ. conclusive, authoritative; precisely defined
Professor Wilson's book is the *definitive* work on ants.

deft ADJ. skillful
The principal praised the teacher's *deft* handling of the difficult situation.

defunct ADJ. no longer existing
Mail service from Weir Junction to Terrapin Station is *defunct*.

degradation N. humiliation; debasement; degeneration
As it develops, China is undergoing great environmental *degradation*.

dehydrate v. to remove water from; dry out
Drink plenty of fluids in hot weather so you don't become *dehydrated*.

deification N. the act of making or regarding as a god
Deification of nature is common in English Romantic poetry.

delectable ADJ. delicious
The desserts all look *delectable*.

delegate v. to give power to others
The manager *delegated* responsibility for foreign sales to his assistant.

deleterious ADJ. harmful
Smoking is *deleterious* to human health.

delineation N. representation, depiction
This writer excels at the *delineation* of complex characters.

Delphic ADJ. relating to Delphi or the oracle of Apollo at Delphi; obscurely prophetic; oracular
She is known for her *Delphic* utterances.

deluge N. a great flood; something that overwhelms
The movie star received a *deluge* of mail.

delusional ADJ. having a false belief
Investigators described John's belief in UFOs as *delusional*.

demagogue N. leader who appeals to emotion or prejudice
Adolph Hitler was a *demagogue*.

demarcation N. establishing limits; limit or boundary
There is a clear *demarcation* between church and state in the United States.

demean v. to degrade, humiliate
The teacher used ridicule to *demean* the student.

demeanor N. way of handling yourself; bearing
The teacher's pleasant *demeanor* made her popular with students.

demise N. death; the end of activity
After his *demise*, Mr. Smith's estate was divided among his children.

demography N. study of human population
Demography is a field that uses insights from a number of other fields.

demote v. to reduce to a lower rank
The corporal was *demoted* to private due to his misconduct.

demotic ADJ. pertaining to the people
The politician is careful to sprinkle his speech liberally with *demotic* idioms.

demur V. to express doubt
When the jury's verdict was announced, only one member *demurred*.

demure adj. reserved and modest in manner
In Asia, females are traditionally encouraged to be *demure*.

demystify V. to remove mystery, clarify
Science seeks to *demystify* the working of nature.

denigrate V. to slur someone's reputation
The rumor was spread to *denigrate* the senator.

denizen N. an inhabitant; a regular visitor
Contrary to popular belief, the *denizens* of New York City are generally friendly and helpful.

denotation N. the most direct meaning of a word
Many words have several *denotations*.

denote V. to serve as a symbol for the meaning of; to signify
A word can *denote* different things depending on how it is used in a sentence.

denouement N. outcome; unraveling of the plot or work of literature
The film's *denouement* explains why the couple decided to divorce.

denounce V. to condemn; criticize
The official *denounced* the enemy attack as barbaric.

denude V. to make bare
The hillside was *denuded* after the fierce battle there.

denunciation N. public condemnation
The president issued a *denunciation* of the improper actions.

depiction N. portrayal
I enjoyed Richard Burton's *depiction* of Alexander the Great in the film.

deplete V. to use up, exhaust
The world is rapidly *depleting* its reserve of fresh water.

deplore V. to regret; disapprove of
The university president gave a speech *deploring* declining standards in education.

deploy V. to spread out over an area
Troops were *deployed* in the city to restore order.

depose V. to remove from high position
The king was *deposed* in the revolution.

depraved ADJ. corrupted; wicked
The film was condemned as being *depraved*.

depravity N. moral corruption
The church leaders condemned the *depravity* of modern society.

deprecate V. to belittle, disparage
The patriot *deprecated* every country in the world except his own.

depredation N. damage or loss
China is undergoing great environmental *depredation*.

deride V. to mock
Joe's friends *derided* his dream of becoming a movie star.

de rigueur ADJ. required by custom or fashion
In the 1960s miniskirts were *de rigueur*.

derision N. ridicule
Joe's ambition to become a major league baseball player is treated with *derision* by his friends.

derivative ADJ. unoriginal
The critic dismissed the new novel as *derivative* and dull.

derogatory ADJ. disparaging, belittling
Stop making *derogatory* remarks.

descry V. to catch sight of something
The bird watcher *descried* an eagle high in the sky.

desecrate V. to violate the sacredness of; profane
Vandals *desecrated* the graveyard.

desiccate V. to dry completely
The dry weather *desiccated* the bones.

desist V. to stop doing something
The judge ordered the man to *desist* from phoning his ex-wife.

despondent ADJ. feeling discouraged
Hal refused to let his poor test score make him *despondent*.

despot N. tyrannical ruler
Mr. Frank runs his classroom like a *despot*.

despotism N. absolute power
Despotism was replaced by democracy in countries like England and France.

destitute ADJ. very poor
Most advanced countries have programs to help the *destitute*.

desuetude N. state of disuse
The house has fallen into *desuetude*.

desultory ADJ. random, disconnected; rambling
Jim's *desultory* efforts to improve his GRE score are not likely to be very effective.

detached ADJ. emotionally removed; indifferent
The detective listened, *detached*, to the victim's account of the crime.

deter V. to discourage; hinder
Nothing *deterred* Bill from pursuing his ambition of being an actor.

determinant N. something that determines
Scientists have found that the disease has no single *determinant*.

deterministic ADJ. determined inevitably as the consequence of antecedent events
The philosopher argues that there is no room for free will in a *deterministic* universe.

determinism N. the philosophy that all events are inevitably determined by preceding events
Determinism would seem to allow little or no room for the exercise of free will.

deterrent N. something that discourages or hinders
The powerful army is a *deterrent* to enemy aggression.

detrimental ADJ. harmful; damaging
The injury to the star running back is *detrimental* to the football team.

deus ex machina N. any artificial method of solving a difficulty; an improbable element introduced in a story to resolve a situation
Critics complain that the mystery writer unnecessarily used a *deus ex machina* in her story.

deviant ADJ. differing from the norm or the accepted social standards
Psychologists vary on what they consider to be *deviant* behavior.

deviate V. to wander, stray
The teacher has a habit of *deviating* from his lesson plan.

devious ADJ. indirect; cunning
The detective uncovered a *devious* plot to rob the bank.

devise V. think up; plan; invent
The class *devised* an April Fool's Day trick to play on their teacher.

devoid ADJ. totally lacking
The moon is *devoid* of life.

devout ADJ. deeply religious
Sister Marie is the most *devout* person I know.

diabolical ADJ. fiendish, wicked
The police uncovered a *diabolical* plan to poison the city's water supply.

dialect N. regional style of speaking
There are many *dialects* of English.

dialectic N. arriving at the truth by the exchange of logical arguments
Ideally, a debate is a *dialectic*.

diaphanous ADJ. transparent; insubstantial; vague
Bill wore a *diaphanous* shirt to the party.

diatribe N. bitter verbal attack
The class listened to their teacher's *diatribe* about the failings of modern education.

dichotomy N. division into two usually contradictory parts
Some philosophers posit a *dichotomy* between mind and matter.

dictate N. guiding principle
Following the *dictates* of her conscience, Rebecca refused to take part in the protest.

diction N. choice of words
The speech was marred by poor *diction*.

dictum N. authoritative statement
The Supreme Court's *dictum* is final and must be followed by the lower courts.

didactic ADJ. intended to instruct; teaching excessively
The English teacher believes that a novel should be, at least on some level, *didactic*.

diffidence N. shyness; lack of confidence
The new student spoke with *diffidence*.

diffuse ADJ. wordy; rambling; spread out
This essay is so *diffuse* that its argument is difficult to follow.

diffuse V. to spread out
The chemical is able to *diffuse* across a cell membrane.

digress V. to stray from the main point
The chairman *digressed* from his prepared remarks to congratulate the employee on his promotion.

dilapidated ADJ. ruined because of neglect
Nobody can remember who owns the abandoned, *dilapidated* house on the corner.

dilatory ADJ. slow, tending to delay
The senator used *dilatory* tactics to delay a vote on the health bill.

dilemma N. a situation necessitating a choice between two unsatisfactory options or mutually exclusive options
The commander faced a *dilemma*: surrender or fight on with little hope of victory.

dilettante N. a dabbler in a field
Many early scientists were wealthy *dilettantes*.

diminution N. lessening; reduction
We waited for a *diminution* in the thunderstorm before leaving home.

diminutive ADJ. small
It was a bit surprising, but the most *diminutive* player on the basketball court is also the best.

dirge N. funeral hymn
The band played a *dirge* for the dead president.

disabuse V. to free from a misconception
The professor felt her first job was to *disabuse* students of the belief that mathematics is a useless subject.

disaffected ADJ. discontented
The new party leader pledged to reach out to *disaffected* members of the party.

disarm V. to overcome or allay suspicion; win the confidence of
We were *disarmed* by our new boss's easygoing nature.

disbar V. to expel from legal profession
The lawyer was *disbarred* because of his involvement in criminal activities.

discern V. to perceive something obscure
The teacher helped the class to *discern* the meaning of the difficult poem.

disclaim V. to deny
The witness *disclaimed* any knowledge of the events leading up to the crime.

discomfit V. to make uneasy; disconcert
Nothing could *discomfit* the experienced talk show host.

disconcerting ADJ. bewildering and disturbing; perplexing
Déjà vu is a *disconcerting* feeling that you've had that same experience in the past.

discord N. lack of agreement; strife
There was so much *discord* within the political party that it split into three groups.

discordant ADJ. not in tune
The United States is a country in which *discordant* voices are allowed to be heard.

discount V. to disregard
The judge ordered the jury to *discount* the witness's comments.

discourse N. verbal expression
The level of *discourse* in this university is high.

discreet ADJ. having good sense and behavior
An ambassador normally should be *discreet*.

discrepancy N. difference between
The *discrepancy* in results between the two experiments meant that the scientist had to repeat the experiment.

discrete ADJ. constituting a separate thing; distinct
He will lecture on how to determine the *discrete* orbit of a space object.

discretion N. quality of showing self-restraint in speech or actions; circumspection; freedom to act on one's own
The teacher left it to the student's *discretion* how long he should make his research paper.

discriminating ADJ. able to see differences; prejudiced
The art critic has *discriminating* taste in art.

discursive ADJ. wandering from topic to topic
The French writer Montaigne was a master of the *discursive* essay.

disdain N. scorn or contempt

Steve has *disdain* for people who don't work hard.

disheveled ADJ. untidy, unkempt

They were *disheveled* after their two-week expedition.

disinclination N. unwillingness

The employee politely expressed a *disinclination* to complete the job on time.

disingenuous ADJ. not candid; crafty

The prosecutor accused the witness of being *disingenuous*.

disinterested ADJ. unprejudiced; objective

The novelist strives to present a *disinterested* view of modern society.

disjointed ADJ. lacking order or coherence; dislocated

The police officer gradually pieced together the drunk's *disjointed* account of the incident.

disparage V. to belittle

The new student was *disparaged* by his classmates.

disparate ADJ. dissimilar

Science seeks to find order in the *disparate* phenomena of nature.

disparity N. difference; incongruity

The *disparity* in qualifications between the two job applicants means that the better qualified person will probably get the job.

dispassionate ADJ. impartial; unaffected by emotion

The teacher was careful to be *dispassionate* in awarding final grades to her students.

dispel V. to drive out

My doubts about the plan were *dispelled* by the reasonable explanation.

disposition N. tendency; temperament

Nancy has a pleasant *disposition*.

disputatious ADJ. argumentative, fond of arguing

Since you speak clearly and are *disputatious*, perhaps you should join the debating team.

disquiet N. absence of peace; anxiety

Our *disquiet* grew when we realized that our friends were now six hours overdue.

disreputable ADJ. lacking respectability

The *disreputable* agent tricked the young writer into paying him a lot of money.

dissemble V. to pretend; disguise one's motives

Psychologists say that a smile can be used to help a person *dissemble*.

disseminate V. to spread; scatter; disperse

The news was *disseminated* via television and radio.

dissension N. difference of opinion

There is so much *dissension* in the committee that no agreement can be reached.

dissent V. to disagree

One justice *dissented* from the Supreme Court's ruling.

dissident ADJ. disagreeing

The dictator didn't tolerate the expression of *dissident* opinions.

dissipate V. to scatter; pursue pleasure to excess

The crowd's anger *dissipated* as time passed.

dissipated ADJ. wasted; excessive in the pursuit of pleasure

Hugh's doctor recommended that he stop living a *dissipated* life.

dissolution N. disintegration; debauchery

Most religions teach that the *dissolution* of the body at death does not mean the extinction of the individual's spiritual self.

dissonance N. lack of agreement; discord

The conflict between his two beliefs created *dissonance* in his mind.

dissuade V. to persuade someone to alter intentions

Rob's mother tried to *dissuade* him from joining the football team.

distend V. to expand; swell out

The balloon *distended* as it filled with water.

distill V. to purify; concentrate; refine

The book *distills* a lifetime of experience into 300 pages.

distrait ADJ. inattentive; preoccupied

In a *distrait* moment Judy drove her car into the car ahead of her.

distraught ADJ. worried, distressed

Distraught relatives gathered in the airline terminal to await news of the overdue plane.

diva N. operatic singer; prima donna

The *diva* retired after a glorious thirty years in opera.

divergent ADJ. differing; deviating
A healthy democracy is able to tolerate *divergent* views.

diversity N. variety
The newspaper seeks to reflect a *diversity* of opinions.

divest V. to strip; deprive; rid
The court *divested* the company of its overseas assets.

divine V. to foretell
Fortune-tellers claim to be able to *divine* the future.

divisive ADJ. creating disunity
Divisive elements within the political party threatened to destroy it.

divulge V. to reveal; make known a secret
The chef refused to *divulge* her secret recipe.

docile ADJ. submissive
The ferocious lion became *docile* in the hands of the professional trainer.

doctrinaire ADJ. rigidly devoted to theories
The officials of that political party are extremely *doctrinaire*.

doctrine N. principles presented for acceptance; dogma
The bishop discussed church *doctrine* with the cardinal.

document V. to provide with written evidence to support
The teacher told the students to *document* their research papers.

doggerel N. poor verse
The lines, "We seek him here, we seek him there" could be described as *doggerel*.

dogma N. belief asserted on authority without evidence
The findings of modern science have often clashed with religious *dogma*.

dogmatic ADJ. stating opinions without proof
Our teacher asked us to look at the issue with open minds and not be *dogmatic*.

doleful ADJ. sad, mournful
The *doleful* song brought tears to our eyes.

domicile N. home
By law, you must vote in the state where your *domicile* is.

dormant ADJ. inactive
The volcano has been *dormant* for over 100 years.

dour ADJ. sullen and gloomy
Some people seem to be born cheerful, while others have a *dour* personality.

dowager N. an elderly woman of high social station
The *dowager* is a well-known patron of the arts in St. Louis.

doyen N. a man who is the senior member of a group
Professor Parker is regarded as the *doyen* of marine biologists.

draconian ADJ. extremely severe
The economic crisis calls for *draconian* measures.

droll ADJ. amusing in a quaint or odd way
One thing Val likes about Chris is his *droll* humor.

dross N. waste; worthless matter; trivial matter
Tina loves to sift through the *dross* on the bargain rack at the boutique for a good bargain.

dualism N. philosophical belief that reality comprises two fundamental elements, such as mind and matter
The history of philosophy can be seen, at least to some degree, as a debate between the proponents of *dualism* and the advocates of monism—the view that reality is composed of one fundamental element.

dubious ADJ. doubtful
Beth won the *dubious* distinction of "Most Underachieving Student."

dudgeon N. a feeling of offense or resentment
The president is in high *dudgeon* over Congress's refusal to pass the bill.

dulcet ADJ. pleasant sounding
The *dulcet* sound of the rain lulled us to sleep.

dupe V. to deceive, trick
Lew was *duped* into paying a lot of money for an inferior camera.

duplicitous ADJ. deceptive, dishonest
Steve is not above being *duplicitous* to get what he wants.

duress N. threat of force or intimidation
The confession was obtained under *duress*.

dyslexia N. inability to associate letter symbols with sounds
Many people have become very successful despite having *dyslexia*.

dystopia N. an imaginary place in which life is bad
Brave New World is Aldous Huxley's depiction of a *dystopia*.

E

ebullient ADJ. exhilarated, enthusiastic
The baseball player was *ebullient* after pitching a no hitter.

eccentric ADJ. odd; irregular
The English are known for tolerating *eccentric* behavior.

ecclesiastical ADJ. relating to a church
The bishop spent his weekend working on *ecclesiastical* affairs.

eclectic ADJ. selecting from various sources
The English textbook is an *eclectic* collection of literary works.

ecstatic ADJ. joyful
The couple was *ecstatic* after their child was born.

ecumenical ADJ. universal; concerned with promoting unity among churches or religions
The *ecumenical* group is holding a meeting of representatives of six churches to discuss common beliefs.

edict N. a decree issued by an authority having the force of law; formal command
The military government issued an *edict* saying that no one could leave the country.

edification N. intellectual, moral, or spiritual improvement
Sam took a religion class in the hope it would result in his *edification*.

edifice N. building; elaborate conceptual structure
Banks are often impressive *edifices*.

efface V. to erase
The date on the coin had been *effaced*.

effervescent ADJ. bubbly, lively
John's *effervescent* personality livened up the party.

effete ADJ. depleted of vitality; overrefined, decadent
The professor was accused of being an *effete* snob.

efficacious ADJ. efficient, effective
The treatment proved *efficacious*.

efficacy N. efficiency, effectiveness
The trials proved the *efficacy* of the new drug.

effigy N. likeness of a person
The protesters burned an *effigy* of the president.

effrontery N. shameless boldness; presumptuousness
The freshman had the *effrontery* to question the professor's conclusion.

effulgent ADJ. shining brightly
The planet Jupiter is *effulgent* tonight.

effusion N. liquid or other matter poured forth; an unrestrained outpouring of feeling
His poetic *effusions* were interesting for a while but are now becoming tiresome.

effusive ADJ. expressing emotion freely
The teacher was embarrassed by the student's *effusive* expression of thanks.

egalitarianism N. characterized by belief in equal rights for all people
Egalitarianism is an important American value.

egocentric ADJ. self-centered
I could see Jim was *egocentric* because he talked only about himself.

egotistical ADJ. excessively self-centered; conceited
Although Steve is *egotistical*, he is quite popular.

egregious ADJ. obviously bad
The English teacher marks *egregious* errors with a large red "X."

elaborate V. to add details
Try to *elaborate* on the basic points you've made.

elaborate ADJ. intricate and rich in detail
The family made *elaborate* preparations for the wedding.

elation N. joy
Jennifer's *elation* was obvious from her big smile.

elegy N. poem or song expressing lamentation
The poet wrote an *elegy* after her country was occupied by foreign forces.

elevated ADJ. exalted; lofty; noble
The class studied literature dealing with *elevated* themes such as nobility.

elicit V. to provoke, draw out
The teacher's question *elicited* several responses.

elite N. select group of people
Only the *elite* among the recruits were selected for officer training.

elitism N. belief that certain people deserve preferred treatment; control by a select group
The teacher argued for an end to *elitism* in public education.

elixir N. a substance believed to have the power to cure ills
Many people consider aspirin to be an *elixir* for many ills.

Elysian ADJ. blissful; delightful
The poet's *Elysian* vision enthralled a generation of readers.

eloquence N. effective speech
Although I admire the candidate's *eloquence*, I don't plan to vote for him.

elucidate V. to clarify
The student asked the teacher to *elucidate* her explanation.

elusive ADJ. evasive; hard to grasp
The concept is an *elusive* one, but I'm beginning to understand it.

emaciated ADJ. thin and wasted
Jill was *emaciated* after her long diet.

emanate V. to issue forth
Steam *emanated* from the radiator.

emancipation N. freedom
The *emancipation* of slaves was a great milestone in American history.

embellish V. to adorn; decorate; enhance; make more attractive by adding details
In a second account of events, the witness *embellished* his story.

embodiment N. representation in bodily or physical form; incarnation
The movie star is the *embodiment* of the perfect man.

embroil V. to involve in
Don't *embroil* me in your dispute.

embryonic ADJ. rudimentary; in early stages of development
The newly independent country is in an *embryonic* state of development.

emend V. to correct
The editor *emended* the error in the manuscript.

émigré N. person who has left a native country, especially for political reasons
The novel is about Russian émigrés in Paris.

eminence grise N. a person who exercises power or influence without holding an official position
Many people regard a distinguished retired professor, Dr. Chambliss, as the college's *eminence grise.*

eminent ADJ. celebrated, distinguished
The college invited an *eminent* scholar to speak at its graduation ceremony.

emollient ADJ. smoothing; mollifying
The president's *emollient* approach has helped to keep his party unified.

emotive ADJ. appealing to or expressing emotion
Emotive language often makes it difficult to discuss an issue rationally.

empathetic ADJ. of, relating to, or characterized by empathy; sympathetic
The leader of the country asked the people to be *empathetic* to the suffering of the poor.

empathy N. putting oneself in another's place; sympathy
We felt *empathy* for the victims of the disaster.

empirical ADJ. derived from observation or experiment
Empirical evidence supports the theory.

emulate V. to imitate, copy
The young author *emulated* her favorite writer.

enamored ADJ. captivated
Bill became *enamored* of Judy, his co-worker at the office.

encomium N. a formal expression of praise
The dean of students ended the dinner for the retiring professor with an *encomium* about her passion for teaching.

encumber v. to hinder, burden
The business is *encumbered* with heavy debts.

endemic ADJ. inherent, belonging to an area
Malaria is *endemic* in that area.

enervate v. to weaken
The hot weather has *enervated* me.

enfant terrible N. one whose unusual behavior or
ideas disturbs others
The iconoclastic young painter is the *enfant terrible*
of the New York art scene.

engender v. to cause, produce
The scientist tried to *engender* a response
in the test subject.

engrossed ADJ. occupied fully
Stan is *engrossed* in his preparation for the GRE.

enhance v. to increase; improve
Enhancing your vocabulary will improve your
chances of doing well on the GRE.

enigma N. puzzle; mystery
The main character in the novel is an *enigma*.

enigmatic ADJ. deeply puzzling; mysterious; obscure
The student found the character in the novel to be
enigmatic.

enjoin v. to order, urge; officially forbid
The court order *enjoined* the band from producing
more CDs.

enmity N. ill will; hatred
The peace negotiator worked to reduce the *enmity*
between the two countries.

ennui N. boredom
Peter took up several hobbies in order to overcome
ennui.

enrapture v. to fill with delight
The children were *enraptured* by the movie.

ensconced v. settled comfortably
The couple was *ensconced* at a table in the café.

entail v. to involve as a necessary result
Achievement usually *entails* hard work.

enthralling ADJ. captivating; enslaving
His novel is so *enthralling* that I can hardly put it
down.

enticing ADJ. tempting; attractive
The *enticing* candy was waved in front of the child.

entity N. something that exists
We established the company as a legal *entity*.

entomology N. the scientific study of insects
Agriculture is one of the main areas in which
entomology has a practical application.

entreat v. to beg, plead
John's mother *entreated* him not to join the army.

entrepreneur N. a person who organizes a business,
taking the risk for the sake of profit
Some people prefer having a secure job to being an
entrepreneur.

enunciate v. to pronounce clearly
The teacher trained the students to *enunciate* their
words.

eon N. indefinitely long period of time
The Earth existed for *eons* before life appeared
on it.

ephemeral ADJ. short-lived; fleeting
By its nature, journalism is *ephemeral*.

epic N. a long narrative poem in elevated language
celebrating the exploits of a hero
One of the great *epics* of world literature is
Homer's *Iliad*.

epic ADJ. relating to a long narrative poem in elevated
language; heroic or grand in scale or nature
Charles Lindbergh's book *The Spirit of St. Louis*
recounts his *epic* transatlantic flight of 1927.

epicure N. person with refined tastes
Grace prides herself on being an *epicure*.

epicurean ADJ. devoted to pleasure
The store caters to *epicurean* tastes.

epidemic N. a widespread disease
The *epidemic* is spreading from country to country.

epidermis N. the outer protective nonvascular layer
of the skin of vertebrates
In vertebrates, the *epidermis* is made up of many
layers of cells.

epigram N. short and witty saying
A famous *epigram* is Mark Twain's "Rumors of my
death have been greatly exaggerated."

epiphany N. comprehension of reality through
a sudden intuitive realization
The wounded soldier experienced an *epiphany*
as he lay in the hospital.

epistemology N. branch of philosophy that examines the nature of knowledge
Distinguishing justified belief from opinion is one of the tasks of *epistemology*.

epithelial ADJ. relating to the epithelium, membranous tissue composed of one or more compact layers of cells that covers most internal and external surfaces of the body, including its organs
Epithelial tissue is nonvascular.

epithet N. a word or phrase characterizing a person or thing
A popular *epithet* for emperors was "The Great."

epitome N. representative of a group; ideal example
For many people John Wayne is the *epitome* of the rugged American male.

epochal ADJ. of a particular period of history, especially one considered important
The rise of modern China may one day be considered as an *epochal* event.

eponym N. person from whose name something is derived
The mythological figure Romulus is the *eponym* for Rome.

equanimity N. composure, calmness
The leader kept his *equanimity* throughout the crisis.

equilibrium N. a stable, balanced state
Engineers waited for the system to achieve *equilibrium*.

equine ADJ. relating to horses
Mary loves *equine* sports.

equitable ADJ. just and impartial
The lawyers reached an *equitable* settlement in the dispute.

equivocal ADJ. ambiguous; misleading
The general's reply was *equivocal*.

equivocate V. to intentionally use vague language
The judge ordered the witness to stop *equivocating*.

eradicate V. to wipe out
The new government seeks to *eradicate* all opposition to its rule.

errant ADJ. mistaken; straying from the proper course
The safety officer destroyed the *errant* rocket by remote control.

erratic ADJ. unpredictable; wandering
The student's performance on tests is *erratic*.

erroneous ADJ. mistaken; wrong
The teacher corrected the student's *erroneous* statement.

ersatz ADJ. being an imitation or substitute
That soap opera is a good place to see displays of *ersatz* emotion.

erudite ADJ. learned; scholarly
Professor Walsh is so *erudite* he knows something about practically everything.

erudition N. deep and wide learning
Professor Wilson possesses vast *erudition*.

eschew V. to abstain from, avoid
Bob *eschews* dessert when he's dieting.

esoteric ADJ. hard to understand; known only to a few
Jill enjoys reading *esoteric* poetry.

espouse V. to support, advocate
I find it interesting to read newspapers that *espouse* views different from my own.

esprit de corps N. team spirit
To build *esprit de corps*, the battalion has a party every month.

essay V. to make an attempt; subject to a test
The director asked the grumpy actor to *essay* a smile.

essentialism N. the practice of regarding something (as a presumed human trait) as having innate existence or universal validity rather than as being a social, ideological, or intellectual construct; a philosophical theory ascribing ultimate reality to essence embodied in a thing perceptible to the senses
The sociologist describes *essentialism* as the tendency to ascribe some invisible essence to all members of a particular group.

esteem V. to value; respect
The professor is *esteemed* by his students

estimable ADJ. admirable; possible to estimate
The two countries see one another as *estimable* adversaries.

estranged ADJ. alienated
The *estranged* couple rarely see each other.

ethereal ADJ. insubstantial, intangible; spiritual
The ghost lives an *ethereal* existence.

ethical ADJ. conforming to moral standards
The job demands high *ethical* standards.

ethnic ADJ. relating to cultures or races
The country is torn by *ethnic* conflict.

ethnocentric ADJ. based on the attitude that one's group is superior
It's easy to make *ethnocentric* assumptions when studying other cultures.

ethnologist N. scientist who studies and compares human cultures
Claude Lévi-Strauss was a French anthropologist and *ethnologist* who has been called the "father of modern anthropology."

ethologist N. scientist who studies animal behavior
Konrad Lorenz was a pioneering *ethologist*.

ethos N. beliefs or character of a group
The new director wants to create a new *ethos* in the company.

etiology N. causes or origins
The disease has a complex *etiology*.

etymology N. origin and history of a word
A good dictionary gives the *etymology* of words.

eugenics N. study of the hereditary factors that influence the hereditary qualities of the human race and ways to improve these qualities
One of the early critics of the philosophy of *eugenics* was the Roman Catholic writer G.K. Chesterton.

eulogy N. high praise, especially of a person who has recently died
The teacher's *eulogy* was delivered by the school principal.

euphemism N. use of inoffensive language in place of unpleasant language
"Rest room" is a *euphemism* for "toilet."

euphony N. pleasant and harmonious sound
Euphony is a notable feature of this poem.

euphoria N. a feeling of extreme happiness
There was *euphoria* in the city after the home team won the World Series.

euthanasia N. mercy-killing
Euthanasia is one of the important moral issues in modern medicine.

evanescent ADJ. transitory, short-lived
The theme of this poem is that life is *evanescent*.

evince V. to show plainly
The teacher asked the class to *evince* three reasons for the failure of the experiment.

eviscerate V. to disembowel; take away a vital part
The dictator ordered the prisoner to be *eviscerated*.

evocative ADJ. tending to call to mind or produce a reaction
The poem is *evocative* of childhood.

evoke V. to produce a reaction; call to mind; create anew
The smell of leaves *evoked* memories of football games from his childhood.

exacerbate V. to aggravate, make worse
Moving around will *exacerbate* your injury.

exacting ADJ. extremely demanding
My English teacher has *exacting* standards for compositions.

exalted ADJ. raised in rank or dignity
Fred was still humble despite his *exalted* position in the company.

excommunicate V. to deprive of membership in a group
Dave was *excommunicated* from the church.

excoriate V. to criticize strongly
The shocking behavior of the official was *excoriated* in the media.

exculpate V. to clear of blame, vindicate
The hearing's finding *exculpated* the accused soldier.

execrable ADJ. detestable, abhorrent
The judge sentenced the man to life imprisonment for his *execrable* crime.

exegesis N. critical interpretation or explanation
The Bible scholar wrote an *exegesis* of the Gospel of Luke.

exemplar N. example worth imitating
Shakespeare's work has been an *exemplar* for writers for hundreds of years.

exemplary ADJ. commendable; worthy of imitation
The soldier won a medal for his *exemplary* conduct.

exemplify V. to show by example
The principal urged the seniors to *exemplify* good conduct for the younger students.

exercise V. to absorb the attention of; upset
The math problem has *exercised* my mind all day.

exhort V. to urge by strong appeals
The captain *exhorted* her teammates to make a greater effort.

exhume V. to remove from a grave
The judge ordered the remains *exhumed*.

exigency N. crisis; urgent requirements
The civil defense team is prepared for all *exigencies*.

exigent ADJ. requiring immediate action or remedy
Exigent circumstances allow the police to search the house without a warrant.

existential ADJ. having to do with existence; based on experience; having to do with the philosophy of existentialism
Several forms of *existential* psychotherapy have been developed.

exodus N. departure of a large number of people
After the government collapsed there was an *exodus* of people from the capital.

exogenous ADJ. originating externally
Carcinogens are *exogenous* factors

exonerate V. to absolve, clear of blame
The trial *exonerated* all of the accused.

exorbitant ADJ. greater than reasonable
The doctor's fees are *exorbitant*.

exorcise V. to expel evil spirits; free from bad influences
Writing a story about her bad experiences helped to *exorcise* the memory of them from her mind.

exotic ADJ. foreign, romantic, unusual
Jean enjoys visiting *exotic* places.

expansive ADJ. sweeping, comprehensive
We have an *expansive* view from our house on the hill.

expatiate V. to speak or write at length
The biologist *expatiated* on ecology for two hours.

expatriate N. someone living outside his or her land
There are many *expatriates* living in former British colonies such as Singapore and Hong Kong.

expedient ADJ. suitable; related to self-serving methods
The *expedient* course of action is not always the moral one.

expeditious ADJ. done with speed and efficiency
Carry out the plan in the most *expeditious* way possible.

expiate V. to atone for
Tom performed an act of penance to *expiate* his sins.

explicable ADJ. able to be explained
The new theory makes the observations *explicable*.

explicit ADJ. very clear; definite
The instructions are *explicit*.

exploit V. to unfairly use others to gain advantage; to use to the greatest possible advantage
The company was accused of *exploiting* its workers.

exponent N. a person who champions or advocates
Senator Smith is an *exponent* of free trade.

exponential ADJ. very great; becoming more and more rapid
The population is increasing at an *exponential* rate.

expository ADJ. explanatory
The teacher asked the students to write an *expository* essay on the topic.

expostulation N. scolding; reproof
The principal's *expostulations* lasted half an hour.

expound V. to elaborate
The professor *expounded* on his theory.

expunge V. to cancel; remove
His name was *expunged* from the records.

expurgate V. to censor
Certain scenes have been *expurgated* from the movie.

extant ADJ. in existence; not lost
The college library has all of the *extant* writing of Willa Cather.

extemporaneous ADJ. unrehearsed
The competition requires you to give an *extemporaneous* talk.

extenuating ADJ. mitigating, reducing in severity
The judge considered the *extenuating* circumstances in the case.

extirpate v. to root up; destroy
The prosecutor vowed to *extirpate* corruption in state government.

extol v. to praise
Critics *extolled* the new novel.

extort v. to obtain something by threat
Jim *extorted* money from the old man.

extraneous ADJ. not essential
Eliminate *extraneous* information from your report.

extrapolate v. to estimate by projecting known information
Extrapolating from present trends, the Earth will be uninhabitable in a few hundred years.

extravagant ADJ. excessive; beyond reasonable limits
The Elliots spent an *extravagant* amount of money on their daughter's wedding.

extremity N. farthest point
The North Pole and the South Pole are two of the Earth's *extremities*.

extricate v. to free from
We wondered how we could *extricate* ourselves from the awkward situation.

extrinsic ADJ. not inherent or essential
Extrinsic motivation through money and presents improved John's school performance.

exuberance N. unrestrained enthusiasm; abundance; lavishness
I admire the *exuberance* of the young composer's work.

exude v. to give off
The cheerleaders *exude* enthusiasm.

exult v. to rejoice
The coach allowed his team a day off from practice to *exult* in the victory.

F

fabricate v. to construct; to fake, falsify
The jury believed that the witnesses' story was *fabricated*.

facade N. the front of a building; face; superficial appearance
The boy's brave *facade* crumbled after the fight began.

facet N. aspect; side
The class discussed every *facet* of the issue.

facetious ADJ. humorous
Two boys sat in the back of the class making facetious comments.

facile ADJ. easy; superficial
I find their argument *facile*.

facilitate v. to make less difficult
Adequate rest *facilitates* learning.

facility N. ability
I have limited *facility* in mathematics.

faction N. a group of people forming a minority within a larger group
A vocal *faction* is against the proposal.

faculty N. ability; power
The ability to reason is one of our greatest *faculties*.

fait accompli N. something done about which it is too late to argue
The CEO presented the merger to the board as a *fait accompli*.

fallacious adj. false
Recent studies have proven the theory to be *fallacious*.

fallacy N. incorrect idea
It is a *fallacy* that the sun orbits the Earth.

fallow ADJ. plowed but not sowed; uncultivated
The field lies *fallow*.

fanaticism N. excessive enthusiasm or zeal
The historian studies religious *fanaticism*.

farcical ADJ. absurd, ridiculous
The performance was so bad it was *farcical*.

Fascism n. a system of government with centralization of power under a dictator, strict control of the economy, suppression of the opposition, and often a policy of belligerent nationalism and racism
Fascism flourished in Mussolini's Italy and Hitler's Germany.

fastidious ADJ. very fussy; concerned with detail
The teacher is *fastidious* in her preparation for class.

fatalism N. belief that events are determined by forces beyond one's control
The theme of *fatalism* reoccurs in the works of that novelist.

fathom V. to penetrate to the meaning or nature of; comprehend
Science has begun to *fathom* the mysteries of nature.

fatuous ADJ. foolishly self-satisfied
Nobody laughed at the *fatuous* comment.

fauna N. animals of a period or region
The guidebook describes the *fauna* of the area.

faux pas N. a social blunder
The lieutenant committed a *faux pas*, addressing the colonel as major.

fawning ADJ. trying to please by flattering and behaving in a servile manner
The *fawning* congressmen gathered around the president.

faze V. to disconcert, bother
The quarterback wasn't *fazed* by the fierce pass rush.

fealty N. loyalty owed by a vassal to his feudal lord
The king is generous to subjects as long as they pledge *fealty* to him.

feasible ADJ. possible
Someday a voyage to Mars may be *feasible*.

feckless ADJ. ineffective; irresponsible
The police department was criticized for its *feckless* attempts to catch the embezzler.

fecund ADJ. fertile, productive
The novelist's *fecund* imagination produced a wonderful fantasy world.

federal ADJ. related to a system of government in which power is divided between a central government and constituent states; related to federal government of a federation
The *federal* system of government has been adopted by many countries.

feign V. to pretend
The boy *feigned* ignorance of the theft.

felicitous ADJ. suitably expressed; appropriate; well-chosen
The writer Oscar Wilde is famous for his felicitous sayings.

felony N. a very serious crime
The *felony* was committed last week.

feral ADJ. existing in a wild or untamed state; having returned to an untamed state from domestication
The abandoned dog became *feral*.

fervent ADJ. full of strong emotion; impassioned
His protest was *fervent* but not very logical.

fervid ADJ. passionate, intense
He is known for his *fervid* devotion to the movement.

fervor N. warmth and intensity of emotion
Sheila embraced the movement with *fervor*.

fetid ADJ. having a bad smell
The fisherman didn't like the look of the black and *fetid* water of the lake.

fetter V. to bind, confine
The police *fettered* the suspect.

fey ADJ. having a magical or fairy-like quality
The hero meets a *fey* girl who says nothing and smiles enigmatically.

fiasco N. disaster
The party was a *fiasco*.

fiat n. arbitrary order; authorization
The king issued a *fiat* banning the use of fireworks in celebrations.

fictitious ADJ. imaginary
The story sounded believable but turned out to be *fictitious*.

fidelity N. loyalty; exact correspondence
Fidelity is a virtue that many people admire.

fiefdom N. estate of a feudal lord; something over which a dominant person or group has control
The principal runs the school like his *fiefdom*.

figurative ADJ. using figures of speech, metaphorical
Poets generally use a lot of *figurative* language.

filial ADJ. pertaining to a son or daughter
Mr. Smith's son took his *filial* duties seriously.

filibuster N. use of obstructive tactics in a legislature to block passage of a law
The *filibuster* prevented the bill from being passed by the legislature.

finesse v. to handle with deceptive or evasive strategy; to use finesse, that is refinement, in performance
The diplomat was able to *finesse* the problem.

fission N. splitting into two parts
The first nuclear *fission* reaction was produced in 1942.

fitful ADJ. starting and stopping
I had a *fitful* sleep last night.

flaccid ADJ. lacking firmness; lacking energy
Daily exercise will tone those *flaccid* muscles.

flag V. to grow tired, weak, or less enthusiastic
As the term went on, Sheila's enthusiasm for the subject *flagged*.

flagrant ADJ. conspicuously wicked, outrageous, shameless
It was a *flagrant* violation of the rules.

flamboyant ADJ. flashy, exciting
Ted is a *flamboyant* dresser.

fledgling N. beginner, novice
The *fledgling* chess player surprised everyone by beating an expert player.

fleeting ADJ. passing quickly; ephemeral
For a *fleeting* moment, Professor Johnson thought he understood the meaning of the universe.

flippant ADJ. disrespectfully light-hearted
Joe's *flippant* attitude always got him into trouble with his teachers.

flora N. plants of a region or era
I like the *flora* of subtropical areas.

florid ADJ. ruddy; reddish; flowery
The editor asked the writer to cut back on her *florid* prose.

flounder V. to waver, falter, struggle
The weak student *floundered* in the advanced class.

flourish V. to grow vigorously; thrive
The plant *flourished* after it was replanted.

flout V. to treat scornfully
Don't *flout* school regulations.

fluctuate V. to shift up and down; to come and go
The value of the U.S. dollar *fluctuates* on international money markets.

fluent ADJ. gifted in speaking
The most *fluent* speaker won the speech competition.

flux N. a continuous flowing
Many people picture time as a *flux*.

foible N. minor weakness
John's *foible* is his tending to want to take too long to complete tasks.

foment V. to incite, arouse
The protesters were accused of *fomenting* revolution.

foolhardy ADJ. rash; heedless
We told them that the plan was *foolhardy*, but they went ahead with it anyway.

foreboding N. sense of evil to come
The movie builds up an atmosphere of *foreboding* very effectively.

forensic ADJ. relating to law or debates
Julie is a member of the Charleston *Forensic* Society.

foreshadow V. to suggest beforehand
The novel *foreshadows* certain events early in the story.

foresight N. looking into the future; concern about the future
The student showed *foresight* in planning her study schedule for the month.

forestall V. to prevent, delay
The legislator *forestalled* opposition to the bill.

forlorn ADJ. dreary; unhappy; despairing
After the ship sank there were only three *forlorn* survivors in a lifeboat.

formidable ADJ. menacing, threatening
The enemy has assembled a *formidable* fighting force.

formulate V. to conceive; plan
The economists *formulated* a plan to improve the economy.

forswear V. to renounce; repudiate
The country *forswears* the use of nuclear weapons.

forte N. a person's strong point
Jim's *forte* is his willingness to work hard.

fortuitous ADJ. accidental; occurring by chance
The discovery was *fortuitous*.

foster V. to promote the growth of
The rich man established a museum to *foster* the arts.

founder V. to sink; fail, collapse
The ship *foundered* in the storm.

fracas N. loud dispute

There was a *fracas* outside the house last night.

fractious ADJ. unruly, rebellious

The president tried to control *fractious* elements in the party.

frenetic ADJ. hectic, frantic

There were *frenetic* last minute preparations for the president's arrival.

fresco N. a painting done on plaster

Leonardo DaVinci's *The Last Supper* is a *fresco*.

Freudian ADJ. relating to the psychoanalytic theories or practices of Sigmund Freud

The critic takes a *Freudian* approach to understanding the characters in the novel.

frieze N. ornamental band on a wall

The Parthenon *frieze* represents the procession of the Great Panathenaia, the most important festival of ancient Athens.

frivolous ADJ. lacking in seriousness; relatively unimportant

With only one week left to prepare for the exam, there isn't time for *frivolous* discussion.

froward ADJ. stubbornly contrary; obstinately disobedient

Even the most experienced trainer has trouble handling the *froward* colt.

frugal ADJ. thrifty

Being *frugal* allowed Bill to save twenty percent of his salary every month.

fulminate V. to attack loudly; denounce

The speaker *fulminated* against the growth of government.

fulsome ADJ. excessive, overdone

The award winner was embarrassed by the *fulsome* praise she received.

fundamental ADJ. forming a foundation; basic; essential

First, understand the *fundamental* ideas of the subject.

fundamentalist N. a person who believes in a literal interpretation of the Bible or other holy book.

The scientist and the *fundamentalist* debated the origin of the universe.

funereal ADJ. mournful

The mood at the school was *funereal* after we lost the state championship game.

furor N. general commotion, disorder; frenzy

The arrival of the movie star created a *furor*.

furtive ADJ. sneaky; stealthy

Cheryl keeps stealing *furtive* glances at Peter.

fusion N. merging things into one

The book argues for an approach in which there is a *fusion* of art, science, and religion.

futile ADJ. ineffective; fruitless

"Resistance is *futile*" is the rebel's slogan.

G

gaffe N. social blunder

Jim was so afraid of making a *gaffe* that he barely spoke to anyone at the party.

gainsay V. to deny or dispute

No one can *gainsay* the impact of technology on modern society.

galvanize V. to rouse or stir

The speech *galvanized* support for the plan.

gambit N. a stratagem or ploy

The general decided on the risky *gambit*.

gambol V. to frolic; leap playfully

We watched the dolphins *gambol* in the waves.

gamut N. entire range

The courses at this university run the *gamut* from anthropology to zoology.

gargantuan ADJ. huge; tremendous

There has been a *gargantuan* increase in public debt.

garner V. to gather and store

The candidate *garnered* the greatest support in rural areas.

garrulous ADJ. very talkative

The *garrulous* students were told to leave the library.

gauche ADJ. coarse and uncouth; clumsy

The girls were embarrassed by the boys' *gauche* behavior.

generic ADJ. universal; referring to a group

They are all in favor of the use of *generic* drugs.

genesis N. beginning; origin
Scientists are studying the *genesis* of the human species.

genial ADJ. having a pleasant or friendly disposition
People like Ted's *genial* personality.

genocide N. the systematic killing of a people or nation
The *genocide* was condemned by the United Nations.

genome N. the genetic material of an organism
An analogy to the human *genome* stored on DNA is the instructions stored in a library.

genre N. type, class; distinct literary or artistic category
Amy's favorite *genre* of literature is the novel.

gentry N. people of standing; class of people just below nobility
The king made sure he had the support of the *gentry* before introducing a new policy.

geomorphic N. relating to the study of the evolution and configuration of landforms
Geomorphic processes are influenced by tectonics, climate, ecology, and human activity.

geophysics N. the physics of the Earth and its environment
One of the phenomena studied by *geophysics* is the periodic reversal in polarity of the Earth's magnetic field.

geriatric ADJ. related to the aged or the aging process
As the population ages, *geriatric* medicine is becoming more important.

germane ADJ. appropriate, relevant
The judge ruled that the testimony was not *germane*.

gerrymander V. to divide an area into voting districts in a way that favors a political party
The lawsuit contends that the party's *gerrymandering* violates the state constitution.

gestalt ADJ. relating to a pattern of elements so unified that properties cannot be derived from the sum of its parts
During the 1920s and 1930s artists Paul Klee, Vasily Kandinsky, and Josef Albers explicitly drew upon *gestalt* theory for inspiration in their writings, paintings, and lectures.

gestation N. growth process from conception to birth
Human beings have a long *gestation* period.

gesticulate V. to motion or gesture
I saw the police officer *gesticulating*, so I pulled my car to the side of the road.

gingerly adv. very carefully
The soldier walked through the mine field *gingerly*.

glacial ADJ. like a glacier; extremely cold; slow
The weather man predicts a *glacial* winter this year.

glib ADJ. fluent in an insincere way; offhand
His remark sounded *glib*, but I don't think he meant it that way.

gloaming N. twilight; dusk
In the first *gloaming* of the night we heard a trumpet sound.

gluttony N. excessive eating and drinking
We went to the supermarket to prepare for a weekend of *gluttony*.

gnomic ADJ. expressed in short, pithy sayings
Few of the guru's followers fully understood her *gnomic* aphorisms.

goad V. urge on
The class *goaded* the teacher into telling them the date of her wedding.

gossamer ADJ. sheer; light and delicate, like cobwebs
Her blouse is made of a *gossamer* material.

gourmet N. connoisseur of food and drink
The *gourmet* decided to open a restaurant.

grandiloquence N. pompous language
The old senator was known for his *grandiloquence*.

grandiose ADJ. magnificent; pretentious
The rich man built a *grandiose* house on the hill.

gratify V. to please
The teacher was *gratified* by the student's progress.

gratuitous ADJ. free, voluntary; unnecessary
The viewers complained about scenes of *gratuitous* violence in the movie.

gravity N. seriousness
Perhaps you don't realize the *gravity* of the situation.

gregarious ADJ. sociable
Scientists say that human beings are essentially *gregarious*.

grouse V. to complain
Stop *grousing* about having too much work.

guile N. deception, trickery
Jack is a person who seems to be without *guile*.

guileless ADJ. free of cunning or deceit; artless
The *guileless* child is always being taken advantage
of by older children.

guise N. outward appearance; false appearance;
pretense
Under the assumed *guise* of an army officer,
he gained entry to the enemy base.

gullible ADJ. easily deceived
The con-man targets people who appear *gullible*.

gustatory ADJ. affecting the sense of taste
The restaurant is famous for its *gustatory* delights.

H

habitat N. dwelling place; the area in which an
organism lives
The bears' *habitat* is being threatened by
development.

hackneyed ADJ. worn out by overuse
The politician used the same *hackneyed* phrases
in every speech.

halcyon ADJ. calm and peaceful; happy; golden;
prosperous
On the eve of the battle the soldier's mind took him
back to the *halcyon* years before the war.

hallowed ADJ. holy; sacred
The couple walked through the *hallowed*
battlefield, remembering their son who had
died there.

hamlet N. small village
The president was born in a *hamlet* in Indiana.

hamper V. to obstruct
Economic development has been *hampered* by a
poorly educated work force.

haphazard ADJ. unplanned, happening by chance
The job was done in a *haphazard* way.

hapless ADJ. unfortunate, having bad luck
The *hapless* soldiers were killed by
a powerful explosion.

harangue N. long pompous speech; tirade
The old senator launched into a *harangue* about
the good old days.

harbinger N. precursor, sign of something to come
The fall in the stock market is a *harbinger* of
economic decline.

hardy ADJ. robust, vigorous
The plant is *hardy* enough to withstand the desert
heat.

harrowing ADJ. extremely distressing, terrifying
We had a *harrowing* journey by train along the
mountainside.

haughty ADJ. arrogant and condescending
Few of the employees like the *haughty* manager.

havoc N. widespread destruction; chaos
The explosion caused *havoc* in the city.

headstrong ADJ. reckless; insisting on one's own way
The mother had her hands full with her *headstrong*
toddler.

heathen ADJ. pagan; uncivilized and irreligious
The missionary preaches to the *heathen* people.

hector V. to bully; torment
The bully *hectored* the boy until the boy began
to cry.

hedonism N. pursuit of pleasure as a goal
Brad lived a life of *hedonism*.

heedful ADJ. paying close attention; mindful
Visitors should be *heedful* of the dangers
of a big city.

hegemony N. leadership, domination, usually
by a country
No one challenges the country's *hegemony*
in the region.

heinous ADJ. shocking, wicked, terrible
The *heinous* crime shocked the town.

Hellenism N. the culture and civilization of ancient
Greece
Hellenism had a great influence on all the
civilizations in the Mediterranean region.

hemorrhage N. heavy bleeding
Doctors used stitches to stop the *hemorrhage*.

Herculean ADJ. calling for great strength or courage
The historian started on the *Herculean* task of writing a comprehensive history of the world.

heresy N. opinion contrary to popular belief
The church condemned the belief as *heresy*.

heretical ADJ. opposed to an established religious teaching
The *heretical* beliefs were condemned by the Church.

hermaphrodism N. a condition in animals and humans in which male and female reproductive organs and secondary sexual characteristics are present in the same individual
The word "*hermaphrodism*" originates from the name of the Greek minor deity, Hermaphroditus.

hermeneutic ADJ. explaining; interpreting
The two literary critics disagree on which of the two approaches is the best *hermeneutic* approach.

hermetic ADJ. tightly sealed; magical
The scholar is studying the *hermetic* tradition associated with the Egyptian pyramids.

heterodox ADJ. unorthodox, not widely accepted
The newspaper likes to publish letters expressing *heterodox* views.

heterogeneous ADJ. composed of unlike parts, different, diverse
The school believes in *heterogeneous* grouping of students.

heuristic ADJ. helping to learn
The science teacher uses models of organic compounds as a *heuristic* device.

hiatus N. break, interruption, vacation
There was a *hiatus* in the signal, and then it resumed.

hidebound ADJ. excessively rigid; dry and stiff
The students complain that the principal is so *hidebound* that she won't consider any of their new ideas.

hierarchy N. a series arranged by rank or grade
Some people enjoy the challenge of climbing the company *hierarchy*.

hieroglyphics N. a system of writing in which pictorial symbols represent meaning or sounds; writing or symbols that are difficult to decipher
For many years scholars believed that Egyptian *hieroglyphics* did not represent phonetic characters.

hindsight N. perception of events after they happen
In *hindsight* I should not have bought the stock.

hinterland N. the remote or less developed parts of a country
Early American settlers clung to the East coast, leaving the *hinterland* largely unexplored.

hirsute ADJ. covered with hair
Scientists believe early man was *hirsute*.

histrionics N. exaggerated emotional behavior calculated for effect; theatrical arts or performances
Critics panned the actor's performance as mere *histrionics*.

hoary ADJ. very old; whitish or gray from age
The *hoary* poet read the poem he had written as a young man.

Hobson's choice N. a double bind; that is, a situation in which a person must choose between alternatives that are equally unsatisfactory
Henry Ford famously offered customers *Hobson's choice* in selecting what color Model-T they wanted: Any color as long as it's black.

hoi polloi N. the common people
The billionaire told his son not to mix with the *hoi polloi*.

holistic ADJ. emphasizing importance of the whole and interdependence of its parts
Only a *holistic* approach can solve this complex problem.

holocaust N. widespread destruction, usually by fire
The bombing caused a *holocaust* in the city.

homage N. public honor and respect
On George Washington's birthday we pay *homage* to "the father of our nation."

homeostasis N. automatic maintenance by an organism of normal temperature, chemical balance, etc., within itself
Various processes help the body to maintain tissue *homeostasis*.

homily N. sermon; tedious moralizing
The minister has the habit of writing his weekly *homily* on Wednesday morning.

homogeneous ADJ. composed of identical parts; uniform in composition
Our group is *homogeneous* in terms of age.

homogenize V. to make uniform in composition
Many countries are afraid that globalization will *homogenize* culture.

homonym N. word identical in pronunciation and spelling but different in meaning
The word "bear" and the word "bear" are *homonyms.*

hone V. to sharpen
The young writer *honed* her skills by writing an hour every day.

host N. a great number
The bankruptcy of the large company presented the town with a *host* of problems.

hubris N. overbearing pride; arrogance
Hubris and greed contributed to his downfall.

humane ADJ. merciful, kindly
Many people advocate the *humane* treatment of animals.

humanist N. one who believes in humanism, a system of ideas and values relating to human beings, emphasizing their value and de-emphasizing belief in God
The debate was between a Christian and a *humanist.*

husband V. to farm, manage carefully and thriftily
The expedition *husbanded* their supplies.

hybrid N. something of mixed origin or composition
The new vehicle is a *hybrid*—part car and part helicopter.

hydrological ADJ. concerned with water, especially its effects on the Earth
Life on Earth is dependent on the *hydrological* cycle.

hyperbole N. purposeful exaggeration for effect
The sports writer uses *hyperbole* regularly.

hyperbolic ADJ. relating to purposeful exaggeration for effect
The sportswriter likes to use *hyperbolic* language.

hyperventilate V. to breathe abnormally fast
The patient was *hyperventilating.*

hypochondria N. unfounded belief that one is often ill
The doctor suspected that her patient was suffering from *hypochondria.*

hypocritical ADJ. pretending to be virtuous; deceiving
His teacher scolded him for his *hypocritical* behavior.

hypostatize V. to ascribe physical existence to
The human mind seems to have a tendency to *hypostatize* the self.

hypothermia N. abnormally low body temperature
The survivors of the avalanche were treated for *hypothermia.*

hypothesis N. unproved theory; provisional explanation of facts
The scientist is trying to support his *hypothesis* with evidence.

hypothetical ADJ. based on assumptions or hypotheses
The existence of life on other planets is only *hypothetical.*

I

icon N. image; representation
The Statue of Liberty is an icon known around the world.

iconoclast N. one who attacks traditional or popular ideas or institutions
The writer is an *iconoclast* who continually questions the established order.

iconography N. the traditional or conventional images or symbols associated with a subject, especially a religious or legendary subject
In Hindu *iconography* the rotation of the Swastika in four directions has been used to represent many ideas, but it primarily describes the four directions, the four Vedas, and their harmonious whole.

idealistic ADJ. relating to the pursuit of noble goals
There is an *idealistic* element in American culture.

ideological ADJ. relating to a set of beliefs forming the basis of a political system
The party is trying to avoid *ideological* disputes.

ideology N. a set of beliefs forming the basis of a political system
The country's *ideology* was shaped by its culture.

idiom N. expression whose meaning as a whole differs from the meanings of its individual words
"Out-of-the-blue" is an *idiom* meaning "unexpected."

idiosyncrasy N. peculiarity of temperament, eccentricity
Everyone has some *idiosyncrasies*.

idiot savant N. a mentally retarded person who exhibits extraordinary talent in one field
The *idiot savant* startled the mathematics teacher by almost instantly calculating the square root of 23,787 in her head.

idolatry N. idol worship; blind or excessive devotion
The young lover places her lover on a pedestal and worships him with honest *idolatry*.

idyllic ADJ. simple and carefree; tranquil
The couple lives an *idyllic* life in Tahiti.

igneous ADJ. produced by fire; volcanic
Geologists identified the rock as *igneous*.

ignoble ADJ. dishonorable, not noble in character
His *ignoble* act disgraced his family.

ignominious ADJ. disgraceful and dishonorable
His life came to an *ignominious* end.

ilk N. type or kind
People of that *ilk* are often misunderstood.

illicit ADJ. illegal, improper
The car was searched at the border for *illicit* drugs.

illimitable ADJ. limitless
On a clear night the stars seem *illimitable*.

illuminate V. to make understandable
The English professor's lecture *illuminated* the poem.

illusion N. erroneous belief or perception
The magician created the *illusion* that the car had disappeared.

illusory ADJ. deceptive; not real
It took Mr. Rogers nearly a lifetime to realize that he was pursuing an *illusory* goal.

illustrious ADJ. famous, renowned
The *illustrious* basketball player signed autographs at the school.

imbroglio N. complicated situation; an entanglement
The novel's plot is based on how the main character gets into and out of one *imbroglio* after another.

imbue V. to infuse; dye, wet, moisten
The school held a pep rally to *imbue* students with school spirit.

immaculate ADJ. spotless; free from error
Ted's new white shirt is *immaculate*.

immanent adj. existing within
That religion believes that God is *immanent* in nature.

immaterial ADJ. extraneous, inconsequential, irrelevant, nonessential; not consisting of matter
It is *immaterial* to me whether you study or not.

imminent adj. about to happen; impending
The wedding is *imminent*.

immunological ADJ. relating to immune system
Dr. Stevenson is an expert on *immunological* disorders.

immutable ADJ. unchangeable
Scientists believe that the laws of nature are *immutable*.

impartial ADJ. unbiased, fair
The judge tries to be *impartial*.

impasse N. blocked path, dilemma with no solution
After a month of negotiations they reached an *impasse*.

impassioned ADJ. with passion
The convicted man made an *impassioned* plea for mercy.

impassive ADJ. showing no emotion
The novelist sees herself as an *impassive* recorder of human behavior.

impeach V. to charge with misdeeds in public office; accuse
The Senate voted to *impeach* the judge.

impeccable ADJ. perfect
The actor gave an *impeccable* performance.

impecunious ADJ. poor, having no money
The government offers help to those who are *impecunious*.

impede V. to hinder; block
The student's progress is *impeded* by an inability to concentrate on his work.

impediment N. barrier, obstacle
Russ believes that the greatest *impediment* to success is lack of focus on the task at hand.

imperative ADJ. essential; mandatory
It is *imperative* that you follow instructions precisely in an emergency.

imperious ADJ. arrogantly self-assured, domineering, overbearing
No one on the staff likes the boss's *imperious* manner.

impermeable ADJ. impossible to penetrate
The groundskeeper put an *impermeable* covering on the field.

impertinent ADJ. rude
The teacher considered the student's remark to be *impertinent*.

imperturbable ADJ. not easily disturbed
The head emergency room nurse remains *imperturbable* through every medical crisis.

impervious ADJ. impossible to penetrate; incapable of being affected
Most people regard Bart as a terrible writer, yet he continues to churn out stories, *impervious* to criticism.

impetuous ADJ. quick to act without thinking
She regretted her *impetuous* action almost as soon as she did it.

impinge V. to encroach
The Supreme Court ruling was criticized as *impinging* on civil liberties.

impious ADJ. not devout in religion
The ancient Greek philosopher Socrates was accused of being *impious*.

implacable ADJ. inflexible, incapable of being pleased
They were *implacable* in their opposition to the plan.

implausible ADJ. unlikely; unbelievable
The explanation was *implausible* but nevertheless turned out to be correct.

implement V. put into effect
The plan was *implemented* immediately.

implicate V. to involve in a crime, incriminate
Organized crime has been *implicated* in the recent murder.

implication N. that which is hinted or suggested
The *implications* of the decision are not clear.

implicit ADJ. implied; understood but not stated
Implicit in her remark is a criticism of the idea.

implode V. to collapse inward violently
The submarine sank to the sea floor and later *imploded*.

imply V. to hint or suggest
I don't understand what you are *implying*.

impolitic ADJ. not wise or expedient
It would be *impolitic* to present the governor with our decision at this time.

imponderable ADJ. unable to be weighed or assessed
A pragmatist, Jim sees no point in thinking about *imponderable* questions such as "Why do things exist?"

importune V. to ask repeatedly, beg
The student *importuned* the teacher to raise his grade.

impose V. to inflict, force upon
The general *imposed* military rule on the country.

imposing ADJ. dignified, grand
Government buildings are often designed to be *imposing*.

imposition N. something inflicted or forced upon
The request was regarded as an *imposition* by many.

impotent ADJ. powerless, ineffective, lacking strength
The country launched a full-scale nuclear attack, seeking to render the enemy *impotent*.

impound V. to seize and confine
The car was *impounded* because its owner didn't make the monthly payment.

impoverish V. make poor or bankrupt
The citizens of the state complained that high taxes were *impoverishing* them.

imprecation N. curse
The witch uttered an *imprecation*.

impregnable ADJ. totally safe from attack, able to resist defeat
The commander believes the base to be *impregnable*.

impresario N. a sponsor or producer of public entertainments
He is at an *impressionable* age.

impressionable ADJ. easily influenced or affected
He is at an *impressionable* age.

imprimatur N. official approval to publish; sanction
The Nobel laureate's introduction to the young scholar's book served as a sort of *imprimatur*.

impromptu ADJ. spontaneous, without rehearsal
The teacher asked the students to give *impromptu* speeches.

improvident ADJ. without planning or foresight, negligent
Because Jim was *improvident*, he had no savings.

improvise V. perform without preparation; make from available materials
The actor was forced to *improvise* when he forgot his lines.

imprudent ADJ. unwise or indiscreet
The coach's decision to start a freshman as quarterback was criticized as *imprudent*.

impudent ADJ. arrogant, audacious
The teacher punished the student for her *impudent* remark.

impugn V. to call into question, attack verbally
The newspaper article *impugned* the judge's integrity.

impunity N. exemption from penalty, punishment, or harm
After the enemy's air defenses were destroyed, our airplanes bombed their targets with *impunity*.

impute V. to relate to a particular cause or source; attribute the fault to; assign as a characteristic
The audience *imputed* an evil intention to the character.

inadvertent ADJ. careless, unintentional
The mistake was clearly *inadvertent*.

inalienable ADJ. incapable of being surrendered
The U.S. Constitution guarantees citizens certain *inalienable* rights.

inane ADJ. silly; senseless
The English teacher told the class that *inane* comments would not receive credit.

inanimate ADJ. not exhibiting life
In the cartoon *inanimate* objects come alive.

inanition N. exhaustion
In one of the Sherlock Holmes stories, Dr. Watson says about Holmes, "My friend had no breakfast himself, for it was one of his peculiarities that in his more intense moments he would permit himself no food, and I have known him presume upon his iron strength until he has fainted from pure *inanition*."

inarticulate ADJ. incapable of giving coherent, clear, or effective expression to one's ideas or feelings
Timothy was so upset that he became *inarticulate*.

inaugurate V. to begin or start officially; induct into office
The new president will be *inaugurated* in January.

incalculable ADJ. impossible to calculate; unpredictable
There are an *incalculable* number of stars in the universe.

incandescent ADJ. shining brightly
Thomas Edison invented the first commercially practical *incandescent* lamp.

incarcerate V. to put in jail; confine
The judge ordered that the prisoner be *incarcerated*.

incarnadine ADJ. blood-red in color
The dragon's flashing *incarnadine* eyes terrified the young knight.

incarnate V. to give bodily, especially human form to
The ancient Greeks believed that the goddess *incarnated* as a beautiful girl on the island of Naxos.

incendiary ADJ. combustible, flammable, burning easily
Incendiary bombs were dropped on the city.

incense V. to infuriate, enrage
The actor was *incensed* by the bad review of his performance.

inception N. beginning
Since its *inception* the paper has been unsuccessful.

incessant ADJ. continuous, never ceasing
I am going to complain about the *incessant* barking of my neighbor's dog.

incest N. sexual intercourse between persons too closely related to marry legally
Nearly every society has taboos against *incest*.

inchoate ADJ. imperfectly formed or formulated
The plan is still *inchoate*.

incidental ADJ. not essential; minor
The company will pay for the *incidental* expenses of your trip.

incipient ADJ. beginning to exist or appear; in an initial stage
It is difficult to diagnose the disease in its *incipient* stage.

incisive ADJ. perceptive; penetrating
This book offers an *incisive* analysis of the issue.

incite V. to arouse to action
The prisoner *incited* his fellow inmates to riot.

inclusive ADJ. tending to include all
Its leaders are working to make the political party more *inclusive*.

incognito ADJ. in disguise, concealing one's identity
The detective went to the party *incognito*.

incoherent ADJ. unintelligible; illogical
Your argument is *incoherent*.

incommunicado ADJ. deprived of communication with other people
The prisoner is being held *incommunicado*.

incompatible ADJ. inharmonious
The couple divorced because they were *incompatible*.

inconceivable ADJ. impossible, unthinkable
All-out nuclear war would cause *inconceivable* destruction.

inconclusive ADJ. not certain; open to doubt
The results of the experiment were *inconclusive*.

incongruity N. something that doesn't fit in
The detective looked for an *incongruity* in the suspect's story.

incongruous ADJ. not fitting
The old-fashioned furniture is *incongruous* in the modern office.

inconsequential ADJ. insignificant; unimportant
One dollar is an *inconsequential* amount of money to a billionaire.

inconspicuous ADJ. not readily noticeable
The new student made herself as *inconspicuous* as she could.

incontrovertible ADJ. indisputable
The findings of the commission are *incontrovertible*.

incorrigible ADJ. uncorrectable
The *incorrigible* student was sent to the principal.

incredulity N. skepticism, doubtfulness
Imagine our *incredulity* when we were told that a UFO had landed nearby.

incredulous ADJ. skeptical, doubtful
We were *incredulous* when the newspaper reported that a UFO had landed on the White House lawn.

incremental ADJ. relating to an increase
Countries are taking *incremental* steps toward eliminating environmental pollution.

inculcate V. to teach, impress in the mind
Schools try to *inculcate* good values in students.

inculpate V. to blame, charge with a crime
Andrew was *inculpated* in the crime.

incumbent ADJ. holding a specified office, often political
It is generally difficult for a challenger to defeat an *incumbent* president.

incursion N. sudden invasion
The country's defenses are prepared to resist an enemy *incursion*.

indefatigable ADJ. never tiring
Lucy was *indefatigable* in her efforts to improve her vocabulary.

indelible ADJ. permanent, not erasable
My first grade teacher made an *indelible* impression on me.

indeterminate ADJ. uncertain; indefinite
The witness described the man as being of an *indeterminate* age.

indicative ADJ. showing or pointing out, suggestive of
The speaker's tone is *indicative* of her attitude toward the subject.

indict V. to charge
Ten people were *indicted* for criminal activity.

indifferent ADJ. unmoved or unconcerned; mediocre
Many people are *indifferent* to events that occur far away.

indigenous ADJ. native, occurring naturally in an area
The *indigenous* Trees introduced from Europe are driving out *indigenous* ones in many parts of Australia.

indigent ADJ. very poor
The *indigent* family applied for food stamps.

indignant ADJ. angry, incensed, offended
The student was *indignant* at the suggestion that she had copied her assignment.

indiscriminate ADJ. random; not properly restrained
The city is troubled by acts of *indiscriminate* violence.

indoctrinate V. to imbue with a partisan point of view
The company tries to *indoctrinate* new workers.

indolent ADJ. habitually lazy, idle
The manager fired the *indolent* worker.

indomitable ADJ. fearless, unconquerable
The *indomitable* explorer refused to give up.

indubitable ADJ. unquestionable
The facts of the case are *indubitable*.

inducement N. act or process of persuasion or bringing about
No *inducement* could get the child to go to school.

induct V. to place ceremoniously in office; to admit to military service
The all-star basketball player was *inducted* into the hall of fame.

induction N. the process of deriving general principles from particular facts
The problem was solved by the use of *induction*.

inductive adj. related to induction
The following is an example of *inductive* reasoning: All of the ice we have examined so far is cold. Therefore, all ice is cold.

indulge V. to give in to a craving or desire
I went to the ice cream parlor to *indulge* my craving for chocolate ice cream.

indulgent ADJ. humoring; lenient; tolerant
The *indulgent* parents spoiled their child.

inebriated ADJ. drunk, intoxicated
Julia was arrested for driving when she was *inebriated*.

ineffable ADJ. incapable of being expressed
The poem is trying to express the *ineffable*.

ineffectual ADJ. not effective; weak
The steps taken to reduce unemployment were *ineffectual*.

ineluctable ADJ. not to be avoided or escaped; inevitable
The *ineluctable* conclusion of the research is that the comet will strike the Earth in 22 years.

inept ADJ. clumsy, awkward; incompetent
The actor's performance was *inept*.

inert ADJ. unable to move; sluggish
After the feast we sat at the table, *inert*.

inertia N. resistance to action or change
The *inertia* in the education system makes change slow.

inestimable ADJ. too great to be estimated
The diamond's worth is *inestimable*.

inevitable ADJ. unavoidable
It is *inevitable* that we will die.

inexorable ADJ. inflexible, unyielding
Nothing could stop the *inexorable* advance of the invading army.

inexplicable ADJ. difficult or impossible to explain
The *inexplicable* event left us all puzzled.

inextricable ADJ. incapable of being disentangled
Politics and economics are often *inextricable*.

infallible ADJ. incapable of making a mistake
No one is *infallible*.

infamous ADJ. notoriously bad
Adolph Hitler is one of history's *infamous* characters.

infamy N. reputation for bad deeds
Hitler and Stalin are names that will live in *infamy*.

infantile ADJ. childish, immature
The teacher scolded the student for his *infantile* behavior.

infatuated ADJ. strongly or foolishly attached to, inspired with foolish passion
Sheila is *infatuated* with Bill.

inference N. deduction; conclusion
What *inference* can we make from the statement?

infidel N. a person who does not believe in a religion
The knight went on a crusade against the *infidels*.

infiltrate V. to pass secretly into enemy territory
The spy *infiltrated* enemy headquarters.

infinitesimal ADJ. extremely tiny
A year is an *infinitesimal* amount of time in the life of the universe.

infirmity N. disease, ailment
The *infirmities* of the elderly are a major problem for society.

inflated ADJ. exaggerated
Bill has an *inflated* idea of his importance.

infrastructure N. an underlying foundation; basic facilities needed in a community
The poor country received a loan to improve its *infrastructure*.

infringement N. act of encroaching or trespassing; transgression, violation
The Supreme Court ruled that the law is an *infringement* of individual rights.

infuriate V. to enrage, provoke, outrage
The failing grade on the test *infuriated* the student.

ingenious ADJ. clever
The plan was *ingenious*.

ingénue N. a naive, innocent girl or young woman
The actress plays the part of the *ingénue* who falls in love with a Casanova.

ingenuous ADJ. naive and trusting; lacking sophistication
The *ingenuous* young heiress fell in love with the scheming Casanova.

ingrate N. ungrateful person
The *ingrate* refused to acknowledge the help he had received.

ingratiate V. to bring oneself purposely into another's good graces
The new employee tried to *ingratiate* himself with his boss.

ingress N. entrance
No means of *ingress* could be found on the UFO.

inherent ADJ. firmly established by nature or habit
The religion teaches the *inherent* goodness of human nature.

inhibit V. to prohibit; restrain
The plant's growth was *inhibited* by poor soil.

inimical ADJ. injurious or harmful; hostile, unfriendly
The policy was criticized as *inimical* to the country.

inimitable ADJ. defying imitation; matchless
No writer has matched the *inimitable* works of William Shakespeare.

iniquity N. wickedness, evil act
The preacher urged them all to avoid *iniquity*.

initiate V. to begin, introduce; enlist; induct
The question of which country had *initiated* hostilities didn't seem to matter much after the war started.

injunction N. command, order
The teacher's *injunction* was clear.

inkling N. hint; vague idea
We had only an *inkling* of what the future would bring.

innate ADJ. inborn
Most people probably have *innate* abilities that they don't fully develop.

innocuous ADJ. harmless
Many bacteria are *innocuous*.

innovation N. something newly introduced
Gabe likes to keep up with *innovations* in electronics.

innuendo N. indirect and subtle criticism, insinuation
The businessman used *innuendo* to undermine his rival's reputation.

innumerable ADJ. too many to be counted
The editor found *innumerable* errors in the manuscript.

inopportune ADJ. untimely; poorly chosen
The phone call came at an *inopportune* time.

inquest N. investigation; court or legal proceeding
The army began an *inquest* into the soldier's death.

insatiable ADJ. never satisfied
The student's demand for knowledge is *insatiable*.

inscribe V. to write or mark on a surface
The pen has my name *inscribed* on it.

inscrutable ADJ. impossible to understand fully
This poem is difficult to understand because it contains many *inscrutable* lines.

insensible ADJ. unconscious; unresponsive
A hard left hook to his head rendered the prize fighter *insensible*.

insentient ADJ. unfeeling, unconscious
The boxer was *insentient* after being hit with a hard right hook.

insidious ADJ. sly, treacherous, devious; causing harm in a way that is not apparent
The gangster's *insidious* plan was to infiltrate the police force.

insinuate V. to suggest, say indirectly, imply
Are you *insinuating* that I should improve my vocabulary?

insipid ADJ. lacking in flavor; dull
Joe was so tired all he felt like doing was watching *insipid* shows on television.

insolent ADJ. insulting and arrogant
The *insolent* student was suspended from school.

insoluble ADJ. not able to be solved or explained
The mathematician concluded that the problem was *insoluble*.

insolvent ADJ. bankrupt, unable to pay one's debts
The bank was forced to close when it became *insolvent*.

insouciant ADJ. indifferent; lacking concern or care
The teenager's *insouciant* attitude annoys her teachers.

instigate V. to incite, urge, agitate
The president vowed to bring those who had *instigated* the rebellion to justice.

instinctual ADJ. related to or derived from instinct
Much of human behavior is *instinctual*.

instrumental ADJ. serving as a means or a cause
Instrumental in our success was good planning.

insubstantial ADJ. modest, insignificant
Our meal was *insubstantial*.

insular ADJ. narrow-minded; isolated
The *insular* country allows no foreign newspapers to be sold.

insuperable ADJ. insurmountable, unconquerable
Despite seemingly *insuperable* obstacles, our team won the state championship.

insurgent ADJ. rebellious, insubordinate
The *insurgent* forces took over the capital.

insurrection N. rebellion
The *insurrection* was led by generals unhappy with the country's leadership.

intangible ADJ. not material
The nurse finds the *intangible* rewards of her job more satisfying than the tangible ones.

integral ADJ. central, indispensable
The engine is an integral part of a car.

integrity N. uprightness; wholeness
The witness testified to the *integrity* of the accused.

intemperate ADJ. not moderate
Try not to be *intemperate* in eating.

inter V. to bury
The bodies of the victims of the disaster were *interred* in a mass grave.

interdict V. to forbid, prohibit
The *interdicted* goods were seized by border police.

interject V. to interpose, insert
The comedian *interjected* humorous remarks during the speech.

interlocutor N. someone taking part in a dialogue
My *interlocutor* looked me directly in the eye.

interloper N. trespasser; meddler in others' affairs
Some of the older workers regarded the new boss as an *interloper*.

interminable ADJ. endless
After years of *interminable* debate, the bill was passed.

intermittent ADJ. starting and stopping
The rain is *intermittent*.

internecine ADJ. deadly to both sides
Centuries of *internecine* wars left both countries weak.

interpolate V. to insert; change by adding new words or material
The editor *interpolated* some information to clarify the writer's reference.

interpose V. to insert; intervene
The referee *interposed* himself between the two boxers.

interregnum N. interval between reigns; gap in continuity
The *interregnum* between empires lasted 100 years.

interrogate V. to question formally
The police detective *interrogated* the suspect.

intersperse V. to distribute among, mix with
Plain clothes agents were *interspersed* among uniformed policemen.

intervene V. to come between
The governor *intervened* in the dispute between the company and the labor union.

intimacy N. close acquaintance
Fred is afraid of *intimacy*.

intimate V. make known subtly and indirectly; hint (n. intimation)
The boss *intimated* that he would not approve my application for unpaid leave.

intimate ADJ. marked by close acquaintance
They have been *intimate* for five years.

intimation N. clue, suggestion
The first *intimation* we had that a problem existed was when the teacher called us.

intimidate V. fill with fear; inhibit by threats
The coach told his team not to be *intimidated* by the opponent's reputation.

intractable ADJ. not easily managed
The *intractable* student was assigned to a special class.

intramural ADJ. within an institution such as a school
Jane plays on the *intramural* basketball team.

intransigent ADJ. uncompromising, refusing to be reconciled
Both sides in the dispute were *intransigent*.

intrepid ADJ. fearless
The *intrepid* mountain climber refused to be driven back by the snowstorm.

intricate ADJ. complex; tangled
The lawyer was familiar with all the *intricate* details of the case.

intrinsic ADJ. inherent, internal
The philosopher believes in the *intrinsic* worth of all human beings.

introspective ADJ. contemplating one's own thoughts and feelings
Mary becomes *introspective* when she writes in her diary.

introvert N. someone given to self-analysis
The *introvert* was uncomfortable giving a speech.

intrusive ADJ. relating to trespass or invasion of another's privacy
I did not appreciate Tom's *intrusive* questions about my involvement with the group.

intuitive ADJ. instinctive, untaught
The mathematician solved the problem by an *intuitive* process.

inundate V. to cover with water; overwhelm
The rock star was *inundated* with fan mail after his concert.

inure V. to harden; accustom; become used to
The peasants have become *inured* to hardship.

invalidate V. to negate or nullify; cancel
New evidence has invalidated the theory.

invariable ADJ. unchanging
The journalist's *invariable* practice is not to reveal her sources.

invective N. verbal abuse
The moderator warned the debaters not to engage in *invective*.

inveigh V. to disapprove; protest vehemently
The critic *inveighed* against the decline in standards in music.

inveigle V. to win over by flattery or coaxing
Sam managed to *inveigle* his father into letting him borrow his car.

invert V. to turn upside down or inside out
The road sign was *inverted* by a gang of teenagers.

invest V. to endow with authority
The U.S. Constitution *invests* great power in the president.

investiture N. ceremony conferring authority
The student council holds its *investiture* in October.

inveterate ADJ. confirmed, long-standing, deeply rooted
An *inveterate* USC football fan, Steve never misses their games.

invidious ADJ. likely to provoke ill will, offensive
The *invidious* comments are likely to provoke a reaction.

invincible ADJ. invulnerable, unbeatable
The army believes it has assembled an *invincible* fighting force.

inviolable ADJ. safe from violation or assault
At the core of his values was a set of *inviolable* beliefs.

inviolate ADJ. not violated; intact
Certain central principles are *inviolate*.

in vitro ADV. and ADJ. outside the living organism in an artificial environment
Over the past thirty years scientists have made great advances in *in vitro* fertilization.

in vivo ADV. and ADJ. within a living organism
The researchers are conducting their studies of human metabolism *in vivo*.

invocation N. prayer
The *invocation* was given by a Navy chaplain.

invoke V. to call upon, request help
In his speech the president *invoked* the spirit of the country's Founding Fathers.

iota N. very tiny amount
There's not an *iota* of evidence to support the theory.

irascible ADJ. easily angered
Everyone is careful not to criticize Rick since he's such an *irascible* character.

irate ADJ. extremely angry; enraged
The *irate* customer demanded an immediate refund.

iridescent ADJ. showing many colors
The diamond is *iridescent*.

ironic ADJ. related to an incongruity between what might be expected and what occurs
It is *ironic* that the bus driver died as a passenger on a bus.

irony N. hidden sarcasm or satire; use of words conveying a meaning opposite to literal meaning
The writer makes frequent use of *irony*.

irreconcilable ADJ. cannot be accepted or resolved
The differences between the two sides are *irreconcilable*.

irredeemable ADJ. incapable of being remedied or reformed
The high school principal refused to believe that the boy's behavior was *irredeemable*.

irrefutable ADJ. impossible to disprove
Their argument was *irrefutable*, so we had little choice but to agree.

irrelevant ADJ. not applicable; unrelated
The editor cut *irrelevant* material from the story.

irreproachable ADJ. blameless
One of the reasons he was made a judge is his *irreproachable* character.

irresolute ADJ. unsure of how to act
Seeing that everyone else was *irresolute* in the crisis, the president's chief of staff took action in the president's absence.

irresolvable ADJ. unable to be resolved; not analyzable
The scientist concluded that the problem was *irresolvable*.

irreverent ADJ. disrespectful
The cartoonist takes an *irreverent* approach in portraying public figures.

irrevocable ADJ. conclusive, irreversible
The president took the *irrevocable* step of breaking diplomatic relations with the country.

isotope N. one of two or more atoms having the same atomic number but different mass numbers
Elements are composed of one or more naturally occurring *isotopes*.

itinerant ADJ. wandering from place to place, unsettled
Itinerant workers picked most of the grapes.

itinerary N. route of a traveler's journey
The boss's secretary confirmed his *itinerary*.

J

jaded ADJ. tired by excess or overuse; slightly cynical
A life in police work left Bill *jaded*.

jargon N. nonsensical talk; specialized language
Jargon makes it easier for specialists in a field to talk to one another.

jaundiced ADJ. having a yellowish discoloration of the skin; affected by envy, resentment, or hostility
He is a talented writer, but his *jaundiced* view of life becomes tiresome after a while.

jejune adj. not interesting; childish
The art critic called Ellen's painting, "*Jejune*, at best."

jettison v. to cast off, throw cargo overboard
Alice moved from New York to San Francisco, completely *jettisoning* her old life.

jihad N. A Muslim holy war; a crusade
Jihad can often refer to an internal struggle to correct one's own mistakes.

jingoism N. extreme support of one's country
The war film was widely criticized as an exercise in *jingoism*.

jingoist N. person who supports his or her country in an extreme way
The director of the controversial war film was accused of being a *jingoist*.

jocose ADJ. given to joking; merry
Fortunately most people at the holiday party were *jocose*.

jocular ADJ. jovial, playful, humorous
The class laughed at the teacher's *jocular* comment.

joie de vivre N. joy of living
Sally describes herself as, "87 years young and still full of *joie de vivre*."

jubilee N. special anniversary
The church had its *jubilee* last year.

judicious ADJ. having sound judgment
The president made a *judicious* decision in selecting the highly experienced general to lead the army.

juggernaut N. huge force destroying everything in its path
The 2004 USC football team was a *juggernaut*, going undefeated and winning the national championship.

juncture N. point where two things are joined; turning point
At this *juncture* in the country's history, we must carefully consider our course.

junta N. group of people united in political intrigue
The country's ruling *junta* has postponed the scheduled elections.

jurisdiction N. power to interpret and apply law; control
The court has no *jurisdiction* in this state.

jurisprudence N. philosophy of law
The student of *jurisprudence* is researching the effect of modern technology on the legal system.

justify v. proved to be right; to declare free of blame
The employee *justified* the expenditure by saying that it would save the company money in the long run.

juxtaposition N. side-by-side placement
Juxtaposition of the two photographs of the landscape showed the changes that had taken place.

K

Kafkaesque ADJ. characterized by distortion and impending danger
Many of Alfred Hitchcock's movies could be described as *Kafkaesque*.

karma N. a person's life force that determines his destiny in the next life
According to the law of *karma*, what we do in the present determines our future.

keynote N. note or tone on which a musical key is founded; main idea of a speech
The *keynote* of the president's speech was the need for all citizens to work together for the common good.

kindle v. to set fire to or ignite; excite or inspire
The team's first victory *kindled* the fans' interest.

kinetic ADJ. relating to motion; characterized by movement
The engineer measured the system's *kinetic* energy.

kismet N. fate; destiny
"I'm sure our love is *kismet*," the heroine told the hero.

knell N. sound of a funeral bell; omen of death or failure
The defeat was the death *knell* of the empire.

kudos N. fame, glory, honor
The instructor won *kudos* from students for her creative approach to teaching.

L

labile ADJ. likely to change
Tom's *labile* personality can make him difficult to get along with.

labyrinth N. maze
The office building was like a *labyrinth*.

laceration N. cut or wound
The child was treated for *lacerations* suffered in the accident.

lachrymose ADJ. tearful; sad
The mood at the funeral was *lachrymose*.

lackadaisical ADJ. idle, lazy; apathetic, indifferent
Stuart is a *lackadaisical* student.

lackluster ADJ. lacking brightness or vitality
His performance this year has been *lackluster*.

laconic ADJ. using few words
The *laconic* scientist was not an ideal guest on the talk show.

laissez-faire ADJ. relating to a doctrine that opposes government interference in the economy; noninterference in the affairs of others
The principal asked the teacher to take a less *laissez-faire* approach to students.

Lamaism N. Tibetan Buddhism
The term "*Lamaism*" probably derives from the Chinese "lama jiao" used to distinguish Tibetan Buddhism from Han Chinese Buddhism, "fo jiao."

Lamarckism N. a theory of biological evolution holding that acquired traits can be inherited
A form of *Lamarckism* was revived in the Soviet Union of the 1930s when Trofim Lysenko promoted Lysenkoism, which suited the ideological opposition of Joseph Stalin to genetics.

lambaste v. to thrash verbally or physically
The champion boxer *lambasted* his opponent.

lament v. to grieve; express sorrow; regret deeply
The poem *laments* the death of the poet's son.

lamentable ADJ. distressing; deplorable
There has been a *lamentable* increase in air pollution.

lampoon v. to attack with satire, mock harshly
The movie *lampoons* the country's leaders.

languid ADJ. lacking energy, indifferent, slow
Time moves at a *languid* pace at this tropical island resort.

languish v. to become weak; to live in disheartening conditions; to be neglected
A small part of the population was left to *languish* in poverty.

languor N. lassitude
They were overcome by weakness and *languor* during their stay in the tropics.

lapidary ADJ. relating to precious stones
Mr. Saunders sells *lapidary* equipment to jewelers in the New York area.

larceny N. theft of property
Bob was charged with *larceny*.

larder N. place where food is stored
It's a good idea to keep some canned food in the *larder* in case of emergency.

largess N. generosity; gift
As a result of the billionaire's *largess*, our town has a new public library.

larynx N. organ containing vocal cords
The *larynx* plays a vital role in speech.

lascivious ADJ. lustful
The movie appeals primarily to the *lascivious* impulses in people.

lassitude N. lethargy, sluggishness
I'm often overcome by *lassitude* on Sunday afternoon.

latent ADJ. present but hidden; potential
The program is designed to bring out the student's *latent* talent.

laud v. to praise
Julia's mother *lauded* her daughter's effort to improve her vocabulary.

laudable ADJ. praiseworthy
The student made a *laudable* effort to improve his vocabulary.

lavish ADJ. liberal; wasteful
The company president put a stop to *lavish* spending by his staff.

lax ADJ. careless
Lax safety standards were partially to blame for the accident.

layman N. a nonprofessional
The *layman* could not understand the technical language in the scientist's paper.

leery ADJ. suspicious
The child was taught to be *leery* of strangers.

legacy N. a gift made by a will; something handed down
Tom's watch is a *legacy* from his grandfather.

legerdemain N. trickery
The magician's *legerdemain* entertained the audience.

legible ADJ. readable
Make sure your handwriting is *legible*.

legion ADJ. constituting a large number
The number of atoms in the universe is *legion*.

legislate V. to decree, mandate, make laws
The primary purpose of Congress is to *legislate*.

legislation N. laws, decrees, mandates
The *legislation* was passed unanimously.

legitimate ADJ. in accordance with established standards; genuine; reasonable
The New York Jets have a *legitimate* chance to win the Super Bowl this year.

leitmotif N. a dominant, recurrent theme
Staircase imagery is a *leitmotif* in T.S. Eliot's writings.

lethargy N. inactivity
After a summer of *lethargy*, the students had difficulty adjusting to school work.

levitate V. to rise in the air or cause to rise
The magician made his assistant appear to *levitate*.

levity N. light manner or attitude
The principal told the students she wanted no *levity* during the exam period.

lexicon N. dictionary, list of words
The teacher compiled a *lexicon* of words that appear frequently on the GRE.

lexis N. vocabulary; the set of words in a language
Professor Summers is an expert in the field of *lexis* and grammar.

liaise V. to communicate and maintain contact
One of Amy's tasks as county librarian is to *liaise* with local libraries.

libel N. defamatory statement; act of writing something that smears a person's character
The writer was sued for *libel*.

liberal ADJ. tolerant, broad-minded; generous, lavish
Humanism is generally credited with creating a more *liberal* populace in Europe.

liberation N. freedom; emancipation
The *liberation* of the political prisoners was celebrated around the world.

libertarian N. one who believes in unrestricted freedom
The *libertarian* believes that government is an unnecessary evil.

libertine N. one without moral restraint
The young *libertine* was condemned by members of his community.

libidinal ADJ. relating to sexual desire
The court ruled that the movie appeals solely to *libidinal* impulses.

libido N. sexual desire
The research team is studying the effects of the drug on the male *libido*.

libretto N. the text of a dramatic musical work
The opera's *libretto* was translated from French into English.

licentious ADJ. immoral; unrestrained by society
Tom's *licentious* behavior threatened his good standing in the community.

lien N. right to possess and sell the property of a debtor
The court ordered a *lien* to be put on the property.

Lilliputian ADJ. extremely small
The doll house contains *Lilliputian* dishes on the dining table.

limn V. to draw; describe
The art teacher asked her students to *limn* the model's torso.

limpid ADJ. clear, transparent
Looking into the lake's *limpid* water, Paul saw fish swimming near the bottom.

lineage N. ancestry
The family has an ancient *lineage*.

linear ADJ. having one dimension; straight
Time can be imagined as moving in a *linear* fashion.

lingua franca N. a language used for communication among peoples speaking different languages
In Asia, English is often used as a *lingua franca* in business.

linguistics N. study of language
Linguistics studies such topics as the origin and structure of language.

liniment N. medicinal liquid used externally to ease pain
The trainer applied *liniment* to the football player's strained muscle.

lionize V. to treat as a celebrity
After winning the Nobel Prize for Literature, the writer was *lionized*.

lissome ADJ. easily flexed, limber, agile
The *lissome* gymnast warmed up for her performance.

listless ADJ. lacking energy and enthusiasm
The class was *listless* on the hot July afternoon.

litany N. a lengthy recitation; repetitive chant
The student repeated his usual *litany* of excuses.

literate ADJ. able to read and write; well-read and educated
The government started a program to increase the proportion of *literate* people.

literati N. scholarly or learned persons
The London *literati* united to defend one of its members.

lithe ADJ. moving and bending with ease; graceful
We admired the dancer's *lithe* movements.

litigation N. legal proceedings
The government discouraged *litigation* in order to conserve the court's resources.

livid ADJ. discolored from a bruise; reddened with anger
Tom's father was *livid* after learning that his son had been caught stealing.

loath ADJ. unwilling or reluctant; disinclined
Russ is *loath* to change his major so late in his academic career.

loathe V. to abhor, despise, hate
Gavin *loathes* snakes.

lobbyist N. person who attempts to influence legislators or other public officials toward desired action
The Congressman ignored the *lobbyists* and voted the way he wanted to.

locomotion N. movement from place to place
Humankind has devised many means of *locomotion*.

locus N. locality; center of great activity
The *locus* of the bomb blast was the town center.

lofty ADJ. very high; noble
Ralph has *lofty* ideals.

logo N. corporate symbol
The company recently changed its *logo*.

loiter V. to stand around idly
The principal doesn't allow students to *loiter* around the school after 5 P.M.

loquacious adj. talkative
The people on the bus were so *loquacious* I had trouble doing any work.

Lothario N. seducer
Henry has a reputation on campus as something of a *Lothario*.

low V. to make a deep sustained sound like a cow, moo
As I went to sleep I heard the sheep *lowing* in the field.

lucid ADJ. bright; clear; intelligible
This is a *lucid* piece of writing.

lucre N. money or profits
Modern men and women spend a lot of their time in pursuit of *lucre*.

ludicrous ADJ. laughable, ridiculous
For many years the idea of space flight was considered *ludicrous*.

lugubrious ADJ. sorrowful, mournful
We listened to the *lugubrious* notes of the bagpipes.

lumber V. to move slowly and awkwardly
The child ran ahead, her grandfather *lumbering* behind.

luminary N. a person who has achieved eminence in a specific field.

Every year science *luminaries* gather in Stockholm, Sweden, to receive the Nobel Prize.

luminous ADJ. bright, brilliant, glowing
Witnesses said that the UFO suddenly became *luminous.*

lunar ADJ. relating to the moon
The astronomy department recently appointed a specialist in *lunar* science.

lurid ADJ. harshly shocking, sensational
The newspaper account left out the *lurid* details of the murder.

lurk V. to prowl, sneak
The thief *lurked* outside the store.

luxuriant ADJ. marked by lavishness
The *luxuriant* palace contains priceless antiques.

luxuriate V. take luxurious pleasure; indulge oneself
Sally *luxuriated* in a bubble bath.

lyric ADJ. suitable for poetry and song; expressing feeling
The English poet John Keats wrote excellent *lyric* poetry.

M

macabre ADJ. grim and horrible
The film was too *macabre* for my taste.

Machiavellian ADJ. crafty; double-dealing
The country's leader proceeds on the assumption that other leaders are as *Machiavellian* as he is.

machinations N. plots or schemes
The novel describes the *machinations* behind the merger of the two companies.

macrocosm N. the universe
Both the hexagram and the Rose Cross are traditional symbols of the *macrocosm.*

maelstrom N. whirlpool; turmoil
The civilians were sucked into the *maelstrom* of war.

magisterial ADJ. authoritative
The book is a *magisterial* analysis of *Hamlet.*

magnanimous ADJ. generous, noble
Our team was *magnanimous* in victory.

magnate N. powerful person
The business *magnate* owns his own airplane.

magnitude N. extent, greatness of size
We didn't realize the *magnitude* of the problem until it was too late to do anything about it.

magnum opus N. the greatest single work of a writer, composer, or artist
The professor's *magnum opus* is the five-volume *An Economic History of Europe.*

maladroit ADJ. clumsy, tactless
The *maladroit* play of the basketball team means it's headed for a losing season.

malady N. illness
A cure for the *malady* has not been found.

malaise N. feeling of discomfort; general sense of depression
A *malaise* has descended on the country.

malapropism N. humorous misuse of a word
The audience burst into laughter on hearing the speaker's *malapropism.*

malcontent N. discontented person
The principal appealed to the *malcontents* among the students to improve their attitude.

malediction N. curse
The witch uttered a *malediction.*

malefactor N. doer of evil
We identified the *malefactor* by his guilty look.

malevolent ADJ. causing evil
Early humans seemed to have believed in the existence of *malevolent* spirits.

malfeasance N. misconduct
Several incidents of *malfeasance* are being investigated by the police.

malice N. animosity, hatred
The soldier feels no *malice* for his enemy.

malicious ADJ. full of animosity and hatred
The *malicious* soldiers tortured their captives.

malign ADJ. evil
The church teaches that there are *malign* supernatural forces at work in the world.

malign V. to speak evil of
Don't *malign* him behind his back.

malinger V. to feign illness to escape duty
The soldier was accused of *malingering.*

malleable ADJ. capable of being shaped; impressionable
Confucius believed that human nature is fairly *malleable*.

mandate N. authoritative command
The election is a *mandate* for change.

mandatory ADJ. required, necessary
Voting is *mandatory* in some countries.

Manichaeism N. a dualistic religious philosophy taught by the Persian prophet Manes
Manichaeism was one of the major Iranian Gnostic religions.

manifest ADJ. obvious
The reasons for his choice are *manifest*.

manifest V. to occur in reality; make evident
The unusual symptoms *manifested* early in her pregnancy.

manifestation N. occurrence in reality
The symptoms are the first *manifestation* of the illness.

manifold ADJ. diverse, comprised of many parts
The newly proposed bill would benefit citizens in *manifold* ways.

manna N. spiritual nourishment
The holy man's writings are *manna* for his followers.

manumission N. freedom from slavery
The *manumission* of the slaves was slow in that state.

martial ADJ. warlike
The army trains recruits in the *martial* arts.

martinet N. strict disciplinarian
The teacher was considered a *martinet*.

masochist N. one who enjoys pain
Herb is not enough of a *masochist* to take a job teaching incorrigible criminals.

matriarchy N. a family or community governed by women
Few societies in history have been *matriarchies*.

matriculate V. to enroll in a college
Which university do you plan to *matriculate* at?

matrilineal ADJ. tracing ancestry through the mother's line

Susan is researching *matrilineal* societies for her sociology paper.

maudlin ADJ. overly sentimental
The *maudlin* movie brought tears to many eyes.

maven N. an expert
The newspaper's editor-in-chief is considered a language *maven*.

maverick N. dissenter
We tried to persuade the *maverick* that his view was mistaken.

mawkish ADJ. very sentimental
The story is a bit *mawkish* for my taste.

maxim N. a concise statement of a fundamental principle
"Never do to others what you would not like them to do to you" is a well-known *maxim*.

mea culpa N. an admission of a personal fault or mistake
The CEO's *mea culpa* included an apology to customers who had been adversely affected by the company's mistake.

meager ADJ. scanty; inadequate
We can't survive on such *meager* rations.

meandering ADJ. winding back and forth, rambling
We rode down a *meandering* stream.

medieval ADJ. pertaining to the middle ages
Sarah is majoring in *medieval* studies at the university.

meditation N. reflection; thought
After some *meditation* on the issue, I realized that my view was mistaken.

medley N. mixture
The concert featured a *medley* of popular songs from the 1960s.

megalith N. huge stone used in prehistoric structures
Ten *megaliths* were discovered on the island.

megalomania N. delusions of power or importance
In the grip of *megalomania*, the country's leader ordered the invasion of the much more powerful neighboring country.

melancholy ADJ. sad, depressed
The mood was *melancholy* after the tragedy was announced.

mélange N. mixture
The soup is a *mélange* of ingredients.

menagerie N. a variety of animals kept together
Mr. Smith has a *menagerie* in his backyard.

mendacious ADJ. dishonest
The *mendacious* shopkeeper was reported in the newspaper.

mendicant N. beggar
The *mendicants* went from house to house asking for food.

mentor N. wise advisor
The president listened closely to his *mentor's* advice.

mercenary N. soldier hired for battle
The army was composed mainly of *mercenaries*.

mercenary ADJ. greedy
I suspect that his motives are largely *mercenary*.

mercurial ADJ. quick, unpredictable
Jim's moods are *mercurial*.

meretricious ADJ. gaudy; plausible but false; specious
We rejected the argument as *meretricious*.

meridian N. imaginary circle that passes through the North and South Pole
The *meridian* passes through the poles at right angles to the equator.

meritocratic ADJ. relating to a system in which advancement is based on achievement
Free market economies tend to be *meritocratic*.

meritorious ADJ. deserving praise
The nurse's dedication to her patients is *meritorious*.

mesmerize V. hypnotize
The continuous movement of the windshield wipers nearly *mesmerized* the driver.

metamorphose V. to change, transform
The small town has *metamorphosed* into a city over the past fifty years.

metamorphosis N. change, transformation
Our town has undergone a *metamorphosis* over the last fifty years.

metaphor N. figure of speech that compares two different things
The English teacher pointed out the *metaphor* in the first paragraph of the story.

metaphysic N. an underlying philosophical or theoretical principle
The book proposes a new *metaphysic* of literary criticism.

metaphysical ADJ. pertaining to speculative philosophy
Metaphysical issues lie outside the field of science.

metaphysics N. speculative philosophy about the nature of reality
The conclusion in the area of *metaphysics* reached by the British philosopher John McTaggart is that the world is composed of nothing but souls, each soul related to one or more of the others by love.

meteorological ADJ. concerned with the weather
Tim wants to pursue a career in *meteorological* science.

methodology N. a particular procedure or set of procedures
Perhaps you used the wrong *methodology* to try to solve the problem.

meticulous ADJ. very careful; fastidious
Meticulous planning went into the Japanese attack on Pearl Harbor.

mettle N. courage, endurance
The battle tested the soldiers' *mettle*.

mettlesome ADJ. full of courage and fortitude; spirited
The general is proud of his *mettlesome* soldiers.

microcosm N. a small system having analogies to a larger system; small world
The principal told the students that the school was a *microcosm* of the larger world.

milieu N. environment; surroundings
Social realist novelists describe the *milieu* of a society.

militant ADJ. combative; bellicose
Militant members of the party argued for stronger measures.

militate V. to work against
Several unlucky events *militated* against his rising to stardom.

millennium N. a span of one thousand years; a hoped for period of joy, justice, and prosperity

Let's hope that this *millennium* is more peaceful than the last one.

minatory ADJ. threatening; menacing
The stranger's *minatory* gestures alarmed the woman.

minuscule ADJ. very small
The critic described the film as "artless comedy shot on a *minuscule* budget."

minute ADJ. very small
Elementary particles are *minute*.

minutia N. petty details
Sally enjoys the *minutia* of office work.

mirth N. gaiety
The party was an occasion of great *mirth*.

misanthropy N. hatred of humanity
The travelers avoided visiting the village because its inhabitants had a reputation for *misanthropy*.

misapprehension N. a misunderstanding
Laura is under the *misapprehension* that she's one of the world's great poets.

miscellany N. mixture of writings on various subjects
The volume is a *miscellany* of sports writing.

misconstrue V. to misunderstand
The student deliberately *misconstrued* what the teacher said.

miscreant N. villain; criminal
The new mayor has vowed to use the full power of the law to go after the *miscreants*.

misdemeanor N. a misdeed
He was fired for a *misdemeanor*.

miserly ADJ. stingy, mean
The prisoners receive a *miserly* amount of food every day.

misgiving N. doubt, sense of foreboding
We had some *misgivings* about taking such a difficult course.

misnomer N. incorrect name
Korean jade is a *misnomer* for serpentine.

misogynist ADJ. characterized by a hatred of women
To some people all-male clubs reflect *misogynist* attitudes.

missive N. letter
I've received your *missive*.

mitigating ADJ. causing to become less harsh, severe, or painful; alleviating
The judge considered the *mitigating* circumstances in the case.

mnemonic ADJ. related to memory; assisting memory
Try using *mnemonic* devices to remember difficult words.

modicum N. limited quantity
There is not even a *modicum* of truth in his story about the lost term paper.

modus operandi N. a method of operating or proceeding
The company's *modus operandi* is to identify potential rivals early and drive them out of business.

mollify V. to soothe
The manager *mollified* the angry customer.

momentous ADJ. very important
July 4, 1776, is a *momentous* date in American history.

monarchy N. government by a monarch; a state ruled by a monarch
The country's *monarchy* was established in 1415.

monastic ADJ. related to monks or monasteries; removed from worldly concerns
Hugh led an almost *monastic* existence.

monism N. philosophical belief that reality is comprised of one fundamental substance
By the term "neutral monism" modern philosophers mean the view that the physical and the mental can both be reduced to a third substance.

monochromatic ADJ. having one color
This novel portrays a monochromatic view of life.

monogamy N. marriage to one person at a time
In some cultures *monogamy* is considered abnormal.

monolithic ADJ. solid and uniform; constituting a single, unified whole
The *monolithic* structure was built centuries ago by the original inhabitants of that island.

monologue N. speech performed by one actor
The *monologue* lasts for five minutes.

montage N. composite picture
The *montage* portrays life in different periods of history.

moot ADJ. debatable, previously decided
The point is *moot*, so let's not waste time debating it.

moratorium N. an authorized delay of a specific activity
The nation agreed to a *moratorium* on testing biological weapons.

morbid ADJ. gruesome, unhealthily gloomy
Let's not dwell on the *morbid* details.

mordant ADJ. bitingly sarcastic
The comedian's *mordant* humor appeals to some people but not others.

mores N. customs
Mores vary from culture to culture.

moribund ADJ. dying
Scientists are studying the *moribund* culture.

morose ADJ. ill-humored; sullen
Preparing to surrender, the general was *morose*.

morphology N. the form and structure of an organism
Dr. Cutler is an expert on the *morphology* of ants.

mosaic ADJ. relating to a design made up of small pieces of various colors
Mosaic materials and techniques is the topic of today's lecture.

mote N. tiny particle
Tom has a *mote* in his eye.

motif N. a main theme for development; a repeated figure
There are three *motifs* in this novel.

motley ADJ. many colored, made up of many parts
The association was a *motley* collection.

multifaceted ADJ. made up of many parts
The problem is *multifaceted*.

multifarious ADJ. diverse
Science attempts to make sense of *multifarious* phenomena.

multiplicity N. state of being numerous
There is a *multiplicity* of explanations for the origin of the world.

mundane ADJ. worldly as opposed to spiritual; concerned with the ordinary
The priest has little interest in *mundane* concerns.

munificent ADJ. generous
The library thanked the *munificent* donor for his large donation.

muse V. to consider something at length; ponder
Amber *mused* about which of the men she should go out with.

mutability N. changeability
The *mutability* of the weather is a common topic of conversation.

mutable ADJ. changeable
The astrological sign Gemini is called "*mutable*" because it occurs as spring changes into summer.

mutation N. significant genetic change
The *mutation* caused a birth defect.

muted ADJ. silent; toned down
The atmosphere was *muted*.

myopic ADJ. near-sighted, unable to anticipate events
The *myopic* adviser had no idea of the great changes to come.

myriad ADJ. of a large number or multitude
The child is trying to count the *myriad* grains of sand on the beach.

mystic N. a person who undergoes profound spiritual experiences
The *mystic* recorded his experiences in a diary.

mystical ADJ. stemming from direct communion with ultimate reality or God
The psychologist is studying *mystical* experiences.

N

nadir N. lowest point
Jim's life reached its *nadir* when he went bankrupt.

naive ADJ. lacking sophistication and worldliness
The *naive* customer believed everything that the salesperson told her.

naiveté N. lack of sophistication and worldliness
For an adult, Florence displays remarkable *naiveté*.

narcissistic ADJ. having excessive love for oneself
Narcissistic Ray loved to stand in front of the mirror admiring himself.

narrative N. account, story

The book is largely a *narrative* of the explorer's life.

nascent ADJ. starting to develop, coming into existence

The government is supporting the *nascent* industry.

natal ADJ. relating to birth

The astrologer calculated his client's *natal* chart.

nebulous ADJ. vague, cloudy

The argument is *nebulous*.

necromancy N. black magic

Necromancy is widely practiced on the island.

necropsy N. autopsy

The Roman physician Antistius performed one of the earliest *necropsies* on record when in 44 B.C. he examined Julius Caesar and documented twenty-three wounds, including a final fatal stab to the chest.

nefarious ADJ. vicious, evil

The *nefarious* plot to blow up the building was uncovered.

negate V. cancel out; nullify

The team's victory in the second game *negated* their opponent's victory in the first game.

negligent ADJ. careless, inattentive

There is evidence that the defendant was *negligent* in performing his duties.

negligible ADJ. not worth considering

It is a *negligible* amount of money for a rich person.

nemesis N. an unbeatable enemy; a source of injury

The team suffered its sixth straight loss to its *nemesis*.

neologism N. new word or expression

The dictionary is updated regularly to include recent *neologisms*.

neonate N. newborn child

The parents are caring for the *neonate*.

neophyte N. novice, beginner

Despite being a *neophyte* at tennis, Gail put up a good fight in her first match.

ne plus ultra N. the perfect or most extreme example of its kind

Many people consider Jimi Hendrix the *ne plus ultra* of electric guitarists.

nepotism N. favoritism to a relative

The law makes *nepotism* in hiring illegal.

nescience N. absence of knowledge; ignorance

"No student will leave my class in a state of *nescience*," the teacher told her class.

Nestorianism N. a religious belief system holding that within Jesus are two distinct persons, divine and human, rather than a single divine person

Nestorianism was condemned at the Council of Ephesus in 431.

nether ADJ. located under or below

Hell is often pictured as located in the *nether* regions of the Earth.

nettle V. to irritate

I was *nettled* by the continually ringing cell phones.

neurosis N. a mental disorder arising without evidence of organic disease

In *The Future of an Illusion* Sigmund Freud describes religion as "the universal *neurosis*."

nexus N. a means of connection; a connected group or series; a center

To enhance security, the army's communication system does not have a *nexus*.

nicety N. elegant or delicate feature; minute distinction

The legal *niceties* of his case were of little interest to the condemned man.

niche N. recess in a wall; best position for something

It is important for a person to find his own *niche* in society.

niggardly ADJ. stingy

We received *niggardly* portions of food.

nihilism N. belief that existence and all traditional values are meaningless

The book explores the topic of *nihilism* in Western thought.

nihilistic ADJ. relating to the belief that existence and all traditional values are meaningless.

Nihilistic thought might increase during times of social stress.

nirvana N. an ideal condition of rest, harmony, or joy

Deep in meditation, the holy man sought *nirvana*.

noblesse oblige N. obligation of persons of high birth or rank to act nobly and benevolently

A strong sense of *noblesse oblige* motivated the billionaire to donate half of his fortune to charity.

nocturnal ADJ. pertaining to night; active at night
The expedition was studying *nocturnal* animals.

noisome ADJ. stinking, putrid
We live by a *noisome* swamp.

nomadic ADJ. moving from place to place
The *nomadic* tribe moves with the seasons.

nomenclature N. terms used in a particular science or discipline
Before each physics unit our teacher goes over the important *nomenclature* in it.

nominal ADJ. existing in name only; negligible
I didn't mind paying the *nominal* entrance fee.

nonchalant ADJ. casual, unconcerned
Tim is *nonchalant* about his studies.

nondescript ADJ. lacking interesting or distinctive qualities; dull
The suspect wore a *nondescript* coat.

nonpareil ADJ. having no match or equal
He is a movie director *nonpareil*.

nonplussed ADJ. bewildered; confused
Harry stood, *nonplussed*, the letter still in his hand.

non sequitur N. conclusion not following from apparent evidence
The essay is filled with *non sequiturs*.

norm N. a standard or model considered typical for a group
The *norm* for this school is a class size of thirty.

normative ADJ. related to or prescribing a norm or standard
The sociologist believes that her job is to describe society and not make *normative* judgments.

nostalgia N. a sentimental longing for a pastime
The movie appeals to people who feel *nostalgia* for the 1960s.

nostrum N. a medicine or remedy of doubtful effectiveness; supposed cure
The advertisement claims that the *nostrum* cures a cold.

notoriety N. disrepute; ill fame
The criminal gained *notoriety* for stealing more money than anyone in history.

notorious ADJ. known widely and unfavorably
The criminal is *notorious* for stealing more money than anyone else in history.

nouveau riche N. one who has recently become rich
As so often happens, the long-established families in the town resent the intrusion of the *nouveau riche*.

novel ADJ. new or original
This essay takes a *novel* approach to the subject.

novice N. apprentice, beginner
For a *novice*, he's doing rather well.

novitiate N. state of being a beginner or novice
During their *novitiate* the men kept a vow of silence.

noxious ADJ. harmful, unwholesome
The truck spewed out *noxious* fumes.

nuance N. shade of meaning; subtle distinction
The teacher explained the *nuances* of the words.

nugatory ADJ. of no value or importance
The lack of funds for the new program will render it *nugatory*.

nullify V. to make invalid
The score was *nullified* by a penalty.

numismatics N. coin collecting
Sean has learned a lot about history from his hobby, *numismatics*.

nuptial ADJ. relating to marriage
The *nuptial* arrangements are going well except for the selection of bridesmaids.

nurture V. to nourish; foster; educate
The school has *nurtured* young people for over one hundred years.

nutritive ADJ. relating to nutrition or health
This snack has little *nutritive* value.

O

obdurate ADJ. stubborn
They remained *obdurate* about their position.

obeisance N. deference or homage
Once a year the king's subjects pay him *obeisance*.

obfuscation N. act of confusing, obscuring
The witness used *obfuscation* to hide the truth.

objectify V. to present or regard as an object or make objective or external
The idea of justice is *objectified* in the novel.

objective ADJ. not influenced by emotions; fair; unbiased
The judge was *objective* in evaluating the evidence.

objet d'art N. object with artistic value
During the war the museum stored its most valuable *objets d'art* in a vault.

oblique ADJ. indirect, evasive; misleading, devious
Many people missed the writer's *oblique* reference.

obliterate V. to destroy completely
The explosion *obliterated* the house.

oblivion N. state of not being aware
We experience *oblivion* when we sleep.

oblivious ADJ. not aware
The audience was *oblivious* of the events occurring backstage.

obloquy N. abusively detractive language; ill repute
Obloquy was heaped on the negotiators for failing to prevent the war.

obscure ADJ. dim, unclear; not well-known
The reference was to an *obscure* author.

obscure V. to make dim or unclear; conceal in obscurity
The view of the valley is *obscured* by the high-rise apartments.

obsequious ADJ. overly submissive
The servants are *obsequious*.

obsequy N. funeral ceremony
Obsequies were held for the slain soldier.

obsolescent ADJ. becoming obsolete
It's hard to find spare parts for the *obsolescent* model.

obsolete ADJ. outmoded; no longer used; old-fashioned
That model car became *obsolete* last year.

obstinate ADJ. stubborn
Jim is *obstinate* about not wanting to rewrite his essay.

obstreperous ADJ. troublesome, boisterous, unruly
The crowd became *obstreperous*.

obtrusive ADJ. pushy, too conspicuous
The teacher supervising the exam tried not to be *obtrusive*.

obtuse ADJ. insensitive, stupid, dull
His *obtuse* remark showed how stupid he could be.

obviate V. to make unnecessary; anticipate and prevent
The increase in revenue has *obviated* the need for a price increase.

occlude V. to shut, block
The cloud is *occluding* the moon.

occult ADJ. related to supernatural phenomena; secret
The religious teacher revealed his *occult* knowledge to his closest followers.

Ockham's razor N. the principle that no more assumptions than necessary should be made in explaining a phenomenon
Most philosophers would probably agree that *Ockham's razor* should be used with great care.

odious ADJ. hateful, contemptible
The man was sentenced to life imprisonment for his *odious* crime.

odyssey N. a long adventurous voyage; a quest
Tom's *odyssey* took him to over fifty countries.

oeuvre N. the sum of the lifework of an artist
The professor is writing a study of the author's *oeuvre*.

officious ADJ. too helpful, meddlesome
We're tired of the *officious* fools interfering in our affairs.

ogle V. to stare at
The man *ogled* the pretty girl.

olfactory ADJ. concerning the sense of smell
The air pollution has impaired his *olfactory* sense.

oligarchy N. government by a few
After the coup d'état the generals formed an *oligarchy* to run the country.

oligopoly N. a situation in which there are few sellers so that action by any one of them will affect price
The government is investigating the situation to see if an *oligopoly* exists.

ombudsman N. a person who investigates complaints and mediates settlements between parties

Some Americans advocate the more widespread use of *ombudsmen* in this country.

ominous ADJ. threatening
There were *ominous* troop movements on the country's border.

omnipotent ADJ. having unlimited power
The emperor feels he is virtually *omnipotent*.

omniscient ADJ. having infinite knowledge
Many novels use an *omniscient* narrator.

omnivorous ADJ. eating everything; absorbing everything
Human beings are *omnivorous*.

onerous ADJ. burdensome
The judge has the *onerous* duty of sentencing convicted criminals to prison.

onomatopoeia N. formation or use of words that imitate sounds of the actions they refer to
The words *hiss, buzz,* and *whack* are examples of *onomatopoeia*.

ontology N. theory about the nature of existence
Ontology is a subject for philosophy, not science.

onus N. a difficult responsibility or burden
"The *onus* is on each of you to master the material," the professor told the class.

opalescent ADJ. iridescent, displaying colors
The diamond is *opalescent*.

opaque ADJ. not transparent; obscure; unintelligible
The prose of the French structuralist can be described as *opaque*.

operative ADJ. functioning, working, most important
The *operative* word in the phrase "greatest living writer" is "living."

opine V. to express an opinion
The newspaper columnist *opines* on every topic under the sun.

opportune ADJ. appropriate, fitting
It is an *opportune* time for a coffee break.

opportunist N. person who sacrifices principles for expediency by taking advantage
Opportunists took advantage of the disaster to raise prices.

opprobrium N. disgrace; contempt
The cowardly act brought *opprobrium* on the soldier.

opulence N. wealth
The wedding allowed the family to display its *opulence*.

oracle N. person who foresees the future and gives advice; prediction of the future
Lucy consulted an *oracle* to find out when she would be married.

oracular ADJ. prophetic; uttered as if with divine authority; mysterious or ambiguous
None of us understood the *oracular* utterance.

oration N. lecture, formal speech
The subject of the senator's *oration* is foreign policy.

orb N. spherical body; eye
The astronauts are in orbit around a large *orb*.

orchestrate V. to arrange music for performance; coordinate, organize
The election campaign was *orchestrated* by the White House.

ordain V. to make someone a priest or minister; order
Father O'Brien was *ordained* in 1992.

ornate ADJ. elaborately ornamented
The art pieces are too *ornate* for my taste.

ornithologist N. scientist who studies birds
The *ornithologist* discovered a new bird species.

orthodox ADJ. traditional; conservative
The new book challenges *orthodox* thinking on the subject.

oscillate V. to move back and forth
The governor is *oscillating* between two positions on the issue.

osmosis N. diffusion of a fluid; gradual assimilation or absorption
Learning a language is to some degree a process of *osmosis*.

ossify V. to turn to bone; become rigid; make rigidly conventional
The dead animal's skin *ossified*.

ostensibly ADV. apparently; professedly
The purpose of the test was *ostensibly* to measure the students' improvement.

ostentatious ADJ. showy; trying to attract attention; pretentious

The billionaire urged his family to avoid *ostentatious* displays of wealth during the recession.

ostracism N. exclusion, temporary banishment
The warrior faces *ostracism* from his tribe.

ouster N. expulsion, ejection
The *ouster* of the country from the United Nations was applauded around the world.

outré ADJ. unconventional; eccentric
The town is not as bohemian as in the past, but the *outré* spirit does survive.

overt ADJ. open and observable
The CIA has detected no *overt* signs of an invasion.

overture N. musical introduction; proposal, offer
The company rejected the merger *overture*.

overweening ADJ. presumptuous; arrogant; overbearing
The tragic hero is brought down by his *overweening* pride.

overwrought ADJ. agitated, overdone
Don't make the decision in your *overwrought* condition.

oxymoron N. the combining of incongruous or contradictory terms
The phrase "deafening silence" is an *oxymoron*.

P

pacific ADJ. calm; peaceful
Canada and the United States enjoy *pacific* relations.

pacifist N. person opposed to war or violence between nations
Pacifists demonstrated against the war.

pacify V. to restore calm, bring peace
The leader's promise *pacified* the angry crowd.

paean N. a song of joy or triumph; a fervent expression of joy
The poem is a *paean* to the beauty of nature.

pagan N. someone who has no religion
The missionary was sent to the country to preach to the *pagans*.

painstaking ADJ. being very careful
Painstaking research goes into the preparation of a GRE test.

palatable ADJ. pleasant to the taste or mind
The dishes George cooks can most kindly be described as *palatable*.

palatial ADJ. like a palace; magnificent
The actor's house is *palatial*.

palaver N. idle talk
"Let's stop this *palaver* and get to work," the boss said.

paleontology N. study of past geological eras through fossil remains
Paleontology makes use of the knowledge of a number of other sciences, such as geology.

paleoseismology N. the study of the timing, location, and size of prehistoric earthquakes
Developments in the science of *paleoseismology* have improved humanity's ability to assess the likelihood of an earthquake occurring in a particular area.

palette N. board for mixing paints; range of colors
We found the colors on the painter's *palette* more interesting than the picture that she was painting.

palisade N. fence made up of stakes
The *palisade* helps to prevent intruders.

pall V. to lose strength or interest
Playing checkers every night began to *pall*.

pall N. covering that darkens or obscures; coffin
After the nuclear explosion, a *pall* descended on the city.

palliate V. to make less serious, ease
The doctor prescribed drugs to *palliate* her patient's suffering.

palliative N. something that relieves the symptoms without curing the disease
Aspirin is a commonly used *palliative*.

pallid ADJ. lacking color or liveliness
Becky looked *pallid* after she saw a ghost.

palpable ADJ. obvious; real; tangible
No *palpable* evidence of alien spacecraft has been found.

palpitation N. trembling; shaking
The patient has heart *palpitations*.

paltry ADJ. pitifully small or worthless
Mr. Jones can barely survive on his *paltry* salary.

panacea N. cure-all

Some people consider aspirin to be a *panacea*.

panache N. flamboyance, verve

Dwight does everything with *panache*.

pandemic N. disease spread over a whole area

Doctors are working to bring the *pandemic* under control.

panegyric N. elaborate praise; formal hymn of praise

The poem is a *panegyric* on the soldier's bravery.

panoply N. impressive array

The military force displayed a *panoply* of weapons.

panorama N. broad view; comprehensive picture

The book provides a *panorama* of the middle ages.

pantheist N. a person who believes that manifestations of the universe are God

Many people believe that the writers Wordsworth, Emerson, and Whitman were *pantheists*.

pantheon N. all the gods of a people; a group of highly regarded persons

In the *pantheon* of English poets, few rank higher than John Milton.

papacy N. the office of the pope

The *papacy* will be vacant until a new pope is elected.

parable N. a short, simple story that teaches a moral lesson

The holy man uses *parables* to teach his followers.

paradigm N. model; example; pattern

The famous scientific experiment has served as a *paradigm* for many other experiments.

paradisiacal ADJ. heavenly; wonderful

Hawaii is often portrayed as a *paradisiacal* land.

paradox N. contradiction, incongruity; dilemma

The saying "the more things change, the more they remain the same" is an example of a *paradox*.

paradoxical ADJ. relating to a contradiction, an incongruity, or a dilemma

It is paradoxical that a river always changes yet always remains the same.

paragon N. model of excellence or perfection

The saint is a *paragon* of virtue.

paramount ADJ. supreme, dominant, primary

The military's *paramount* mission is to defend the country.

parenthetical ADJ. clarifying or qualifying

The speaker's *parenthetical* remarks clarified his point.

pariah N. outcast

The traitor is a *pariah* in his country.

parity N. equality

The arms buildup is designed to achieve military *parity* with the enemy.

parlance N. a particular manner of speaking

In newspaper *parlance*, a story can be "killed."

parley N. discussion, usually between enemies

The opposing general agreed to a *parley*.

parochial ADJ. narrow in outlook; provincial

Many of the people in this town are *parochial*.

parody N. humorous imitation

The poem is a *parody* of T.S. Eliot's *Four Quartets*.

paroxysm N. fit or attack of pain, laughter, or rage

The joke made Ruth double over in *paroxysms* of laughter.

parry V. to ward off or deflect

The boxer *parried* his opponent's punches.

parsimony N. stinginess

The cheapskate's *parsimony* is legendary.

partisan ADJ. one-sided; committed to a party, group, or cause; prejudiced

The columnist usually takes a *partisan* position.

partisan N. a fervent supporter or proponent of a party, group, or cause

Partisans of all the candidates were invited to the debate.

parvenu N. a newly rich person who is regarded as an upstart

The landed aristocracy felt superior to the *parvenu*.

passé ADJ. old-fashioned

New electronic gadgets often quickly become *passé*.

passive ADJ. not active; not acted upon

The activists used *passive* resistance to protest the policy.

pastiche N. piece of literature or music imitating other works

The poem is a *pastiche* of famous twentieth-century poems.

pastoral ADJ. rural; charmingly simple and peaceful; portrays country life in an idealized way
The artist painted a *pastoral* scene.

patent ADJ. obvious, unconcealed
Her story was a *patent* lie.

paternal ADJ. fatherly
The veteran pitcher is keeping a *paternal* eye on the young rookie.

paternalistic ADJ. providing for the needs of people without giving them rights and responsibilities
Most people don't want the government to be too *paternalistic*.

paternity N. fatherhood; descent from father's ancestors
A DNA test established the man's *paternity*.

pathogen N. agent that causes disease
Researchers have identified the *pathogen*.

pathogenic ADJ. capable of causing disease
The bacteria are being tested to see if they are *pathogenic*.

pathological ADJ. departing from normal condition
Lying has become *pathological* with the boy.

pathology N. the manifestation of a disease; departure from normal condition
The test determined that *pathology* was present.

pathos N. pity, compassion
It was a play of such *pathos* that everyone in the audience was in tears.

patois N. a regional dialect; nonstandard speech; the jargon of a group
The people in that area speak a local *patois*.

patriarchal ADJ. relating to a family or community governed by men
Most human societies are *patriarchal*.

patrician N. aristocrat
The *patrician* feels a duty to help the poor.

patricide N. murder of one's father
Many scholars believe that Alexander the Great became king through *patricide*.

patrimony N. inheritance or heritage derived from one's father
Doug spent his *patrimony* on a Ferrari and a yacht.

patronizing ADJ. condescending, disparaging; buying from
The class felt that the teacher was *patronizing*.

patron saint N. a saint who is regarded as an intercessor in heaven for a person, nation, etc.
Saint Luke is considered the *patron saint* of doctors.

paucity N. scarcity
In China there is a *paucity* of women for men to marry.

pauper N. very poor person
Ralph lives like a *pauper* so that he can build up his savings.

peccadillo N. minor sin or offense
The police officer ignored the *peccadillo*.

peculation N. theft of money or goods
The gang planned a lot of *peculation* in the summer.

pecuniary ADJ. relating to money
David spends so much time writing poetry not from a *pecuniary* motive but rather for the satisfaction of expressing himself.

pedagogue N. teacher
The curriculum was designed by *pedagogues*.

pedagogy N. art or profession of teaching
Gilbert Highet's *The Art of Teaching* is a well-known book on *pedagogy*.

pedant N. uninspired, boring academic
The *pedant* never has an original idea; he just repeats the ideas of others.

pedantic ADJ. showing off learning
The class resented the teacher's *pedantic* insistence on old-fashioned grammar rules.

pedantry N. pedantic attention to learning or formal rules
The scholar didn't include footnotes in his new book to avoid the appearance of *pedantry*.

pedestrian ADJ. commonplace
Most of the ideas in the book are *pedestrian*.

pediatrician N. doctor specializing in children and their ailments
Mrs. Moore took her child to a *pediatrician*.

pediment N. triangular gable on a roof or facade
The building's *pediment* is modeled on one found in an ancient Greek temple.

peer N. contemporary, equal, match
Kim has the respect of her *peers*.

peerless ADJ. unequaled
Shakespeare was a *peerless* writer.

pejorative ADJ. having bad connotations; disparaging
We didn't like the *pejorative* comments about us.

pelagic ADJ. living in open oceans or seas rather than waters adjacent to land or inland waters
The scientists are studying the migration patterns of *pelagic* birds.

pellucid ADJ. transparent; translucent; easily understood
I saw to the bottom of the *pellucid* stream.

penance N. voluntary suffering to repent for a wrong
The sinner performed *penance*.

penchant N. inclination
Steve has a *penchant* for writing.

penitent ADJ. expressing sorrow for sins or offenses, repentant
The convicted man was *penitent* about the wrong he had done.

pensive ADJ. thoughtful
Valerie is in a *pensive* mood.

penultimate ADJ. next to last
Our team occupies the *penultimate* place in the league standing.

penumbra N. partial shadow
During the eclipse we watched the *penumbra* move across the moon's surface.

penurious ADJ. poverty-stricken; destitute
The city government has set up shelters for *penurious* old people.

penury N. extreme poverty
The lawsuit reduced Mr. Wilson to *penury*.

perambulation N. walking about
The park is a good place for *perambulation*.

percipient ADJ. discerning, able to perceive
A *percipient* onlooker noted the license number of the car.

perdition N. complete and utter loss; damnation
The sermon warned of *perdition* to come.

peregrination N. a wandering from place to place
Mr. Theroux's *peregrinations* took him around the world.

peremptory ADJ. imperative; leaving no choice
No one in the company questioned the colonel's *peremptory* order.

perennial ADJ. present throughout the years; persistent
Pollution is a *perennial* problem in the city.

perfidious ADJ. faithless, disloyal, untrustworthy
The boss dismissed the *perfidious* employee.

perfidy N. deliberate breach of faith or violation of trust
Our ally's *perfidy* came as a shock to everyone.

perfunctory ADJ. superficial; not thorough; performed really as a duty
The pilot had time only for a *perfunctory* check of his aircraft before takeoff.

perigee N. point in an orbit that is closest to the Earth.
The probe will be launched so that upon its arrival Mars will be at *perigee*.

perihelion N. point in orbit nearest to the sun
The Earth is approaching *perihelion*.

peripatetic ADJ. moving from place to place
The *peripatetic* professor has taught at twenty colleges.

peripheral ADJ. not central; of minor importance
The issue is only of *peripheral* importance.

periphery N. perimeter
The poor often live on the *periphery* of society.

periphrastic ADJ. containing too many words
The critic called the translation of the French poem into English "*periphrastic*."

perjure V. to tell a lie under oath
The judge concluded that the witness had *perjured* himself.

permafrost N. permanently frozen subsoil
The U.S. Department of Interior's permafrost network in Alaska is part of a global network of *permafrost* monitoring stations.

permeable ADJ. penetrable
The frozen soil is not *permeable*.

permeate V. to spread or flow through
The new CEO's personality has begun to *permeate* through the firm.

pernicious ADJ. very harmful
The talk is on the *pernicious* effects of alcohol abuse.

perpetual ADJ. endless, lasting
The inventor claims that he has built a *perpetual* motion machine.

perpetuate V. to cause to continue indefinitely
The false idea was *perpetuated* in several publications.

perpetuity N. time without end; eternity
The lease was granted in *perpetuity*.

persona N. a person's public image
The politician is trying to improve his *persona*.

personification N. act of attributing human qualities to objects or abstract qualities
Calling the wind "angry" is an example of *personification*.

perspicacious ADJ. shrewd, astute, keen-witted
The *perspicacious* lawyer won the majority of his cases.

perspicacity N. acuteness of perception or understanding
Perspicacity helped the lawyer to win the case.

pert ADJ. lively and bold
Joan plays the role of the *pert* young law student.

pertinacious ADJ. persistent, stubborn
Richard's *pertinacious* character is a major factor in his success.

perturb V. to disturb greatly; make uneasy or anxious
Observations showed that the satellite's orbit had been *perturbed*.

perturbation N. disturbance
The *perturbation* in the star's orbit is evidence for the existence of a large planet in the vicinity.

perusal N. close examination
The editor's *perusal* of the manuscript revealed several errors.

peruse V. to examine closely
Sherlock Holmes *perused* the newspaper for a clue.

pervade V. to spread throughout every part
Hydrogen *pervades* the universe.

pervasive ADJ. spread throughout every part
The influence of the West is *pervasive*.

perverse ADJ. stubborn, intractable, contradicting without good reason
The girl seems to have a *perverse* desire to be expelled from school.

pervert V. to cause to change in immoral way; misuse
The interpretation *perverts* the poem's meaning.

perverted ADJ. changed in immoral way; misused
The group follows a *perverted* version of its founder's teachings.

pestilence N. epidemic, plague
The *pestilence* spread rapidly to neighboring countries.

petty ADJ. trivial; very small; unimportant
Let's forget about this *petty* matter.

petulantly ADV. in a rude or peevish manner
The child stamped her feet and frowned *petulantly*.

phalanx N. massed group of soldiers, people, or things
A *phalanx* of soldiers prevented the mob from entering.

phallocentric ADJ. centered on men or on a male viewpoint
The critic described *The Odyssey* as *phallocentric*.

phantasmagoria N. a fantastic sequence of haphazardly associative imagery
She described her dream as "a *phantasmagoria*."

pharmacopoeia N. a collection of drugs
The *pharmacopoeia* contains many drugs derived from plants.

phenomena N. observable occurrences
Scientists try to understand natural *phenomena*.

philanderer N. pursuer of casual love affairs
Jerry has a reputation as a *philanderer*.

philanthropist N. lover of humanity; humanitarian
The *philanthropist* who donated the money for the new college library prefers to remain anonymous.

philanthropy N. love of humanity; generosity to worthy causes
The tax system encourages *philanthropy*.

philatelist N. stamp collector
The *philatelist* has a stamp collection valued at over $30,000.

philistine N. narrow-minded person, someone lacking appreciation for art or culture
The *philistines* voted against the funds for the arts program.

philology N. study of words
English *philology* owes a great deal to the *Oxford English Dictionary.*

phlegmatic ADJ. calm in temperament; sluggish
The *phlegmatic* librarian merely raised an eyebrow when a fire broke out in the reference section.

phobia N. irrational fear
The patient was treated by a psychologist for his *phobia.*

phoenix N. mythical, immortal bird that lives for 500 years, burns itself to death, and rises from its ashes
Our winless football team will rise like a *phoenix* next year.

phonetics N. study of speech sounds
Knowledge of *phonetics* is helpful to a reading teacher.

phonic ADJ. relating to sound
The stories are designed to develop children's *phonic* knowledge.

physiognomy N. facial features
Some people believe that a person's *physiognomy* reflects his or her character.

physiology N. study of living organism; the functions of a living organism
A good understanding of human *physiology* is important for a medical doctor.

pidgin N. a simplified form of speech
The people of the country speak French and a *pidgin* that is based on English.

piety N. devoutness
We all admire his *piety.*

pilfer V. to steal
Someone *pilfered* my copy of *Wordfest!*

pillage V. to loot, especially during a war
The enemy soldiers *pillaged* the town.

pinnacle N. peak, highest point of development
The writer is at the *pinnacle* of her career.

pious ADJ. dedicated, devout, extremely religious
The *pious* worshipper attends church every day.

piquant ADJ. appealingly stimulating; pleasantly pungent
The chef's *piquant* tomato sauce is popular with diners.

pique N. fleeting feeling of hurt pride
She'll soon get over her *pique.*

pique V. to provoke, arouse
His eighth grade teacher *piqued* his interest in the English language.

piscivore N. a fish-eating animal
An example of a *piscivore* is the Aquatic Genet.

pithy ADJ. forceful and brief
Grandfather usually sits quietly observing, occasionally making a *pithy* comment.

pittance N. meager amount or wage
Tom's allowance is a *pittance.*

placate V. to lessen another's anger; pacify
Nothing would *placate* their anger.

placebo N. a substance with no medication given to a patient
One group of people in the experiment was given a *placebo.*

placid ADJ. calm
George has a *placid* disposition.

plagiarism N. theft of another's ideas or writing
A few students in the class think that there's nothing wrong with *plagiarism.*

plaintiff N. injured person in a lawsuit
The *plaintiff* is seeking ten million in damages.

planetesimal N. any of numerous small celestial bodies that may have existed at an early stage of the development of the solar system
Many astronomers believe that the planets have evolved by aggregation from *planetesimals.*

plasticity N. condition of being able to be shaped or formed; pliability
Behaviorist psychologists such as B.F. Skinner tend to stress the *plasticity* of human beings.

platitude N. stale, overused expression
"Might makes right" is a *platitude.*

platonic ADJ. spiritual; without physical desire; theoretical

James and Emma used to be lovers, but now their relationship is *platonic*.

plaudits N. enthusiastic praise or approval
The actor's performance won the *plaudits* of the critics.

plausibility N. validity, likeliness, or acceptability
The scientist questioned the *plausibility* of the claim.

plebeian ADJ. crude, vulgar, low-class
Ralph's tastes are *plebeian*.

plenary adj. complete in all respects; fully attended by all qualified members
The chief minister called a *plenary* meeting of the council.

plenitude N. abundance, plenty
The new immigrants were amazed by Australia's *plenitude*.

plethora N. excess, overabundance
There is a *plethora* of jobs in the booming economy.

pliant ADJ. pliable, yielding
Garth has a *pliant* nature.

ploy N. an action to gain an advantage indirectly or deviously
The *ploy* helped us to gain the advantage.

plucky ADJ. courageous, spunky
The *plucky* soldier charged the enemy machine gun position.

plumb V. to determine the depth; to examine deeply
The poem *plumbs* the depths of human nature.

plummet V. to fall, plunge
The dead bird *plummeted* to Earth.

pluralistic ADJ. including a variety of groups
The United States is a *pluralistic* society.

plurality N. being plural; a large number
The candidate received a *plurality* of the votes.

plutocracy N. society ruled by the wealthy
America is described by some people as having some of the characteristics of a *plutocracy*.

ply V. to use diligently; engage; join together
The tailor *plies* his trade in a nearby town.

pneumatic ADJ. relating to air; worked by compressed air

The workmen used a *pneumatic* drill to dig through the surface of the road.

poach V. to steal game or fish; appropriate something as one's own; cook in boiling liquid
The track coach accused the football coach of *poaching* his athletes.

podium N. platform or lectern for orchestra conductors or speakers
The person on the *podium* looked small from where we were sitting.

pogrom N. an organized massacre or persecution of a minority group
The *pogrom* was carried out over one year.

poignant ADJ. emotionally moving
The survivors told *poignant* stories.

polar ADJ. relating to a geographic pole; exhibiting contrast
The expedition studied the *polar* region.

polarize V. to tend toward opposite extremes
The candidate's stand on the controversial issue has *polarized* voters across the state.

polemic N. controversy, argument; verbal attack
His works are *polemics* in support of the present policy.

polemical ADJ. relating to controversy, argument, or verbal attack
The politician wrote a *polemical* article on the issue.

politic ADJ. discreet, tactful
The *politic* diplomat was chosen to lead the negotiation.

polity N. an organized society having a specific form of government
The *polity* is devoted to freedom of speech and expression.

polyandry N. the practice of having more than one husband at one time
The form of polyandry in which a woman is married to two or more brothers is known as "fraternal *polyandry*," and it is believed by many anthropologists to be the most frequently encountered form.

polygamy N. having more than one wife or husband at a time

Polygamy is practiced in Australia's aboriginal culture.

polyglot N. speaker of many languages
The *polyglot* speaks French, German, Italian, Spanish, and English.

polytheist N. a person who believes in more than one god
Many people in ancient Rome were *polytheists*.

pompous ADJ. marked by excessive self-esteem or exaggerated dignity
Stan plays the part of the *pompous* Milfoil in the schools' production of Shakespeare's *Twelfth Night*.

ponder V. to weigh carefully in the mind; reflect deeply
Susan is *pondering* the meaning and purpose of existence.

ponderous ADJ. weighty; unwieldy; labored
How long will this boring, *ponderous* speech last?

pontificate V. to speak in a pretentious manner
Mr. Sanders likes to *pontificate* in his history class.

portent N. omen
The sailors saw the storm as a bad *portent*.

portentous ADJ. foreboding; exciting wonder and awe
The diary records the *portentous* events of 1776.

portly ADJ. stout, dignified
A *portly* gentleman entered the room.

poseur N. a person who tries to impress others by affecting a manner, attitude, etc., other than his or her true one
Sharon's reputation as a *poseur* makes it hard to take her seriously.

posit V. to assume or affirm the existence of; postulate; to propose as an explanation
The science fiction novel *posits* the existence of an advanced race living on Mars one billion years ago.

positivism N. a philosophical doctrine that says that sense perceptions are the only valid basis of human knowledge
Positivism holds that science is humanity's highest intellectual achievement.

posterior ADJ. later in time
The evidence shows that the crime occurred *posterior* to the meeting.

posterity N. future generations; all of a person's descendants
How will *posterity* judge us?

posthumous ADJ. occurring or continuing after one's death; published after a writer's death
He received a *posthumous* award for bravery.

Postmodernism N. theory that involves a radical reappraisal of modern assumptions about culture, identity, history, or language; in the arts, any of various movements in reaction to modernism that are typically characterized by a return to traditional materials and forms
The article discusses the view that *Postmodernism* is no longer an important theory.

post mortem N. medical examination of a dead body; autopsy
The *post mortem* revealed the cause of death.

postulate N. a principle provisionally adopted as a basis for argument; a presupposition; basic principle
We accepted the *postulate* for the sake of discussion.

postulate V. to assume as a premise
The science fiction novel *postulates* that an advanced civilization once lived on the moon.

potable ADJ. drinkable
The water is *potable*.

potent ADJ. strong; powerful
The *potent* drug must be used carefully.

potentate N. monarch or ruler with great power
The *potentate* ordered an invasion of the neighboring country.

pragmatic ADJ. practical
The English have a reputation as a *pragmatic*, down-to-earth people.

pragmatism N. practical way of approaching situations or solving problems
Pragmatism can be described as a fancy word for common sense.

prate V. to talk idly; chatter
The fool *prated* on, showing his ignorance of the subject.

prattle N. meaningless, foolish talk
I've had enough of this *prattle*; let's get to work.

precarious ADJ. uncertain
Our position is *precarious*.

precedence N. right of preceding; priority
This latest case must take *precedence* over the earlier ones.

precedent N. a model for that which follows
The lawyer found a *precedent* for the case.

precept N. principle; law
The class studied the *precepts* of good writing.

preceptor N. teacher
The young writer's *preceptor* is a famous novelist.

precipice N. edge, steep overhang
The car went off the *precipice*.

precipitate ADJ. rash; hasty; sudden
The man's friend urged him not to be *precipitate* in coming to a decision.

precipitate V. to cause to happen; throw down from a height
The rumors *precipitated* a rebellion.

precipitation N. water droplets or ice particles condensed from atmospheric water vapor that falls to Earth
There has been a lot of *precipitation* this winter.

precipitous ADJ. hasty, quickly, with too little caution
The *precipitous* decision nearly led to disaster.

précis N. short summary of facts
The governor asked his aid to prepare a *précis* of the report.

preclude V. to make impossible; prevent
The snowstorm *precludes* having the celebration tonight.

precocious ADJ. unusually advanced at an early age
The *precocious* child was enrolled in the school's gifted program.

preconception N. an idea formed in advance of actual knowledge; a prejudice
Education can encourage us to examine our *preconceptions*.

precursor N. forerunner, predecessor
The League of Nations was a *precursor* to the United Nations.

predator N. one that preys on others, destroyer, plunderer
The tiger is one of nature's most deadly *predators*.

predatory ADJ. marked by preying on others
The *predatory* salesperson watched the shoppers carefully.

predecessor N. former occupant of post; something that has been succeeded by another
The new governor met with his *predecessor*.

predicament N. difficult situation
There is no easy way out of the *predicament*.

predicate V. to found or base on
Our argument is *predicated* on several assumptions.

predicate N. one of the two main constituents of a sentence or clause, modifying the subject
The students learned to identify the subject and *predicate* in a sentence.

predictive ADJ. relating to prediction, indicative of the future
The experiment will test the theory's *predictive* power.

predilection N. preference, liking
I have a *predilection* for reading books about language.

predisposed ADJ. having a tendency
The judge is *predisposed* to be lenient.

predisposition N. tendency, inclination
He has a *predisposition* to be happy.

predominance N. ascendancy, importance; prevalence
Japan's *predominance* in Asia is being challenged by China.

preeminence N. condition of being superior to or notable above all others
Most experts agree on Shakespeare's *preeminence* among English playwrights.

preface N. introduction to a book; introductory remarks to a speech
In her *preface* the author explains why she wrote the book.

prehensile ADJ. capable of grasping
The animal's *prehensile* tail allows it to hang from the branches of trees.

prejudge V. to judge beforehand or without all the evidence
The jurors were told not to *prejudge* the case.

prelude N. an introductory performance, action, or event preceding and preparing for the principal or a more important matter
We enjoyed the *prelude* to the performance.

premeditate V. to consider, plan beforehand
The jury found that the accused had *premeditated* the murder.

premise N. a proposition upon which an argument is based
The argument is based on a faulty *premise*.

premonition N. forewarning; presentiment
The woman had a *premonition* of disaster.

preordained ADJ. decided in advance
The philosopher believes that the events of our lives are *preordained*.

preponderance N. majority in number; dominance
There is a *preponderance* of science majors at the college.

prepossessing ADJ. attractive, engaging, appealing
They were a *prepossessing* group of students.

preposterous ADJ. absurd, illogical
What a *preposterous* plan!

prerequisite N. something necessary as a prior condition
An advanced math course is a *prerequisite* for physics.

prerogative N. a special right or privilege
Formerly, voting was a *prerogative* of certain groups.

presage V. to foretell, indicate in advance
The legend *presages* a golden age.

prescience N. foresight
Mrs. Tan had the *prescience* to bring an umbrella to the lacrosse game.

prescribe V. to order the use of
Make sure you get the list of books *prescribed* by the examiners for the exam.

presentiment N. premonition, sense of foreboding
Several people said they felt a *presentiment* of the tragedy.

prestidigitation N. sleight of hand
The magician amazed the audience with his feats of *prestidigitation*.

presume V. to assume to be true
We *presumed* that the account was accurate.

presumption N. belief based on reasonable evidence
My *presumption* is that you are telling the truth.

presumptuous ADJ. rude, improperly bold
The student was *presumptuous* in criticizing the instructor's teaching technique.

presuppose V. to assume or suppose something in advance
The essay makes the mistake of *presupposing* what it is trying to prove.

presupposition N. something assumed or supposed in advance
Modern biology accepts evolution as a *presupposition*.

pretentious ADJ. ostentatious; showy
Herb's big car is *pretentious*.

preternatural ADJ. beyond the normal course of nature; supernatural
There were rumors of *preternatural* occurrences in the graveyard.

pretext N. excuse, pretended reason
Hugh used his question as a *pretext* to meet Erica.

prevalent ADJ. widespread
The disease is *prevalent* in Europe.

prevaricate V. to quibble, evade the truth
The witness *prevaricated* under questioning from the detective.

prima facie ADV. at first sight; ADJ. true at first sight; evident without proof
In view of the strong *prima facie* evidence, the detective has decided to proceed with the investigation.

primeval ADJ. ancient, primitive
This history of the world starts from *primeval* time.

primordial ADJ. original, existing from the beginning
The astronomer is studying the *primordial* universe.

pristine ADJ. untouched, uncorrupted
The computer is in *pristine* condition.

privation N. lack of usual necessities or comforts
The soldiers suffered *privation* during the long winter campaign.

probity N. honesty, high-mindedness
The official's *probity* is beyond question.

proclivity N. tendency, inclination
Tom's *proclivities* are toward the arts.

procrastinator N. one who continually and unjustifiably postpones
The student is a *procrastinator*.

procure V. to obtain
We need to *procure* a copy of the textbook before classes begin.

prodigal ADJ. wasteful, extravagant, lavish
The celebration was criticized as *prodigal*.

prodigious ADJ. vast, enormous, extraordinary
The scientist has made a *prodigious* effort to prove his theory.

prodigy N. highly gifted child; marvel
The violin *prodigy* is giving a concert tonight.

profane V. to treat with irreverence or disrespect; degrade or abuse
The sign instructed tourists to remove their shoes so as not to *profane* the sanctity of the temple.

profligacy N. corruption, degeneration; wild extravagance
The government was accused of *profligacy* in spending ten million dollars on the celebrations.

profound ADJ. deep; not superficial
Profound thinking is needed to understand this poem.

profundity N. the quality of being deep, not superficial
Few would doubt the *profundity* of Spinoza's philosophy.

profuse ADJ. lavish, extravagant
He was embarrassed by the *profuse* compliments.

profusion N. great quantity; abundance
There is a *profusion* of fresh fruit available this summer.

progenitor N. originator, forefather, ancestor in a direct line
The tribe follows the teachings of its *progenitors*.

progeny N. offspring, children
Those who come after us are our *progeny*.

prognosis N. prediction of disease outcome; any prediction
The doctor's *prognosis* is favorable.

prognostication N. prediction through use of present condition as a guide
His *prognostication* was that there would be a recession.

progressive ADJ. favoring progress or change; moving forward, going step by step
The government has taken a *progressive* approach to lowering taxes.

prohibition N. a law or order that forbids something
There is a *prohibition* on selling alcoholic beverages after 10 P.M.

proletariat N. the class of industrial wage earners who must sell their labor to survive
The writer's sympathies are with the *proletariat*.

proliferate V. to increase rapidly
Weeds are *proliferating* on the front lawn.

prolific ADJ. abundantly fruitful
The *prolific* author Isaac Asimov wrote more than 300 books.

prolix ADJ. tending to speak or write at excessive length; wordy
The writer's main fault is that he is *prolix*.

prologue N. introductory section of a literary work or play
The novel's *prologue* sets the scene.

promontory N. piece of land or rock higher than its surroundings
From the *promontory* we could see far across the desert.

promulgate V. to make known publicly
The new policy was *promulgated* last month.

propaganda N. the systematic dissemination of ideas reflecting a particular view or interest
The film has been criticized as being *propaganda* for the government.

propensity N. inclination, tendency
The student has a *propensity* to exaggerate his academic achievements.

prophecy N. a prediction
The fortune teller's *prophecy* turned out to be incorrect.

propinquity N. nearness
My partner's *propinquity* makes working together convenient.

propitiate V. to win over, appease
The sacrifice *propitiated* the angry gods.

propitious ADJ. favorable, advantageous
The full moon was regarded as *propitious*.

proponent N. person who argues for something; advocate
Proponents of the plan argue that it will be cost-effective.

propriety N. correct conduct; fitness
Propriety demands that we dress correctly.

prosaic ADJ. relating to prose; dull, commonplace
The *prosaic* writer has produced no bestsellers.

proscribe V. to condemn; forbid, outlaw
The law *proscribes* gambling.

proscriptive ADJ. relating to restriction or restraint
This grammar book takes a *proscriptive* approach rather than a descriptive one.

prose N. ordinary language used in everyday speech
The essay is written in clear *prose*.

proselytize V. to convert to a particular belief or religion
Students are not allowed to *proselytize* on campus.

prosification N. converting (poetry, etc.) into prose
The teacher is working on a *prosification* of *Hamlet*.

prostrate ADJ. lying face downward, lying flat on ground
The wounded soldier was *prostrate* on the battlefield.

protagonist N. main character in a play or story; hero
The novel's *protagonist* is based on a person the author knew in high school.

protean ADJ. readily assuming different forms or characters
The *protean* actor performed thirty roles in his one-man show.

protégé N. person receiving protection and support from a patron
The championship tennis player trains her *protégé* every day.

protestation N. strong expression of disapproval; formal declaration
Tom made a *protestation* of his love to Debbie.

protocol N. ceremony and manners observed by diplomats
Protocol demands that the president be seated at the head of the table.

prototype N. original work used as a model by others
The *prototype* of the new aircraft is being built in France.

protract V. to prolong
The meeting was *protracted*, ending at 9 P.M.

protrusion N. something that sticks out
Geologists are investigating the large *protrusion* on the Earth's surface.

proverbial ADJ. widely referred to
Oscar Wilde's wit is *proverbial*.

provident ADJ. providing for future needs; frugal
In Singapore employees and employers contribute to the Central *Provident* Fund to provide economic security for retirees.

province N. range; scope
The book ranges over the entire *province* of human knowledge.

provincial ADJ. limited in outlook; unsophisticated
Many people in the town are *provincial*.

provisional ADJ. provided for the time being
The two sides reached a *provisional* agreement.

proviso N. a condition or qualification
John bought the used car with the *proviso* that it would be repainted.

provocative ADJ. arousing anger or interest; annoying
The *provocative* statements were designed to start a debate on the subject.

prowess N. bravery, skill
The actor's *prowess* was recognized when he won an Academy Award.

proximate ADJ. very near
Since your home is *proximate* to mine, we should get together more often.

proximity N. nearness
The two areas of the brain are in close *proximity*.

proxy N. authorized agent; power to act as a substitute for another

The businessman's lawyer will act as his *proxy* at the hearing.

prude N. one who is excessively proper or modest
The play pokes fun at *prudes* who never want to have fun.

prudent ADJ. cautious; careful
It is *prudent* to prepare well for the GRE.

prurient ADJ. lustful, exhibiting lewd desires
The movie has mainly a *prurient* appeal.

pseudonym N. pen name; fictitious or borrowed name
The scholar writes mystery books under a *pseudonym*.

psyche N. the mind
The book explores the mysteries of the human *psyche*.

psychic ADJ. perceptive of non-material, spiritual forces; originating in the mind
The scientist is studying *psychic* phenomena.

psychosis N. a severe mental disorder characterized by derangement of personality and loss of contact with reality
The new drug promises to offer an effective control for several forms of *psychosis*.

pubescent ADJ. reaching puberty
The *pubescent* boys are becoming interested in girls.

puerile ADJ. childish, immature, silly
The seniors are tired of the freshman's *puerile* jokes.

pugilism N. boxing
Pugilism is an Olympic sport.

pugnacious ADJ. quarrelsome, eager and ready to fight
The *pugnacious* boy is always getting into fights.

puissance N. power
Freedom is an idea of great *puissance*.

pulchritude N. beauty
Helen of Troy was famous for her *pulchritude*.

pulverize V. to pound, crush, or grind into powder; destroy
The artillery barrage *pulverized* the town.

pummel V. to pound, beat
The men seized the thief and *pummeled* him.

punctilious ADJ. careful in observing rules of behavior or ceremony
The host was *punctilious* in seating the guests.

pundit N. critic; learned person
Most *pundits* agree that the policy was sound.

pungent ADJ. strong or sharp in smell or taste
The *pungent* aroma was coming from the kitchen.

punitive ADJ. having to do with punishment
Punitive measures have been taken against the rebellious students.

purgation N. catharsis, purification
The hero of the play performed acts of *purgation*.

purge V. to cleanse or free from impurities
Party leaders want to *purge* disloyal members.

puritanical ADJ. adhering to a rigid moral code
The actor plays the *puritanical* servant Malvolio in Shakespeare's *Twelfth Night*.

purported ADJ. alleged; claimed; reputed or rumored
The *purported* occurrences cannot be verified.

pusillanimous ADJ. cowardly
The general warned the president that he must give the enemy no suggestion that he was *pusillanimous*.

putative ADJ. generally regarded as such; supposed
The *putative* reason he gave for leaving the firm is that he had found a better job.

putsch N. a sudden attempt by a group to overthrow a government
After the military *putsch* in 1991, she left the country.

Q

quack N. faker; one who falsely claims to have medical skill
The *quack* claims that he can heal broken bones in one week.

quadruped N. animal having four feet
Most mammals are *quadrupeds*.

quaff V. to drink with relish
The thirsty man *quaffed* a large bottle of water.

quagmire N. marsh; difficult situation
The castle's best defense was the *quagmire* around it.

quail V. to cower; lose heart
The invaders began to *quail* in face of the enemy's withering artillery barrage.

quaint ADJ. old-fashioned; picturesque; odd
The girls find the old man's ideas about women *quaint*.

qualification N. limitation; restriction
I can agree with your statement provided that you accept my *qualifications* to it.

qualified ADJ. limited or restricted
The concert was a *qualified* success.

qualify V. to provide with needed skills; modify, limit
It is often necessary to *qualify* a statement to make it true.

qualitative ADJ. related to quality
The governor ordered a *qualitative* analysis of the situation.

qualm N. uneasy feeling about the rightness of an action
The witness has *qualms* about testifying against her friend.

quandary N. state of uncertainty; dilemma
Shirley is in a *quandary* about whether to take physics or chemistry.

quantify V. to determine or express the amount
Opinion polls try to *quantify* public opinion.

quantitative ADJ. expressed as a quantity; able to be measured
Many historians now use *quantitative* methods.

quantum leap N. a sudden advance
The theory of plate tectonics was a *quantum leap* in geology.

quarry N. object of a hunt; victim
The detective tracked down his *quarry* and arrested him.

quell V. to crush or subdue
National Guard troops *quelled* the uprising.

querulous ADJ. inclined to complain, irritable
Everyone avoided the *querulous* old man.

query N. question
The teacher promised to answer the student's *query* later.

quibble V. to argue about insignificant and irrelevant details.
Let's not *quibble* over details.

quid pro quo N. a favor given in return for something
Tom's *quid pro quo* for helping Sam in French was for Sam to help him in physics.

quiescence N. inactivity, stillness
The physicist believes that the universe alternates between periods of activity and *quiescence*.

quintessence N. most typical example; concentrated essence
Sarah is the *quintessence* of politeness.

quintessential ADJ. most typical
Mr. Miller is the *quintessential* teacher.

quip N. a brief and often impromptu witty remark
This *quip* of Mark Twain's is often quoted: "Always do right. This will gratify some people and astonish the rest."

quixotic ADJ. overly idealistic, impractical
One world government is regarded by many as a *quixotic* idea.

quorum N. number of members necessary to conduct a meeting
The House of Representatives couldn't vote on the bill because there wasn't a *quorum*.

quotidian ADJ. occurring daily; commonplace
The novel attempts to describe the *quotidian* details of one day in a character's life.

R

raconteur N. witty, skillful storyteller
The *raconteur* was surrounded by people listening to his story.

radial ADJ. radiating from or converging to a common center
Many flowers and plants exhibit *radial* symmetry.

radical ADJ. extreme; favoring great change in society
The *radical* plan calls for abolishing taxes.

rail V. to scold with bitter or abusive language
The speaker *railed* against social injustice.

raiment N. clothing
The waiters in the restaurant are all clad in blue *raiment*.

raison d'être N. justification for existing
The writer defines philosophy as the search for humanity's *raison d'être*.

ramification N. implication
The law student's paper deals with the *ramifications* of the Supreme Court's decision.

rampant ADJ. unrestrained; occurring widely
Cheating is *rampant* in the college.

rancid ADJ. spoiled, rotten
The smell of *rancid* meat is very unpleasant.

rancor N. bitter hatred
There was *rancor* on both sides of the dispute.

rapacious ADJ. taking by force; greedy
The *rapacious* landlord doubled our rent.

rapport N. relationship of trust and respect
There is great *rapport* between Tom and Beth.

rapprochement N. establishment of harmonious relations
After the war ended there was a *rapprochement* between the two countries.

rapt ADJ. deeply absorbed
The children listened to the story with *rapt* attention.

rarefied ADJ. refined
It was difficult to understand the professor's *rarefied* discussion.

ratify V. to approve formally, confirm
The treaty was *ratified* by the Senate.

ratiocination N. methodical, logical reasoning
Some scientists believe that human beings are the only species capable of *ratiocination*.

rational ADJ. logical, reasonable
Scientists are searching for a *rational* explanation of the strange phenomenon.

rationale N. fundamental reasons
What is the *rationale* for changing our plans?

rationalization N. act or practice of providing self-satisfying but incorrect reasons for something
The excuse you gave is nothing but a *rationalization*.

raucous ADJ. harsh-sounding; boisterous
The crow's *raucous* calls make it hard to concentrate.

ravage V. to destroy, devastate
The disease *ravaged* the population of Europe.

ravenous ADJ. extremely hungry
After fasting all day, Rick is *ravenous*.

ravine N. deep, narrow gorge
The town plans to build a footbridge over the *ravine*.

raze V. to tear down, demolish
The area was *razed* so it could be redeveloped.

reactionary ADJ. marked by extreme conservatism
The *reactionary* group opposes any form of change.

rebuff V. to snub; beat back
Holly *rebuffed* Luke's offer of marriage.

rebuke V. to reprimand, scold
The teacher *rebuked* the student for her poor behavior.

rebuttal N. refutation; response with contrary evidence
The debater's *rebuttal* of her opponent's argument was persuasive.

recalcitrant ADJ. resisting authority or control
The UN Security Council plans to take action against the *recalcitrant* country.

recant V. to retract a statement, opinion, etc.
The medical board ordered the doctor to *recant* his statement.

recapitulate V. to review by a brief summary; in biology: to appear to repeat the evolution of the species during the embryonic development of the individual
The English teacher *recapitulated* the events of the novel for her class.

recidivism N. tendency to relapse into previous behavior
The rate of *recidivism* is increasing.

reclusive ADJ. seeking seclusion or isolation
The *reclusive* writer hates to give interviews.

reconciliation N. a settlement or resolution; act of making compatible or consistent
Negotiations brought *reconciliation* between the two opposing sides.

recondite ADJ. abstruse; profound
The course is an introduction to Kant's *recondite* philosophy.

reconnaissance N. survey of enemy by soldiers; reconnoitering

The scout conducted a *reconnaissance* of the enemy position.

recount V. to narrate or tell
The novel *recounts* the story of three generations of the Galbraith family.

rectify V. to correct
Once the problem with the engine is *rectified*, we will be on our way again.

rectitude N. moral uprightness
The country expects its leaders to be people of *rectitude*.

redolent ADJ. odorous; fragrant; suggestive of an odor
This white wine is *redolent* of lemon.

redoubtable ADJ. formidable; arousing fear; worthy of respect
Glenda is a *redoubtable* debater.

redress N. relief from wrong or injury
The court ordered payment as *redress* for the injury he suffered.

reductionism N. attempt to explain complex phenomena by simple principles
The statement "A person is nothing but a combination of chemicals" is an example of *reductionism*.

reductionistic ADJ. attempting to explain complex phenomena by simple principles
The idea that the brain is nothing but a bunch of chemicals can be regarded as *reductionistic*.

redundant ADJ. exceeding what is necessary; unnecessarily repetitive
The engineers built several *redundant* systems into the spacecraft.

refectory N. room where meals are served
The family had breakfast in the *refectory*.

refined ADJ. cultivated; elegant
Professor Hunter is a woman of *refined* taste in literature.

refract V. to deflect sound or light
Water *refracts* light more than air does.

refractory ADJ. stubborn; unmanageable; resisting ordinary methods of treatment
Only the stable's most experienced trainer could deal with the *refractory* horse.

refulgent ADJ. brightly shining; resplendent
The mystic had a vision of a *refulgent* being.

refurbish V. to renovate
We are planning to *refurbish* our home next year.

refutation N. disproof of opponent's argument
The lawyer's *refutation* of the argument was clear and effective.

refute V. to contradict; disprove
The man's lawyer *refuted* the charges against his client.

regale V. to entertain
The bride's family hired a jazz band to *regale* the guests.

regimen N. government rule; systematic plan
Susie is sticking to her *regimen* of learning ten advanced words a day.

regimented ADJ. systematized; made uniform
The study shows that students who take a *regimented* approach do best.

regression N. a movement backward; reversion to an earlier form or state
Bill was disappointed by the *regression* in his GRE scores.

reification N. treatment of an abstraction as if it had material existence
The psychologist believes that the human mind has a natural tendency toward *reification*.

reiterate V. to say or do again, repeat
The teacher *reiterated* her statement for emphasis.

rejoinder N. response
The comedian is always ready with a *rejoinder* to comments from the audience.

rejuvenate V. to make young again; renew
Our vacation *rejuvenated* us.

relegate V. to consign to an inferior position
The veteran baseball player was *relegated* to a backup role.

relevance N. pertinence; connection with a matter under consideration
That case has little *relevance* to this one.

relic N. surviving remnant; memento
Tom keeps his old tennis racquet as a *relic* of his playing days.

relinquish v. to renounce or surrender something
The boxer was forced to *relinquish* his title because he failed to defend it.

relish v. to enjoy greatly
Everyone in the family *relished* their Thanksgiving dinner.

remediable ADJ. capable of being corrected
Luckily, your errors are *remediable*.

reminisce v. to remember past events
The couple *reminisced* about their first date.

remission N. lessening, relaxation
The disease went into *remission*.

remonstrate v. to object or protest
The columnist regularly *remonstrated* about social injustice.

remorseless ADJ. having no pity; merciless
We watched the *remorseless* advance of the invading force.

remuneration N. pay or reward for work, trouble, etc.
The job doesn't offer adequate *remuneration*.

renaissance N. rebirth or revival
In recent years poetry has enjoyed a *renaissance* in America.

renascent ADJ. reborn, coming into being again
After many years of dictatorship in the country, democracy is now *renascent* there.

render v. to provide; give what is due; represent in drawing or painting
The artist *rendered* his subject as a young woman.

rendition N. artistic interpretation of a song, etc.; translation
The singers gave an interesting *rendition* of the well-known song.

renegade N. traitor, person abandoning a cause
Government troops captured the *renegades* and brought them to trial.

renege v. to go back on one's word
When our partner *reneged* on the agreement, he was sued by the other parties.

renounce v. to give up or reject a right, title, person, etc.
One member of the family *renounced* her right to the property.

renown N. fame, widespread acclaim
The novelist enjoys international *renown*.

reparation N. amends; compensation
The peace treaty stipulates that the vanquished country will pay *reparations* to the victorious country.

repast N. meal or mealtime
On Sundays my family enjoys a big *repast*.

repentant ADJ. apologetic, guilty, remorseful
The priest asked the sinner if he was *repentant*.

repertoire N. pieces that an artist or artists are prepared to perform; a person's range of skills
The pianist's *repertoire* includes pieces by Chopin.

repine v. to fret; complain
She is no longer invited to their parties but she doesn't greatly *repine*.

replete ADJ. abundantly supplied
My new car is *replete* with every gadget imaginable.

replica N. duplication, copy of something
Herb built a miniature *replica* of a Boeing 747.

repose N. relaxation, leisure
On Sundays we enjoy a day of *repose*.

repository N. place things are put for safekeeping
Libraries are *repositories* of human knowledge.

reprehensible ADJ. blameworthy, disreputable
The invasion was condemned around the world as a *reprehensible* act.

repressive ADJ. causing or inclined to cause repression
The *repressive* government was overthrown.

reprimand v. to scold
The teacher *reprimanded* the class for talking.

reprise N. repetition, esp. of a piece of music
We enjoyed the *reprise* of the last movement of the symphony.

reproach v. to find fault with; blame
The platoon leader *reproached* the soldier for disobeying orders.

reprobate N. morally unprincipled person
Most people shun the man as a *reprobate*.

reprove v. to criticize or correct
The teacher *reproved* the student for not paying attention.

repudiate v. to reject as having no authority
The court *repudiated* the decision reached by the citizens' committee.

repugnant ADJ. distasteful; offensive
The views expressed in this book are *repugnant* to most people.

requiem N. hymns or religious service for the dead
A *requiem* was held for the dead soldier.

rescind v. to cancel
The bank has *rescinded* Tom's credit card.

reserve N. self-control; formal but distant manner
Ms. Smith's *reserve* makes her difficult to get to know.

residual ADJ. remaining, leftover
The organization decided to donate the *residual* funds to charity.

resigned ADJ. unresisting; patiently submissive
Bob is *resigned* to failing math again this year.

resilient ADJ. able to recover quickly after illness or misfortune
The *resilient* boxer was back on his feet again right away after being knocked down by his opponent.

resolute ADJ. determined; with a clear purpose
Laura is *resolute* in her determination to become a scientist.

resolve v. to determine to do something
Sue *resolved* to obtain a Ph.D.

resonate v. to echo
The speaker's words *resonated* through the hall.

respire v. to breathe
The accident victim was not *respiring*.

respite N. interval of relief
The teacher gave the class a five-minute *respite*.

resplendent ADJ. splendid, brilliant
The royal couple looked *resplendent* in their golden robes.

restitution N. act of compensating for loss or damage
As *restitution* for his crime, Steve performed community service.

restive ADJ. impatient, uneasy, restless
The audience grew *restive* when the speaker hadn't appeared.

restorative ADJ. having the power to renew or revitalize
The herbalist believes in the *restorative* power of ginseng.

restrained v. controlled, repressed, restricted
Security guards *restrained* the angry customer.

resurrection N. rising from the dead; revival
The book begins the *resurrection* of long-forgotten ideas.

resuscitate v. to revive, bring back to life
Paramedics *resuscitated* the woman who had collapsed at the mall.

resurgent ADJ. rising again
The political scientist analyzed the effects of a *resurgent* Russia on international relations.

reticence N. reserve; reluctance
The star's *reticence* annoyed the journalist who interviewed him.

retinue N. group of attendants with an important person
The queen arrived with a *retinue* of servants.

retiring ADJ. shy, modest, reserved
Few successful politicians are the *retiring* type.

retort N. cutting response
The comedian is a master of the quick *retort* to comments from the audience.

retrench v. to regroup, reorganize
The company is making plans to *retrench*.

retribution N. something demanded in repayment; punishment
As *retribution* for setting fire to the granary, the villagers demanded his house and possessions.

retrograde ADJ. having a backward motion or direction
Planets sometimes appear to have a *retrograde* motion due to the fact that planets travel at different speeds around the sun.

retrospect N. review or contemplation of the past
In *retrospect*, I wish I had studied more in high school.

reveille N. the sounding of a bugle early in the morning to awaken and summon people
Reveille was sounded at 6:00 A.M.

revelation N. something revealed
The woman was stunned by the *revelation* that he was now married.

revelry N. boisterous festivity
The *revelry* continued past midnight.

reverie N. daydream
The student's *reverie* was broken by the teacher's question.

reversion N. return to an earlier state; regression
To avoid *reversion* to his past behavior, special steps have been taken.

revile V. to criticize with harsh language, verbally abuse
The candidates *reviled* each other in their debate.

revivify V. give new life or energy
The vacation *revivified* the students.

revulsion N. strong feeling of repugnance or dislike
Tom feels *revulsion* for violence.

rhapsodize V. to speak or write in an exaggeratedly enthusiastic manner
The speaker *rhapsodized* about the beauty of nature.

rhapsody N. emotional literary or musical work
The poem is a *rhapsody* on the beauty of nature.

rhetoric N. persuasive use of language; pretentious language
The politician's speech was full of empty *rhetoric*.

rhetorical ADJ. related to effective communication; insincere in language
All the *rhetorical* devices in the world won't make you a good writer unless you have something to say.

ribald ADJ. humorous in a vulgar way
The *ribald* jokes are not suitable for a young audience.

rife ADJ. widespread, prevalent; abundant
Reports of cheating are *rife*.

riposte N. a retaliatory action or retort
The enemy's attack brought a quick *riposte* from our side.

risqué ADJ. bordering on being inappropriate or indecent
The principal thought the show was too *risqué* for a young audience.

robust ADJ. strong and healthy; hardy
The man was eighty years old and still enjoyed *robust* health.

rococo ADJ. very highly ornamented
The writer's *rococo* style has fallen out of fashion.

romanticize V. to interpret romantically
People seem to have a tendency to *romanticize* the past.

rotund ADJ. round in shape; fat
The *rotund* man has trouble climbing stairs.

rubric N. title or heading; category; established mode of procedure
The new policy falls under the *rubric* of law and order.

rudimentary ADJ. related to the basic principles of something; elementary; in early stages of development
Ivan's essay is still at a *rudimentary* stage of development.

rue V. to regret
The old man *rues* the day he dropped out of college.

rueful ADJ. full of regret
The old man reminisced about his lost opportunities with a *rueful* smile.

ruminate V. to contemplate, reflect upon
The philosopher *ruminated* all day about the idea.

ruse N. trick; crafty stratagem; subterfuge
The *ruse* allowed the prisoners to escape.

rustic ADJ. rural
Phil and Sue love to have picnics in *rustic* settings.

S

saccharine ADJ. excessively sweet or sentimental
The love story is too *saccharine* for Bill's taste.

sacrilege N. the desecration of something holy
The robber committed the *sacrilege* of opening the saint's tomb.

sacrosanct ADJ. extremely sacred; beyond criticism
The idea of freedom is *sacrosanct*.

sagacious ADJ. having insight; wise
Many young students seek the advice of the *sagacious* professor.

sagacity N. insight; wisdom
Socrates is remembered as a person of great *sagacity*.

saga N. prose narrative
The novel tells the *saga* of the settling of America by Europeans.

sage N. wise older person
The *sage* advised the students to seek the truth within themselves.

salacious ADJ. lascivious; lustful
The film's *salacious* content got it an X rating.

salient ADJ. prominent or conspicuous
Your opening paragraph should outline the *salient* points of your argument.

sallow ADJ. sickly yellow in color
The long illness left Bob looking *sallow*.

salubrious ADJ. healthful
After she enjoyed the *salubrious* climate of Western Australia, Jill's health was restored.

salutary ADJ. effecting an improvement; favorable to health
Regular exercise had a *salutary* effect on Joan's health.

salutation N. greeting
"Hi" has become a popular e-mail *salutation*.

sanctify V. to set apart as holy; consecrate
The church was *sanctified* by the bishop.

sanctimonious ADJ. pretending to be pious or righteous
We were annoyed by the *sanctimonious* newspaper editorial.

sanction V. to approve; ratify; permit; penalize
The governor *sanctioned* the use of force to stop the riot.

sanction N. approval; ratification; permission; penalization
The drug has received the *sanction* of health officials.

sanguine ADJ. ruddy; cheerfully optimistic
Most economists are *sanguine* about the economy.

sardonic ADJ. cynical, scornfully mocking
The *sardonic* article criticizes government policy.

sartorial ADJ. pertaining to tailors
Professor Parker's small *sartorial* rebellion is to wear jeans during his tutorials.

satiate V. to satisfy
The university library has more than enough books to *satiate* your hunger for knowledge.

satire N. use of ridicule to expose vice or foolishness
The movie is a *satire* on consumers in modern society.

satirical ADJ. relating to the use of ridicule to expose vice or foolishness
The drama society performed a *satirical* anti-war skit.

saturnine ADJ. gloomy
The mood on campus after the big loss was *saturnine*.

satyr N. a creature that is half-man, half-beast with the horns and legs of a goat; a lecher
Joan's friends urged her to steer clear of the *satyr*.

savant N. learned person
The *savant* has written books on many subjects.

savoir faire N. ability to behave appropriately in social situations
A big part of the actor's appeal is his remarkable *savoir faire*.

savory ADJ. agreeable in taste or smell; morally respectable
Only *savory* characters are accepted to the teacher's college.

scabbard N. sheath for sword or dagger
After slaying the dragon, the knight returned his sword to its *scabbard*.

scathing ADJ. harshly critical; painfully hot
The opposition party was *scathing* in its criticism of government policy.

scenario N. plot outline; possible situation
In this *scenario*, the company loses money for awhile but gains in the long run.

schematic N. an outline or diagram
The engineer made a *schematic* of the radio's circuit.

schism N. division; split
The *schism* in the party eventually led to its breakup.

scintilla N. trace amount
There is not one *scintilla* of evidence to support the case.

scintillate V. to sparkle, flash
The actor's performance was adequate but did not *scintillate*.

scion N. descendant or heir
The *scion* of the billionaire established a foundation to help the poor.

scourge N. source of widespread affliction or devastation
War was one of the *scourges* of the twentieth century.

scrivener N. professional copyist
With modern technology, *scriveners* are not in much demand.

scruple N. conscientious feeling that tends to hinder action
His *scruples* don't allow him to participate in war.

scrupulous ADJ. conscientious; very thorough
The *scrupulous* editor discovered many errors in the manuscript.

scrutinize V. to examine closely and critically
The teacher *scrutinized* the student's exam paper.

scurrilous ADJ. vulgar, low, indecent
There were *scurrilous* rumors about the girl.

secrete V. to produce and release substance into an organism
The physiologist is studying the mechanisms by which the body *secretes* digestive juices.

sect N. a group of people forming a distinct unit within a larger group due to distinctions of belief
The religious *sect* has doubled its membership over the last twenty years.

sectarian ADJ. narrow-minded; relating to a group or sect
The president does not want his decision on the issue to be influenced by *sectarian* interests.

secular ADJ. not specifically pertaining to religion
The church has a department to take care of *secular* matters.

sedentary ADJ. inactive, stationary; sluggish
A *sedentary* lifestyle is not healthy.

sedimentary ADJ. relating to or containing sediment, that is material deposited by water, wind, or glaciers
Geologists are studying the *sedimentary* rocks.

sedition N. behavior promoting rebellion
The writer was accused of *sedition*.

sedulous ADJ. diligent
Karen has a reputation as a *sedulous* worker.

segregation N. separation from others; policy of separating races in society
Segregation was ended in America in the middle of the last century.

seismology N. science of earthquakes
Advances in *seismology* may some day allow scientists to make accurate predictions of earthquakes.

self-indulgent ADJ. relating to excessive gratification of desires
Lucy has become so *self-indulgent* that she doesn't care about work anymore.

self-perpetuating ADJ. having the power to renew itself
The scientists are creating a *self-perpetuating* robot.

semantics N. the study of meaning in language
The debate on democracy was largely a discussion of *semantics*.

semblance N. outward appearance; resemblance
Although this book has a *semblance* of scholarship, if you examine it closely, it contains falsehoods and errors.

seminal ADJ. relating to the beginning or seeds of something; containing the seeds of later development
The scientist did *seminal* work in the field of biophysics.

semiotic ADJ. related to semiotics or the production of meanings by sign systems
Umberto Eco's *The Name of the Rose* could be described as a *semiotic* novel.

semiotics N. the study of signs and symbols as elements of communication
The advertising firm has hired an expert on *semiotics* as a consultant.

Semitic ADJ. related to Semites, members of any of a number of peoples of ancient southwestern Asia

including the Akkadians, Phoenicians, Hebrews, and Arabs or to a descendant of these peoples
The most widely spoken *Semitic* language today is Arabic.

senescent ADJ. aging, growing old
The government is trying to help *senescent* industries.

sensibility N. receptiveness to impression; refined awareness and appreciation in feeling
Visiting a good art gallery can improve your artistic *sensibility*.

sensual ADJ. satisfying or gratifying the senses; suggesting sexuality
Heather's father doesn't want her to wear such *sensual* outfits.

sensuous ADJ. relating to the senses; operating through the senses
Barbara loves the *sensuous* feeling of silk on her skin.

sententious ADJ. having a moralizing tone
The speaker wants to talk about moral issues without sounding *sententious*.

sentience N. awareness, consciousness, ability to perceive
The scientists are studying what produces *sentience* in the human brain.

sentient ADJ. aware, conscious, able to perceive
No one knows if there's *sentient* life on other planets.

sentiment N. general attitude toward something; a view based on emotion rather than reason; emotion
The teacher asked the students to express their *sentiments* about the budget cuts.

sequester V. to remove or set apart; put into seclusion
The class was *sequestered* after being exposed to the virus.

seraphic ADJ. angelic, pure, sublime
The infant gave her mother a *seraphic* smile.

serendipitous ADJ. resulting from a fortunate discovery by chance
It was a *serendipitous* discovery.

serendipity N. habit of making fortunate discoveries by chance

The scientist thanked *serendipity* for helping her make the discovery.

serenity N. calm, peacefulness
Many people enjoy the *serenity* of nature.

serpentine ADJ. serpent-like; twisting, winding
The stream takes a *serpentine* course through the valley.

serrated ADJ. saw-toothed, notched
Use a *serrated* knife to cut the wood.

servile ADJ. submissive, obedient
The boss likes employees who are cooperative without being *servile*.

sextant N. navigation tool that determines latitude and longitude
A *sextant* is often used to sight the sun and moon to find one's latitude.

shaman N. a person who acts as intermediary between the natural and supernatural worlds, controls spiritual forces, and cures illnesses
The *shaman* went into a trance, hoping to get the spirit's help to heal the dying child.

shard N. piece of broken glass or pottery
The scientist found a *shard* she thought was part of an ancient Greek vase.

shibboleth N. a belief or custom that distinguishes a certain group, especially one regarded as outmoded
Members of the party have begun to break with the *shibboleths* of the left.

sibyl N. one of a number of women regarded as oracles or prophets by the ancient Greeks and Romans; a woman prophet
One of the main characters in the novel is a *sibyl* who seems to know what is going to happen to most of the other characters.

sidereal ADJ. relating to the stars
Astronomers generally use *sidereal* time in their work.

simian ADJ. ape-like; relating to apes
Human beings evolved from *simian* creatures.

simile N. comparison of one thing with another using "like" or "as"
A *simile* from the French writer Balzac: "She snatched her happiness like swimmer seizing a

willow branch overhanging the river to draw himself to land and rest for a while."

simper V. to smirk, smile foolishly
The director told the actress to stop *simpering*.

sinecure N. well-paying job or office that requires little or no work
The former government official was offered a *sinecure*.

singular ADJ. unique; extraordinary; odd
The appearance of the UFO was a *singular* event.

sinister ADJ. suggesting or threatening evil; ominous
The country's troop buildup was seen by many observers as *sinister*.

sinuous ADJ. winding; intricate, complex
The road follows a *sinuous* path over the mountain.

Sisyphean ADJ. endlessly laborious or futile
The housekeeper aptly described his job as *Sisyphean*.

skeptic N. one who doubts
Lynn is a *skeptic* when it comes to UFOs.

skeptical ADJ. doubting; suspending judgment
The investigator takes a *skeptical* approach to alleged occult phenomena.

skewed ADJ. distorted in meaning
His interpretation of the poem might be *skewed* by his religious beliefs.

skulk V. to move in a stealthy or cautious manner; sneak
We saw two men *skulking* around outside our house.

slavish ADJ. servile; blindly imitative
The teacher warned the students that they couldn't make a *slavish* copy of the test.

slipshod ADJ. careless, hasty
The barber gave Tom a *slipshod* haircut.

sloth N. sluggishness, laziness
Rick's *sloth* means that he will never succeed.

slough V. to discard or shed
The snake *sloughed* off its skin.

slovenly ADJ. untidy, messy
Ted will never get the job with his *slovenly* appearance.

smelt V. to melt metal in order to refine it
The ore is *smelted* to obtain copper.

snippet N. tiny part, tidbit
I've included *snippets* from several books in the article.

sobriety N. seriousness
The judge is a man of great *sobriety*.

sobriquet N. nickname
The center on our basketball team was given the *sobriquet* "The Tower."

Socratic irony N. profession of ignorance while questioning another person in order to discover the truth
The detective puts *Socratic irony* to good use when she questions suspects.

sodden ADJ. thoroughly soaked; saturated
The *sodden* field made it difficult to play soccer.

soiree N. an evening party
The poets had a *soiree* at which they read their poems.

sojourn N. visit, stay
My *sojourn* to Australia lasted two weeks.

solace N. comfort in sorrow; consolation
The relatives of the soldiers killed in the battle drew *solace* from the knowledge that they had died for a noble cause.

solarium N. room or glassed-in area exposed to the sun
We enjoy eating breakfast in the *solarium* in the winter.

solecism N. grammatical mistake
Even good writers sometimes commit *solecisms*.

solicitude N. concern, attention; eagerness
The students appreciate their teacher's *solicitude*.

soliloquy N. literary or dramatic speech by one character, not addressed to others
Playwrights sometimes use a *soliloquy* to convey something about a character's inner life.

solipsism N. belief that the self is the only reality
Solipsism raises many interesting philosophical issues.

solipsistic ADJ. relating to the belief that the self is the only reality

Critics see her poems as *solipsistic* and self-absorbed.

solstice N. shortest and longest day of the year
In a week, the winter *solstice* will occur.

soluble ADJ. capable of being solved or dissolved
Sugar is *soluble* in water.

solvent ADJ. able to meet financial obligations
Mr. Lesh is happy to still be *solvent* after paying for his four children's college education.

somatic ADJ. relating to or affecting the body
The psychologist investigated the patient's complaint to see if there were any *somatic* symptoms.

somber ADJ. dark and gloomy; melancholy, dismal
Ted tried to break the *somber* mood by cracking a joke.

somnambulist N. sleepwalker
The *somnambulist* doesn't remember what he did last night.

somnolent ADJ. drowsy, sleepy; inducing sleep
The drug made Liz *somnolent*.

sonic ADJ. relating to sound
The jet fighter created a *sonic* boom when it broke the sound barrier.

sonorous ADJ. producing a full, rich sound
The audience enjoyed listening to the speaker's *sonorous* voice.

sophist N. person good at arguing deviously
The debater accused her opponents of being *sophists*.

sophistical ADJ. relating to deceptive reasoning or argumentation
The debater's *sophistical* reasoning didn't confuse the judges.

sophistry N. deceptive reasoning or argumentation
Good debaters should not need to resort to *sophistry*.

sophomoric ADJ. immature and overconfident
The judge called the lawyer's presentation *sophomoric*.

soporific N. something that produces sleep
Jim took a *soporific* to help him get to sleep.

sordid ADJ. filthy; contemptible and corrupt
The actress tried to keep the *sordid* affair out of the newspapers.

sovereign ADJ. having supreme power
Singapore became a *sovereign* nation in 1965.

Spartan ADJ. austere, severe, grave; simple, bare
The soldiers live in *Spartan* quarters.

spate N. a sudden outpouring
There has been a *spate* of violence recently.

spawn V. to generate, produce
The new invention soon *spawned* many imitations.

speciation N. the evolutionary formation of new biological species
There is a debate within evolutionary biology about the rate at which *speciation* events occur over time.

specious ADJ. seeming to be logical, sound, etc., but not really so
The debate team used a *specious* argument.

specter N. an apparition; a threatening possibility
Increasing international tension has led to the *specter* of war.

spectrum N. band of colors produced when sunlight passes through prism; a broad range of related ideas or objects
The electromagnetic *spectrum* is one of our precious natural resources.

speculate V. take something as true based on insufficient evidence
The astronomer doesn't like to *speculate* about life in outer space.

spendthrift N. a person who spends money recklessly
Richard's reputation as a *spendthrift* didn't help him to get a bank loan.

spontaneous ADJ. on the spur of the moment, impulsive
In a *spontaneous* act of gratitude, the student hugged the teacher.

sporadic ADJ. irregular
Sporadic gunfire could still be heard in the city.

sportive ADJ. frolicsome, playful
Sportive children danced on the lawn during the celebration.

sprightly ADJ. lively, animated, energetic
The *sprightly* actress gave a lively performance.

spur v. to prod
Failure on the exam *spurred* Carol to study harder for the next one.

spurious ADJ. lacking authenticity; counterfeit, false
The salesperson's claims are *spurious*.

spurn v. to reject; scorn
Marcia *spurned* Wayne's offer of marriage.

squalid ADJ. filthy; morally repulsive
The family lives in *squalid* conditions.

squander v. to waste
The student *squandered* time in the exam daydreaming.

staccato ADJ. marked by abrupt, clear-cut sounds
We heard the *staccato* sound of the drum approaching.

staid ADJ. self-restrained to the point of dullness
The banker wears *staid* clothes to work.

stanch v. to stop or check the flow of
Use a tourniquet to *stanch* the bleeding.

stark ADJ. bare, empty, vacant
The writer concentrates best in a *stark* environment.

stasis ADJ. motionless state; standstill
The family settled into the dull *stasis* of country life.

static ADJ. at rest
The airplane engine was subjected to a *static* test.

stature N. status; achieved level
The professor has achieved a high *stature* in the field.

status quo N. existing condition
The election results suggest the majority doesn't want to change the *status quo*.

stentorian ADJ. extremely loud
The orator's *stentorian* voice echoed through the hall.

stigma N. mark of disgrace or inferiority
Divorce is no longer the *stigma* it was fifty years ago.

stilted ADJ. stiff, unnatural
Avoid *stilted* language when you write an essay.

stint N. period of time spent doing something
Joe had a two-year *stint* in the Peace Corps.

stipend N. a regular fixed payment
His father receives a monthly *stipend* from the government.

stipulate v. to specify as an essential condition
The contract *stipulates* that Ms. Smith teaches for two years.

stoic ADJ. indifferent to or unaffected by emotions
The monk has a *stoic* acceptance of life's misfortunes.

stolid ADJ. having or showing little emotion
The soldier was *stolid* despite being severely wounded.

stratagem N. trick designed to deceive an enemy
The enemy's *stratagem* was to make us think that they were retreating.

stratify v. to arrange into layers
The scientist studied how the layers of soil had *stratified*.

stratum N. layer
John knows people in the highest *stratum* of society.

striated ADJ. marked with thin, narrow grooves or channels
The geologist believes that the rock is *striated* because of flowing water.

stricture N. something that restrains; negative criticism
The writer refuses to be bound by the *strictures* of modern taste.

strident ADJ. loud, harsh, unpleasantly noisy
There were several *strident* objections to the proposal from the audience.

stultify v. to impair or reduce to uselessness
If you keep changing your views, you will *stultify* yourself.

stupefy v. to dull the senses of; stun, astonish
The artillery barrage *stupefied* the soldiers.

stupor N. daze; state of mental confusion
They stole his watch when he was in a drunken *stupor*.

stygian ADJ. dark and gloomy; hellish
The soldier's memoir describes the atmosphere of the battlefield as *stygian*.

stylized ADJ. conforming to a particular style
Kabuki is a Japanese drama that is performed in a *stylized* manner.

stymie V. to block or thwart
The proposal was *stymied* by congressional opposition.

suave ADJ. smoothly gracious or polite; blandly ingratiating
Ralph's *suave* manner makes him popular.

subdued V. suppressed, stifled
The rebellion was finally *subdued.*

subjective ADJ. taking place within a person; particular to a person
The analysis is regarded as too *subjective* to be of much scientific value.

subjugate V. to conquer, subdue; enslave
The ruler's ambition was to *subjugate* China.

sublethal ADJ. almost lethal
The victim had been given a *sublethal* dose of poison.

sublime ADJ. awe-inspiring; of high spiritual or moral value
The professor has spent much of his life studying the *sublime* work of Shakespeare.

subliminal ADJ. subconscious; imperceptible
Studies suggest that violence on television has a *subliminal* effect on children.

sublimity N. nobility; majesty; high spirituality or moral value
Rarely has an artist produced a work of such *sublimity.*

subpoena N. notice ordering someone to appear in court
Peter received a *subpoena* yesterday.

substantiate V. support with proof or evidence
The writer *substantiates* his claims with eyewitness accounts.

substantive ADJ. essential; pertaining to the substance
The two sides are in agreement on the *substantive* issues.

subsume V. to include or incorporate in something else
Most of the phenomena can be *subsumed* under three broad categories.

subterfuge N. trick or tactic used to avoid something
The enemy general's *subterfuge* allowed most of his forces to escape.

subterranean ADJ. hidden, secret; underground
Geologists found a vast *subterranean* store of fresh water not far from the city.

subtlety N. quality or state of being hard to detect or describe
The *subtlety* of the poem makes it too advanced for a high school class.

subversive ADJ. intended to undermine or overthrow, especially an established government
The intelligence agency is monitoring *subversive* activity.

subvert V. to undermine or corrupt
The group was accused of *subverting* the government.

succinct ADJ. terse, brief, concise
The lawyer prepared a *succinct* account of events.

succor N. help and support in times of hardship and distress
The prisoners of war were freed by friendly forces and given *succor.*

succulent ADJ. juicy; full of vitality or freshness
The steak is *succulent.*

succumb V. yield; give in; die
The old man finally *succumbed* to the disease.

sufferable ADJ. bearable
The long journey was made *sufferable* by the good novel I had brought.

suffrage N. the right to vote
Suffrage was extended to women in the early twentieth century.

suffragist N. one who advocates extended voting rights
Nineteenth-century *suffragists* campaigned to extend the right to vote to women.

suffuse V. spread through
His writing is *suffused* with irony.

sui generis ADJ. one of a kind; unique
Many critics regard the book *Wuthering Heights* as *sui generis.*

sullen ADJ. brooding, gloomy
The boy was *sullen* after being told that he had not been selected for the football team.

sully V. to soil, stain, tarnish; taint
The players' uniforms were *sullied* after the soccer match.

summa bonum N. the greatest good
For millennia human beings have searched for the *summa bonum*.

sumptuous ADJ. lavish, splendid
We enjoyed a *sumptuous* Christmas dinner.

sundry ADJ. various
"There are *sundry* reasons I don't want to go to graduate school, " Amy said.

superannuated ADJ. too old, obsolete, outdated
The *superannuated* teacher works as a volunteer in the school.

supercilious ADJ. arrogant, haughty, overbearing, condescending
Nobody likes the boss's *supercilious* attitude.

supererogatory ADJ. more than needed; superfluous
The coach decided that any more practice would be *supererogatory*.

superfluity N. overabundance; excess
There is a *superfluity* of males of marriageable age in China.

superfluous ADJ. excessive; overabundant; unnecessary
The teacher wrote a single page of comments about the essay; any more would be *superfluous*.

supernal ADJ. celestial; heavenly
The fantasy novel describes voyages to a *supernal* world.

supersede V. to take the place of; replace
The teacher announced that the latest test result would *supersede* the earlier one.

supine ADJ. lying on the back; marked by lethargy
The long distance runner was *supine* on the track after the race.

supplant V. to replace, substitute
Our school's main rival has *supplanted* us in first place.

supple ADJ. flexible, pliant
The gymnast does stretching exercises to keep her body *supple*.

suppliant ADJ. beseeching
The king looked down from his throne at the *suppliant* face of his subject.

supplicant N. one who asks humbly and earnestly
The *supplicant* asked the king to pardon her son.

supplication N. humble and earnest entreaty
The referee was deaf to the coach's *supplications*.

supposition N. the act of assuming to be true or real
The investigation was conducted on the *supposition* that the victim was murdered.

supposititious ADJ. hypothetical; not genuine; suppositious
The critic described the linguist's work as "the *supposititious* reconstruction of a dead language."

surfeit N. excessive amount
We have such a *surfeit* of food for the picnic that we'll be eating all day.

surly ADJ. rude and bad-tempered
The boy told the *surly* man a joke to make him laugh

surmise V. to make an educated guess
The teacher *surmised* that the student had not studied by the test result.

surmount V. to conquer, overcome
With steady work you will be able to *surmount* the obstacles.

surreal ADJ. fantastic; bizarre
The science fiction novel describes a *surreal* futuristic world.

surrealistic ADJ. irrational and fantastic
The futuristic movie contains several *surrealistic* scenes.

surreptitious ADJ. secret
The lovers had a *surreptitious* date.

surrogate ADJ. relating to a substitute
Ms. Hughes volunteered to be a *surrogate* mother for the orphan.

swagger V. behave arrogantly or pompously; walk proudly
Ted *swaggered* down the aisle of his office.

swarthy ADJ. having a dark complexion
The witness said she saw a *swarthy* man at the scene of the crime.

sybarite N. person devoted to pleasure and luxury
The *sybarite* spends most of his money on food and entertainment.

sycophant N. self-serving flatterer, yes-man
The *sycophant* was surprised when he didn't get the promotion.

syllogism N. form of deductive reasoning that has a major premise, a minor premise, and a conclusion
The statement "All dogs are animals; all animals have four legs; therefore all dogs have four legs" is a *syllogism*.

sylvan ADJ. related to the woods or forest
The play has a *sylvan* setting.

symbiotic ADJ. relating to cooperation; mutually helpful
Over the years the couple developed a *symbiotic* relationship.

symmetry N. balance of parts; harmony
The architect strives to achieve *symmetry* in her designs.

symposium N. meeting with short presentations on related topics
The *symposium* on health care will be held in Hawaii.

synchronous ADJ. occurring at the same time; moving at the same rate
The celebrations in New York and Los Angeles will be *synchronous*.

syncopation N. temporary irregularity in musical rhythm
The song has unusual *syncopation*.

syncretistic ADJ. composed of differing systems of belief
The new religion is a *syncretistic* blend of the beliefs of three existing religions.

syndrome N. a group of symptoms that indicate an abnormal condition
The doctor recognized the patient's *syndrome*.

synergy N. the interaction of two or more forces so that their combined effect is greater than the sum of their individual effects

The two companies believe that *synergies* will come out of their merger.

synopsis N. brief summary
The *synopsis* makes the book sound interesting.

synoptic ADJ. providing an overview; summary
The historian wrote a *synoptic* account of the middle ages.

syntactic ADJ. related to syntax
Proficient readers make use of *syntactic* clues.

syntax N. the way in which words are put together to form phrases and sentences
Her *syntax* suggests that she is not a native English speaker.

synthesis N. blend, combination
The new philosophy is a *synthesis* of several earlier philosophies.

systematic ADJ. based on a system; orderly
A *systematic* study of the problem should produce a solution.

systemic ADJ. relating to systems; affecting the entire body
Unfortunately, his illness appears to be *systemic*.

T

tableau N. vivid description, striking incident or scene
The dancers formed a *tableau* in the shape of a diamond.

taboo N. a ban as a result of a social custom
That society has a *taboo* against men and women displaying affection for each other in public.

tabula rasa N. condition of mind free from ideas or impressions; something that is new and not marked by external influence
The professor regards each new class of students as a *tabula rasa*.

tacit ADJ. silently understood or implied
There was a *tacit* agreement between the couple not to bring up the subject.

taciturn ADJ. uncommunicative, not inclined to speak much
Vermonters have a reputation for being *taciturn*.

tactile ADJ. relating to the sense of touch
The soldier's burned hands had lost their *tactile* sensitivity.

talisman N. charm to bring good luck and avert misfortune
Chase's *talisman* is a rabbit's foot that he brings to exams.

talon N. claw of an animal, esp. a bird of prey
The eagle held a chicken with its *talon*.

tandem ADJ. one behind the other
The cyclists rode around the track in *tandem*.

tangent N. digression, diversion
The speaker keeps going off on *tangents*.

tangential ADJ. digressing, diverting
Try to avoid discussing *tangential* issues in your essay.

tangible ADJ. able to be touched
The judge asked for *tangible* evidence to be produced.

tantamount ADJ. equivalent in value or significance; amounting to
Offering him five dollars for the watch is *tantamount* to saying the watch is a fake.

tattoo N. a signal sounded on a drum or a bugle to summon soldiers to their quarters at night; a continuous even drumming
The *tattoo* sounded at 9:00 P.M.

tautological ADJ. needlessly repetitious
Try to avoid *tautological* expressions in your writing.

tautology N. unnecessary repetition
The phrase "repeat again" is often a *tautology*.

tawdry ADJ. gaudy, cheap, showy
Mandy loves to wear *tawdry* jewelry.

taxonomy N. science of classification; in biology, the process of classifying organisms in categories
The Swedish scientist Carolus Linnaeus developed the system of *taxonomy* used by scientists today.

technocracy N. government by scientists and engineers
Some observers believe that the United States is becoming a *technocracy*.

technocrat N. a scientist or technical expert who has a lot of power in politics or industry
The Indian Prime Minister Dr. Manmohan Singh has been described as a *technocrat*.

technophile N. person who is enthusiastic about technology
The *technophile* always buys the most advanced cell phone available.

tectonic ADJ. related to structural deformation of the Earth's crust
The Mid-Atlantic Ridge *tectonic* plate boundary runs down the center of the Atlantic Ocean.

teleology N. belief in a purposeful development toward an end
Teleology is a recurring issue in biology.

temerity N. boldness; rashness
The professor had the *temerity* to suggest that sports have little place at a university.

temper V. to moderate; restrain; tone down or toughen
The critic *tempered* her negative remarks about the book by saying that it showed some promise.

temperament N. disposition; characteristic frame of mind
By *temperament* Steve is not the type of person likely to become a writer.

temperance N. restraint, self-control, moderation
Hardship taught the family the value of *temperance*.

temperate ADJ. marked by moderate temperatures, weather, or climate; moderate in degree or quality
Tired of the hard winter, Mr. Smith moved to a *temperate* climate.

tempered ADJ. moderated, restrained
His *tempered* support for the war is due to the fact that his son is in the army.

tempestuous ADJ. stormy, raging, furious
The movie portrays the couple's *tempestuous* relationship.

template N. pattern for making a copy
This *template* has produced 10,000 copies of the product.

temporal ADJ. related to time; not eternal
The monastery is organized so that *temporal* matters occupy little of the monks' time.

temporize V. to act evasively to gain time, avoid an argument, or postpone a decision

The board of governors *temporized* so long that our company lost the contract.

tenable ADJ. defensible, reasonable
This is *tenable* if we proceed cautiously.

tenacious ADJ. stubborn, holding firm
Our team's *tenacious* defense is allowing less than seven points a game.

tendentious ADJ. biased; designed to further a cause; having an aim
The columnist's *tendentious* article sparked a debate on the issue.

tenet N. belief, doctrine
The philosophy has three basic *tenets*.

tensile ADJ. capable of withstanding physical stress
The engineer designed a test to check the product's *tensile* strength.

tenuous ADJ. weak, insubstantial
Scientists have established a *tenuous* connection between achievement and IQ.

tepid ADJ. lukewarm; showing little enthusiasm
The suggestion received a *tepid* response.

terra firma N. solid ground
After the fourteen-hour flight we were glad to be back on *terra firma*.

terra incognita N. an unexplored region or area of knowledge
Modern researchers are steadily exploring the *terra incognita* of the brain.

terrestrial ADJ. earthly; down-to-earth, commonplace
The *terrestrial* tracking station monitors the space probe.

terse ADJ. concise, brief, free of extra words
The *terse* reply to our question simply said, "No."

tête-à-tête N. a private conversation between two people
Lawyers for each of the parties met for a *tête-à-tête*.

theism N. belief in the existence of a god
Surveys show that most Americans believe in some form of *theism*.

theocracy N. government by priests representing a god
Some European settlers wanted to establish a *theocracy*.

theological ADJ. concerned with the study of religion
The book discusses *theological* issues such as whether God is all-powerful.

theoretical ADJ. abstract; not verified; not practical
So far the plan is only *theoretical*.

therapeutic ADJ. having healing powers
Many doctors consider swimming to be *therapeutic*.

thermal ADJ. pertaining to heat
The generator runs on *thermal* energy from the sun.

thesaurus N. book of synonyms and antonyms
The *thesaurus* groups similar words around a single shared meaning.

thesis N. a proposition put forward for consideration
The *thesis* of the book is that women should have the duty as well as the right to serve in the military.

thespian N. an actor or actress
Our school's *thespians* will perform the musical *South Pacific* next month.

timbre N. the characteristic quality of sound produced by a particular experiment or voice
The guitar maker uses a special type of wood to give the instruments he makes a particular *timbre*.

timorous ADJ. timid, shy, full of apprehension
The *timorous* girl became more confident and outgoing when she went to college.

tirade N. long violent speech; verbal assault
The principal's *tirade* lasted over an hour.

titan N. person of colossal stature or achievement
Bill Gates is one of the *titans* of the computer industry.

titanic ADJ. of colossal stature, strength, or achievement
The play depicts a *titanic* struggle between good and bad.

titillate V. to excite pleasurably
Several scenes in the movie are designed to *titillate* viewers.

titular ADJ. holding of title without obligations; nominal
The country's *titular* ruler hosted a dinner for foreign guests.

toady N. flatterer, hanger-on, yes-man
The *toady* agrees with everything her boss says.

tome N. book, usually large and academic
The *tome* contains twenty long essays on Shakespeare's play.

topography N. art of making maps or charts; physical features of a place
The country's rugged *topography* makes land travel difficult.

torpid ADJ. lethargic; unable to move; dormant
The snakes are *torpid* in the winter.

torpor N. lethargy; dormancy; sluggishness
The bear slowly recovered from the *torpor* caused by its long hibernation.

torque N. a turning or twisting force
The engine generates a lot of torque, making it excellent for use in vehicles designed to tow heavy loads.

torrid ADJ. burning hot; passionate
The actor's *torrid* affair is the subject of a popular movie.

torsion N. act of twisting and turning
The race car uses a bar that provides *torsion* to stabilize when it corners.

tortuous ADJ. having many twists and turns; highly complex
The road takes a *tortuous* path through the mountains.

totalitarianism N. a system of government in which one political group maintains complete control
Communism and Fascism were the two major forms of *totalitarianism* during the twentieth century.

totem N. a natural object or animal believed to have spiritual significance
The clan keeps a wooden pole on which *totems* are carved.

touchstone N. a quality or example used to test the genuineness or excellence of others
The *touchstone* I use in judging a poem is a Shakespearean sonnet.

tout V. to promote or praise energetically
The salesperson *touted* this product as the best of its type.

toxin N. poison
The *toxins* were stored safely away from children.

tract N. region of land; pamphlet
The 100-acre *tract* was sold for ten million dollars.

tractable ADJ. obedient, yielding
The children became more *tractable* as the year progressed.

transcendent ADJ. rising above, going beyond; superior; beyond the material
Many people believe that human beings possess a soul that is *transcendent*.

transcription N. copy, reproduction; record
The *transcription* of the speech will be available next week.

transfix V. to render motionless, as with awe, terror, or amazement
The crowd watched, *transfixed*, as the gigantic UFO landed.

transgress V. to trespass, violate a law
Be careful not to *transgress* against the local laws.

transient ADJ. temporary, short-lived, fleeting
Each individual life seems to be *transient*.

transitory ADJ. short-lived, existing only briefly
Rainbows are normally *transitory*.

translucent ADJ. partially transparent
We could see the fish quite well through the *translucent* glass.

transmogrification N. change from one shape or form to another
The story describes Joe's *transmogrification* into a werewolf.

transmutation N. change in appearance, shape, or nature
Art involves the *transmutation* of the ordinary into the extraordinary.

trappings N. outward decorations; ornaments
The president enjoyed the *trappings* of office, such as flying in a special jet plane.

travail N. work, especially arduous work; tribulation; anguish
The book tells the story of the *travail* of a slave in America.

travesty N. parody, exaggerated imitation, caricature
The new play is a deliberate *travesty* of *Hamlet*.

treatise N. article treating a subject systematically and thoroughly

The *treatise* argues that countries most often go to war for economic reasons.

tremulous ADJ. trembling, quivering; fearful, timid
Gail was *tremulous* as she waited to get her GRE score.

trenchant ADJ. acute, sharp, incisive; forceful, effective
The student took her teacher's *trenchant* criticism of her writing to heart.

trepidation N. fear and anxiety
The soldier looked forward to the battle with *trepidation*.

trifling ADJ. of slight worth, trivial, insignificant
Don't worry about this *trifling* matter.

trite ADJ. unoriginal
Try to avoid *trite* language when you write.

trivial ADJ. unimportant
Things that seemed important before the war now seem *trivial*.

trope N. a figure of speech using words in a nonliteral way
The writer uses the two Americas *trope* to highlight the difference between rich and poor.

trophic ADJ. related to nutrition
The *trophic* level of an organism is the position it occupies on the food chain.

tropism N. the movement of an organism or part of an organism toward or away from an external stimulus
In one type of *tropism*, gravitropism, plant movement occurs in response to gravity.

troupe N. group of actors
The *troupe* has performed three Shakespearean comedies.

truculence N. state of violent agitation
The child's *truculence* began when his mother took away his favorite toy.

truism N. a statement that is obviously true and that says nothing new
The salesperson often utters the *truism* to customers "You get what you pay for."

truncate V. to cut off, shorten by cutting
The editor *truncated* the long novel by eliminating long descriptions.

tryst N. agreement between lovers to meet; rendezvous
The lovers arranged a *tryst*.

tsunami N. a very large wave caused by a seismic disturbance of the ocean floor
With coastal areas around the world becoming increasingly populated, *tsunamis* are posing a great risk to human life.

tumid ADJ. swollen; distended
Images of starving children with *tumid* bellies captured the world's attention.

tumult N. state of confusion; agitation
There was *tumult* in the streets when the enemy invasion began.

tundra N. treeless plain found in arctic or subarctic regions
The explorers walked across the frozen *tundra*, searching for oil.

turbid ADJ. muddy; opaque; in a state of confusion
They rowed down the silty, *turbid* waters of the Congo River.

turbulence N. commotion, disorder; agitation
The 1960s was a period of *turbulence* in American history.

turgid ADJ. swollen, bloated
The publisher rejected the book because it was written in *turgid* prose.

turmoil N. great commotion; confusion
There was *turmoil* in the city when invaders reached the edge of town.

turpitude N. inherent vileness, foulness, depravity
The novelist portrays the *turpitude* human beings are capable of.

tutelary ADJ. serving as a guardian or protector
The ancient Romans believed that everyone has a *tutelary* spirit.

typology n. a theory of types
The linguist's *typology* of language classifies languages by grammatical features rather than common ancestry.

tyrannical ADJ. oppressive; dictatorial
The men took up arms to end the dictator's *tyrannical* rule.

tyro N. beginner, novice
The students tried to take advantage of the teacher because she was a *tyro*.

U

ubiquitous ADJ. being everywhere simultaneously; widespread
Hydrogen is *ubiquitous* in the universe.

ulterior ADJ. unstated; situated beyond
The country has an *ulterior* motive for invading its neighbor.

ultimate ADJ. final
No one knows for sure what the *ultimate* fate of the universe will be.

umbrage N. offense, resentment
The writer is quick to take *umbrage* at criticism of her work.

unadulterated ADJ. absolutely pure
The mountain spring contains *unadulterated* water.

unambiguous ADJ. clear; not uncertain
The court refuses to take an *unambiguous* stand on the issue.

unanimity N. state of total agreement or unity
The jury couldn't reach *unanimity* on a verdict.

unappealing ADJ. unattractive, unpleasant
Pollution makes the city an *unappealing* place to live.

unassailable ADJ. not open to attack or question
The essay's main argument is *unassailable*.

unavailing ADJ. hopeless, useless
Efforts to rescue the captured soldier were *unavailing*.

unbiased ADJ. impartial
The commission was asked to give an *unbiased* report on the issue.

uncanny ADJ. mysterious; strange
Joe has an *uncanny* ability to guess the correct answer to multiple-choice questions.

unconscionable ADJ. unscrupulous; shockingly unfair or unjust
The protestors believe that it is *unconscionable* that only males must register for the draft.

unctuous ADJ. greasy, oily; smug and falsely earnest
The *unctuous* salesman said we were the nicest folks he had ever met.

undaunted ADJ. not discouraged
The coach is *undaunted* despite the fact that his team hasn't won a game yet this season.

undefiled ADJ. not corrupted or contaminated
The saint is *undefiled* by sin.

undermine V. to weaken
The lawyer's case was *undermined* by weak evidence.

understatement N. a restrained statement
"War is unpleasant" is an *understatement*.

undifferentiated ADJ. not distinguished from something else
I couldn't hear her in the *undifferentiated* hubbub of voices.

undocumented ADJ. not certified, unsubstantiated
Only one case of the disease has been reported, and that is *undocumented*.

undulating ADJ. moving in waves
The sailor rowed across the sea's *undulating* surface.

unequivocal ADJ. absolute, certain
The judge asked the witness for an *unequivocal* statement.

unfathomable ADJ. incomprehensible; impenetrable
The reason he committed the crime is *unfathomable* to me.

unfeigned ADJ. not false; not made up; genuine
Everyone enjoyed the look of *unfeigned* surprise on the child's face when he opened the present.

unfetter V. set free
The prisoner promised that if he was *unfettered* he wouldn't try to escape.

unfrock V. to strip of priestly duties
The priest was *unfrocked* for improper conduct.

ungainly ADJ. lacking grace; clumsy; unwieldy
The airplane looks *ungainly* on the ground, but it's graceful in the air.

unheralded ADJ. unannounced, unexpected, not publicized
The president's arrival in the town was *unheralded*.

uniformity N. sameness; lack of variation
The reporter got her information from an *uniformity* in the laws of nature.

unimpeachable ADJ. beyond question
The reporter got her information from an *unimpeachable* source.

unimpeded ADJ. not obstructed
If you take the new road, your journey will be *unimpeded*.

uninhibited ADJ. unrepressed
The children's *uninhibited* laughter could be heard all throughout the school.

uninitiated N. people who are not familiar with an area of study
To the *uninitiated*, computer programming can seem frighteningly complex.

unique ADJ. one of a kind
This author is the only person to have taken that *unique* approach to the subject.

universal ADJ. characterizing or affecting all; present everywhere
Fear of death is *universal*.

unmitigated ADJ. not lessened or moderated in intensity; without qualification
The *unmitigated* horrors of the war he saw action in turned Bill against war for any cause.

unobtrusive ADJ. inconspicuous; not obvious
Our houseguest is *unobtrusive*.

unorthodox ADJ. breaking with tradition
The new school takes an *unorthodox* approach to education.

unpalatable ADJ. distasteful; disagreeable
Most people find the idea of child soldiers *unpalatable*.

unprecedented ADJ. not seen before; original
There was an *unprecedented* increase in economic growth last year.

unrequited ADJ. not reciprocated
In Shakespeare's *Twelfth Night*, Malvolio's love for Olivia is *unrequited*.

unscathed ADJ. unharmed
The soldier came through the war *unscathed*.

unscrupulous ADJ. dishonest
The millionaire obtained her wealth by *unscrupulous* means.

unsolicited ADJ. not requested
The magazine does not publish *unsolicited* manuscripts.

unsullied ADJ. undefiled; untainted
The president completed his term *unsullied* by charges of corruption.

untainted ADJ. not polluted or contaminated
The new administration is *untainted* by corruption.

untenable ADJ. indefensible
The plan to invade the country is militarily *untenable*.

untoward ADJ. not favorable; troublesome; adverse; unruly
Although he was concerned about the malfunctioning engine, the airline pilot acted as though nothing *untoward* had happened.

untrammeled ADJ. not limited or restricted
No country allows its citizens *untrammeled* freedom.

unwarranted ADJ. unjustified; groundless; undeserved
Many people believe that the draft is an *unwarranted* restriction of the human rights of males.

unwitting ADJ. unconscious; unintentional
The *unwitting* suspect was captured when he was strolling in the park.

unyielding ADJ. firm, resolute
The president is *unyielding* in his determination to find a peaceful solution to the conflict.

upbraid V. to scold sharply
The soldier was *upbraided* by her commander for not carrying out orders properly.

uproarious ADJ. loud and forceful
The *uproarious* comedy had everyone laughing loudly.

urban ADJ. related to a city
In World War II *urban* areas of Germany were heavily bombed.

urbane ADJ. refined, sophisticated, suave
The writer's *urbane* humor is not appreciated by everyone.

usurp V. to seize by force
Paths intended for pedestrians are being *usurped* by cyclists.

usury N. practice of lending money at exorbitant rates
The credit card company was accused of *usury* because it charges 22% interest per year.

utilitarian ADJ. concerned with usefulness rather than beauty
To some people a car is strictly a *utilitarian* vehicle.

utopia N. perfect place
The novel portrays a *utopia* based on moral ideals.

utopian ADJ. visionary; referring to a utopia, that is, a perfect place; ideal but impracticable
The plan to provide free medical coverage for everyone was criticized as *utopian*.

V

vacillate V. to waver, show indecision
Ben *vacillated* between pursuing a law degree and a medical degree.

vacuole N. a small cavity in cell cytoplasm, bound by a single membrane and containing water, food, or metabolic waste
Most mature plant cells have one large central *vacuole* that typically occupies more than 30 percent of the cell's volume.

vacuous ADJ. empty, void; lacking intelligence, purposeless
The speech contains his usual *vacuous* remarks.

vagary N. an unpredictable or erratic action or occurrence
Baseball is subject to the *vagaries* of the weather.

vagrant N. poor person with no home
There are hundreds of *vagrants* in the city.

valedictory ADJ. pertaining to a farewell
The retiring principal gave a *valedictory* speech.

valor N. courage and boldness; bravery
Valor is traditionally regarded as a masculine virtue.

vanguard N. forerunners; advance forces
John and Bill are in the *vanguard* of the animal rights movement.

vanquish ADJ. conquered, defeated
The *vanquished* soldiers were imprisoned by their captors.

vantage ADJ. relating to a position likely to provide superiority or give an overall view
The invaders captured a *vantage* point overlooking the city.

vapid ADJ. tasteless, dull
The politician gave her usual *vapid* speech.

variable N. something that varies or is prone to variation
The scientist is trying to identify the important *variable*.

variation N. varying; change in form, extent, etc.
There has been a lot of *variation* in the weather recently.

variegated adj. varied; marked with different colors
The picture shows a *variegated* autumn landscape.

vaunted ADJ. boasted about, bragged about
For all of medicine's *vaunted* achievements, disease is still widespread.

Veda N. any of the oldest and most authoritative sacred texts of Hinduism
The various Indian philosophies and sects have taken differing positions on the *Vedas*.

Vedic ADJ. relating to the Veda
The Vedas are composed in *Vedic* Sanskrit.

vehemently adv. strongly, urgently
The accused man *vehemently* denied the charge.

venal ADJ. bribable; mercenary; corruptible
That country's customs officers are notoriously *venal*.

vendetta N. prolonged feud marked by bitter hostility
The *vendetta* between the two families goes back more than a century.

venerable ADJ. respected because of age
The *venerable* professor is the subject of a recent documentary.

veneration N. adoration, honor, respect
A service was held in *veneration* of the saint.

veracious ADJ. truthful, accurate
The testimony was accepted as *veracious*.

veracity N. accuracy, truthfulness
The *veracity* of the testimony was supported by a witness.

verbatim N. word for word
The student copied the lecture *verbatim*.

verbiage N. an excess of words for the purpose; wordiness
The editor checked the manuscript for *verbiage*.

verbose ADJ. wordy
The *verbose* speech ran an hour over the scheduled time.

verdant ADJ. green with vegetation; inexperienced
Our plane flew over the *verdant* landscape.

verdure N. fresh, rich vegetation
In spring the desert is covered with a luxuriant *verdure*.

verisimilitude N. quality of appearing true or real
The producer of the movie spared no expense in his quest for *verisimilitude*.

verity N. truthfulness; belief viewed as true and enduring
Philosophy has been described as the search for eternal *verities*.

vermin N. small creatures offensive to humans
Vermin got into the food supplies.

vernacular N. everyday language used by ordinary people; specialized language of a profession
Almost all modern novelists write in the *vernacular*.

vernal ADJ. related to spring
April usually brings *vernal* showers.

vertigo N. dizziness
Heights give some people *vertigo*.

vestige N. trace, remnant
Scientists discovered *vestiges* of an ancient civilization on the island.

vestigial ADJ. remaining
The species has a *vestigial* tail.

vexation N. irritation, annoyance; confusion, puzzlement
The students' chatter was a source of *vexation* for the teacher.

viable ADJ. practicable; capable of developing
The boss wants a *viable* plan for increasing sales on his desk by Friday.

viaduct N. series of elevated arches used to cross a valley
In Italy we saw the ruins of Roman *viaducts*.

vibrant ADJ. throbbing with life or activity; vigorous and lively
San Francisco is a modern, *vibrant* city.

vicarious ADJ. substitute, surrogate; enjoyed through imagined participation in another's experience
Movies give viewers *vicarious* enjoyment.

vicissitude N. change or variation; ups and downs
Try to remain calm through life's *vicissitudes*.

vie V. to compete, contend
The two teams *vied* for the championship.

vigilance N. attentiveness, watchfulness
After the attack the commander ordered increased *vigilance*.

vignette N. decorative design; short literary composition
The English teacher asked his class to write a *vignette*.

vilify V. to slander, defame
The woman sued after the newspaper article *vilified* her.

vim N. energy, enthusiasm
The director wants the actors to put more *vim* into their performance.

vindicate V. to clear of blame; support a claim
The defendant was *vindicated* by the evidence.

vindictive ADJ. spiteful, vengeful, unforgiving
The *vindictive* old woman had held the grudge for fifty years.

virile ADJ. manly, having qualities of an adult male
Bill joined the army to prove that he's *virile*.

virtuoso N. someone with masterly skill; expert musician
Loud applause followed the *virtuoso's* performance.

virulent ADJ. extremely poisonous or pathogenic; malignant; hateful
Immediate action must be taken to control the *virulent* disease.

visage N. countenance; appearance; aspect
The actor's handsome *visage* made him popular with moviegoers.

visceral ADJ. deep; profound; instinctive
Tom has a *visceral* hatred of violence.

viscous ADJ. thick, syrupy and sticky
The maple syrup is *viscous*.

vision N. intelligent foresight; mental image produced by the imagination
The president's *vision* is of a nation united and at peace.

vitiate V. to impair the quality of; corrupt morally; make inoperative
The effects of the policy have been *vitiated* by poor compliance on the part of some members.

vitriolic ADJ. burning, caustic; sharp, bitter
The critic's *vitriolic* review angered the author.

vituperative ADJ. using or containing harsh, abusive censure
What began as a simple criticism turned into a *vituperative* attack.

vivacious ADJ. lively, spirited
The *vivacious* actress entertained the audience.

vivisection N. dissection, surgery, or painful experiments performed on a living animal for the purpose of scientific research
The laboratory has stringent regulations on experiments involving *vivisection*.

vociferous ADJ. loud, vocal and noisy
Protests against the war grew more *vociferous* as the death toll mounted.

vogue N. prevailing fashion or practice
There seems to be a *vogue* for pointy shoes.

void N. emptiness, vacuum
The astronomer peered into the *void* of space.

void V. to cancel, invalidate
The contract allows either side to *void* it with one-month's notice.

volatile ADJ. tending to vary frequently; fickle
I don't want to invest in the *volatile* stock market.

volcanology N. the scientific study of volcanoes
A major aspect of *volcanology* is studying in great detail the remains of past eruptions at dormant or dead volcanoes.

volition N. free choice, free will; act of choosing
The woman joined the army of her own *volition*.

volley N. flight of missiles, round of gunshots
The first *volley* of musket fire killed most of the enemy soldiers.

voluble ADJ. speaking much and easily, talkative; glib
The *voluble* talk show guest entertained the audience for an hour.

voluminous ADJ. bulky; large
The professor's *voluminous* writings cover much of human history.

Voodooism N. a religion that is derived from African polytheism and ancestor worship and is practiced chiefly in Haiti
Voodism is a syncretistic religion.

voracious ADJ. having a great appetite
Beth has a *voracious* appetite for knowledge.

vortex N. whirlpool; whirlwind; center of turbulence
Many people were sucked into the *vortex* of violence in World War II.

W

waffle V. speak equivocally about an issue
When pressed for his view on the issue, the senator *waffled*.

waive V. to refrain from enforcing a rule; give up a legal right
The defendant *waived* his right to a jury trial.

wallow V. to indulge oneself excessively, luxuriate
Peter refused to *wallow* in self-pity after all of his bad luck.

wan ADJ. sickly pale
The virus has left Sam looking *wan*.

wane V. decrease gradually
Some experts believe that Japan's power will *wane* as China's increases.

wanton ADJ. undisciplined, unrestrained, reckless
The soldiers were punished for the *wanton* killing of civilians.

warrant V. attest to the accuracy or quality of something; justify; grant authorization
The auditor *warrants* that the report is comprehensive.

warranted ADJ. justified
Some people believe that the tax increase is *warranted*.

wary ADJ. careful, cautious
Children should be *wary* of strangers.

watershed N. the region draining into a river, river system, or other body of water; an important point of division or transition between two phases or conditions.
The Civil War was a *watershed* in American history.

wax V. to increase gradually
Some experts believe that China's power is *waxing* as Japan's is decreasing.

wayward ADJ. erratic, unrestrained, reckless
The house is a shelter for *wayward* teenagers.

weather V. to endure, undergo
The city *weathered* the enemy bombardment.

Weltanschauung N. a comprehensive conception of the universe and of humanity's relation to it; world view
Albert Einstein said that the philosopher Spinoza was the philosopher who had the most influence on his *Weltanschauung*.

Weltschmerz N. feeling of melancholy and world-weariness
The novel describes the protagonist's *Weltschmerz*.

whet V. to sharpen, stimulate
Going to the play *whetted* Dan's appetite for the theatre.

whimsical ADJ. fanciful; unpredictable
The *Wizard of Oz* is a *whimsical* movie.

whimsy N. playful or fanciful idea
The fantasy writer follows her *whimsy* when writing a story.

wile N. clever stratagem or trick to deceive
The submarine commander used *wile* to avoid the enemy destroyers.

windfall N. sudden, unexpected good fortune
The tax rebate was a *windfall* for the rich.

winnow V. separate good parts from bad; sift
Contenders for the scholarship have been *winnowed* to five.

winsome ADJ. charming, happily engaging
Audrey is a *winsome* young woman who is popular with everyone in school.

wistful ADJ. vaguely longing; sadly thoughtful
The book is a *wistful* look at a long-vanished period of history.

witticism N. a witty remark
The audience laughed at the speaker's *witticism*.

wizened ADJ. withered, shriveled, wrinkled
The *wizened* old man could barely walk.

wrath N. anger
Students who are always late to school become the object of the principal's *wrath*.

wrench V. pull at the emotions; pain
The scenes of the injured soldiers *wrenched* viewers' hearts.

writ N. written document, usually in law
The lawyer obtained a *writ* of seizure from the judge.

writhe V. twist in coils; contort in pain
The injured woman *writhed* in pain.

wry ADJ. amusing, ironic
Some people don't appreciate Uncle Bill's *wry* sense of humor.

X

xenophobia N. fear or hatred of foreigners or strangers
The government appealed to *xenophobia* to build support for the war.

Y

yahoo N. a coarse or brutish person
Those *yahoos* are fighting again.

yen N. strong desire; yearning or craving
Steward and his wife have a *yen* to travel.

yoga N. a school of Hindu philosophy advocating a course of physical and mental disciplines for attaining liberation from the material world and union of the self with the Supreme Being or ultimate principle
Many Westerners practice *yoga* to improve both their physical and spiritual life.

yoke v. to join together; to harness
The horses were *yoked* to the plough.

Z

zany ADJ. absurd; ludicrous
Children love the clown's *zany* antics.

zeal N. enthusiastic devotion to a cause
The candidate thanked the campaign workers for their *zeal*.

zealot N. one who is fanatically devoted to a cause
Anti-war *zealots* demonstrated outside government offices.

zealous ADJ. enthusiastically devoted to a cause
Bill and Ron are *zealous* in their opposition to the policy.

zeitgeist N. the outlook characteristic of a period
The book argues that individualism is the *zeitgeist* of our era.

zenith N. highest point, summit
The writer is at the *zenith* of her career.

zephyr N. a soft gentle breeze
On the hot August evening we all welcomed the *zephyr* blowing from the west.

zoologist N. scientist who studies animals
The *zoologist* is an expert on mice.

zooplankton N. plankton that consists of animals, including the corals and jelly-fish
Although *zooplankton* are primarily transported by ambient water currents, many have some power of locomotion and use this to avoid predators.

Zoroastrianism N. religion founded by the sixth century B.C. Persian prophet Zoroaster teaching the worship of Ahura Mazda in the context of a struggle between the forces of light and darkness
"*Zoroastrianism* is the oldest of the revealed world-religions, and it has probably had more influence on mankind, directly and indirectly, than any other single faith." Mary Boyce, *Zoroastrians: Their Religious Beliefs and Practices.*

Acknowledgments

The author gratefully acknowledges the following copyright holders for permission to reprint material used in reading passages:

Page 14: From *Ferdinand De Saussure* by Jonathan Culler. Copyright © 1986. Reprinted by permission of Cornell University Press.

Page 24: From *Evolutionary Humanism* by Julian Huxley. Reprinted by permission of SLL/Sterling Lord Literistic, Inc. Copyright by Julian Huxley Peters Fraser & Dunlop A/A/F.

Page 26: From "Cloudy with a Chance of Stars" by Erick T. Young in *Scientific American*, February 2010. Reprinted with permission. Copyright © 2010 Scientific American, a division of Nature America, Inc. All rights reserved.

Page 32: Reprinted with the permission of The Free Press, a Division of Simon & Schuster, Inc., from THE CASE FOR MARS by Robert Zubrin. Copyright © 1996 by Robert Zubrin. All rights reserved. (U.S., its territories and dependencies, the Philippines, and Canada)

Page 32: Reprinted with the permission of the Linda Chester Literary Agency, from THE CASE FOR MARS by Robert Zubrin. Copyright © 1996 by Robert Zubrin. All rights reserved. (World)

Page 34: From "The Enduring Power of Traditional Art" by Janadas Devan in *The Straits Times*, February 1, 2004. Source: The Sunday Times © Singapore Press Holdings Limited. Reprinted with permission.

Page 119: From *Hinduism and Buddhism: An Historical Sketch* by Sir Charles Eliot. Copyright 1921. Routledge & Kegan Paul LTD, London.

Page 120: From "Microbial Communities and Carbon Cycling in Response to Global Change" by Dr. Mark Waldrop, US Geological Survey, 2010.

Page 121: From *Barchester Towers* by Anthony Trollope. Copyright 1857. Longman, London.

Page 122: From "The Spiritual Ebb and Flow Exhibited in English Poetry from Chaucer to Tennyson and Browning" in *An Introduction to the Study of Robert Browning's Poetry* by Hiram Corson, 1886.

Page 124: From "The Art of Fiction" in *Partial Portraits* by Henry James. Copyright 1894. Macmillan & Co, London and New York.

Page 125: From "Contaminant Immune Functions," USGS Western Ecological Research Center, Keith A. Miles, US Geological Survey, 2010.

Page 126: From *Insights: A Comprehensive Approach to the General Paper* by Peter Saunders and Philip Geer, Longman, 1982.

Page 126: From pp. 1–2 of *Pidgins and Creoles* by Loreto Todd. Copyright 1990. Reprinted by permission of Cengage Learning EMEA Ltd.

Page 127: From "Understanding Contaminants Associated with Mineral Deposits" by Mark R. Stanton, US Geological Survey, 2008.

Page 128: From "The Will to Believe" by William James, copyright 1896.

Page 130: Excerpt by CEM Joad from *A Guide to Modern Thought* (© CEM Joad, 1976) is reproduced by permission of PFD (www.pfd.co.uk) on behalf of the Estate of CEM Joad.

Page 131: From *Insights: A Comprehensive Approach to the General Paper* by Peter Saunders and Philip Geer, Longman, 1982.

Page 132: From *The Balkans, a History of Bulgaria—Serbia—Greece—Rumania—Turkey* by Nevill Forbes, Arnold J. Toynbee, D. Mitrany, and D.G. Hogarth, 1915.

Page 134: From *The Sense of Beauty: Being the Outline of Aesthetic Theory*, George Santayana, 1896.

Page 136: From "Age of the Earth" by William L. Newman, US Geological Survey, 1997.

Page 138: From "The Professionalization of Poetry" in *Heavy Lifting* by David Alpaugh. Copyright © 2007 Alehouse Press. Reprinted by permission of the author.

Page 141: From "The Icy Satellites of Jupiter and Saturn" by Keith S. Noll, US Geological Survey, 2010.

Page 143: Excerpt from "What Is Feminist Criticism?" by Linda H. Peterson, in Emily Bronte's *Wuthering Heights,* Bedford/St. Martin's Case Studies in Contemporary Criticism. Second edition copyright © 2003 by Bedford/St. Martin's. Used with permission of the publisher.

Page 145: From "Age & Reproduction in Three Reef-Dwelling Serranid Fishes of the Northeastern Gulf of Mexico Outer Continental Shelf" by Kenneth J. Sulak, US Geological Survey, 2004.

Page 147: From "Arctic Now Traps 25% of World's Carbon—But That Could Change" by Christine Buckley, Catherine Puckett, and David McGuire, US Geological Survey, 2009.

Page 149: From *The Golden Bough* by Sir James George Frazer. Copyright 1890.

Page 170: From "Postmodern Blackness" by Bell Hooks in *Post Modern Culture* 1:1 (1990). © 1990 bell hooks. Reprinted with permission of The Johns Hopkins University Press.

Page 172: From "The Naked Truth" by Nina G. Jablonski in *Scientific American*, February 2010. Reprinted with permission. Copyright © 2010 Scientific American, a division of Nature America, Inc. All rights reserved.

Page 173: From "The Spiritual Ebb and Flow Exhibited in English Poetry from Chaucer to Tennyson and Browning" in *An Introduction to the Study of Robert Browning's Poetry* by Hiram Corson, 1886.

Page 174: From *The Life of Reason: Reason in Religion* by George Santayana, 1905.

Page 178: From "Organic Origins of Petroleum" (Energy Resource Program—Geochemistry & Geophysics), US Geological Survey, 2010.

Page 179: From *Hinduism and Buddhism: An Historical Sketch* by Sir Charles Eliot. Copyright 1921. Routledge & Kegan Paul LTD, London.

Page 180: From *The Life of Reason: Reason in Art* by George Santayana, 1905.

Page 182: From "The Art of Bacterial Warfare" by B. Brett Finlay in *Scientific American*, February 2010. Reprinted with permission. Copyright © 2010 Scientific American, a division of Nature America, Inc. All rights reserved.

Page 200: From *The Souls of Black Folk* by W.E.B. Du Bois, 1903.

Page 201: From *Manual of Egyptian Archaeology and Guide to the Study of Antiquities in Egypt* by G. Maspero, D.C.L. Oxon, 1895.

Page 202: From "The Delivery of Volatiles & Organics from Earth to Exoearths in the Era of JUST" by Michael Mumma, US Geological Survey, 2010.

Page 203: From *Interpretations of Poetry and Religion* by George Santayana, 1900.

Page 208: From *Case Studies on Climate Change and World Heritage*, UNESCO, 2007.

Page 209: "Complexity and Collapse" by Niall Ferguson, originally published in *Foreign Affairs*. Copyright © 2010 by Niall Ferguson, used with permission of The Wylie Agency LLC.

Page 211: From *Insights: A Comprehensive Approach to the General Paper* by Peter Saunders and Philip Geer, Longman, 1982.

Page 212: From "Red Mountain Volcano—a Spectacular and Unusual Cinder Cone in Northern Arizona" by Susan S. Priest, Wendell A. Duffield, Nancy R. Riggs, Brian Poturalski, and Karen Malis-Clark, US Geological Survey, 2002.

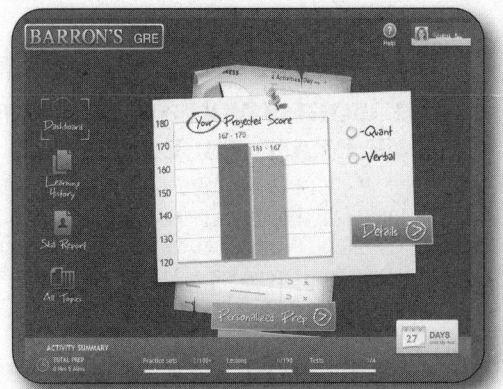

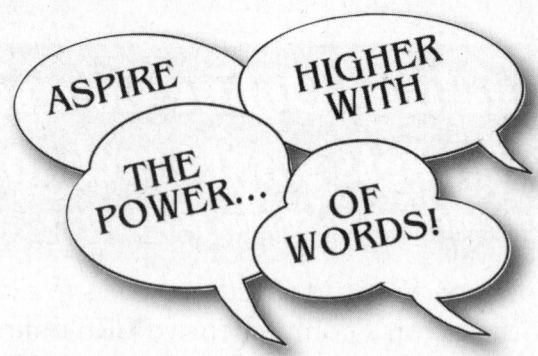

504 ABSOLUTELY ESSENTIAL WORDS, 6th Edition

Builds practical vocabulary skills through funny stories and cartoons plus practice exercises.

ISBN 978-0-7641-4781-4, $12.99, *Can$14.99*

601 WORDS YOU NEED TO KNOW TO PASS YOUR EXAM, 5th Edition

This new edition hones students' English language skills with 40 updated lessons that include definitions, pronunciation notes, and more. A new section called "Panorama of Words" shows how some of the 601 words are used in a variety of resources, from newspapers to speeches.

ISBN 978-1-4380-0169-2, $13.99, *Can$15.99*

1100 WORDS YOU NEED TO KNOW, 6th Edition

This book is the way to master more than 1100 useful words and idioms taken from the mass media.

ISBN 978-1-4380-0166-1, $13.99, *Can$15.99*

AMERICAN SLANG DICTIONARY AND THESAURUS

This unique reference volume is two books in one: an A-to-Z slang dictionary and a slang thesaurus. Words are coded with symbols to help readers distinguish between objectionable and milder slang, and all synonyms are coded for their level of formality.

ISBN 978-0-7641-3861-4, $14.99, *Can$17.99*

A DICTIONARY OF AMERICAN IDIOMS, 5th Edition

Over 8,000 idiomatic words, expressions, regionalisms, and informal English expressions are defined and cross-referenced for easy access.

ISBN 978-1-4380-0157-9, $16.99, *Can$19.50*

HANDBOOK OF COMMONLY USED AMERICAN IDIOMS, 5th Edition

With 2500 popular idioms, this book will benefit both English-speaking people and those learning English as a second language.

ISBN 978-1-4380-0167-8, $8.99, *Can$9.99*

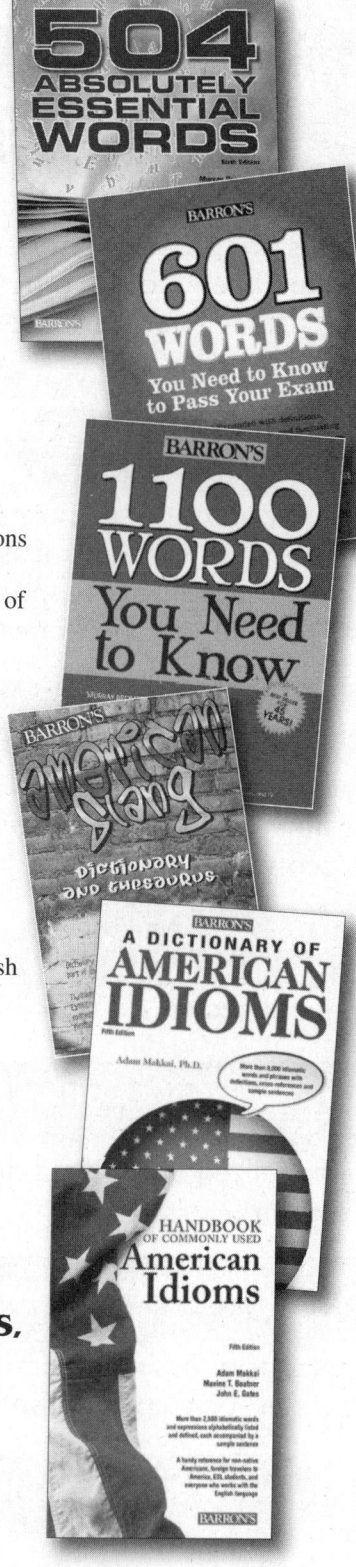

Available at your local book store
or visit **www.barronseduc.com**

BARRON'S EDUCATIONAL SERIES, INC.
250 Wireless Blvd.
Hauppauge, N.Y. 11788
Order toll-free: 1-800-645-3476
Order by fax: 1-631-434-3217

In Canada:
Georgetown Book Warehouse
34 Armstrong Ave.
Georgetown, Ontario L7G 4R9
Canadian orders: 1-800-247-7160
Order by fax: 1-800-887-1594

Prices subject to change without notice.

(#14) R 6/13